# C A S E
# STUDIES
# IN SERVICE
# QUALITY

WHEN AMERICA DOES IT RIGHT

*Case Studies in Service Quality*

*Updated with a new chapter by Dr. Spechler*

**JAY W. SPECHLER**

Industrial Engineering and Management Press
Institute of Industrial Engineers
Norcross, Georgia

**Library of Congress Cataloging-in-Publication Data**

Spechler, Jay W., 1934-
    When America does it right : case studies in service quality / Jay W. Spechler ; updated with a new chapter by Dr. Spechler.
        p.   cm.
    Includes bibliographical references and index.
    ISBN 0-89806-100-8
    1. Customer service--United States--Case studies. 2. Quality assurance--United States--Case studies. I. Title.
    HF5415.5.S625    1991
    658.8'12--dc20                                            91-26624
                                                                   CIP

Additional copies may be obtained by contacting:
Institute of Industrial Engineers
Publication Sales
25 Technology Park
Norcross, GA  30092
USA

*Quantity discounts available.*

*This book is dedicated to the people of American Express. Their performance provided the foundation upon which this book was constructed.*

# Table of Contents

## WHEN AMERICA DOES IT RIGHT: Case Studies in Service Quality

# Table of Contents

# Preface

In recent years, articles and books have appeared with increasing frequency criticizing the quality of service provided by U.S. companies. But there is another side of the story that deserves to be told.

A number of American companies are making quality a top priority. *Fortune* magazine's annual survey of the United States' most admired companies includes service quality as one of eight selection criteria. In addition, last year *Fortune* devoted a major feature to "Companies That Serve You Best".

Within this context, it occurred to me that many businesses could benefit from learning how the most admired companies achieve outstanding service quality. Working through the Institute of Industrial Engineers (IIE), I invited each of the most admired companies to submit its quality story for a book called, *When America Does It Right*.

The result is the collection of case studies in this volume. They tell the inside story of what it takes to be a quality company—from executive commitment and corporate policy statements to the nuts and bolts of delivering quality—transaction by transaction. The common message is that when employees work together creatively through a shared quality process to consistently meet customer requirements, that's "When America Does It Right".

Jay W. Spechler, Ph.D., P.E.
American Express Travel
Related Services Company, Inc.

# Acknowledgements

In 1985 a colleague said to me, "Why don't you write a book on service quality"? That was the beginning of a mental process that led to the concept for *When America Does It Right*.

Since writing a book is not part of my job description at American Express, all of the organizational and writing effort was accomplished during evenings, weekends, and in lieu of vacations. It is with gratitude and love that I acknowledge my wife, Marilyn's, encouragement through it all. Even more important, however, were the editorial and structural recommendations that she made.

I am indebted to *Fortune* magazine for focusing on the subject of service quality at just the right time. I had been conducting research into the quality processes of major companies when the January 19, 1987 issue of *Fortune*, highlighting the most admired companies in the country, appeared. This listing containing almost three hundred firms spanning thirty-three industrial classifications, identified the group I was looking for—the superior performers whom others could model. While the *Fortune* article provided the names of the most outstanding companies that I wanted to contact, it did not provide the names of their CEO's nor their addresses. My son Lee, spent several days in the library getting the latter information together. The quality of his effort may be seen in the fact that not one letter addressed to the CEO's was returned by the Post Office.

Since joining American Express, I have worked under three Senior Vice Presidents who have been responsible for the Ft. Lauderdale operations center. Each of these executives have been unfailing in their support of the quality mission originated by our Chairman, James D. Robinson III. They are: Terrence J. Smith, Keith Halliday and Edwin E. Sherin. Without their dedication and that of other centerheads around the world, it is unlikely that the company would have the outstanding reputation for service quality that it enjoys today.

A very special note of appreciation to MaryAnne Rasmussen, Vice President of Worldwide Quality Assurance at American Express for expressing her belief in the value of this effort and for her most constructive ideas.

I am glad to have this opportunity to express appreciation to Lieutenant General Kenneth L. Tallman, President of Embry-Riddle Aeronautical University and former Superintendent of the Air Force Academy for demonstrating a leadership model that applies to all situations where people have to work together to get a quality job done.

It is important to make mention of the extraordinary efforts of my secretary, Elaine Abdo. Over the last two years this book has resulted in an enormous extra workload. Elaine has been unfailing in preparing the manuscript and in communicating with the numerous individuals connected with this project.

My gratitude to everyone connected with the project for their creative thinking and ability to make things happen, and to Ed and Maryann Reese for their incomparable training in communications.

# Key Strategies and Success Factors In Improving Service Quality Performance

The case studies in this volume include so many examples of service quality excellence that identifying the key service quality success factors among them is like sifting through gold nuggets to find the largest and purest of the lot. Nevertheless, we have selected six of the most significant factors that can help the reader achieve quality service in his or her own environment.

In addition, there are several overall strategies for quality service mentioned frequently and prominently in the case studies and during discussions with the authors.

## SERVICE QUALITY STRATEGIES

Developing effective, lasting service quality is a job that is never finished. Unlike product and process quality control where dimensional and operating standards may remain fixed for a long time, service quality requirements change with customer perceptions and needs over relatively short periods.

The constant adjustments necessary to achieve service quality mean that all companies, whether manufacturing or service organizations, have found implementing service quality to be difficult. The task is particularly hard for manufacturers who, in addition to achieving product quality objectives, must also live up to marketing promises after the sale. In this context, manufacturers find it necessary to expand their concept of quality to cover the total service life of their products. It's one thing, for example, to build a computer. It's quite another to staff a telephone center to respond to customer inquiries about how to use the computer.

Achieving service quality requires a well-defined purpose, patience and discipline. Quality assurance in the service sector and in the customer service aspect of manufacturing businesses is relatively new. Few companies have a long-established, service quality assurance process in place, and starting one within a traditional organization structure is very, very difficult. Top level commitment is essential. Unlike traditional functions such as finance or manufacturing, service quality assurance exists at the pleasure of the policymaker—without the CEO's attention and support, service quality efforts can be neglected and wither away.

The case studies prove that when service quality is achieved, the direct and indirect benefits are enormous. Direct cost savings resulting from implementing quality improvement processes yield on the order of a 10-to-1 return on investment. Further, these savings have a high leverage factor, resulting in ongoing economic benefits (i.e. small capital investment and development costs frequently result in comparatively significant long-term savings on items such as labor and cash management expenses.) Increased market share often is a major indirect benefit of improved service quality, as customers use quality to differentiate services and select which to purchase.

## KEY SUCCESS FACTORS

Achieving quality customer service is based on six key ingredients. The first is the formulation of a quality strategy, and a commitment throughout the organization to put the strategy to work. The second is the use of technology to improve communication with customers and reduce human error. Third is the creation of quality measurements to ensure that customer requirements are met and track the level of service that the organization is providing. Fourth is the use of feedback mechanisms that tell how the customer perceives service. Fifth is the establishment of an organization that enables the service quality initiatives to succeed. The sixth factor is the use of training to give personnel the skills and knowledge necessary to reach the company's service quality goals.

## STRATEGY

There are many illustrations in this book of how the key success factors are being used to achieve superior service quality. The process starts with a strategy, and impetus to develop and implement a service quality strategy must come from the chief executive officer. There isn't a single case in this collection where quality developed from a bottom-up approach. It is also clear that the CEO can never walk away from maintaining a direct, highly-visible, and pervasive involvement in quality. Otherwise, lower-level executives who are pressed to deliver short-run financial gains, productivity improvements or new marketing programs may reduce budget allocations needed to introduce and maintain quality improvement programs and/or loosen quality performance standards.

The CEO's continuing involvement can be expressed through such vehicles as: Chairman's quality awards, with recipients given cash or other incentives, as well as recognition dinners at headquarters; quality councils composed of senior executives within the company and/or customers; and, the CEO's personal monitoring of quality objective setting and performance measurement.

## TECHNOLOGY

Quality service companies recognize that technology can be an important tool to help employees better meet customer requirements. They focus on applying technology, not for its own sake, but to improve service by increasing reliability, responsiveness, and customer choices, while reducing operating costs. By enabling employees to do their jobs more effectively and serve each other better as internal customers, technology also helps improve employee morale and performance quality.

The rapid pace of technological change gives a competitive edge to companies which quickly recognize the applicability of new technology and put them to work to improve quality.

## MEASUREMENT

The case studies demonstrate that quality measurement has received important attention from management.

Many of the authors believe that service measurement is the foundation upon which service quality excellence is built. Their most consistent message is that a company must design a service quality measurement system if it is to have any chance of becoming a service leader, and many point to their measurement systems as a vital part of their corporate survival strategies.

Measurement systems must look at internal customer service performance as well as external customer satisfaction. Service quality audits are vital to maintaining the integrity and validity of the measurement system. They prevent drifts from established procedures and provide an opportunity to evaluate areas for service improvement.

A subtle but important ingredient to the successful utilization of measurement systems is how employees perceive the information will be used—will it be a club to enforce performance, or a tool for guidance and development to help them improve service quality? It is important that the purpose of service quality measurement be clearly communicated.

## Feedback

The leading service quality companies devote considerable effort and resources to checking customers' perceptions of their service. As one author expresses it, "Quality will be judged by the user, not announced by its maker." Through executives meeting directly with customers to obtain their perceptions of the company's services, focus groups, questionnaires and telephone interviews, service quality leaders use customer feedback mechanisms to ensure that the customers' requirements are being met.

## Organization

The top management commitment required to establish and maintain focus on quality service includes support for organizational changes necessary to reinforce the quality process. Many companies are creating new executive positions to bring focus to the service quality issue.

Whatever organizational structure is selected, the companies in this book are focusing on customer needs and perceptions to arrive at what they consider to be the best organizational approach. The results being achieved in terms of customer satisfaction are impressive.

## Training

Training individuals throughout the company in quality management and application techniques is essential for quality to take hold. The diverse aspects of service quality training programs are described in this book. The case studies show that having training programs may not guarantee success in achieving high levels of quality, but not having them will guarantee underachievement.

## MAKING QUALITY WORK

In applying the service quality characteristics and key success factors, companies employ a number of approaches. For example:

**Belief systems.** Quality credos collected from companies included in this book define belief systems that focus all efforts of the company on quality. They integrate strong beliefs in the value of customer service with a strategic emphasis on service quality.

**Marketing.** A number of companies use service quality to enhance marketing efforts and beat competitors in the race for market share. Testimonials to the importance of quality in marketing are found throughout the case studies. Differentiating products and services on the basis of quality is an important way to meet the challenge of intense global competition.

**Vendor quality assurance.** An evolving area of importance in achieving high customer service levels is controlling the product or service quality provided by company suppliers or vendors. A number of case studies explain how companies are improving quality and controlling costs with vendor quality assurance programs.

**Productivity, quality, and effectiveness.** The leading service quality companies are coming to grips with a long-standing management taffy-pull: the view that productivity and quality are mutually exclusive goals. Polar positions on the issue traditionally have made it almost impossible to achieve quality and productivity objectives simultaneously. Each side has seen itself competing with the other for the same resource, i.e. labor. The view has been that major productivity gains, particularly in service, must come from force reductions. Conversely, those promoting quality have believed in the need for additional people to ensure quality. Increased competition and the negative effect of the business cycle have only added fuel to the fire. In the past, only marginally effective solutions to this dilemma were found, such as mergers that increased plant utilization and eliminated redundant labor, more mechanization and occasional breakthroughs in automation.

Even within the outstanding companies represented in this book, the battle for financial and human resources goes on. There is never enough money to satisfy all needs and wants. However, many companies have resolved the practical and philosophical differences over productivity and quality by implementing strategies that have established the principle that productivity and quality are mutually complimentary goals. They have adopted a "quality first" strategy. In order to send a consistent message to the work force on quality, management's marching orders are that if something in the process or workflow breaks down and either quality or quantity has to suffer, it must not be quality.

Through that philosophy of eliminating unnecessary and do-over work, quality processes can lower overall costs while better meeting customer requirements. This reframing of the issue has won its adherents rich rewards in increased profitability, reduced management stress, enhanced labor relations, and improved market share.

Yet, as the true relationship of productivity and quality becomes clear, awareness of a new management dilemma is also emerging. It centers on *effectiveness*.

Several of the authors mention the term, effectiveness, in relation to improved productivity and quality. There is an underlying sense that a company could experience high levels of productivity and quality, and yet still fail to achieve bottom-line success. Effectiveness success factors include: increased customer loyalty and market share, high employee morale and low turnover, as well as greater utilization of human and capital resources that results in lower unit cost. Quality effectiveness, then, is the ultimate objective of today's quality service leaders.

# Aerospace

Boeing Commercial Airplane
R. N. Karnes, J. R. Black, J. V. Imre, and J. H. Wires

Lockheed Corporation
Richard S. Sapp

# Boeing Service Quality: An Evolving Tradition

**R. N. Karnes, J. R. Black, J. V. Imre, J. H. Wires**

Boeing Commercial Airplane

Boeing Commercial Airplane is a division of The Boeing Company which was founded in 1916. The Boeing Company is a manufacturer of commercial jet airplanes and is located in Seattle, Washington. The Commercial Airplane division employs approximately 48,000 individuals.

## Background

Boeing Commercial Airplane (BCA) has a seventy-one-year tradition of service quality that has resulted in a comprehensive worldwide customer support network. Management has learned a lot from its relationships with customers, and continues to apply that knowledge to business relationships within company walls—among their departments and people. Each employee has customers, and each in turn is someone else's customer. By applying continuous improvement based on internal customer feedback, as it has with commercial and military customer feedback, Boeing plans to meet the stiffer challenges of tomorrow's competitive environment.

## The First Decades of Customer Service

In the industry's early days, customers both operated and maintained their own aircraft. Early planes were mechanically simple. However, in 1933 Boeing introduced the Model 247—the first monoplane transport, which was all-metal, had nacelles blended into the wing, and utilized retractable landing gear. Aircraft became more complex, and it became necessary to begin to emphasize customer service.

## Formation of Worldwide Customer Support Network

In 1934 Boeing began marketing the Model 281 commercial version of the P-26 "Peashooter" fighter (pursuit) craft. Eleven were sold to China in 1935, so a China-based Boeing representative was hired to uncrate and assemble the planes and train Chinese mechanics to service them.

The service unit was formed within the engineering department in 1936. Its mission was to provide a link between Boeing and customers once the sales and manufacturing departments had completed their tasks. The increasing size and complexity of company products made after-sale customer attention essential. For example, the Pan American Clipper had fifty-thousand parts and a wingspan of 152 feet. In addition, the first B-17 "Flying Fortress" orders had come in. There were twenty-four people in the service unit by the end of 1936.

Boeing sent twenty B-17Cs to Britain in 1940, along with two people who went as the first official field representatives. Their jobs were to keep the bombers flying and to relay information back to Seattle as a basis for continual improvements to the B-17 product line.

In the spring of 1943 the service unit was reorganized as the Boeing Service Department. It then had forty-five field representatives, of whom sixteen were assigned overseas. Its five main organizations were the handbook unit, field service section, training section, administration section, and spare parts unit. Although military products dominated, commercial airplanes were supported as well. In July 1944 a commercial group within the service department was formed to assure that commercial products would continue to receive the proper attention.

By spring of 1945 there were 134 field representatives (32 of whom were overseas), supporting a fleet of 12,700 B-17s (5,700 built under license by Douglas and Vega) and 4,000 B-29 "Super Fortresses" (1,200 built under license). Training had become a vital component of customer service. Initial training for field representatives, upgrade training on improved systems and newer planes, military maintenance training, and operations personnel training were provided. The "Fortress" school in Seattle and Boeing Mobile Technical Training units were also implemented.

## Feedback from Customers

Recall that in 1940 the official mission of overseas field representatives was to relay information back to Seattle as a basis for continual improvements to the B-17. At war's end this mission was greatly enhanced. The resources of the entire service department were extended to all Boeing airplane operators, military as well as commercial. The department's objectives were redefined in two ways: first, assist to the largest extent possible those using Boeing airplanes; second, return data to the Boeing engineering division to enable constant product improvement leading to superior design of future aircraft.

The 1945 service department reorganization provided a number of services: instructional courses for flight and ground personnel prior to the first-plane delivery; a check-out of customer flight personnel prior to delivery; assignment of service engineers to domestic and overseas bases per customer specification for helping with maintenance and operational problems during the first year of service; and the preparation of handbooks on pilot operating procedures, aircraft maintenance techniques, parts catalog, service bulletins, and assistance in spare-part selection. Ever since, Boeing's reputation for quality service has been based on the priority placed on obtaining and fully responding to feedback from customers.

## Customer Service in the Jet Transport Era

In 1956 the transport division was formed to produce both the KC-135 jet tanker and the 707 jet transport. At that time the service department was reorganized into two units, one for military and the other for commercial airplanes. Relying on ten years of experience with large military jets (B-47, B-52), the commercial unit was quickly put into operation. An engineering support group was added to assist airlines in making the transition to jet aircraft. A new spirit invigorated the service department as the first 707 went into service for Pan Am in 1958. Every aspect of customer service from training to publications to field service was brought up-to-date to reflect the new era of international transportation that the jets would bring.

The increased complexity of each successive new model (and its variations) brought with it better customer support services. In 1970 a new customer support organization, separate from the engineering department, was formed within the commercial airplane group. Field support was reorganized into eight geographical regions, each with a regional director, in order to be more sensitive to customer needs in each region.

A further restructuring in 1979 created the customer services division, which added flight test engineering and flight operations to the existing customer support functions. Today customer services employs twenty-eight hundred people. However, the basic support philosophy as set forth by the service department in 1936 has not changed very much. The main objective is still to assist Boeing airplane operators to the largest extent possible. To this end, Boeing requires field experience for all service personnel.

## THE QUALITY IMPROVEMENT (QI) METHOD

### The Modern Challenge

The company's commitment is to listen and to respond when customers need them. Boeing's continued success requires repeat business, which in turn depends upon customers' perceptions of services. In 1980-1984, Boeing had averaged about 8% productivity improvement per year, largely because of the quality and reliability of both its products and customer service.

However, three phenomena in the last half-dozen years have changed the picture. First, the domestic airline industry has been deregulated. Fares, previously fixed at comfortably high levels, were suddenly subjected to market-pricing pressures. One result was that domestic airlines shifted their equipment acquisition criteria away from superior product engineering to superior product pricing. Second, an increasing customer demand for special features, more stringent government requirements, and rapidly advancing technology have combined to force Boeing's development costs to increase more rapidly than the domestic inflation rate. Third, the heavily subsidized Airbus Industrie was transforming itself into a full-fledged competitor, sharpening price-consciousness among Boeing's European customers.

Competitors' products and services are very good indeed; consequently, the strong customer focus that has helped give Boeing a reputation for superior quality is no longer sufficient to meet today's challenges. The company had to find a way to restore its profit margin and to reduce upward price trends at the same time.

### Internationalization of Customer Orientation

Boeing's management realized the need to increase the advantage of dealing with BCA. The previous focus was not good enough. Aggressively priced competition needed to be offset by eliminating non-value-added labor and material at home. Also, as their awareness of the Japanese *total quality* management approach grew, they began to see elements of the total quality approach in their own customer service practices. They began to recognize that the people within BCA are both suppliers and customers with respect to the others they deal with all the time. Everyone's output at BCA is someone else's input. Everyone at BCA has customers, whether they are airlines, the Boeing organization in the next building, or the person at the next desk. In order to streamline operations, they had to listen more effectively to their own people.

This new customer focus is now extended to all BCA internal customers. Getting everyone involved in finding ways to improve at-home efficiency will reduce product costs and prices, and in turn increase the customers' return per new-aircraft dollar. In short, what's good for quality customer service is good for the whole company.

## Current Efforts

The notions of quality and customers are essentially being redefined companywide. This process means analyzing both internal and external customers' perceptions and launching improvement programs at home and abroad and spending time on self-examination. Where are we going? Why are we in business? What do we do? Why do we do it that way? How can we do it smarter, better, and more efficiently? The company is educating its people, and management is providing leadership from-the-top-down in the philosophy, approach, and techniques of total quality improvement. Success will be founded on self-improvement based on customer feedback—the same formula that has seemed to work so well with airline and military customers over the past seventy-one years, except this time Boeing is listening to internal customers, too.

**Old versus new.** Traditional cost-reduction methods generally rely on either exhortation or any of a variety of objective management techniques. Exhortation (for example, do better, work smarter, zero defects) provides only temporary relief, since anyone can reduce costs by 5% while the pressure is on; moreover, concurrent management participation is lacking. No basic changes occur, and once management's attention is diverted elsewhere, things go back to normal.

Objective methods condition people to negotiate conservative objectives which they know they can meet. Padding creeps into estimates, driving out creative risk-taking. Inefficient but essential work components are shifted to other organizations; worthwhile ongoing capital improvement gets derailed; essential services are curtailed.

By contrast, the quality improvement (QI) method gets people working together *on the system* (of management, production, administration, etc.) to improve it permanently. The object is to provide internal and external customers with the quality of products and services they require, expect, and deserve, rather than to give them excuses.

**Variation.** The primary tangible benefit of the quality improvement method is the reduction of variability to a minimum. Traditionally, Boeing has relied upon inspection to weed out defective products (reports, parts, service), thus providing "quality" output to the next customer. This is simply removing variation after it has been created. By contrast, QI provides a rational method to minimize variation. For example, depending on the situation, it can enable them to reduce or eliminate after-the-fact inspections; implement self-inspection before the next process step; automate the inspection before the next process step; change processes to reduce variability; and eliminate the non-value-added processes altogether. The results are reduced scrap and rework. The resources thus recovered are available for additional productivity. The result, of course, is lower unit costs.

**Waste.** Where does variability come from in the first place? Enterprises generally do not start out with built-in waste. However, once an enterprise becomes too unwieldy for one person to manage, several departments are created for specialized purposes, each with its own manager. Left to their own inclinations, each department tends to focus on its own mission exclusively, and each therefore begins to see its context differently. Energies are turned in part to sustaining and solidifying the organization. Routines become "standard practice." Changing requirements result in additional duties and staff, rather than altered business processes.

At BCA, management began to realize that it was working on sporadic problems while tolerating a high variation in basic departmental performance. It began to put non-management people to work on defining problems and finding ways to eliminate the sporadic problems; then management teamed up with these groups to improve the basic performance level.

## Steps in the Quality Improvement Strategy

Boeings continuous improvement process focuses on constancy of purpose, internal and external customers, continuous improvement of processes and products, and a participative work environment. The process includes the following steps.

**Departmental task analysis (DTA).** This analysis begins with a number of questions. What is your department's mission? Responsibilities? Activities? Who are its customers? Suppliers? What do your customers require of you? Are your activities consistent with these expectations? What do you require from your suppliers? Are your suppliers' activities consistent with your requirements? Next, calibrate your answers with your customers and suppliers. Repeat the process until everything is in balance, and revise your traditional responsibilities and activities accordingly.

Do this at all organizational levels. Ideally, it should start at the top, ending with individual employees. Often, some non-value-added activities become immediately obvious, and improvement teams can be set to work to devise and implement permanent changes.

**Business process analysis (BPA).** Identify your organization's processes. Flowchart the way you actually do business (not how you are "supposed" to do it). Obtain agreement on responsibilities from those affected.

Using the flowchart as a basis for change, identify non-value-added activities such as inspection, delays, inventory storage, and transportation. Define measurement points and implement measurements to determine where the most attention should be applied. Identify problem areas to be worked in order of priority.

Both DTA and BPA are "consensus processes" that take a lot of time but produce superior, permanent results. In a consensus process, nothing of substance is decided by majority vote. Everyone affected is included. Everyone is heard, and problems are discussed, debated, and resolved so that everyone subscribes to the results and is able to live with them.

**Problem solving.** Based on the DTA and BPA results, set priorities and select the problems to solve. If the solution is known, implement it. If not, field a problem-solving team to analyze causes, identify and collect solutions, select the best solution, and implement it. Then measure and evaluate the results of the implemented solution. If the situation is not yet under control, reexamine the problem and go through the process again. If it is under control, then subject the process to continuous measurement and improvement. Improvement opportunities never cease.

**Control.** When a process is under control, its variability is within calculable limits based on the standard deviation of measured data. This is quite different from being within specification. Only measurement will tell you whether your process is within control or out of control (in which case you need to look for special sporadic causes like nonuniform mold temperature, fluctuating power levels, or office distractions). If it is under control, could the results nevertheless be improved (i.e., for a quicker turnaround, a lower defect rate, fewer changes, a higher yield)? Measurement should always be in place, whether for periodically interviewing customers or instrumenting a machine tool.

**Participative involvement.** Doing all of this requires thorough employee involvement. To begin with, employees are naturally motivated. If increased personal commitment to the company can be developed, it leads to higher morale and improved work performance. If employees are better informed, they make more effective decisions. Since people are naturally creative, they can learn to solve work-related problems on the job. Personal development and growth are important to employees and benefit the organization, too. But such individual potential is realizable only when freedom, initiative, and creativity are encouraged by management through participative techniques.

Participative involvement is synonymous with group decision making (consensus). Nobody votes; everyone agrees, buys into the decision, and therefore has a stake in the results. Generating consensus can be a lengthy process, but the payoff is always worthwhile.

Participants should include all of those affected; those with relevant skills, knowledge, and experience; those with needed resources; those with the authority to implement the results; and those who might otherwise thwart implementation. Participative involvement should be used when decisions affect daily work, when several people have the combined knowledge and experience which could contribute to a better decision, and when several people's support and commitment are required for successful implementation.

Teamwork is not second nature. The orchestration of participative consensus sessions to minimize interpersonal emotion and chain-of-command intimidation is essential. Trained facilitators and team leaders are requisite for success, and BCA has a compulsory training program for all team leaders and members of management.

## VISION

Boeing is doing no less than forging a company consensus on a total quality vision. One of Boeing's high-priority actions is to convert the middle manager from being an expert and functional organization protector to a facilitator and barrier eliminator. The traditional organizational pyramid must be inverted so that senior management works to support middle management and front-line workers.

The successful implementation of this vision will transform Boeing's organizational emphasis into a horizontal management system with only one purpose: to identify, quantify, and eliminate waste and prevent its return—in other words, continuous improvement. The test of Boeing's success will be its position in tomorrow's marketplace.

# Star Quality
# The Lockheed Way

**R. S. Sapp**

Lockheed Corporation

The Lockheed Corporation, headquartered in Calabasas, California, is a broad-based aerospace firm with over ninety-nine thousand employees. In recent years the corporation has consistently ranked among the top ten Department of Defense and NASA contractors. In 1987, Lockheed had net earnings of $421 million on sales of $11.3 billion. The operation of its various companies include the research, design, testing, production, and support of aircraft, missiles, satellites, electronic systems, space systems, ocean systems, information systems, and ships. The United States and foreign government business (91% of sales) and commercial business (9% of sales) also include technical and support services to these customers. While the majority of the Lockheed companies are located in the United States, customer support and related product support serve an international market. The variety of customers, products, and services, when combined with the need to meet customer quality expectations, are the major drivers for "Star Quality - The Lockheed Way."

## LOCKHEED CUSTOMERS

Quality means satisfying customer expectations. The Lockheed customers are many and varied. To satisfy all customer expectations, you need to know all of your customers, commercial and government. On the commercial side, Lockheed customers range from airlines whose planes are refueled by Lockheed Air Terminal, to users of CADAM (Computer Aided Design and Manufacturing) software packages, to IBM which obtains computer peripheral equipment from CalComp. On the government side, Lockheed's major customer is the Department of Defense. However, some lines of its business are with other U.S. Government agencies, such as the Federal Aviation Agency and NASA, and some are with foreign governments.

When dealing with the U.S. Government, particularly the DOD, you find there are multiple customers. These customers range from the government personnel stationed in many of our plants, to the government personnel at the procurement offices, and to the individual users of military hardware. For example, Sanders Associates, a Lockheed company in Nashua, New Hampshire, has its DOD contracts administered by a resident team from the Defense Contract Administration Services; Lockheed Aeronautical Systems Company-Burbank Division by the Navy Plant Representatives Office; and at Lockheed Missiles and Space Company in Sunnyvale, California, the Space Systems Division's contracts are administered by personnel from the Air Force Plant Representatives Office. In turn, these contracts are issued from various buying offices across the United States: from NAVAIR in Washington, D.C., to the Air Force Space Division in Los Angeles, California. Then, there are special "customer representatives," such as the Defense Contract Audit Agency. Finally, the ultimate customer is the individual soldier, sailor, or aviator—anywhere in the world.

Another customer category includes other companies, either internal or external to the Lockheed Corporation. For example, the Lockheed Aeronautical Systems Company is a major supplier to McDonnell-Douglas on the C-17 aircraft program with a subcontract, which exceeds one billion dollars, to manufacture major sections of the wings. The C-17 work will be done by two divisions within Lockheed: one in Burbank, the other in Georgia. Thus, one division becomes a customer to the other. There are many other examples where one Lockheed company does work for another through the "Intercompany Work Transfer System," thereby making one company a customer, the other a supplier.

This principle also extends down within the companies to departments, and ultimately to individuals. Each of us is a customer and a supplier. Each customer has quality expectations that must be satisfied. Whether you provide a product, a service, or both, the key is to know your customers, especially their expectations of quality and the extent those are fulfilled.

## SERVICE QUALITY

Service quality means different things to different people. For the sake of clarity, the following explanation is offered. Service quality in a narrow sense means the quality of the service(s) delivered to a customer. For example, in this narrow context, it means the quality of health care delivered to a patient in a hospital, or to Lockheed, the quality of launch services provided to NASA on the Space Shuttle Program. In this context, people are doing "something" for others; that "something" is service. There is no "product" involved. Service quality in the broader sense includes everything done to deliver what a customer is expecting. It can involve a product, a service, or a product and a service combined.

For example, many of the Lockheed contracts include product support. For a weapons system that has been fielded, Lockheed provides spare parts and modification kits. It may or may not be contracted also to install those parts or kits. If so, then the customer expects service quality in the total operation. The customer expects it to work; the parts should be good, as should the installation and checkout. The customer does not distinguish between the two kinds of service quality. Therefore, the Lockheed view is that service quality encompasses everything that is done to satisfy the customer: the provision of hardware, software, services, or any combination of these.

The criteria used to judge Lockheed service quality are numerous. They depend on the customer and on the product and the service being delivered. There are two general categories: those criteria that are internal to the corporation and those that are external. For example, internally, data on scrap, rework, and test costs are used; externally, Lockheed receives feedback on problems with its products from its own field support teams and from customers. There are also frequent audits by customers, e.g., contractor operations reviews by the Air Force, and contractor system status reviews and cost of quality audits by the Defense Contract Administration Services. In all cases, this information is assembled within the corporation in order to determine overall customer satisfaction. The bottom line is the saying, "Quality will be judged by its user, not announced by its maker."

## STAR QUALITY CONTINUUM

Star Quality - The Lockheed Way is a continuum. It had a beginning, and it has no end. It is comprised of a Quality Policy and Quality Business Strategy.

## Policy

The policy of the Lockheed Corporation is to provide products and services to its customers that satisfy their quality expectations.

## Approach

In order to fulfill the mission, goals, and long-term objectives of the corporation, the products and services Lockheed provides its customers must satisfy their quality expectations and be price competitive. To achieve the required level of quality at a competitive price, an integrated, comprehensive, organizational, quality strategy is required. That means employees need to be aware of, committed to, and actively involved in the quality improvement process. Each employee is treated as a customer and a supplier. However, the major focus is on the ultimate end-customer. The pursuit of quality improvement is a continuous process with measurable objectives.

## Responsibilities

The business approach of the Lockheed Corporation is to place the responsibility and commensurate authority for the success of each Lockheed company with its president. Likewise, the quality policy and strategy is the responsibility of the company president. More specifically, each president is held accountable for the following:

- Defining specific responsibilities for quality
- Developing and implementing a quality strategy
- Communicating the policy, responsibilities and strategy to each employee
- Involving suppliers and other business partners in the quality process
- Providing awareness, education, and training in quality
- Monitoring and improving the level of customer satisfaction
- Monitoring and reducing the cost of quality.

The corporate vice presidents are responsible for providing direction and other assistance in implementing the policy in their respective functional areas and in ensuring policy compliance.

## Corporate Quality Strategy

The goal of Lockheed's corporate quality strategy is to provide products and services that satisfy customer expectations better than anyone else. To achieve this goal, the following objectives must be met:

- Know what the customer wants
- Build products and provide services better than anyone else does
- Ensure that the customer got what was expected
- Tell the customer, stockholders, and employees about it.

To implement this strategy, two methods are used. At the company level, each president is responsible for developing and implementing a strategy appropriate to their customers, products and services, workforce and environment, and for doing so in concert with overall corporate plans.

At the corporate level, there are five thrust areas in implementing the strategy. They are the following:

1. Customer expectations and satisfaction. Corporate executives meet with the customers to discuss their quality expectations and their satisfaction with Lockheed products and services.

2. Supporting policy and guidance. The minimum direction and guidance necessary to ensure a coordinated and consistent policy approach is provided to the Lockheed companies.
3. Communications. Through the communications media available at the corporate level, customers, employees, and stockholders are informed about quality goals, objectives, policy, direction, guidance, and most importantly, performance.
4. Quality improvement. The corporate staff assists management at all levels to continue quality improvement efforts in six major areas:
   - Education and training
   - Motivation
   - Suppliers
   - Technology
   - Tools and methodology
   - Measurement, inspection, and test
5. Compliance. The corporate staff, in their respective functional areas, are responsible for assuring compliance with policy and direction. In addition, the corporate internal auditor offers assistance through its staff based at each Lockheed company.

Within the corporation, five focus groups are responsible for making it all happen. They are:
1. Quality leaders. Every member of the management team, from the first-line supervisor to the CEO and Chairman of the Board, is expected to be a quality leader.
2. Engineering. At Lockheed, design is recognized as the key to quality products.
3. Manufacturing.
4. Support groups. These include all the other functional groups that support engineering and manufacturing.
5. Committees and task forces. Both at the corporate and company level, interdisciplinary and/or functional teams are necessary to address some issues. One team, for example, is the Corporate Quality Assurance Committee, consisting of the quality directors from each Lockheed company. It has five subcommittees that address specific corporate-wide quality issues in education and training, technology, software, supplier activities, and metrology.

## SELECTED COMPANY PROGRAMS
Lockheed companies have various approaches to provide quality services.

## Hardware and Services
One of Lockheed's core programs is the Navy's fleet ballistic missile (FBM). The corporation—more specifically, the Lockheed Missiles and Space

Company/Missile Systems Division in Sunnyvale, California—has provided the industrial capability for the design, production and support of submarine-launched strategic missiles for more than three decades. Production of the Trident I FBM ended in 1986 with delivery of the 570th missile. Lockheed is now over halfway through the six-year, $5.7 billion contract covering the design, fabrication, validation, flight-testing, and production of the first deployable Trident II missiles. Early in 1987, at Cape Canaveral, Florida, Lockheed successfully completed the first flight of the Trident II. U.S. deployment of the Trident II will begin in 1989. This program is noteworthy because of several factors related to service quality. First, to maintain a line of business and a customer for over thirty years means "customer satisfaction." This satisfaction is a direct result of the communications between the U.S. Navy and Lockheed, and the commitment to quality and reliability at an affordable price. The joint Navy-Lockheed management team has stressed continued improvement throughout. This is exemplified in the current contract for the Trident II in which the Navy has implemented incentives for Lockheed to use statistical process controls on key production parameters.

In the fall of 1987, several Lockheed companies that are aeronautically focused were merged for future cost-competitive reasons into the Lockheed Aeronautical Systems Company. Two of the former companies, now called divisions, have excellent, continuing quality improvement processes. Both divisions provide an entire spectrum of products and services.

The Georgia division is currently producing C-5B aircraft for the U.S. Air Force and C-130 aircraft for the USAF as well as other foreign government agencies and commercial concerns. The "Total Quality Improvement Program" (TQIP) is the cornerstone of the division's business strategy. It is a structured, planned approach to continuous quality improvement and establishes an ongoing quality management program in every operation of the division. Its goal is to create a customer-oriented quality culture committed to making quality improvement a permanent way of life for the division. Its major elements are:

- Management commitment.
- Functional organization ownership in approach.
- Employee involvement at all levels.
- Practical measures to track progress.
- Recognition for team and individual performance.
- Ongoing training and communications.

The results of TQIP, which was started in 1987, are mounting. For example, customer satisfaction was evident when the resident Air Force quality organization notified Lockheed in the fall of 1987 that they were eliminating their inspection of the C-130 outer wings because of continued high product quality by Lockheed personnel. Earlier in 1987, the Air Force had spent 319 man-hours in one month inspecting wings with only four squawks found—all minor.

The Burbank division of the Lockheed Aeronautical Systems Company uses "product excellence" to describe its systematic effort to create a culture of continuous improvement in quality, productivity, and employee-management communications. The Burbank division has been a long-time supplier of antisubmarine warfare aircraft, such as the P-3 and S-3, to the U.S. Navy and foreign governments. Also, it was selected by the U.S. Air Force in 1986, along with its team members, Boeing and General Dynamics, as one of two U.S. competitors to design, build, and demonstrate two prototype fighters for the next generation advanced tactical fighter.

Product excellence is aimed at creating an atmosphere of open communication, teamwork, professionalism, and employee recognition which will promote quality workmanship and customer satisfaction. Product excellence is an effort to create in every employee a dedicated attitude and a commitment to produce the highest quality products and services for Lockheed's customers. The Burbank division aims to create this by developing a synergy between management and employees throughout the company. Management goals and objectives are publicized widely and employees are encouraged by several means to make their input. Management lays out the what and the employees respond with the how. Management guidance comes from executive level steering committees and from joint management-employee operating committees that serve to localize and define the objectives for their area. Employees make their input through the employee suggestion system, quality circles, task forces, "skip-level" meetings, after-hours discussion sessions, and periodic employee surveys.

Product excellence is also achieved through special projects. Critical need areas are identified in some cases by the customer—foreign object damage, for example—or by self-audit, a technique that has proven valuable as an internal quality check. Employee recognition plays a vital role as well, allowing any employee to nominate another for exceptional performance. If chosen, an employee receives up to one-thousand dollars for his or her accomplishments.

## Hardware and Services - Commercial

CalComp is a Lockheed company recognized as a world leader in computer graphics. CalComp manufactures computer plotters, digitizers, and graphic display terminals used for product design and other applications in such industries as aerospace, automobiles, electronics and communications, and oil. In addition to making direct sales, CalComp sells its products to original equipment manufacturers. About two-thirds of CalComp's sales are domestic. CalComp has a "continuous process improvement" philosophy to ensure the quality of their service.

Their major focus to date has been on the manufacturing process and its continuous improvement. For example, at the Plotter Products Division in Anaheim, California, in a 24-month period through mid-1987, revenue was up 70% as a result of the continuous improvement philosophy; units delivered were up 130%. Cycle time went from nine weeks to three days. Suppliers were reduced by 45%; overhead spending was down 14%; headcount was flat; space was reduced 45%; inventory turns increased 5.5 from 1.7 and cash flow was up 21 points. The turn-on rate went from 0 to 83%, line inspectors were removed, and field reliability was up 22%. They did not automate, add computers, use consultants, or make heavy capital investments.

Another example of CalComp's drive for quality is their small format raster line. The entire organization recently spent months focusing solely on transforming their work area. Inventory turns have increased threefold— from four to over twelve turns. Completed boxes are no longer moved to another building, but shipped directly from the small raster area. Packaging materials were removed from a parking lot trailer onto the line. Materials unique to small raster are also stocked on line. None of these moves, however, have increased the space requirements. In fact, overall floor space actually decreased by over 20%. This was accomplished by removing all excess material, keeping just what is required for the day's build at the workstation, building subassemblies only when required, and removing all excess furniture (especially storage racks). In other words, there was the beginning of a just-in-time environment.

The assembly and test lines have experienced the greatest changes. The absence of the conveyor allows all the workstations to be closer together. The proximity of stations means there is no space available for stock to build up. The line was reconfigured into a U-shape in order to better accommodate just-in-time production. Changes in both areas have helped improve communications.

Steps to improve system reliability have also been taken on the small raster line. The need for system burn-in has been eliminated, and the test turn-on rate has jumped from 74% to 95%. A stress test was implemented that has proven very effective in shaking out dead-on-arrival failures as is evident from small format raster line's 100% acceptance rate for two months by their number one customer.

The management and staff in the small raster business and operating units have been instrumental in initiating changes in the quality of service, and in promoting an atmosphere which encourages improvements. Daily employee meetings where problems can be highlighted and solutions worked out are attended by everyone in the operating unit. Management, staff, and line operators have completed training in Statistical Process Control. Activity groups have been set up to study process flow and to determine critical variables that need to be monitored. Thus, in a number of ways, CalComp's small format raster line offers a good example of Lockheed's "star quality."

## Software

With more than two-thousand installations in thirty-one countries, Lockheed's CADAM software is a leader in computer aided design and computer augmented manufacturing systems. The CADAM system is an integral part of computer integrated manufacturing, providing powerful design, manufacturing, and analysis capabilities on mainframes, engineering work stations, and personal computers. CADAM, Inc., uses many of the standard, and some innovative, software techniques for quality assurance. However, its key to customer satisfaction, continuing improvement and, "service quality," is CADAM User's Exchange (CUE). CUE is a means for CADAM users to exchange information and to communicate with CADAM, Inc. The users are able to ask each other questions about using CADAM, present success stories about what works for them, and communicate their desires to CADAM, Inc. CADAM, Inc., and its customers meet twice a year in the United States. There are also CUE meetings in Southeast Asia, Japan, and Europe once a year. CADAM, Inc., sponsors CUE and usually gives over one-fourth of the presentations. The presentations are usually on technical information, new product introductions, or company directions. CUE meetings have played a major role in leading to improved CADAM installation guides, user reference manuals, and overall customer satisfaction.

## Services

The Lockheed Engineering Management Services Company (LEMSCO), based in Houston, Texas, provides technical services to a variety of government customers. For two decades LEMSCO has been NASA's primary research and development support contractor at the Johnson Space Center in Houston. LEMSCO also provides technical and engineering services to NASA at the White Sands Test Facility in New Mexico, the Army at the White Sands Missile Range and Dugway Proving Ground in Utah, and the Environmental Protection Agency in Las Vegas. For its support of NASA at the Johnson Space Center in 1986 and 1987, the Engineering and Science Program Office of LEMSCO was selected as a finalist for the NASA Excellence Award for Quality and Productivity. In 1986, it was the only service contractor selected as a finalist. The NASA award followed two criteria: performance achievements and improvements, and productivity improvement and quality enhancement process attainments. The first criterion has three elements: customer satisfaction, quality, and productivity.

The LEMSCO goal is to be, and to be recognized as, the service industry quality and productivity leader. Its approach is to improve methods of performing tasks within management, engineering, and scientific process flows. LEMSCO constantly strives to reexamine process methods and to apply new ideas and technology to improve operations. Its productivity programs provide the training and tools to facilitate analysis and improvement. To achieve its goal LEMSCO uses a structured program which includes

- Performance development teams
- Cost reduction program
- New technology program
- Process evaluation program
- Training and information exchanges
- Professional societies
- Technical excellence program
- Distinctions of Leadership program
- Skip level communications process
- Quality of work life
- Lockheed information for employees/performance enhancement recommendation system
- Lockheed wellness facility

This program helps LEMSCO keep its commitment to excellence.

## SUMMARY

The challenge for a large corporation today is to assure that it is satisfying its customers in a cost-effective manner that will allow the corporation to remain competitive, continue to grow, and return to its employees and owners a fair return on their investment. Quality, and its continuing improvement, is one of the key business strategies that will successfully meet this challenge. For a corporation that is diverse, such as Lockheed, and works on a decentralized principle of operation that holds company presidents accountable for profit and loss, and has the government as its major customer—the task is especially large. However, we believe the Lockheed quality policy and business strategy set forth above will prove essential in meeting the challenge.

# Beverages

Anheuser-Busch, Inc.
William L. Rammes

# Making Friends is Our Business

**William L. Rammes**
Anheuser-Busch, Inc.

Anheuser-Busch, Inc. is the brewing subsidiary of Anheuser-Busch Companies, Inc. Its products include, Budweiser and Bud Light, Michelob, Michelob Light and Michelob Classic Dark, Busch, Natural Light, LA and King Cobra beers. Anheuser-Busch's headquarters are in St. Louis, Missouri, where the company was founded in 1852. In the 1870s Anheuser-Busch introduced pasteurization to the American brewing industry, thus allowing beer to retain its quality through climate change and long distance shipping. Currently, Anheuser-Busch Companies, Inc. employs 42,000 people, 15,000 of whom are employed in the brewing division.

## INTRODUCTION

At Anheuser-Busch Companies, Inc., "Making friends is our business" is more than just a corporate slogan. In fact, it defines a longstanding commitment to produce the finest family of quality beers, supported by the highest level of service in the brewing industry. "Quality is the single most important, unyielding commitment at Anheuser-Busch," says August A. Busch III, chairman and president of Anheuser-Busch Companies. Consistent service is an important means of demonstrating the company's overall dedication to excellence throughout the beer distribution system, from the brewery to the consumer's glass.

Anheuser-Busch and its nationwide network of over 950 beer distributors provide a myriad of services which address three general objectives:

- First, assure that the quality and reputation of Anheuser-Busch beers are carefully maintained throughout the beer distribution system.
- Second, assist wholesalers and their retail accounts in making their operations more successful, thereby improving the consumer's accessibility to and perception of Anheuser-Busch products.
- And third, actively participate in public service programs. This demonstrates appreciation for consumer loyalty to Anheuser-Busch and generates community good will.

## QUALITY ASSURANCE

Brewing quality beer has been viewed as an art and a science at Anheuser-Busch for over a century. Protecting that quality continues to be the company's highest priority in terms of customer service. The commitment to quality begins with the selection of superior ingredients. Anheuser-Busch uses what it considers the finest and most costly ingredients available, obtained on the basis of stringent requirements and specifications.

All Anheuser-Busch beers are produced according to its traditional "Old World" brewing method, a long, natural process taking up to thirty days or longer. It is probably the most costly brewing process in the industry. "It may appear old-fashioned to brew beer principally the same way for over a hundred years, but we have never found a better way than by combining the finest ingredients with slow, precise steps which give nature the time it needs to create great beer," said the company's chief brewmaster, Gerhardt A. Kraemer.

### Brewing Quality

For example, while many brewers use only a single fermentation, Anheuser-Busch uses a centuries-old European process called *kraeusening*. This secondary fermentation matures the beer's flavor and provides natural carbonation. The St. Louis-based brewer is also the only major beer producer in the world using the traditional beechwood-aging process to age and naturally carbonate its beers. A layer of beechwood chips is spread on the bottom of the lager tank to provide more surface area for the action of the yeast during fermentation. The yeast settles on the chips and continues to work until the beer is completely fermented.

While some brewers use modern shortcuts—such as forcing fermentation by mechanical agitation, using enzyme preparations for chillproofing, or artificially injecting carbon dioxide to create carbonation—these techniques do not create great beer. While it has chosen not to use *chemical* advances to cut corners in brewing, Anheuser-Busch has always been innovative in the use of science to promote quality. Today the company's traditional brewing process is strictly maintained using modern technology in a rigorous program of quality assurance.

No scientific test, however, can replace tasting as the final judgment of quality. "Flavor panels" meet daily at each of the company's eleven breweries to judge the aroma, appearance, and taste of beer. In addition, samples from each brewery are regularly flown to the company's headquarters for taste evaluation by a panel of expert brewmasters. Anheuser-Busch was the first American brewer to establish a brewery research laboratory. Now more than a century old, this laboratory exemplifies the company's sincere dedication to product quality.

## Distributor/Wholesaler Training

Brewing quality, however, is only the first step. Anheuser-Busch works closely with its wholesaler and retailer network to ensure that the quality, taste, and freshness achieved in the brewhouse are protected throughout the distribution system until the beer reaches the consumer. To assure this quality, the company offers extensive training to its wholesalers in the proper handling of beer, both packaged and draught. This instruction focuses on such topics as the proper storage temperature for beer, methods to stack products in the warehouse, and proper delivery procedures. The company's beer marketing seminars also have a strong quality orientation. Wholesalers learn what goes into a quality beer, and why the success of Anheuser-Busch, its distributors, and their retail accounts depends on consistently delivering a quality product to the consumer.

Wholesalers, in turn, extend training in quality control to their retail customers wherever it is legal, either in the retailer's establishment or in the wholesaler's own distribution facility. Many Anheuser-Busch distributors, in fact, equip their warehouses with special seminar rooms designed specifically for training.

Retailer training covers a wide range of beer-handling and customer service tips. Servers at on-premise accounts, such as bars, taverns, and restaurants, receive instruction on the proper way to store beer, the temperature at which it should be served, the serving of a "beer clean" glass, and the way to pour beer so that a pleasing head of foam enhances taste and aroma.

Retailers also learn how to clean draught beer lines, or in states where it is legally permitted, wholesalers perform this service at no cost to their customers. To ensure that customers always receive a fresh beer, wholesalers also provide regular stock rotation, both in their own warehouses and in retail accounts. This rotation program includes a date code on every can. The code identifies the day, year, and fifteen-minute time period of production; the plant at which the product was brewed and packaged; and the production line. For off-premise retailers, such as grocery stores and other packaged liquor accounts, training focuses primarily on product knowledge, merchandising techniques, and profitability.

Among the company's training services is a unique mobile training program for retail accounts. It consists of three customized motor coaches, each equipped with a television and a VCR for playing instructional tapes, a working draught-beer system, glassware, and other teaching aids. Each year, the mobile training coaches visit 130 to 150 markets across the country, providing training for fifteen-hundred employees of retail accounts, usually at their own establishments. In addition, the program offers training courses for college students on marketing and on alcohol awareness.

To maximize the shelf life of packaged beer, most Anheuser-Busch distributors operate refrigerated facilities called "controlled environmental warehouses," or CEWs. The conversion to refrigerated warehousing is another indication of the company's commitment to unsurpassed quality. To assist wholesalers in building and expanding their CEWs, Anheuser-Busch created an in-house engineering consulting group which offers technical expertise in such areas as facility design, insulation, and refrigeration requirements. Engineers offer assistance by hotline telephone service as well as on-site visits. As Anheuser-Busch Companies has expanded its business to market snacks and other non-beer products in recent years, the technical group has also assisted wholesalers in meeting their warehouse needs for these products.

## SERVICE AND PROFITABILITY

Anheuser-Busch provides many services designed to improve productivity of its wholesalers and to help retail accounts build sales and profitability. The wholesaler services department offers more than forty different programs related to productivity and efficiency. Besides improving wholesaler profitability, higher productivity helps hold down the need for price increases and enables wholesalers to use their resources to improve customer service. For example, the department offers a detailed analysis of wholesalers' operations—examining every facet of the business from deployment of sales personnel to a review of expenses by department. This financial and operational overview results in specific recommendations to help wholesalers make their businesses more efficient.

Computerized routing assists beer distributors in minimizing their travel time during beer deliveries. The company provides routing experts while wholesalers use their own computer systems to provide daily routes. The routing system takes into account a distributor's sales volume, number of accounts, and driving distances, as well as special requests from retailers who want to receive their beer deliveries at a certain time of the day. By reducing travel time, wholesalers can spend more productive time servicing their accounts. In addition, increased efficiency may help wholesalers avoid the significant manpower, vehicle, and other delivery costs of assigning additional routes, while still maintaining the highest quality of service available. Computerized routing is also useful when a wholesaler is planning to add a satellite warehouse location. The routing system can determine the best site for the new facility based on the number and location of existing accounts, distribution costs, and related factors.

Recognizing that sales and delivery account for the greatest portion of wholesaler's controllable expenses, Anheuser-Busch also offers a sophisticated delivery-analysis service. Company engineers spend three to five days in a wholesaler's market, riding routes and observing the wholesaler's delivery system and that of the competition. Recommendations are then made on ways to increase the existing delivery system's efficiency, and lastly alternative delivery systems are identified, evaluated, and recommended in order to improve productivity, sales, and retailer service.

The same attention to service extends to retail customers, both on and off the premises. Anheuser-Busch wholesalers concentrate on developing a personal relationship with their retail accounts, on understanding the needs of their business, and on emphasizing a team approach. This approach recognizes that the wholesaler and retailer share a common goal. Both want smooth and efficient service, with minimum problems and maximum positive results. In short, they want to form a winning team, complementing each other's efforts to be successful in the marketplace.

Anheuser-Busch wholesalers offer their retail accounts probably the most extensive customer service in the brewing industry. In addition to services related to delivery, stock rotation, and other quality assurance, distributors provide and set up merchandising displays and point-of-sale materials. Effective merchandising not only improves a retail account's appearance, but also helps consumers locate their favorite beer brands, alerts them to special offers or promotions, and serves as a key factor in generating impulse purchases which add to a retailer's sales and profitability.

The company also offers retail accounts a unique computerized shelf-management system. This system, likely the most sophisticated stocking and merchandising tool in the beer industry, is designed to minimize out-of-stock costs, decrease restocking labor costs, and organize products for ease of consumer selection. The basic key to successful retailing is having what customers want, when they want it. The retailer's challenge is to anticipate these consumer desires and to present the product in an appealing, easy-to-find manner. However, these simple goals require complex recordkeeping, analysis, and planning.

Currently used by more than five hundred of the company's wholesalers, the "shelf space evaluation tool" program analyzes a store's inventory and sales data. A computer then generates a bar graph and photographic composite showing how the beer shelf or cooler should be aligned to maximize sales and profitability. A well-balanced department matches the space allocated for each brand of beer and its package type with a product's market share in a particular store, a region, or the general market. Among their services to retailers, wholesalers also provide "hot shot" or special deliveries to deal with out-of-stock conditions, as well as troubleshooting for any other problems which may suddenly arise.

To ensure that distributors maintain the highest level of service, the company requires that principals of every wholesalership personally visit their retail accounts on a periodic basis. This enables wholesaler management to monitor the performance of their sales and delivery personnel, and to address any special retailer issues or concerns.

Retailer surveys are another important means of measuring the company's service performance. Anheuser-Busch, its company-owned beer branches, and wholesalers have used retail trade surveys for several years to obtain from retail accounts direct feedback about selling programs and services. Properly implemented, a retailer survey can be used as both a problem solver and motivation tool, reinforcing the wholesaler-retailer relationship and ultimately leading to stronger support for marketing programs and for increased sales.

The company utilizes independent research firms which contact retail accounts in a given market or region of the country. Anheuser-Busch is not identified as the source of the survey; rather, retailers are asked to evaluate all of the major brewers in their market from the standpoint of product quality and service. Results are analyzed and wholesalers are informed of the findings through the company's field sales staff. If necessary, corrective steps are taken to shore up any areas of weakness. As a rule, however, Anheuser-Busch wholesalers earn high marks for service, particularly in such areas as delivery, stocking, and call frequency.

## PUBLIC SERVICE

After the great San Francisco earthquake of 1906, Adolphus Busch donated one hundred thousand dollars to aid the victims of the disaster. Today, as then, the company is committed to public service as another important component of its total service orientation. During 1987, the company and its charitable foundations contributed approximately nineteen million dollars to many non-profit organizations in the fields of education, health care, medical research, community service, cultural enrichment, leadership development, and other programs.

In cities where it operates a brewery or company-owned beer distributorship, Anheuser-Busch offers an innovative program called "Operation Brightside." This program, which provides summer employment for youth to perform beautification and other community service jobs, has been recognized by the White House Office on Private Initiatives as an excellent example of the progress which can be achieved through a public-private partnership.

Among the company's major charitable involvements is the Muscular Dystrophy Association. In 1987, Anheuser-Busch and its wholesalers raised $3.4 million for the annual Jerry Lewis Labor Day telethon, making the company's total MDA contributions exceed $20 million over the past ten years. As the founder and national sponsor of the Lou Rawls Parade of Stars telethon, Anheuser-Busch has helped the United Negro College Fund raise more than $40 million in gifts and pledges. And, in 1986, the company became the largest corporate supporter of the National Hispanic Scholarship Fund, with a commitment of $1 million. In addition, it has an active minority-banking program and hosts regional seminars for minority entrepreneurs under its "Partners in Economic Progress" program.

Social responsibility has been another area of major concern. Anheuser-Busch is a leader in the brewing industry in developing programs to promote responsible drinking and to discourage alcohol abuse. The company's Operation A.L.E.R.T." program (Action and Leadership Through Education, Responsibility, and Training) is a multifaceted public service effort to address drunk driving and related alcohol abuse. Key components of the program include:

- "Know when to say when," a nationwide consumer campaign consisting of films, blood alcohol charts, party guides, and other educational materials designed to help consumers who choose to drink, to do so responsibly.
- A media campaign about moderation, with ads on network television, radio, outdoor billboard, and print during major holiday periods. The T.V. ads feature celebrity spokespersons, such as Dan Marino of the Miami Dolphins and actor John Schneider, reminding the public to "know when to say when."
- The "Buddy System," a program to promote responsibility among college students and other young adults of legal drinking age.
- Retailer training to instruct employees of bars and other retail accounts how to serve alcoholic beverages responsibly, and thereby how to help prevent drunk driving incidents.

The Operation A.L.E.R.T. campaign also features a designated driver program, a cab program, sponsorship of the national Students Against

Driving Drunk (SADD) organization, funding for alcoholism research, responsible guidelines for beer marketing to college students, and many other efforts to address this issue in a positive manner. "Millions of Americans enjoy beer responsibly every day, but as the leader of our industry, it is only right that we take a leading role in helping to solve the problem," states Stephen K. Lambright, a vice president at Anheuser-Busch. Although the vast majority of beer drinkers act responsibly, alcohol abuse remains a serious concern. Anheuser-Busch believes the issue can be successfully addressed with realistic programs involving a cooperative effort of the public and private sectors.

## CORPORATE SERVICE ORIENTATION

The service orientation supporting the company's beer business also extends to other Anheuser-Busch subsidiaries, including those related to brewing. The company's aluminum can manufacturer, Metal Container Corporation (M.C.C.), supplies aluminum cans to Anheuser-Busch as well as to customers in the soft drink industry. In addition to extensive quality controls relating to can production, M.C.C. provides customer service representatives who closely monitor the performance of those containers in customers' plants. Given the light weight of aluminum cans and the high speed of modern can-filling lines, such on-site visits are an important means of assuring the quality and integrity of M.C.C.'s products.

Busch Agricultural Resources, which supplies rice and barley malt used in the brewing process, provides a number of services to assure a dependable supply of the highest quality ingredients. The subsidiary works closely with its barley and rice growers to review Anheuser-Busch's quality requirements and to discuss proper techniques for handling and storing crops. Busch Agricultural also operates several country elevators throughout the West and upper Midwest in order to store barley and other grains, and to provide a means of carefully controlling the quality and varieties of barley used in the Anheuser-Busch brewing process.

Barley breeding has proven to be another successful and promising program. Busch Agricultural is continually researching and developing new varieties of barley seeds that will not only improve the flavor and quality of barley malt, but also help growers achieve greater crop yields. A similar program has also been launched for rice suppliers.

Effective retailer service is a high priority not only for the beer division but also for the company's snack division, Eagle Snacks, Inc., and its baking subsidiary, Campbell Taggert, Inc., the nation's second largest commercial baker. Because it is estimated that at least 80% of snack sales result from impulse purchases, successful merchandising is critical in the snack industry. Eagle Snacks distributors, who include Anheuser-Busch wholesalers and Campbell Taggert route salesmen, emphasize effective use of point-of-sale materials, special displays, and other merchandising techniques to draw shoppers to the snack aisle and to generate incremental sales.

Snack and bread delivery personnel also offer direct store delivery, stock rotation, shelf maintenance, and other services that retailers themselves must provide for many other types of food products. Because bread has a shorter shelf life than beer or snacks, Campbell Taggert route salesmen call on major accounts twice a day—usually in the morning to make a delivery, and then again in the afternoon to straighten and merchandise a shelf or display. In addition, all delivery personnel participate in training programs to review product handling and other quality issues.

Whether the business is brewing beer or marketing snacks, producing aluminum cans or helping barley growers achieve a better crop, quality and service are the two most important values within the Anheuser-Busch corporate family. As a saying at the company goes, "Somebody still cares about quality."

# Cable Television

American Television and Communications Corporation
Patricia Karpas

# Customer Service Strategies

**Patricia Karpas**
American Television and Communications Corporation

American Television and Communications Corporation (ATC) provides cable television service to 3.54 million basic cable television households, including three million premium television customers, in thirty-two states nationwide.

ATC began as a publicly owned company in 1968 and became a wholly owned subsidiary of Time Inc. in 1978. In 1986 the company assumed its current publicly held status, with Time Inc. owning 82 percent of its common stock.

Headquarters operations, based in Englewood, Colorado, are performed by a staff of three-hundred while a nationwide staff of nine thousand run the cable television operations.

## INTRODUCTION

Cable television, received by 50 percent of American TV households, is a ten billion dollar business, and continued growth is expected. At the same time, a competitive challenge in the form of video tape rentals, competition from neighboring cable systems, and the satellite dish business, will continue to grow. However, it is the 50 percent of American TV homes not yet subscribing to cable television that represents the industry's principal challenge.

ATC has made great strides in addressing historical technical and billing problems and has made a strong commitment to customer satisfaction, improved programming, and quality service.

Quality service means:

- Staying in touch with and understanding the consumer perspective.
- Providing unique, exceptional quality programming that meets the demands of viewers nationwide.
- Offering an increasingly wider variety of high quality, differentiated programming—something to satisfy each person's special interests.
- Delivering reliable service with trained and committed employees who follow through to meet the needs of each and every customer.

ATC has taken several steps over the last several years to ensure quality, service delivery. This commitment involves:

- A *mission statement* demonstrating the company's vision and philosophy, including a powerful orientation toward the needs of the customer.
- A *senior management commitment* to support customer service initiatives.
- A *decentralized organizational structure* allowing key consumer-related decisions to be made in communities by a management team sensitive to local needs.
- An ongoing comprehensive and independent *customer satisfaction tracking program* designed to measure customer perception of service delivery.
- A *set of performance standards*, Indicators of Quality Service (IQS), to ensure that operational procedures meet required standards of good service.
- A *set of locally developed initiatives* to guarantee quality service is a top priority.

Customer service has been, and will continue to be, a top priority for ATC.

Two of ATC's division presidents appropriately state the attitude toward service delivery. According to Randall Fraser, president of the Raleigh/Durham, North Carolina division, "Customer service isn't a job description. It's an attitude, an attitude that each and every one of us brings to the job and every customer transaction. We're here to satisfy the entertainment and information needs of our customers; professional, efficient and friendly service helps us to meet the consumer's needs." Stephen McMahon, president of the Jackson/Monroe, California division, points out that "Management places a very high priority on customer service and this is communicated to each employee. In fact, we borrowed Lee Iacocca's phrase, 'The pride is back,' and try to communicate the pride we feel about our company in every customer transaction. If the employees feel it, it's easy to translate it to the customers."

## A MISSION STATEMENT

ATC has developed a statement of its vision, its mission, its value, and philosophy to provide direction within the organization so that all employees can work toward consistent goals, including the delivery of top-notch service (see table 1).

## A SENIOR MANAGEMENT COMMITMENT

ATC's senior management commitment to customer service is demonstrated in several ways. Since 1984, the corporate headquarters office in Englewood, Colorado, has been the home of a customer service department that is dedicated to serving ATC divisions nationwide. This group's objectives are:

- To provide information and expertise to divisions in order to increase the understanding and awareness of service-oriented issues and activities.
- To develop measurement tools to assess the impact of excellent service on profitability objectives.
- To support the development of outstanding customer service training programs, for example, Professional Customer Service Skills, for line managers, supervisors, and customer contact staff.
- To design and implement recognition and incentive programs to promote outstanding service performance by customer contact staff.
- To collect and disseminate information on succesful service programs from within and outside of ATC.
- To provide ongoing support to divisions in the evaluation of new equipment available to support efficiency in customer service operations.

Having a group in the corporate headquarters dedicated to the goal of achieving outstanding customer service levels exemplifies the commitment of senior management to customer service at ATC.

## A DECENTRALIZED ORGANIZATION STRUCTURE

In 1983 ATC began to evaluate its organizational structure to determine if it served company objectives most effectively. Technical problems and poor customer service were commonplace, and a new organizational structure was needed to address many of these issues.

TABLE 1
MISSION STATEMENT

---

ATC VISION

Working together to provide entertainment and information choices.

ATC MISSION

We develop, market, deliver, and service in a quality and profitable manner
a broad selection of electronic entertainment and information
for as many customers as possible in our communities.

ATC VALUES AND PHILOSOPHY

| **We believe in our:** | **We will operate our business so that:** |
| --- | --- |
| Heritage of high performance. | In all we do, we strive to be the best. |
| Customers, the most important part of our business. | We provide our customers with quality entertainment and information choices and service at fair prices. |
| People, our greatest resource. | We treat people in all positions with fairness and dignity, and we give them room to grow and achieve. Our people are proud of their high standards and are rewarded equitably for high performance and contributions. |
| Communities–they and we both benefit from our contributions. | Our communities benefit from our service and from our individual and company commitment and activities. |
| Growth–it provides vitality to our enterprise. | Our company grows by adding new customers, building new businesses and serving more communities. |
| Financial strength from efficient and profitable operations. | We provide stable and fair returns to our shareholders, stable employment and opportunity for our people, and quality facilities and services to satisfy our customers. |
| Adaptability in a competitive and changing world. | We test and try new concepts and services. We understand that one of our key strengths is our ability to identify and benefit from change. |
| Integrity in all our actions. | We treat our customers, people, communities, and suppliers with fairness and honesty. |
| Teamwork, it enables each of us to be more effective. | We communicate openly and with trust in mutually pursuing opportunities and solving problems. Each person is important to the success of the ATC team. |

A reorganizational plan that would place decision-making responsibilities at the local cable operation (where the customer lives) was the solution. But, before a decentralized effort could be accomplished, a separate but complementary effort had to take place. The company began to reorganize its inventory by selling smaller, scattered cable systems and acquiring or trading for cable systems in contiguous franchises in targeted metropolitan areas. Dubbed ATC's "clustering" strategy, it provided economies of scale in marketing services and provided a greater challenge to attract, hire, and retain outstanding local management. The positive results of the strategy confirm that clustering not only is the most efficient and effective way for ATC to operate, but is also the most customer-sensitive way to operate. The completion of the clustering activity provided the framework for the formation of what are now twenty-four largely autonomous divisions, each headed by a president and staffed with excellent managers in every major discipline. Additionally, ATC manages five Paragon Communications (joint venture ATC and Houston Industries) divisions similarly organized. This decentralized operating structure allows ATC to be closer to its customers and encourages more personal customer contact.

## A CUSTOMER SATISFACTION TRACKING PROGRAM

ATC's Customer Satisfaction Tracking (CST) program was initiated in 1984 to survey customers' satisfaction with their local (ATC owned and operated) cable companies. It is designed to provide management a means of evaluating and tracking service performance—from the customers' perspective. The survey effort has strategic implications that influence how ATC does business in communities. Over time, the survey also provides management with a norm by which to evaluate new customer service programs.

The biannual survey by an independent research company measures twenty-four ATC divisions and five Paragon Communications divisions, and interviews more than seven thousand customers. Questions fall into the following categories:

1. When contact is made with the ATC office:
   - Courtesy of the customer service representative
   - Ability and rapidity of the customer service representative to solve problems
   - Ease of getting through by phone
2. When visited at home by cable installers or technicians:
   - Courtesy and professional appearance of the service technicians
   - Competence and rapidity of the field work performed
3. General cable company questions:
   - Signal reception
   - Comprehensibility of cable bills
   - Company image in the community
   - Overall service

Since the initiation of the study, customer service, as assessed by our customers, has been on an upward trend. The measurement process, including the ranking of divisions, has provided impetus for improvement in several areas. In fact, both the spirit of friendly competition between divisions and the fact that a component of compensation is tied to scores have helped to motivate this positive trend. The following graphs show various improvements:

TABLE 2
ATC CST RATINGS TREND
by Survey

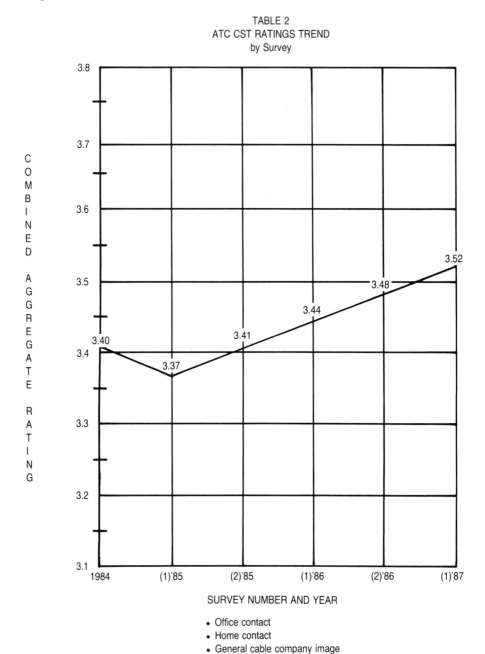

SURVEY NUMBER AND YEAR

- Office contact
- Home contact
- General cable company image

Table 2 shows total aggregate ratings improved from 1984 to 1987 (3.40 to 3.52).

TABLE 3
ATC CST RATINGS TREND
by Survey

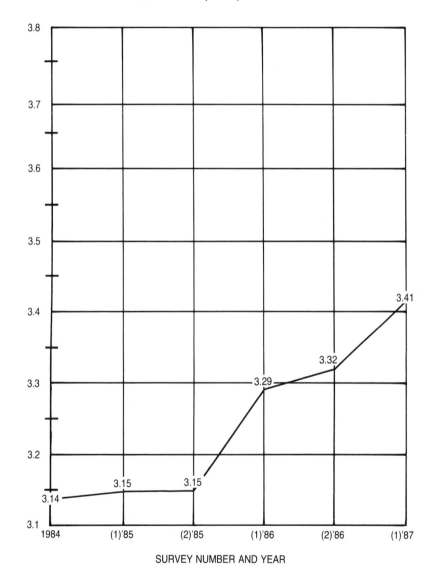

SURVEY NUMBER AND YEAR

- Courtesy of the customer service representative
- Ability and rapidity of the customer service representative to solve problems
- Ease of getting through by phone

Table 3 depicts total office contact ratings improved from 3.14 to 3.41 during the period 1984 to 1987.

TABLE 4
ATC CST RATINGS TREND
by Survey

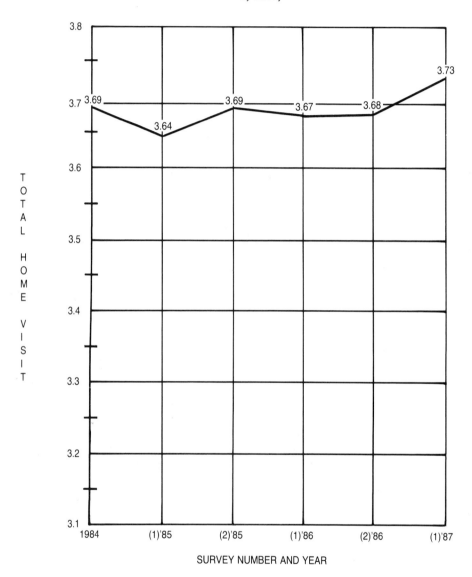

SURVEY NUMBER AND YEAR

- Courtesy and professional appearance of the service technicians.
- Competence and rapidity of the field work performed

In Table 4 the total home contact ratings improved from 1984 to 1987 (3.69 to 3.73).

TABLE 5
ATC CST RATINGS TREND
by Survey

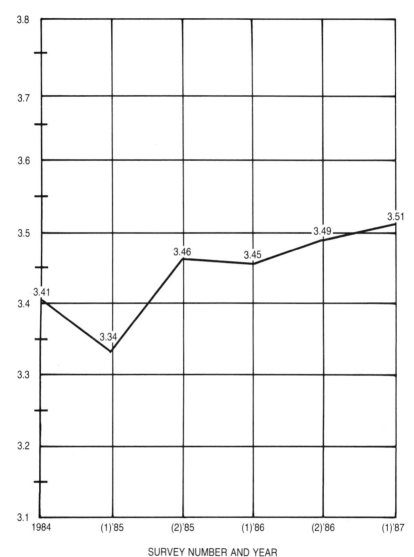

SURVEY NUMBER AND YEAR

- Signal reception
- Comprehensibility of cable bills
- Company image in the community
- Overall service

Table 5 represents the total general cable company ratings improvement through 1984 1987 (3.41 to 3.51).

49

## A Set of Performance Standards

Customer service standards, indices, benchmarks, etc., have been used to measure performance in most service-oriented companies. They are used to measure a company's ability to satisfy customers and to scrutinize consistently the results of each customer contact. ATC has developed performance standards called Indicators of Quality Service (IQS). The IQS serve as a framework for each operating division, which can customize them to fit specific local needs and opportunities. Every measurement is based on the individual circumstances of the organization, as well as on the public's perception of good service. Key indices are maintained through healthy commitment by employees and through management's desire to keep service at optimum levels.

A goal in the development of the IQS was to focus on what were identified as the key customer contact points—the incoming *telephone call*, the *installation* or connection of cable service, and the *repair* of cable service. ATC used the information learned from the CST studies in order to develop specific IQS. ATC believes that the Customer Satisfaction Tracking program and the following Indicators of Quality Service jointly provide information needed to stay close to the customer's perspective:

1. *Incoming call management indicators*—to ensure accessibility to the cable company via the telephone.
   - *Hold time*—the length of time, in seconds, that a customer waits on the line before the call is handled.
   - *Abandonment rate*—the percentage of customers who hang up once a call has been accepted into the system, but before it is handled by a customer service representative or other agent.
   - *Busy rate*—the percentage of time that all trunk lines are busy and that customers are unable to make contact with the system.
2. *Outages*—to measure the reliability of service delivered on a consistent basis and to assess the frequency, duration, and impact of service interruptions.
3. *Picture and audio quality*—to measure the reliability of the product being delivered to the customer's home.
4. *Percentage of service requests completed per customer*—to reduce the number and percentage of service requests.
5. *Response time to service requests*—to ensure timeliness in response to service requests.
6. *Installation completion percentage*—to ensure that customers are connected with cable service as scheduled.
7. *Installation lead time*—to ensure timeliness in response to connection requests.

Each one of these indicators was developed with the intent to strive toward providing all ATC customers with 100% reliability.

# A SET OF LOCALLY DEVELOPED INITIATIVES

ATC manages over thirty divisions encompassing more than one hundred cable companies throughout the country. Each operating divison has made its own commitment to quality, as evidenced through its specific programs or activities designed to improve service delivery to customers. Different divisions initiated various actions in four areas:

**Accessibility.** Office hours were expanded to maximize customer access to the company; the number of incoming telephone lines serving customers were increased and investments were made in Automatic Response Units and Automatic Call Distributors; customer service reps and technical staff were increased where appropriate; and remote payment centers for the convenience of outlying customers were added.

**Reliability.** Training programs for employees were improved in the areas of interpersonal communications, technical competence, product knowledge, sales development, complaint management and resolution, and professional customer service skills. Also, the level and quality of preventive maintenance was increased.

**Customer education.** Customer information handbooks and literature were developed; business reply cards soliciting customer feedback on performance were designed; and the quality of program guides delivering product information was improved.

**Employee motivation.** Recognition and incentive programs to reward outstanding customer contact professionals were initiated. Also, a sixteen-page, company-wide, quarterly newsletter to highlight outstanding customer service performance was produced.

The divisions have also realized the importance of "upward" and "downward" communications, both by advocating a customer service philosophy and cheerleading for customer contact people. In addition, several divisions initiated their own Commitment to Quality programs. The statement of "Commitment to Quality" by ATC's Rochester division illustrates one of many programs designed to get all employees behind the quality effort (see table 6).

TABLE 6
Commitment to Quality

At Greater Rochester Cablevision (GRC), service to our customer is our number one concern. Our quality of service depends upon

1. Being courteous to every customer and using the customer's name during each contact.
2. Reflecting a positive attitude toward our customers, our product, and fellow employees.
3. Displaying a consistently professional appearance while on the job.
4. Expressing concern for the company's image and reputation, and accepting the concept that "the employee is the company."
5. Exerting the extra effort to follow through, not expecting that someone else will do it.
6. Being the customers' agent and knowing that our job is to solve our customers' problems.
7. Bending the rules sometimes, when the rules get in the way of servicing the customer effectively.
8. Providing feedback to each customer about what action has been or will be taken.
9. Continuously seeking knowledge about our products and our industry to inform and serve our customers better.
10. Demonstrating pride in workmanship that results in the highest level of quality and productivity.

As an employee of GRC, I support these ten quality measurements and acknowledge my commitment to uphold these principles in my daily work performance.

*At time of publication, ATC was in the process of reorganizing its operations. The information contained here relates to programs designed and implemented between 1984 and June 1988.*

# Chemicals

BASF Corporation
Manfred Buller

Dow Chemical Company
Carl C. Thurman and Sam L. Smolik

# Quality Improvement Process at BASF Polymers Group

**Manfred Buller, Ph.D.**
BASF Corporation

BASF Corporation was formed in early 1986, when the company restructured its North American operations by merging BASF Wyandotte Corporation, Badische Corporation, BASF Inmont Corporation, BASF Systems Corporation, and other units.

The company's chemicals division, headquartered in Parsippany, New Jersey is comprised of the former BASF Wyandotte Corp., plus the chemical activities of the former Badische Corp. Included among its products are agricultural chemicals, vitamins, dyestuffs, pigments, ethylene oxide and glycol, antifreeze, functional fluids, intermediate chemicals, expandable polystyrene, polyurethane chemicals and specialties, nonionic surfactants, and catalysts.

The polymers group produces polyurethane chemicals and systems for a number of automotive applications, including car seats, visors, headrests, bumpers, sheathing panels, and other related products. The polymers group is also a major supplier to the packaging, furniture, and construction industries.

## INITIATION OF A QUALITY IMPROVEMENT PROGRAM

When the polymers group of the chemicals division of BASF Corporation formally launched its Quality Improvement Process (QIP) in 1984, it was building on a tradition of quality service to customers and end-users dating back more than a century, when its parent company was founded in Germany as Badische Anilin- & Soda-Fabrik.

In late 1984, executives of the polymers group came to the conclusion that employees were not sufficiently aware of the urgent need for systematic defect prevention and an overall improvement of quality. These concerns were triggered by the fact that U.S. automakers were finding themselves increasingly challenged on quality issues by Japanese competitors and were demanding quality improvements from their suppliers. It was widely perceived that the domestic auto companies were producing vehicles inferior to those of the quality-conscious Japanese.

To help rectify this critical problem, a quality improvement program was implemented at polymers group facilities. The effort was named Quality Improvement Process (QIP) because the word *process* implies an ongoing, increasing commitment. As its educational base, the polymers group chose Philip Crosby's *Quality Education System*, which stresses the importance of quality in all departments of a company. This system coincided with the polymers group's objective of using an across-the-board approach aimed at achieving quality improvements in product development, manufacturing, shipping, and service. In addition, emphasis was placed on helping key personnel to acquire the specific tools of quality management. Many, accordingly, were schooled in the use of statistical process control techniques, failure mode and effect analysis, process flow diagrams and control plans, and other quality assurance methods.

Simply stated, statistical process control (SPC) is a technique through which process variables are monitored and the data obtained are statistically analyzed. The process can then be fine-tuned to control the variables. Because the system relies on continuous and consistent recordkeeping, it helps to point to cause-and-effect relationships. Also, because it actively involves employees in this ongoing effort, it helps to make them aware of their contributions to the quality improvement process.

Failure mode and effect analysis (FMEA) takes a given process and hypothesizes all the various failures that could take place. For each potential mishap, an estimate is made of the effects it could have on the final product, and proposals for countering the specific defects are reviewed.

As a further impetus for immediate quality assurance improvements, polymers group management worked out a formula to determine the approximate cost of nonconformances in quality. By indexing expenses related to scrap, excess inventory, and reshipments against total company sales, it was found that nonconformances were responsible for a substantial drain on the group's resources. The QIP, then, could be justified on a strictly profit-related basis. It was time to invest that same money in preventing defects.

## DEFECT PREVENTION

The QIP began to take shape with a basic outline of what needed to be accomplished. It was recognized that significant attitudinal changes had to be brought about in the workforce toward the importance of quality in service as well as in all other operations.

### *Zero Defects* as a Standard

For a working definition of quality, polymers group management decided to reject the widely used standard for acceptable quality levels (AQL) of *less than 2%* for a process, because such levels would still lead to excessive reshipments and inventories. Instead, sights were set on *zero defects* as the standard. This meant that an immediate alert would be issued upon detection of any defect, and a system implemented to prevent its recurrence.

In the key area of customer service, no industry standard for acceptable quality existed. So the polymers group formulated its own definition, basing its standard for quality service on the specific needs expressed by the individual customer.

Customer satisfaction would be virtually guaranteed through close adherence to this quality benchmark, the company reasoned. Whether in regard to products or services, the polymers group's QIP approach is grounded on the principle of defect prevention. Management firmly believes that a successful quality improvement effort must be based on preventing mistakes before they occur, rather than solving problems after the fact. The educational thrust of the process, therefore, has been to instill in the entire polymers group workforce a keen awareness of the importance of defect prevention.

### Quality Improvement Teams

The day-to-day business of the QIP is overseen by Quality Improvement Teams (QITs) consisting of selected managers recruited from each plant or business group. The polymers group has eleven such teams, representing five product groups and six plants, with a maximum of ten managers per team. These teams play a pivotal role in identifying nonconformances and providing liaison between the workforce and top management. They also interact directly with workers to effect solutions. A steering committee composed of polymers group administrative staff provides the QITs with input grounded on upper management's objectives.

If a specific problem is identified—a recurring customer service error, for example—the QIT immediately appoints a subcommittee to take action. Applying methods learned through the Quality Education System, the subcommittee initiates a corrective action system which defines the problem, applies a quick fix, identifies the root cause, and implements a solution. The subcommittee then evaluates and follows up on the problem to prevent any possibility of a recurrence.

To maintain a fresh perspective and evaluate progress, QITs interact with one another at periodic meetings. The gatherings serve to assure that each team is adhering to the specified approach. When teams complete the implementation of quality improvements in their respective areas, the entire procedure is repeated in order to fine-tune the improved products and services. Approximately 25 to 50% of the team is replaced after each cycle in order to gain new perspectives.

Clearly, the overall success of the process depends on effective education. Defect elimination, the ultimate goal of the QIP, cannot take place without vigilance on the part of the workforce and the abilities to recognize nonconformances and to solve resulting problems. Initially, therefore, workers throughout the polymers group were apprised of the new quality improvement policies and of management's commitment to the QIP at group sessions; the vice president of the polymers group personally attended these sessions that his staff had organized at all of the plant sites. As the effort has expanded, employees have followed in the footsteps of their managers by attending quality improvement courses, with some receiving training that has enabled them to pass along to fellow employees the principles of the Quality Education System. All polymers group employees are required to attend the in-house training sessions. The course consists of a weekly two-and-a-half-hour session for ten weeks. Among the topics covered are: the need for quality improvement; concepts of quality improvements; how to establish quality requirements; how to permanently eliminate defects; the team approach to defect elimination; the need for an easily understood performance standard; the cost of quality, and the role of the company and the supplier in quality improvement.

## Quality Improvement by Suppliers

In addition to putting its own house in order, however, the polymers group recognized the need to extend quality improvement education to its suppliers. At a seminar held in 1986 in Dearborn, Michigan, the polymers group announced to the more than one hundred supplier representatives present that it would in the future survey the plants of all its suppliers. Those without a comprehensive quality improvement program of their own keyed to defect prevention were urged to initiate such an effort; moreover, the polymers group offered to share what they had learned with them.

Polymers group management thinks their program is the first in the chemical industry; the supplier survey project is expected to include over one hundred plants. It is part of their overall effort to reduce waste and promote greater efficiency. While such surveys may be new to the chemical industry, polymers group plants have been undergoing regular inspections by the automobile industry for the past two years.

A highlight of the polymers group's ongoing supplier plant survey program was the inspection in fall 1986 of the facilities of Du Pont chemicals and pigments department in Beaumont, Texas. Du Pont, which supplies the polymers group with several raw materials, already had its own companywide Total Quality Management Program, which predated polymers' QIP. The result of the interaction between these two quality-conscious companies has proved beneficial to both. Prior to the Du Pont survey, a team of polymers purchasing, production, and quality assurance executives traveled to Beaumont and laid the groundwork for the upcoming plant inspection. While the quality improvement approaches of the two companies differed in some respects, it was discovered that they had much in common, including the goal to work in partnership with customers to provide the best possible service.

## QIP Achievements

Though still in its early stages (a five-year period is considered to be the minimum time span necessary to accurately measure a program's effectiveness), the QIP has already begun to pay dividends for the BASF polymers group. Cost savings at the company's Wyandotte, Michigan, polyols plant alone have been impressive.

The polymers group has determined that its *cost of quality* in 1986—a figure derived by adding the *price of conformance (POC)* to the *price of nonconformance (PONC)*—equaled 17% of sales, with the PONC accounting for 11% and the POC 6%. The POC represents the costs associated with quality prevention systems, and the PONC the costs incurred while not doing jobs right the first time. Subsequent tracking of the cost of quality will enable polymers group management to measure progress in reducing nonconformance and to pinpoint which areas need special attention. The ultimate result should be improved profits for the group.

In addition to its early impact on the polymers group's profit picture, the QIP has elicited highly encouraging responses from key customers such as General Motors and the Ford Motor Company. In 1986, for example, the Wyandotte polyols plant was awarded GM's prestigious Corporate Spear One preferred supplier award, the first time such recognition had ever been given to a chemical company. Less than 2% of GM's thousands of suppliers hold this rating. The Wyandotte plant also has received Ford's *Q1* top quality rating. Following recent audits by GM, moreover, BASF's Livonia, Michigan, urethane specialties plant and Geismar, Louisiana Methylene Diphenylisocyanate (MDI) plant have received GM's Corporate Spear Two award, a distinction given to suppliers judged to have superior product and service quality improvement programs. The likely end-result of such recognition by customers is a share-of-market increase, since purchasers have a way of gravitating to suppliers known for their reliability.

In honor of its successful implementation of the first stages of the QIP, the polymers group this year held a Zero Defects Day celebration for its Wyandotte polyols plant. The festive event marked the completion of a year-long educational process aimed at preparing the workforce to effectively initiate the *zero defects* approach at all levels of production and service. As the first polymers group plant to reach this *change-of-attitude* day, the polyols facility attracted companywide attention as an industry front-runner in the quest for quality. The major value of the occasion, of course, was that it served to symbolize an important beginning, a point from which *zero defects* was to become the only acceptable standard.

## QUALITY STANDARDS IN SERVICE DELIVERY

Since first initiating the QIP, the polymers group has never lost sight of the fact that service quality must be an integral part of the process. Striving for product quality is useless if the company is unable to take and process a correct order, get a shipment delivered on time, or produce a correct invoice. By its very nature, a quality improvement process must encompass mechanisms to provide immediate response to service problems, whether they originate with the supplier or the customer.

### Shipping and Delivery

The polymers group has instituted a number of measures specifically designed to improve the quality of service to its customers. For example, all invoices are reviewed and audited before mailing. Although this is costly, we want to be assured that the customer receives an error-free invoice. In the meantime, a corrective action team is investigating a prevention system designed to guard against future nonconformances in this area.

It is important to keep up-to-date on a customer's shipping requirements. A misunderstanding may cause delays that generate ill will. Here, too, prevention is the key, and this has been accomplished by the use of *customer specification* sheets, which help the polymers group to maintain for each customer up-to-the-minute computerized instructions relating to current product requirements, handling, delivery, and all other pertinent factors. The customer specification sheet gives the specifications for products shipped by tank trucks and tank cars, notes what must be included on the enclosed certificate of analysis, and lists the products ordered by the customer, together with any unusual specifications. In the company's view, failure to follow accepted procedures in issuing required documentation is poor service quality. While one might tolerate occasional oversights, it is not in the best interests of the customer to do so. Therefore, the polymers group is careful to submit all proper papers, including certificates of analysis, when shipping products to a customer.

As part of its overall service quality upgrade, the polymers group is improving the appearance of its delivery systems. Beginning in 1987 with renovations of eighty-five railroad cars at BASF's Geismar Toleune Diisocyanate (TDI) plant, the program will be expanded to include all polymers' cars at the Geismar MDI plant, the Geismar polyol plant and Wyandotte. In all, three hundred railroad cars will be spruced up, tested, and serviced, if necessary. Tank cars will be pressurized to check for leakage, and the lining, which prevents the product from touching metal, will be examined for tears. The guidelines established for the polymers group are more stringent than those of the Association of American Railroads. Under this program all railroad cars will have been serviced at least once by the end of 1988. In the future, all railroad cars will be checked for appearance before the loading of each shipment. The cost of this continuing effort, though significant, is worthwhile because a clean, neat appearance builds customers' confidence in the company and its products.

Ongoing emphasis on quality in both products and services is a powerful competitive weapon in today's global marketplace. It has become clear that the Quality Improvement Process can play a pivotal role in determining the outcome of a battle for share of the market. Service quality can have a particularly important influence in setting a company apart from its competition. For example, one of BASF's plants ensured a continued good relationship with Ford when it was able to ship an emergency order to the company's Utica, Michigan, plant four and one-half hours from the time of the request.

Another example of service quality in the manufacturing sector concerned a General Motors plant that received a shipment of instrument panel resin which was inadvertently contaminated with an inert material, preventing use of the product. A technical service team immediately went to the GM plant and filtered the contaminant from the otherwise usable product on-site to prevent interrupting production. The contamination had not been noticed because the product went right from the pipeline to the tankcar without ever being seen. After this incident, a method was devised and equipment installed to prevent a recurrence. General Motors, in turn, cited BASF's response as the good work of a Spear One supplier.

At the polymers group, technical service people are giving special emphasis to the commitment to quality. They are made available whenever needed to help customers improve their products; this service is being increasingly sought as the polymers group's reputation for quality excellence spreads.

## Customer Feedback

A reputation for excellence, of course, is a result of many factors. Not the least of these is a seemingly simple adjustment in attitude. The polymers group has adopted the attitude that goes along with putting oneself in the customer's shoes. What is involved here, clearly, is a philosophy essentially based on the golden rule, "supply to others what we would like others to supply to us."

Supplying quality service, by its very nature, requires customer feedback. Customer reactions help to ascertain the effectiveness of an effort, including the follow-up systems employed. The best method of determining just how well a job is being done, the polymers group has found, is to ask the obvious question, How can we serve you better?

The polymers group adopted just such an approach two years ago, shortly after the inception of the Quality Improvement Process. With each polyurethane shipment, the paperwork is sent in an envelope that also contains a checklist to specify whether all is in order; among the items included are a certificate of analysis, customer shipping papers, driver shipping papers, safety data, and a customer report form. The envelope also informs the customer of the date on which the shipment was sent and names who loaded, approved, and released the shipment. Emergency phone numbers are given for BASF at Parsippany and Wyandotte, and for the carrier of the shipment.

Contained in that same envelope is a self-addressed stamped card listing a number of questions aimed at rating the quality of service. Customers are asked if the shipment arrived on time; whether it was in good condition and conformed to requirements; if the appropriate paperwork was delivered; if the correct fittings and equipment were on the truck; and if the truck driver was courteous and helpful. Space is provided for comments. All polymers group customers are urged to return these cards so that action can be taken on their suggestions. Usually, upon receipt of the cards, any necessary changes are made immediately to prevent recurrence of the cited problem. Often this involves altering the customer's file or adjusting a computer program by entering new data. Particular attention then is given to insure that subsequent shipments meet all the newly specified requirements. The overwhelming majority of cards returned indicate that there has been no problem with the shipment. Nonetheless, customer responses are statistically evaluated on a quarterly basis with the goal of eliminating all complaints. The Quality Improvement Process with its emphasis on *zero defects* brings this goal well within reach.

Evaluating customer feedback in this manner has been an invaluable tool in the polymers group's ongoing effort to improve quality of service. The cards reveal whether there has been **total** *conformance to requirements*, which is the polymers group's definition of quality service. In working to achieve such conformance, difficulties tend to occur in obtaining *all* the requirements of a particular customer. Customers often assume that certain requirements need not be listed because they are obvious. What is obvious to them, however, sometimes may not be apparent to the supplier. The follow-up cards help to communicate this idea, as well as to bring out latent requirements that even the customer may have neglected to recognize.

Customer requirements, furthermore, may change over time. The cards provide a means of communicating these changes before costly complaint-handling procedures need to be called into play. Interestingly, while problems with the product tend to surface immediately, errors in service are often repressed. Perhaps it is because service problems are not thought of as crucial. Yet they often lead a customer to change suppliers. It, therefore, is clear that such quality-of-service measures as customer feedback cards can play an essential role in cementing a satisfactory relationship between supplier and customer, as well as uncovering a potentially serious problem.

The polymers group learned from one recent feedback card, for example, that despite being delayed because of a problem in the customer's receiving system, the driver who delivered a product remained courteous and helpful. Another card included comments about the "great job" one of BASF's carriers does. Feedback such as this, of course, allows BASF to determine the ongoing effectiveness of its quality improvement efforts and, in turn, helps it to continue providing superior service.

Good suppliers, such as the carriers cited by customers, are a prized asset and demand a relationship of mutual trust and respect. The ultimate manifestation of this attitude, and one that has helped to reinforce the polymers group's belief in the Quality Improvement Process, is reflected in a recent observation by a General Motors representative: "We have enough confidence in your product to accept it without checking it ourselves. That's the kind of supplier we want to do business with."

# The Management of Product Stewardship

**Carl C. Thurman**
**Sam L. Smolik**
The Dow Chemical Company

Dow Chemical Company, founded in 1897, manufactures more than 1,800 products in chemicals, plastics, metals, agricultural and consumer products, and pharmaceuticals. Headquartered in Midland, Michigan, the company employs approximately 50,000 people.

# INTRODUCTION

At Dow Chemical Company, service quality takes on a distinctly different role than in many other manufacturing operations. The products Dow delivers—chemicals—require an extraordinary level of customer service to assure that these products are properly handled. Not only does Dow's business depend on its customers, but its customers depend on Dow to guide them in the use of chemical products that, if improperly handled, could affect the life and health of people far beyond the customer base.

Dow's product stewardship program is its means of assuring delivery of quality customer service. A prime example of this program is the product stewardship program for allyl chloride and epichlorohydrin. It began with the basic concept that Dow's job was to assist its distributors and customers in training their people to safely use and transport these potentially hazardous products.

Product stewardship is a commitment to protect all individuals who utilize Dow Chemical products, as well as to protect the environment. It includes toxicology, ecology, and safe handling of products during manufacturing, shipment, use and disposal. A sound product stewardship program is based on an understanding of what the customer needs and how the product will be used. Technical bulletins, labeling, and material safety data sheets are basic elements of stewardship programs. Other elements include storage recommendations, handling emergencies, equipment guidelines, industrial hygiene, safety audits, and truck driver training.

One example of a comprehensive product stewardship program at Dow involves a group of four chemical intermediates widely used in the coatings industry: allyl chloride, epichlorohydrin, hydroxyethyl acrylate (HEA), and hydroxypropyl acrylate (HPA). Each has specific stewardship concerns—allyl chloride is highly flammable, epichlorohydrin is classified as an animal carcinogen, and HEA and HPA monomers are very reactive and potentially toxic. How does a stewardship program manage a group of products with such diversity in properties and handling characteristics?

A systematic approach to stewardship starts before the customer receives an initial sample. It utilizes a set of stewardship "tools," each designed to provide information, answer customer concerns, and monitor product use. Some of these stewardship tools, as they apply to allyl chloride, epichlorohydrin, HEA and HPA are discussed below.

## Controlled Sampling

No sample of allyl chloride, epichlorohydrin, HEA or HPA can be sent without the authorization of the product steward—and then, only after a conversation with the individual who will actually use it. Two critical items must be established: one, that the product will be used as an intermediate for an environmentally safe end use that complies with governmental regulations; and two, that the company requesting the sample is a legitimate business capable of handling and disposing the materials properly. Once these criteria are established, product properties, labeling, and safe handling are reviewed. A follow-up letter is sent by the service center and includes a Material Safety Data sheet. It is the responsibility of the product steward to provide any additional information required by the customer.

Dow will not sample nor sell a product for selected applications. In this circumstance, an effort will be made to recommend an environmentally safe alternative, along with manufacturing contacts. Influencing and supervising global activities of this nature are carried out through Dow technology centers. Initial sample requests may lead to on-site visitation of potential customers where specific needs are determined by the level of product consumption and end use.

## Product Stewardship Manuals/Customer Training Sessions
One focal point of the intermediates product stewardship program, and an invaluable resource for the customer, is the Product Stewardship Manual. Each is individually numbered, assigned, and computer logged to facilitate revisions. These reference books cover emergency information, employee education, handling practices, storage guidelines, piping and pump design, waste disposal, analytical methods, and medical surveillance testing, among other information.

Generally presented during training and handling seminars, the manual is thoroughly reviewed (along with MSD sheets) with the people actually involved in the day-to-day operations of product handling. These sessions provide the opportunity to discuss any specific concerns the customer may have. If an inquiry requires more data than the manual or the product steward has available, Dow technical experts from research, production, the technical center, and industrial hygiene can respond with follow-up letters.

## Plant Safety Audits
Often requested by customers, plant safety audits are conducted prior to scaling up from drum to tank truck quantities. Materials of construction, electrical grounding, and oxygen content in the storage tank are checked with the plant engineer. Two additional items must be verified—one, that unobstructed safety showers and eye baths are located within 25 feet of the unloading site; and two, that closed loop unloading systems with a nitrogen padded storage tank for allyl chloride and epichlorohydrin are in place. (HEA and HPA do not use nitrogen because it excludes the oxygen necessary to maintain the stabilizer's activity.)

If a plant safety audit turns up unsatisfactory conditions, they are discussed on-site with the engineer, and summarized again in a follow-up letter. Dow offers assistance in amending potential safety problems; however, if the product steward has concerns regarding the health and safety of individuals and environment, Dow may delay sales. In this case, the steward is required to proceed through a series of documented follow-up steps with the customer until the situation is adequately corrected.

## Industrial Hygiene Surveys

Another product stewardship tool for intermediates is a Dow sponsored industrial hygiene survey. Although at considerable expense to Dow, the product steward and certified industrial hygienist will take short term and extended period air samples around process area and personnel for one day. As an example, a survey might include monitoring a complete batch cycle in which allyl chloride, epichlorohydrin, HEA or HPA are used as intermediates. Samples collected throughout the day are returned to Dow labs for analysis and a formal report of the results is sent back to the customer's management.

## Carrier Training Programs

Just as important as proper on-site handling is safe transportation of the product. Toward this end, drivers may not transport the product until trained through a program given at the carrier's terminal four to six times each year. Emphasis is placed on the importance of safety to the carrier's business, as well as to Dow's. Drivers are informed about product handling, regulations, emergencies, and unloading procedures.

Consistent professional and courteous service is an essential ingredient Dow requires of the carrier's drivers. Occasionally, the product steward may show up unannounced at a tank truck unloading simply to watch. At times, the carrier's terminal manager may accompany him. Dow regards its carriers as representatives of The Dow Chemical Company and its stewardship program. To assure all aspects of tank truck delivery are maintained, Dow uses a sole carrier with dedicated tank trucks for allyl chloride and epichlorohydrin.

## Unloading Programs

When scaling up from drum to tank truck quantities, a Dow representative is on hand. The plant safety audit discussed earlier always precedes the initial unloading to ensure that the customer is ready to unload, handle, and use the product properly. Drivers must confirm proper product identification prior to unloading. This may be done by catching a sample for the customer to analyze.

Tank trucks possess both internal and external valves in order to reduce the change of spills. Future plans are to replace onboard pumps with dry disconnects. This will further prevent the chance of spills. The manufacturer of the dry disconnects, the exclusive carrier, and Dow are an active and committed team in making this change a reality.

A short video providing information and demonstrating the use of dry disconnects is available for customers to review at their plants or even at home. The video is proving to be a success in the acceptance and proper use of the dry disconnect. At the first trial unloading in which the video was used to train operators, representatives from all three companies of the "dry disconnect team" attended—only one drop of allyl chloride was lost. To further support the conversion of dry disconnects, a manual including a truck schematic and storage tank is provided.

## STEWARDSHIP FOR SMALL VOLUME CUSTOMERS

Not every customer requires tank truck or rail car quantities of chemical intermediates; however, safe handling of drum accounts is just as important to Dow as bulk volume accounts. Services offered to these customers are the same.

In fact, companies using only a few drums of material a year may represent a higher probability for unfortunate incidents than bulk accounts because their use is often intermittent. If not dealing with the product regularly, safety and handling precautions are not reinforced by repetition and can be forgotten. To circumvent a potential problem, drum customers must review process and products involved before each campaign.

## SUMMARY

The chemical intermediates product stewardship program described here is by no means the only one at Dow. Product stewardship is a fundamental and on-going part of the business. The ultimate goal is to assist people to protect themselves and the environment from potentially hazardous materials in a sound and responsible manner.

This article has reviewed some of the details, spirit, and ideas behind the product stewardship program for allyl chloride, epichlorohydrin, HEA and HPA monomers at The Dow Chemical Company. Basically, all the stewardship tools—manuals, safety audits, hygiene surveys, etc., revolve around a central principle: listen to, respond to, and educate all persons involved with the distribution and use of these products. Continue to improve and revise training programs. Be aware of updated equipment and how it can impact safety. Find new and better ways to communicate stewardship ideas to key personnel. Stay involved. Care.

# Commercial Banking

Citicorp
Dinah Nemeroff

National Westminster Bank, USA
Howard Deutsch and Neil J. Metviner

# Quality in Consumer Financial Services

**Dinah Nemeroff**
Citicorp

Citicorp is a global financial services enterprise serving the financial needs of individuals, businesses, governments, and other financial institutions in 90 countries. In order to meet the challenges of the marketplace, Citicorp has organized its activities around customer-oriented core businesses: the Individual Bank, which serves consumers; and the Institutional Bank, Investment Bank, and Information Business which work together to serve other customers.

## SERVICE QUALITY OVERVIEW

In Citicorp's Individual Bank, the overall goal is to set and consistently meet service performance standards that satisfy customers and profit the corporation. One overriding belief guides all efforts: Execution wins it. According to Richard S. Braddock, head of the worldwide Individual Bank, "Each employee *is* Citicorp to each customer. Therefore, in our attitude, behavior, and sensitivities we always must work to ensure customer satisfaction."

To accomplish this, Citicorp's Individual Bank uses a comprehensive, five-part approach in its businesses worldwide: an explicit service strategy, service statesmanship, a service management process, major investments in technology, and major investments in people. Each of these elements, and ongoing implementation challenges, will be discussed in the following pages.

## SERVICE STRATEGY

The Individual Bank's approach to service is based in part on research into companies renowned for their service performance: Disney, McDonald's, Federal Express, Singapore Airlines, and many others. This research included visits to the companies and in-depth interviews with company managers. Regardless of their diverse industry lines, these companies share a common approach to service and follow certain imperatives:

- *Practice service statesmanship* — senior management actively works to build service excellence into the organization.
- *Put efficient tools in place* — service personnel are given the necessary information, systems, and materials to deliver quality service.
- *Establish service professionalism* — employees are motivated, skilled, and rewarded so they reliably serve customers.
- *Use service performance standards and measures* — these checks on performance determine if quality is being delivered, and are used to manage corrective programs.

The Individual Bank uses all of these principles and also has conducted customer research. Thousands of consumers doing business with Citicorp and competitors have been surveyed. This research has shown that consumers worldwide want problem-free service, delivered competently, in a timely manner. Consistently delivering such service is the Individual Bank's root service performance strategy.

This objective is communicated throughout the organization in many ways. A worldwide graphic keeps all employees aware of what is termed the *Service Fundamentals.* This approach allows a particular business to feature a special service initiative targeted at its employees. Because Citicorp is a decentralized organization, the combination of a universal strategy and local implementation variations is most appropriate (see figure 1).

# *CITICORP✛*
## *Quality Service Worldwide.*
## *Competent. Problem-free.Timely.*

# *CITICORP✛*
## *Quality Service Worldwide.*
優質服務・稱譽全球
## *Competent. Problem-free.Timely.*
資深熟鍊・疑難盡消・快捷妥善

# *CITICORP✛*
## *Calidad De Servicio Mundial.*
## *Competente. Sin Problemas. Expedito.*

FIG. 1. WORLDWIDE SERVICE LOGOS

Within each business, managers detail for their employees how the Service Fundamentals must be delivered to customers. What problems could a student have when trying to secure a loan? How can employees ensure such problems do not occur? What do branch banking customers regard as competent behavior by tellers and service representatives? What does a timely mortgage commitment mean to an applicant? Such questions are answered for employees and also translated into service performance standards. Thus, Citicorp begins with a strategy based on consumer needs and ultimately translates this into service performance geared to generate high customer satisfaction.

## SERVICE STATESMANSHIP

A perceptive comment on service statesmanship came from a CEO who said, "When the fish stinks, it stinks from the head." At Citicorp, senior management—and by extension all management—actively work to make service quality the reality of how business is done with every customer. Service statesmanship must be vigorously expressed, in both philosophy and personal action.

In terms of philosophy, each Citicorp consumer business has a service mission statement. It is part of the business charter and tells all employees how to do business with customers.

For example, Citicorp Savings of California has formulated this mission statement:

To consistently deliver a differentiated level of service so exceptional and so unexpected that it becomes a vehicle for the acquisition of profitable new relationships as well as the retention and growth of existing ones.

Additional communications spell out the commitment of California's senior management:

Service excellence is a non-negotiable requirement of Citicorp Savings' strategic plan. It is no more an option for the organization than is operational control. It is an essential and uncompromisable element in our future success. It is up to every manager to actively and visibly support the achievement of service standards, and it is up to every manager to coach employees in being sensitive to service in all aspects of our business—service to our customers as well as service to each other. . . .

In the Northeast Division of the U.S. Consumer Bank, all staff have signed a service excellence pledge:

- I pledge to make quality service a way of life at Citicorp
- . . . To exhibit the virtues of good service—caring, attentiveness, patience, and a desire to walk the extra mile.
- . . . To treat my customers and fellow employees with respect and dignity.

- . . . To be responsive and attentive to customer needs, both spoken and unspoken; and to make every effort to satisfy every customer in every way.
- And to deliver all my efforts to the goal of excellence in all aspects of service.

In terms of actions, senior managers serve as role models. Senior executives review service performance as frequently as they review financial results. They inspire, convince, and when necessary, insist that others join the cause. At times, a dramatic gesture is the most successful: Steve H. Price, the head of 250 branches in New York City, spent two weeks one summer as a branch manager, replacing vacationing managers; he was so successful that the branch employees threatened to hold him hostage and not permit him to return to headquarters. Robert D. Horner, the head of St. Louis based Citicorp Mortgage, Inc., took another approach: he sent highly valued baseball playoff tickets to very special people in his organization—those who had won corporate service excellence awards for particularly meritorious performance. Steve Price's investment of time and Bob Horner's recognition of the service stars in his organization are two examples of what makes service statesmanship a powerful reality. As Peter Drucker has suggested, people perform to the standards of their leaders. It is service statesmanship that sets the pace for all other aspects of service quality.

## SERVICE MANAGEMENT PROCESS

Individual accountability for achieving explicit, quantifiable service performance goals—and the rigorous measurement of this achievement—are at the heart of Citicorp's service management process. Accountability is established in managers' annual management-by-objective (MBO) work contracts. Individual staff members' accountability is spelled out in their job descriptions and work unit standards.

A business manager typically has two types of service goals: first, the percent of high customer satisfaction to be achieved, that is, the percent of interviewed customers who report they are highly satisfied with their Citicorp branch or mortgage service, for example; second, the percent of service performance standards, measured internally, to be achieved on a monthly basis. These typically measure service *accuracy, responsiveness,* and *timeliness* (ART). For instance, the accuracy of customer statements is ascertained by quality checks; the responsiveness of customer service letters is measured against incoming queries; and the timeliness of loan approvals is assessed against the initial application date. While these indicators can be measured internally, the most significant measurements are from the customer's point of view.

The timeliness of lost or stolen credit card replacement, for example, is assessed from the date of the initial customer request to the receipt of the new card. While productivity measures may reflect only intermediate steps in the multistep chain of service delivery, true service indicators measure the entire experience from the customer's perspective.

Results measured against these service goals are reported daily at the work unit level and aggregated monthly as part of the regular business review cycle. In standard documentation, on service scorecards, these results are reported all the way up the organization and, ultimately, are discussed at monthly sector-level reviews. Even though external measurements of customer satisfaction are made far less frequently, the monthly service scorecards always include the annual goals as well as the most recent satisfaction measures. This keeps the focus on the all-important customer satisfaction rating, the ultimate service report card.

In actual practice, daily and monthly reviews of service performance focus on shortfalls to goal. Managers formally develop action plans opposite any variances, and track implementation and corrective success.

Goals are taken literally: James W. Hutchinson, a senior customer service manager, once commented to visitors, "Right now we're not in good shape. Our standard is to meet 95% of our indicators, and we're only at 93%. This is a serious shortfall and we're all working extra hard to bring the results up to standard." Subsequently this was achieved.

Annual appraisals for managers and staff evaluate performance against quantitative service goals and other types of objectives. A manager's total MBO, for example, defines financial, people management, and service performance goals, as well as functional responsibilities in marketing, credit, or operations. A manager's success in meeting his MBO determines his merit salary increase and bonus. Because service responsibilities are an explicit part of the goal-setting, evaluation, and compensation process, a powerful service performance motivation is established.

Experience has proven this service management process to be most successful when geared to an individual branch or customer service unit. Every branch manager requires branch-specific feedback from his own customers on how satisfied they are with that branch. This creates automatic ownership for satisfaction findings.

Dramatic improvement in customer branch satisfaction has been achieved with this branch-specific management process. One business's progress is shown in figure 2, which demonstrates the pattern many businesses experience. Typically, branches with poor initial scores move to average, and an excellence "build" begins by the second measurement wave (survey intervals of six to twelve months are common). In subsequent measurements, the problematic bottom rating virtually drops out as few branches weigh in at the lowest level. Instead, there is rapid growth in units achieving high customer satisfaction.

Branch managers depend on the initial survey as a starting point from which to measure improvement. They use diagnostic survey information to

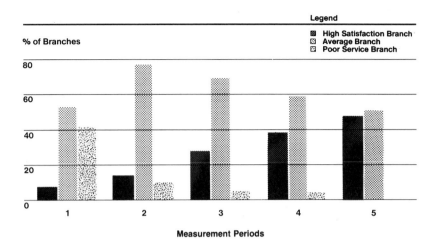

FIG. 2. BRANCH SERVICE STUDY SHOWING INDIVIDUAL BRANCH IMPROVEMENT

develop a practical improvement plan. Managers rally their staffs with hard data and with customer comments from surveys, describing what their customers say about them. And they demonstrate how much they have improved their branches with follow-up surveys. When meeting a senior manager, a branch manager usually describes his branch in terms of business dimensions, sales performance, and his service satisfaction score. These vital statistics describe the full bottom line for a Citicorp branch.

## MAJOR INVESTMENTS IN TECHNOLOGY

Applying technology to achieve service quality is a great challenge and a great opportunity. Choosing from ever-expanding options and then managing the smooth integration of new technology—while delivering uninterrupted service to customers—are major responsibilities for managers. Fortunately, the complexity of these tasks is matched by a handsome return: the double success of improved productivity and increased customer satisfaction.

Service-driven technology serves three constituencies: service managers, service representatives, and customers.

For today's service managers, a state-of-the-art tool kit ranges from space age technology to the mundane. Citicorp's U.S. Card Products managers transmit customer information via satellite on CitiSatCom to service centers across the country. In their command center in Hunt Valley, Maryland, these managers schedule and control the operating systems of widely-dispersed centers. Overcoming historical time and space constraints, this technology enables the organization to manage information and "fly the service machine" on a grand scale.

Individual branches also require sophisticated technology. Engaged in relationship banking, branch staff must provide customers with service after the sale. They must be knowledgeable in real time about more than one hundred products and all customer accounts, and be ready to meet the peaks of demand for customer transactions.

Efficient technology oriented to the branch enables financial service retailers to meet such needs. For example, line-wait measurement systems record both customer arrivals for tellers and session times. These data then afford branch managers the same capacity-planning capabilities used in large customer service centers, based on automated call distributor information.

"If you measure it, it moves," is a common expression in quality literature. Citicorp managers say, "We are what we measure." Line measurement technology has enabled branch managers to significantly decrease customer waiting time for tellers with no increase in staffing and, at times, even with reduced staffing. Feedback indicates the combination of improved information, planning capabilities, and personal accountability produces these results.

Technology must also support service representatives. A rapidly expanding product line characterizes much of the financial services industry today, and no one feels the burden of growth more than the individual employee. Complex products, as well as the scope of the product line, require enhanced workstations and information systems. The basics include up-to-date customer information, efficient order entry, and follow-up tracking.

In a number of Citicorp service centers, new technology has improved information accessibility. One example is the use of quad screen or multiwindow CRTs. This technology brings the representative a multiple view of a customer's relationship during the customer interaction. For example, the representative can view a customer's account history at the same time he enters data for a new order. The result is improved staff competence, customer convenience, and speed of service. Other support software further extends staff on-line competencies. The branch banking businesses, where product lines are most extensive, are building "Systems of Knowledge." Such databases give representatives instant expertise about literally thousands of topics, accessible in seconds.

Help screens provide employees with procedural guidance upon request. Moreover, software with structured, expert protocols now automatically assists representatives as they move through complex transactions. For instance, a customer calling a service center with a dispute will be taken through a multipart information exchange which all Citicorp customer service representatives use. It is based on Citicorp's best customer service representatives' routines and ensures all representatives assist customers in the most efficient and comprehensive manner.

While interpersonal service interactions remain a core delivery channel, technology that directly serves customers is increasing in popularity. Citicorp's automated teller machines, called Citicard Banking Centers, were engineered to be highly responsive to consumers. This even includes language options. Depending on the market, a customer can choose from a language menu of English, Spanish, and Chinese, with German and French options soon to be introduced.

The outstanding performance of the Centers has motivated a large percent of customers to switch to self-service banking. In the New York City market, 80% of Citicorp's retail banking customers use Citicard Banking Centers for more than 50% of their transactions, double the national average. New touch-screen terminals were first introduced in New York City and Hong Kong in 1987. This next generation of Citicard Banking Centers is even easier and faster for customers to use. The future looks extremely bright for customer-activated banking technology.

A guiding principle for all service-driven technology is to afford customers a choice for where, when, and how they can do business with Citicorp. In practical terms, this means offering customers a range of responsive, dependable ways to get information and to complete transactions twenty-four hours a day. Clearly, only through continuing technological innovation can Citicorp provide increased choice and flexibility to customers, backed by dependable quality.

## MAJOR INVESTMENTS IN PEOPLE

Building a worldwide team of sixty-five thousand service professionals is, in many ways, the Individual Bank's greatest service challenge of all. This begins with each staff member understanding that he or she serves customers. The corporation subscribes to the quality maxim, "If you're not serving the customer, you'd better be serving someone who is" (Albrecht and Zemke 1985, 96). Thus, departments whose customers are Citicorp employees must learn their customers' expectations and satisfaction levels. This puts *everyone* in the service business.

The Citicorp approach to service professionalism can be expressed in several ways. First is the belief that the basics of sound people management must be executed energetically. This means conscientiously managing employees starting with their selection and orientation, through training and ongoing coaching, and extending to appraisal and rewards. Because of the immense task of doing this well with a large number of people, Citicorp is constantly working to manage these activities better. Line managers themselves are responsible for such improvement.

The company's research demonstrates that there are four essential ingredients of staff service professionalism:

- Each employee must be personally accountable for service performance; each must believe and portray in his or her actions, *I* am Citibank for the customer.

- Staff must function as a service team because of the inevitable interdependencies of work units.
- Employees must constantly work to communicate and keep each other informed. Most importantly, they must learn from what customers say.
- Citicorp must continuously develop its staff because in the long run they are the greatest resource.

This approach to staff professionalism motivates specific investments and people management practices.

For example, the New York City branch business has upgraded the teller position; existing employees as well as new hires earn significantly higher base salaries.

In recognition of superior service achievement, employees earn the Citicorp Service Excellence Award. Since its inception in 1983, four thousand Individual Bank staff members have won these awards. Winners receive a personalized certificate from Chairman John S. Reed; businesses also honor winners with recognition and, at times, financial rewards.

Reflecting a widespread practice in service-dedicated companies, Citicorp employees meeting the public wear name tags for ease of identification and for accountability. When customer-contact employees become Service Excellence Award winners, they are further distinguished: their silver name tags turn gold. This highly visible practice ensures these service stars always are recognized by their colleagues, as well as their customers, as special people and important role models.

Citicorp, along with other service-successful companies, believes that customer relations mirror employee relations. This means the messages and attitudes passed within an organization are inevitably internalized by customer-contact personnel and then broadcast thousands of times every day to customers. Thus, an organization must take responsibility for such messages as they influence employee, and ultimately customer, satisfaction. As Benjamin Schneider (1980, 63) has noted, "Management emphasis in a service organization cannot be hidden from those who are served: climate shows in service organizations."

This responsibility begins with identifying the messages within the organization. To accomplish this, Citicorp uses frequent employee attitude surveys. Managers and staff members are polled confidentially to determine their experiences on a number of topics, including variables relating to their business as a service organization. For instance, employees are asked their degree of agreement with these statements: I have clearly-defined performance standards; I regularly get feedback from my supervisor on how well or poorly I'm doing on the job; and, the people in my work unit know how to solve problems for our customers.

Managers analyze their work unit results, discuss the findings with their employees, and institute follow-up programs. Results are tracked over time and reported up the line to sector management. Here again, line managers are responsible for implementing this process and achieving acceptable results.

Another investment dictated by the corporation's service strategy is service training. This ranges from programs several weeks long for service representatives, to management training for all levels of executives.

Just as managers are trained in marketing, credit, treasury, and people management disciplines, they also are educated in service quality skills. To date, hundreds of managers have participated in a three and one-half day course entitled Service Management Strategy and Tactics. At each session, thirty-five managers from diverse Citicorp businesses work together at a training location on classroom material, a special case study, and a service simulation game. While this rollout continues, thousands of branch and unit managers are being instructed at home in their own businesses and languages, in a three-day course, Managing Service. This video-based program teaches core service quality skills and increases understanding of a particular business's service program.

## ONGOING CHALLENGES

Citicorp's Individual Bank recognizes the following challenges lie ahead in the effort to further improve service performance.

**Building service quality into corporate values.** Based on fiduciary responsibility and regulatory requirements, banks historically have been control-minded. As Citicorp works to become a customer-driven, global financial services enterprise, a major recasting of values is involved.

Service literature often mentions that to be successful at service you have to be obsessed with service. At Citicorp, the Individual Bank is still working to become service obsessed. Beyond the quality controls and service training formally administered, the commitment of each employee to executional excellence must be built. This commitment must be developed over time to provide a quality safety net, ensuring promises to customers are fulfilled.

**Having the patience to pursue an endless process.** This involves both the length of time needed to make necessary service improvements in the businesses, as well as the realization that the service task is never finished. As Leon Gorman, president of L. L. Bean, expressed it, service is "just a day-in, day-out, ongoing, never-ending, unremitting, persevering, compassionate type of activity" (Uttal 1987, 98). Persistence is key. Top management's recognition of this dynamic sets an important tone. As Sector Executive Rick Braddock said in a speech to the Bank Administration Institute, entitled, *Beyond Lip Service*:

We have a lot to learn. Changes cannot come about on a wholesale basis. They come slowly. We use the phrase 'an inch a day.' And we use it often. At Citicorp, we've hit few home runs, but a lot of doubles and singles, and foul balls. We've also been hit by a few pitches.

We don't have all the answers, but what we have arrived at is a process whereby we *can* improve service quality.

Guarding against complacency. Even in those businesses that meet service-performance goals, the day-in, day-out work continues. The process must be kept energized and the commitment to quality must not be allowed to grow stale.

The Distribution Services Division, which provides service fulfillment for U.S. Card Products, has faced up to this mature service issue. Under Richard G. McCrossen's leadership, this organization constantly reinvigorates the process. For example, tough service performance standards are made even more demanding in innovative ways. Managers now are responsible for more than their own unit's service performance. Shared MBOs mandate that managers all win or lose together. That is, service performance goals for an entire facility such as the Sioux Falls, South Dakota Service Center must be achieved across the board for any manager to meet his or her service objectives. Managers acknowledge that this creates instant teamwork as well as healthy peer pressure. Of course, the ultimate winner is the customer.

Marketing service success. The corporation aims to provide satisfying service and then leverage it for even greater business success. Citicorp, along with many others, is still learning how to market service most effectively. A number of techniques and approaches are being pursued. In Citibank Hong Kong, an advertising campaign has featured the theme, "Caring for people like you." In Citibank Arizona, branch representative signs have proclaimed, "I can help you succeed." This message ties in with Citicorp's national advertising campaign, "Because Americans want to succeed, not just survive."

Citibank Visa and MasterCard television ads stress not only the security of these cards, but also Citicorp's continuing concern for and responsiveness to cardmembers. For instance, viewers are told about increased credit availability for personal emergencies and protection from fraudulent charges on their accounts. They're then reminded, "not just VISA . . . Citibank VISA."

By offering customers a unique set of service features and then superbly delivering on this promise, the goal is to differentiate Citibank service.

One of the most successful executions was the 1977 introduction of the Citicard Banking Centers, affording customers twenty-four-hour convenience and capabilities. The "Citi never sleeps" campaign remains strong in customer recall, and the Citicard Banking Centers continue to enjoy high satisfaction ratings. This is a particularly notable illustration of offering customers a new set of service features, promoting these enhancements, and thereby achieving even greater success through service marketing.

Citicorp Chairman John Reed summarized the ongoing challenge and the significance of service excellence in a 1988 Service Fundamentals video communication to employees:

I'm confident we're building a business that will distinguish itself in the minds of our customers in three ways. First, by the visible reality that customers will sense we are dedicated to them. This is something which in the banking business is not generally perceived to be the attitude of banking institutions. Second, that the level of service interactions with us will be our distinctive competitive advantage. And finally, that this quality value in the organization will say a lot about who wants to work at Citicorp and how much fun it is to work here. I think these three ingredients are the cornerstones of where we're going.

## Works Cited

Albrecht, K., and R. Zemke. 1985. *Service America! Doing Business in the New Economy.* Homewood: Dow Jones-Irwin, 96.

Schneider, B. Autumn 1980. The service organization: climate is crucial. *Organization Dynamics*, 63.

Uttal, B. December 1987. Companies that serve you best. *Fortune*, 98.

*The author thanks her colleagues, particularly C. Gregory Brown and Gary E. Greenwald, for their ongoing support and assistance with this article.*

# Quality Improvement At National Westminster Bank USA

**Howard Deutsch**
**Neil J. Metviner**
National Westminster Bank USA

National Westminster Bank USA is a New York City-based bank with approximately $11.5 billion in total assets. It is a full-service bank with 134 retail branches in the New York metropolitan area and with commercial banking offices in key cities around the United States. It employs forty-eight hundred people. It is a wholly owned subsidiary of National Westminster Bank PLC, the London-based international banking and financial services organization.

# INTRODUCTION

This chapter describes the NatWest USA quality improvement process, which is now in its fourth year. Included are discussions of how the process began and how it has evolved over time. The benefits of the quality improvement process, the emphasis on improved communications among employees and with customers, and an expanded focus on customers are some of the many issues described.

The development of a quality improvement process should not be left to chance, nor should it be hastily constructed because "every company has one," or simply because "it's in next year's plan." Today, it is difficult to find a company that is not implementing or thinking of implementing a quality improvement process. Unfortunately, most of these efforts will fail. This will be due in large part to the failure of many companies to view quality improvement as a perpetual undertaking entailing fundamental changes in corporate culture and attitudes toward customers. Rather, quality improvement is too often looked upon as merely an employee relations exercise in which we get people to smile wider and work faster.

The quality improvement process at NatWest USA is a systematic approach to meeting customer requirements. It encompasses every facet of the business, every employee, every product, every process. Quality is perceived as the key factor by which the bank is differentiating itself in the marketplace. The process is planned, highly structured, and carefully monitored. Specific tasks are identified, and responsibilities and accountability are established.

# QUALITY AWARENESS

In order to work, the quality improvement effort had to affect everyone and become part of everyone's job. The total quality concept recognizes that each individual is responsible for the quality of his or her effort and output and that management is responsible for providing the tools, systems, training, and environment that enable individuals to meet these responsibilities.

Given this philosophy, NatWest USA initiated its quality improvement process with an awareness campaign to spread the word, convert the cynics, and get the organization to become active in the process. A cartoon character named DIRF, an acronym for Do It Right First, appeared on posters displayed in employee lounges and coffee areas, on key rings, and on note pads. A fable titled "The Legend of DIRF" was written and distributed to the staff. DIRF reinforces the precept that doing everything right the first time results in much-improved customer service at reduced or contained costs. In addition, employees participated in a slogan contest for the quality effort. More than three-thousand slogan entries were received, and the winning slogan was "Do it right first—It's the NatWest way." Parties were held for employees with the theme "It's just a beginning," and it soon became apparent to all in the company that the concept of quality was taking hold and the process was gaining momentum. People were beginning to talk about the quality process in the workplace, in the cafeteria, and in staff meetings.

## MANAGEMENT INVOLVEMENT

Before any work gets started it is imperative that the quality effort receive not only the endorsement but the total participation of the company's top executives, including its chief executive officer. Without executive involvement and leadership in quality improvement, the process will never achieve its ultimate goal of restructuring the entire management process and internal workings of the company. In order to succeed, management of generalities must be converted to involvement in specifics. Commitment to quality as a theme goes only so far. Management must involve itself in the nuts-and-bolts activities needed to bring quality out of the closet, or more commonly, the executive conference room, and into the daily work environment. There are a number of steps a company can take to ensure executive involvement in quality improvement.

### Step 1. Make Quality the CEO's Personal Mission

The first and most critical step is to get the chief executive personally involved. The quality improvement effort must become "his or her baby," his or her personal mission. The CEO must recruit and demand the involvement of key executives and personally "sell" the process to the rank and file. Bringing a quality improvement process to life requires changing the culture of the corporation. This cultural alteration must be shaped at the top with the leader's vision translated into strategic action and a change in organizational direction.

Bill Knowles, NatWest USA's chairman, has remained highly visible throughout the first three years of the quality improvement process. He has brought his quality campaign to the staff by appearing in the company's quarterly video magazine and biweekly newspaper. He personally initiated the program with a key address at the "It's just a beginning" parties and addressed both internal and external groups on the need for quality. In addition, he has closely monitored the quality improvement process by holding quarterly meetings with each of the bank's executive vice presidents to discuss the status of their annual quality plans. When NatWest USA introduced a quality and customer-service warranty program backed by cash payouts to customers, Bill Knowles led the way by addressing every employee at a series of celebration parties. He spelled out the details of the warranty program, previewed the upcoming advertising campaign, and personally asked for everyone's support.

### Step 2. Establish a Quality Improvement Steering Committee

The quality effort needs an overseeing body to plan and monitor its progress. The CEO should select and support a committee made up of key executives representing the whole of the organization. This will ensure the participation and accountability of the committee members through an integration of quality improvement goals and practices into the accepted organizational structure. A strong, well-respected individual needs to lead the committee to set direction and keep it on course.

NatWest USA's quality improvement steering committee includes eight executive and senior vice presidents from retail banking, commercial lending, technology and processing, financial management, marketing, human resources, and quality improvement. Meeting monthly, it has been part of every element in the quality improvement process. Each year the committee names a new chairman along with a co-chairman, who becomes chairman the following year. In order to introduce new ideas and direction while ensuring continuity from year to year, two or three committee members are replaced annually. The steering committee's first task was to establish the basic direction and policies of the quality improvement process. Next, it developed a formal organizational structure (discussed later in this chapter) to carry out the committee's plans.

## Step 3. Involve Executives In Quality Improvement Projects

Successful project management has rarely been a key rung in the ladder of executive success. Most executives will readily admit to having a hands-off posture on the projects within their domain, relying on periodic status reports to keep them on top of the situation. Most executives have little background in, and knowledge of, the tools of project management. This is understandable since project management has in the past been relegated to lower levels of the organization.

Failure to include executives in critical projects can result in a number of problems:

- A "we" (staff) versus "them" (management) situation.
- Poorly defined or absent objectives.
- Perceptions among staff of conflicting management priorities.
- Executives out of touch with major problems.
- Executives imposing unrealistic time frames or budgets on project teams.

To remedy these, the CEO might try assigning to each key executive a high priority quality project. The projects should be meaningful and visible and should have a high chance of success. A wish list of quality improvement should be developed and the CEO should make project leaders out of those executives he feels will best see them to fruition. The executives should then be taught project management techniques of planning, organization, and reporting to help the projects run more smoothly. Well-run executive projects that produce positive results can become internal showpieces of the corporation. They visibly show management involvement and action while improving communication and the involvement of the entire staff.

Each of NatWest USA's executive vice presidents was assigned to lead a high priority quality improvement project early in the process. The benefits derived from these projects have included the development of a bankwide quality reward and recognition program, the standardization of many processes, the improved handling of customer inquiries and complaints, and the development of quality measures.

### Step 4. Involve Executives In Quality Improvement Training

First, all executives should receive the same training as other levels of the corporation. This will ensure a uniformity of vocabulary and understanding of quality principles and techniques, which will enable them to fulfill their role as agents of change in achieving a quality culture. The fact that executives attend this training should be well publicized. Articles with pictures and interviews, for example, have appeared in NatWest USA's newsletter, and the involvement of NatWest USA's executives in training has added credibility to the company-wide training effort.

Each quality training course at NatWest USA concludes with an executive devoting a full hour to present his or her personal commitment to quality and then to field questions and listen to comments from employees. This communication forum has not only helped bridge the gap, but it has narrowed the gap that exists between the executive ranks and the bank's wide range of employees.

### Step 5. Require Annual Quality Improvement Plans from Each Executive

A strategy is a planned effort, and if quality improvement is to become a strategic imperative of a corporation, it must be part of a formal planning process. Just as budget and business plans are required from each executive, so must be quality plans. In this light, they must have well-documented objectives, be approved at a higher level, and be formally monitored and reported upon. The executive should be required to personally report to the chairman on the progress of his plan.

Each of NatWest USA's organizational groups is required to develop annual quality plans. These plans, whose progress is reviewed each quarter by the bank's Office of the Chairman, include strategies for

- Improving quality through projects.
- Expanding quality measurement, including the development of standards and targets.
- Increasing staff involvement in the quality improvement process.

By having executives commit themselves to the implementation of these plans, just as they do for budget and business plans, the bank has made quality improvement a key executive priority.

## Step 6. Require Each Executive to Develop a Cost-of-Quality Estimate for His or Her Area

Executives must be made aware of the existence of any waste in their operations and be required to develop plans (Step 5) aimed at its reduction. The cost-of-quality estimates are most important at the outset of the quality improvement process, since the estimation process focuses attention on quality improvement opportunities that offer bottom-line payback. The resulting efficiencies should be visibly communicated to staff and customers. As the quality improvement process takes hold throughout the organization, new improvements in quality and customer service continuously surface without updates to the cost-of-quality calculations.

Each of NatWest USA's top executives was responsible for documenting his or her group's cost of quality during the first months of the quality improvement process. Since quality improvement is now firmly embedded in the culture of the bank, there is no apparent need to continuously quantify the cost of quality opportunities.

## Step 7. Include Discussions about Issues of Quality in All Staff Meetings

Employees understandably place great importance on those issues discussed at staff meetings. These issues are the visible priorities of the individual managers. If quality is to be pushed down the organization, it must be made part of the accepted management process of which staff meetings are usually an integral element. Status reports on quality projects, training plans, and individual quality achievements are part of the agenda in many NatWest USA staff meetings, and this has given both structure, permanence, and priority to the quality improvement process.

## Step 8. Put Executives "In Touch" with the Outside Customer

The benefits of this strategy are two-fold. First the executive, by breaking down the corporate insulation he or she is accustomed to, can see and hear firsthand how well the products and services for which he or she is ultimately responsible meet the needs of the customers. Secondly, customers will in most instances take a much more positive view of a company that is run by "working managers," those leaders who lead through example and involvement.

NatWest USA executives regularly meet with customers and often host breakfasts and luncheons to bring customers together and to solicit constructive feedback. Another program aimed at narrowing the distance between executives and customers is the "EVP and SVP of the Week Program." Executives are responsible on a rotating basis for the handling of all customer inquiries and complaints going into the chairman's office. Customers have made positive mention of the fact that this personal attention by executives is highly appreciated. Further, since the quality improvement process was introduced, the number of customer complaints received has declined dramatically.

## GROUNDWORK FOR A QUALITY IMPROVEMENT SYSTEM

### The Quality Improvement Organization

With the steering committee setting the policy and leading the overall quality improvement process, a quality council made up of managers from each area of the Bank was formed to coordinate interdivisional improvement projects and to further facilitate the process bank-wide. Quality improvement teams, comprising managers at all levels, were developed in each division with responsibility for identifying improvement opportunities and developing teams—"quality action teams"—to analyze the details and implement required changes. These quality action teams are made up of employees from all levels, and by bringing the detail people into the project fold, many superb changes, which may have eluded a high-level officer, have been made with great bottom-line benefit to the Bank.

Last, a quality improvement division with a total staff of nine people was established to train the bank staff, develop and present proposals to the steering committee, facilitate implementation of the approved strategies, and generally help keep the process on track. The division head (Howard Deutsch, co-author of this article) is a senior vice president and permanent member of the quality improvement steering committee.

### Quality Training

Training is of the utmost importance to NatWest USA. All of NatWest USA's employees—including the chairman, president, and every senior and executive vice president—receive quality improvement training. All officers and staff professionals receive two days of training, and the remainder of the staff (tellers, clerks, messengers, etc.) receive one day. Both courses cover the same basic material with the only main difference being the degree of detail provided. This training is vital to ensure a common language and approach and to provide a standard set of tools and techniques to address the opportunities at hand.

Each course begins with a broad-based discussion of quality. Employees are encouraged to share perceptions and experiences as they arrive at a common definition of quality. Another key section of the training involves a discussion of customer-supplier relationships, with an emphasis on identifying and meeting the needs of internal as well as external customers. The cost of quality, including prevention, appraisal, and failure costs, also is discussed, with bank examples cited throughout.

Quality measurement and reporting form another topic, and tools and techniques for data collection, charting, and analysis are explained. Case studies utilizing current bank data and processes are key elements of this section. A discussion of process management and exercises in workflow charting are also part of the seminar; they have proven to be very popular and instrumental in getting the entire staff to analyze and improve their procedures once they return to their workplaces.

## Quality Measurement

If one defines quality as "conformance to requirements," then clearly the cornerstone of a corporate quality improvement process is a comprehensive measurement and reporting system. Without such a system, the assessment of a product's or service's conformance to customer requirements becomes a guessing game. To succeed, the program must grow beyond the constraints of measurement and become part of the overall management process. It must not be directed to its own end but must be integrated into the strategic thrust of the organization.

NatWest USA's quality measurement program includes a combination of many approaches. In broad terms, this program is the means by which the performance of all elements of the bank is assessed: its people, products, and processes. As such, the solution was not one single manual or automated system but a mixture of many subsystems, each tailored to meet the detailed requirements of the specific areas. For example, measuring the reject rates of check-processing equipment and the levels of customer satisfaction in the credit card area could not be performed using the same boiler plate method. Measurement as a true subset of management has become fully integrated into much of the Bank, and it is continuously expanding.

At NatWest USA all employees from the mailroom to the Office of the Chairman receive training on the development and use of measurement tools. These include tools used for data collection, analysis, and charting. Since clerks are the people closest to the detail, they should be the ones collecting the detailed data. It was recognized that in order to succeed, data collection had to be quick and simple. Matrices and check sheets have been of great help. They are easy to design and use, and make data collection simple and fast. Furthermore, when properly constructed they make the summary and transfer of data to other reporting mechanisms a relatively easy task. In a comprehensive survey about quality issues sent to all NatWest employees, in August 1987, 34% of those responding stated they had used data collection check sheets since completing quality training. The bank has seen its use in every area from human resources to commercial lending.

## Let's Get Charting!

A major push over the past few years at NatWest USA has been to get areas to begin charting their functions and then displaying these charts in their work areas. To accomplish this, the Bank designed a standard lucite chart holder, ordered approximately one thousand holders, and permanently installed them in all its departments, including its retail branches, commercial lending offices, operations, and support areas. The goal was to make charts visible to all employees and to get them to feel part of the business. It is not unusual in today's environment to see NatWest USA employees reviewing these wall charts or to hear managers discussing these charts in staff meetings. In many ways, the measurement charts have helped managers communicate more effectively by providing a clear picture of goals, targets, and actual current performance and trends. The chart gives the manager a reason for walking around, for asking questions, and for showing not only commitment to, but also involvement in, the quality improvement process.

## Quality Processes

Effective processes are those that consistently produce top quality products and services at high levels of productivity. To achieve this end, processes cannot be left to chance. They must be well thought out and designed with a full knowledge and understanding of customer requirements. Processes that produce poor quality products and services are characterized by low productivity. This is so because poor quality typically features waste, rework, investigations, lost customers, and a myriad of other undesirable effects.

An excellent way in which to start to improve process quality is to prepare not only workflow charts to examine *what* you are doing but also quality measures to see *how* you are doing. This data will help pinpoint problem areas and their probable causes in each process. Once identified, these problems can be eliminated or reduced. The end-product is a more effective, more efficient high quality process—one that meets the requirements of the customer.

NatWest USA through its quality training effort has instructed each of its forty-eight hundred employees in the use of workflow charts. These charts are simple process schematics and are useful to

• Document processes.
• Identify all process inputs and outputs.
• Study and analyze processes.
• Identify areas of improvement.

While in the past most workflow documentation has been handled by consultants or industrial engineers, every employee—teller, messenger, lender, manager—has the potential to document his or her own processes and make improvements. In the past few years many of the Bank's processes have been improved as a result of individual employees developing workflow charts to analyze and improve upon the processes in their own work areas.

## IMPLEMENTATION OF A QUALITY IMPROVEMENT PROGRAM

### Quality Projects

The vehicle to improve a system or process is the project. In the past, the elements of project management were often left to the individual. Some projects ran well; many, unfortunately, did not. Projects got sidetracked, plans were absent, and inevitably, much fell through the cracks. A standard approach to project management was greatly needed. Today, NatWest USA has that standard approach. Now detailed project plans are developed, project roles are assigned and understood, schedules are documented, and budgets and cost-benefit analyses are performed. Meeting agendas and minutes are now written and distributed to project team members.

With more than one hundred quality action team projects currently in progress and many more already completed, positive change has spread throughout the organization. Lenders are improving their internal operations as well as working with the back office to better serve customers. The mailroom staff has significantly reduced missorts. Errors on transactions of all types generated from the bank's 134 retail branches have been reduced or eliminated. Timeliness of operations such as letters of credit have been greatly improved, with direct bottom-line impact. Also, secretaries are working to improve their effectiveness. Well designed and maintained automated systems are more efficient: they experience less downtime and an improved response time. Automated teller machine (ATM) availability is at its all-time high (over 97%). Unnecessary paper is being systematically eliminated, and through automation and basic process improvement, the number of forms is being reduced. Inquiries are handled more quickly and professionally. Fee capture has dramatically improved, and float losses have been greatly reduced.

People are getting involved, improving their own functions, cutting out the hassles that get in their way, and looking at improving each aspect of their jobs. Managers are finding more time to manage, motivate, and develop the talents of their staffs by reducing the time spent on rework and fire fighting. Contracts with outside suppliers of goods and services include performance standards and, where appropriate, contain quality incentives and penalties. Performance is monitored, and problems are quickly rectified.

## Reward and Recognition for Quality

NatWest USA has redesigned its employee performance evaluation process to emphasize further the importance of quality. Specific sections on quality improvement objectives and attained results are prominent in the new evaluation forms. In addition to formal performance reviews, other mechanisms for reward and recognition have been developed with the following features:

- Useful specific feedback is given on a timely basis.
- Teamwork and individual excellence are encouraged.
- Short-term improvements are identified.
- Successes are publicized.

NatWest USA intends for its employees to see that they can make a difference, that their suggestions can become reality, and that they will be rewarded and recognized for these achievements. Associated with those goals, a formal program of immediate reward and recognition has gotten underway. In this program, managers at all levels and from all bank areas are able to recommend rewards of one hundred dollars for "quality achievers."

In 1987 over seven hundred awards were given out; each recipient was also eligible for a year-end lottery which included the grand prize of an all-expense-paid vacation for two (including extra vacation time) as well as a number of other large runner-up prizes.

## Competitive Benchmarking

Competitive benchmarking is simply the process in which a company measures its products, services, and practices against those of its toughest competitors or against those companies with a reputation of excellence in a particular facet of their business.

Once managers get out and start seeing how each element of their businesses stacks up against those same elements of the competition, the quicker they will then be able to differentiate themselves from the competition. At NatWest USA, each executive vice president began the benchmarking process by personally visiting companies and picking the brains of their top executives. Reports of their findings were then presented to others in executive management. As the quality improvement process evolves, so does the program of competitive benchmarking. Since the benchmarks in the industry are constantly changing—with new products, technologies, and competitors—the program must always be changing.

Whether it is a computer operation or a lending team, a training department or a messenger area, there is probably some company out there that does that function or some aspect of it better. In the mortgage department, for example, a thorough analysis of competitors was undertaken and benchmarks were documented. NatWest USA analyzed marketing brochures and applications kits from fifteen banks and savings and loan institutions and compared those with its own. The result was a new, streamlined application kit that utilizes some good ideas from the competition. Numerous field trips were performed to study the internal processes and uses of automation of other lending institutions. These too became benchmarks for future process and automation changes. The identification of superior competitors and the specification of internal shortcomings has helped NatWest USA articulate the requirements for its own Quality Improvement Process.

## Customer Interviews and Focus Groups

Quality in its simplest form is the ability to meet or exceed customer requirements. To accomplish this, a substantial effort must be undertaken to receive and analyze customer input. Too often companies provide only what they want to offer or simply what they assume the customers require; little or no research is performed, and few if any customers are actually contacted. The bank's experiences have shown that many customers, satisfied or not, provide very valuable information to a company. All you have to do is ask. NatWest USA has made two-way customer communication a corporate priority. Through various means, including market research, suggestion and comment cards on branch counters, personal interviews and focus groups of commercial customers, and hands-on executive involvement, the bank is developing specific customer requirements from which to extract detailed internal specifications and against which to measure quality.

## Quality Assessments

Most companies refer to these exercises as quality audits, but given the negative connotation attached by many (especially in banking) to the word *audit*, the bank elected to go with the term *quality assessments*.

The quality improvement division performs quality assessments on a department-by-departmet basis; it intends not only to analyze the quality of an area's output but also to evaluate the quality improvement process as a procedure. This includes looking at employee commitment to the philosophy of quality improvement, the area's application of the tools and techniques taught in quality training, and the level of staff involvement in quality improvement projects.

There are several objectives of quality assessments:

- Ensure that quality standards exist and that products and services comply with published standards.
- Ensure that the quality standards are realistic, measurable, and attainable.
- Verify that data collection and analytical techniques are optimal.
- Identify opportunities to reduce quality-related costs and improve product conformance.
- Increase quality awareness.
- Provide departments with the methodology and techniques for continued self-assessment.
- Ascertain the existence of accurate, timely documentation for the quality system.
- Analyze the effectiveness of projects and project management.
- Analyze vendor performance.

Quality assessments serve to monitor and document the progress of the quality effort, to identify weaknesses, and to recommend changes. It should be stressed that quality assessments are not intended to be reviews of area management or employee productivity, nor do they take the place of financial or data processing audits. The focus is on reviewing the quality improvement process—to enforce it, perpetuate it, and improve it.

## CONCLUSION

If quality is to improve, the focus on it must become part of the accepted management process and be integrated into the corporate culture. It must be strategically planned for, developed, and maintained. Every level and area of the organization must be involved. Management must establish quality and service standards, use quality measures in their decision making, and communicate these actions to the employees.

Honest, open communications with employees and customers are essential. A wide array of programs is needed to sustain and increase employee participation. NatWest USA has made quality improvement a strategic imperative. Customers are demanding quality banking products and services, and they are willing to pay for it. Without quality, customer loyalty is quickly lost. Likewise, employees are increasingly demanding quality performance from themselves and those they support and work with. Awareness has turned itself into actions, and these have resulted in a more committed work force, dedicated to getting things done right the first time. Bill Knowles, the bank's CEO, envisions quality becoming "a part of the very fabric of the bank, part of the value system, part of the things we believe in."

# Diversified Financial

American Express Company – Southern Region Operations Center
Jay W. Spechler, Ph.D

American Express Company Travel Related Services, Inc.
MaryAnne Rasmussen

# Quality Achievement Strategies and Awareness Programs

**Jay W. Spechler**
American Express Company

The Travel Related Services (TRS) division of American Express markets diversified financial and travel services such as the Gold Card, Platinum Card, Optima Card, American Express Travelers Cheques and Money Orders. The Company has a network of more than 1,400 travel offices worldwide and markets publications including *Travel and Leisure, Food and Wine*, and *New York Woman* magazines.

## INTRODUCTION

The focus of this discussion is to describe key elements in achieving high levels of quality performance at the American Express Regional Operations Center located in Fort Lauderdale, Florida. This facility provides a broad range of customer service activities in support of the Gold and Platinum card products.

The atmosphere at an operations center is dynamic: it is a twenty-four-hours-a-day, seven-days-a-week business—a business that has been growing at double digit rates for years. The operations center has had to adapt to the introduction of numerous new technologies—methods, workflows, computer systems, and products during a period of time when financial services institutions as a whole have undergone extensive structural changes creating extraordinary competitive market forces.

For well over seven years the center has had comprehensive quality and productivity measurement systems in place that enable it to track and manage its performance in these areas. Figure 1 shows the total quality performance achievement of the Southern Region Operations Center (SROC) over the last five years. During this period, the center's total productivity levels (based on engineered standards) have been over 100%.

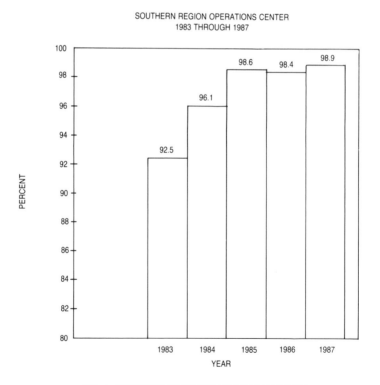

FIG. 1. PERCENTAGE OF QUALITY ACHIEVEMENT

## QUALITY ACHIEVEMENT STRATEGIES

**Measure With Integrity.** It is the company's belief that people will perform to management's high expectations, when given reasonable resources and a credible measurement system which they can use to track their performance and measure the impact of corrective action plans. The integrity of the regional quality measurement and tracking system is enhanced by the fact that headquarters administers an auditing function over the regional centers' measurement practices.

**Join the troops in the trenches.** The quality assurance department samples output spanning one hundred key operating elements twenty-four-hours-a-day, seven-days-a-week. It is vital that the quality assurance function not take the position nor be perceived as merely keeping a score card on others' performance. Within the quality assurance organization, there is a group of improvement specialists whose job it is to assist line managers in making breakthroughs in quality problems. These individuals move horizontally and vertically throughout the organization with total management support.

**Market and Sell Quality.** Achieving high levels of quality performance requires a broad and sustained marketing effort. Quality achievement is not just a matter of displaying statistical performance. The center's quality, statistical tracking report helps employees understand where they have come from and where they are. What is needed, in addition, are quality awareness and education programs that consistently get the message out to everyone in the organization that quality performance is important, and that their jobs depend upon their performance—every hour of every day.

## QUALITY ACHIEVEMENT TACTICS

In order to keep quality awareness fresh and on the minds of everyone at American Express, quality awareness programs have been developed for each level of the organization.

### Quality Awareness Programs

**Weekly executive quality results meetings.** The single most important management tactic towards achieving high quality levels is the weekly executive quality results meeting. There, the senior vice president in charge of the center calls together his senior operating and staff executives to review the most recent quality performance results. This is a hard-ball, no-holds-barred event. Any executive whose department's performance is below 98% explains what went wrong and what the corrective actions for the next period are.

This forum is used as an opportunity to highlight performance difficulties that may be impacting the center from other areas of the company, such as extraordinary marketing promotions or difficulties in computer communications; secondly, the forum may focus on the appropriate responses to overcome these problems. The meeting also serves to bring executives together who can share the human and physial resources needed to meet peaks and valleys in business demand.

**Quality awareness month.** Quality awareness month is an event that involves the entire operating center staff of four thousand people. It brings extraordinary focus on the need for quality achievement. Throughout the month employees receive raffle tickets for all work that is sampled by quality assurance and found to be correct. A budget of thirty thousand dollars is allocated for awards to the people with superior performance. Executives take the staff or units with outstanding quality ratings to dinner at first-class restaurants. Department decoration contests are held on the selected theme for quality awareness month. Last year the theme was "Aim high for quality." This year's theme was "Quality—the difference is me." Functions are held at the end of each week to award outstanding performers. These prizes have included a trip for two to California and to the Bahamas; limousine service to and from work for a week, and a night-on-the-town for two with a chauffeured limousine.

**Quality club.** The quality club is a way of giving recognition to operating units whose quality performance has reached 100% for two consecutive months, or 99% for three consecutive months. The number of units achieving this level of performance has been so high the center recently "raised the bar" and introduced Super Quality Club. Induction into the super quality club requires four consecutive months at 100% achievement or five consecutive months at 99%. Quality club members are given special recognition lunches, pins, and certificates.

**Quality employee of the month.** This program provides departmental members with an opportunity to select one individual as the most outstanding in quality achievement. Once a quarter, the recipients of this award are given a special recognition lunch, certificates, and T-shirts by the quality assurance department.

**Quality tips.** Often, quality assurance analysts detect error patterns and quality problems that need to be communicated throughout a major department or throughout the center as a whole. Quality Tips are a lighthearted approach to bringing about awareness and recognition of important quality issues.

**Quality hot line.** The quality hot line program permits any individual within the center to contact a quality assurance specialist and discuss how to best handle a customer inquiry. A hotline directory shows the list of quality measures, the individual analysts most expert in those measures, and the time of day that they may be reached. Quality assurance handles approximately forty such calls a month from departments all over the center. If counted in the error-sampling statistics as incorrect, the issues handled in these forty calls could make a 1% difference in the center's total quality performance.

**Quality commendations.** As quality assurance personnel monitor telephone communications and evaluate the timeliness, accuracy, and responsiveness to customers, they occasionally detect extraordinary quality performance on the part of an individual. Rather than have this performance go unnoticed, this evaluation is put into the form of a special commendation to that individual. This commendation is sent to the individual and to all levels of management within the center, and is placed in his or her personnel file.

**Broadcast computer system.** While quality assurance publishes weekly quality performance statistics and consolidates them monthly, it is felt that daily quality results need to be communicated to managers, supervisors, and their staffs. An on-line, computer management information system has been developed that shows each manager every error that has been detected by quality assurance for each day of the week. This is translated into a performance statistic so that each manager is able to see his or her current quality performance. Furthermore, every error detected by quality assurance is described in detail by the appropriate quality assurance analyst and given to the appropriate manager within twenty-four hours.

**Video employee service.** Periodically during the year, a video camera crew interviews employees throughout the center and displays the results on strategically located monitors in the building. A current interview theme, for example, is "What quality means to me."

**"Expressway."** *Expressway* is a center newsletter that is widely read by employees for its content on current events and business issues. One objective of the quality assurance department is to have at least one article covering quality achievement published each month. This usually involves photographs of high quality achievers and other noteworthy quality performance activities.

## Quality through new technologies

Listed below are several areas of new technology implementation that have had a significant impact on quality performance.

**Knowledge engineering and the 3-SIGMA concept.** A financial services company has a significantly different workforce from that of the typical manufacturing organization. It tends to require an increasing number of knowledge workers whose analytical efforts and judgments make the difference in achieving successful levels of service quality. Understanding and capitalizing upon these analytical abilities are essential for developing training programs to upgrade the performance of the workforce. American Express has developed a unique approach for determining how its most successful quality achievers are able to accomplish their tasks and utilizes this information to improve the performance of the total group. This approach, the "3-SIGMA" program, is being used for improving both manual and computer-based systems.

**Expert Systems.** Information gained from the company's knowledge engineering efforts and used in its training programs is also employed to develop computer programs that replace repetitive, simple customer-servicing decisions. The application of expert systems has enabled it to achieve productivity increases on the ratio of seven hundred to one, while improving quality levels through greater consistency in the decision-making process.

**Artificial intelligence.** Artificial intelligence systems go one step beyond expert systems in that they permit the computer to make decisions using a composite of available information. This higher order of computerizing human analytical thinking has had the same result as that achieved with expert systems, that is, simultaneously higher levels of productivity and quality.

**Automation.** The large-scale implementation of computerized mechanical systems has greatly improved productivity and quality. The company has, for instance, employed automation in microfilm record retrieval, the generation of correspondence to customers, and the consolidation of outgoing mail by zip code.

**Electronic imaging.** One of the latest innovations in rapid document processing and retrieval is the use of electronic imaging. This technique enables the center to improve upon the timeliness of processing, storing, and retrieving information while greatly enhancing the quality of the document being copied.

# Service Quality: Our Most Strategic Weapon

**MaryAnne Rasmussen**
American Express Travel Related Services Co., Inc.

American Express Travel Related Services Company, Inc. is one of four American Express operating units. The other three are American Express Bank Ltd., Shearson/Lehman/Hutton Inc., and IDS Financial Services, Inc. The company was founded in 1841 and is involved in financial as well as travel related services such as travel agencies. It employs over 84,000 and is headquartered in New York City.

## INITIATION OF A NEW QUALITY ASSURANCE SYSTEM

For nearly 150 years American Express has played a unique role in the financial and travel lives of its customers around the world. The company has dealt in products and services which chiefly involve *a promise to pay* — ranging from the Travelers Cheque, which the company invented in 1891, to the American Express Card, which helped launch the *plastic* revolution in 1958. Its success has been built on two key factors: customer trust in the integrity, security, and reliability of the company: and a culture of putting the customer first.

The history of American Express is filled with dramatic, true tales of fulfilling their promise to pay through two World Wars, the bank holiday of 1933, international monetary crises, revolutions, and natural disasters. They have kept their doors open, sometimes when other financial institutions could not, and built a worldwide reputation for helping customers in emergency situations. In fact, when U.S. citizens have serious problems abroad, often more of them seek help at the American Express office than the U.S. Embassy.

### Quality Starts at the Top

Given this unique role and history, American Express has always viewed quality service as its number one strategic marketing weapon. In fact, company chairman Jim Robinson is fond of saying that American Express's success depends on four factors: quality, quality, quality, and *quality*. Robinson's commitment is a key reason why *Fortune* magazine (December 1987), in an article on "Companies That Serve You Best," called American Express one of the country's best service companies, and why *Time* magazine (February 2, 1987), in a cover story on the generally dismal state of service in the U.S., singled out American Express as one of a handful of "pioneers in reliable service."

Why? Because as many management experts agree, and as a *Business Week* article on *quality* highlighted, "The process of improving quality has to start at the very top and filter down." (Port, 134) Indeed, the experience of American Express confirms the fact that, when it comes to quality, the power of executive leadership cannot be underestimated. Nevertheless, as the article goes on to point out, leadership in and of itself is not enough: "Quality is not evangelism, suggestion boxes, or slogans . . . It is a way of life."

How has quality become a way of life at American Express? To fully appreciate the enormous effort involved, go back to the late seventies and look at the Travel Related Services (TRS) part of the business, best known for its Card, Travelers Cheque, and travel products and services. It was an era of explosive growth. TRS was doubling the size of every facet of its business every three to four years. International expansion was equally phenomenal. So, despite the fact that it was known as a company that went the extra mile for a customer, its need for a uniform, consistent quality assurance (QA) process became more important than ever. There were two reasons for this. First, company management realized that if they delivered poor quality service—which is the same thing as creating unhappy customers—the result would be lost revenues and increased operating expenses; moreover, it would negatively affect the future growth and profitability of the business. Second, they were convinced that since employees really wanted to do a first-rate job, if they were shown how to improve service, they would be happier, prouder, more satisfied, and more productive workers in the long run.

## Launching Quality Assurance

In 1978 the company made the critical decision to launch a new quality assurance methodology—virtually unheard of in this type of business. Its purpose was to track, evaluate, and correct the weak spots in the service delivery of the American Express Card, a product that was growing by leaps and bounds. The goal was to establish a quality assurance methodology which would (a) define company service from the customer's point of view; (b) measure service delivery with the same rigor and objectivity that the company brought to productivity, costs, and revenues; and (c) involve all employees—and staff at every level—in the quality service process.

The study was begun at a single Card Operations Center in Phoenix. The company began to understand that it had been looking at service through the wrong end of the telescope, measuring the work of individual departments rather than the total process. As John Naisbitt wrote in his book *Re-Inventing the Corporation*, "Consumers perceive quality in terms of the whole, not just the parts." That realization launched what the company termed its enlightenment phase. The gap between the old way of thinking and measuring, and the adoption of the customer's perspective was obvious. It was time to break down the walls between departments and start tracking the flow of paper and information: a credit card application, for example, from one end of the operations center to the other.

The next big step involved segregating the credit card service into discrete transactions visible and measurable to customers, such as billing card members, paying retail establishments, and replacing lost or stolen cards. Card replacement was especially important because, without a card a customer cannot do business with American Express. It would be like sending a customer to the competition. The goal used to be to replace a card in ten days; it soon became replacement in one day.

## Setting Quality Standards

The company's market research and analysis of customer communications showed that, for customers, quality in the card business revolved around three characteristics: timeliness, accuracy, and responsiveness. That is, not only did people want on-time, error-free responses to their billing inquiries, but also knowledgeable, caring, and polite company representatives. When setting standards, the guideline was—and continues to be—to set exceptionally high standards that are noticeably superior to the competition and above customer expectations.

## Measuring Quality Standards

Once it set performance standards, the company implemented a system to measure and monitor performance on an ongoing basis. This system, now in place worldwide, statistically tracks performance for key transactions affecting the two groups of external credit card customers—card members and service establishments.

Measuring service performance had profound effects on the way the company did business: it changed workflows, eliminated unnecessary steps; examined root causes, and restructured organizations by changing reporting lines to focus better on the customer. In every case, it came up with new methods, procedures, and ideas. The goals were simple: to satisfy the customer and turn a profit.

This process of transformation took a full year to accomplish at the first Card Operations Center. Senior management was supportive all the way. The company chairman received monthly reports, read all of them, and even flew out to Phoenix to meet with employees and share ideas about quality and service. So did the director of the new quality assurance program (Lou Gerstner, who is now the president of American Express). However, it is one thing to sell QA to management, quite another to sell it to employees. As Casey Stengel put it, "It's easy to get the players. Gettin 'em to play together, that's the hard part."

## Changing Employee Behavior

Transforming employee attitudes and behavior required a complex series of steps. First, management did not simply impose new rules and workflows upon employees without explanation or consultation. Instead, they involved employees in the QA process from the start, bringing them together from different departments to identify new possibilities for better service through service improvement teams. This helped to minimize anxiety and resentment.

Second, the company launched an extensive internal educational and communication process through written and visual material. They used— and continue to use—everything from posters, buttons, and cartoons to highly visible progress charts. The process began with a program called "Quality—I take it personally"; each employee received a *ticket to quality* with a message from the company chairman. They developed a video program which is used worldwide during employee orientation. To get employees to seriously buy into the process, they also explained and communicated the reasons for the standards. In addition, each employee needed to understand what was expected of him or her and how performance expectations, measured against established standards, would be an important part of each performance appraisal.

Management communicated to employees the costs of poor quality, emphasizing that quality is as bottom-line as a company can get. For example, they showed how reducing *non-revenue generating input*—that is, rework due to not meeting customers' expectations in the first place—productivity and customer satisfaction improved, and revenues increased. (Reducing non-revenue generating input can be viewed as the service equivalent to reducing "rejects" in manufacturing.)

## Recognition Programs

The company developed, and continues to use, over one hundred different recognition and reward programs for employees. They are both narrowly focused—so that people in every location can see fellow workers being honored—and companywide. At a large operations center, there may be a Quality Month, during which a variety of recognition awards are distributed, a Quality Employee of the Month elected by peers, and a video crew on location to tape employees' definitions of quality for subsequent telecasts.

TRS' Great Performer Awards honor those individuals who have performed exceptional services for customers. The range of these feats is astonishing. They have included:

- Improvising a travel office in the middle of a downtown street for travelers caught in Mexico City's earthquake;
- Aiding hundreds of tourists who were caught in a civil war to safety by communicating with the outside world despite local curfews and travel prohibitions;
- Personally housing a group of stranded tourists whose belongings had been stolen while on holiday;
- Working night and day to reissue lost travel documents to a traveler and reunite him with his tour group.

Employees who win Great Performer Awards are flown to New York, wined and dined in the city, and given cash awards at a lavish banquet attended by TRS' top executives. Equally important, their extraordinary actions are communicated worldwide, thereby inspiring others to take actions way beyond the normal call of duty on behalf of our customers.

## Bottom-Line Results

Three years after the company implemented the QA program in operations centers in the U.S. and abroad, the bottom-line results revealed a dramatic story. Not only had quality of service delivery improved 78% but at the same time expenses per transaction decreased 21%. Within two years, for example, the card member application processing time dropped by 37%;

this single improvement has added up to more than seventy million dollars in increased revenues over the past ten years and built customer loyalty right from the start of their relationship with American Express.

With hundreds of millions of dollars added to the bottom line, there was no further need to sell QA within the company. Everyone became eager to apply it to their line of business. So QA, which had begun with the credit card department, expanded to Travelers Cheques and other company businesses.

## MONITORING QUALITY ASSURANCE: INTERNAL METHODOLOGY

Monitoring, tracking, and ensuring worldwide quality delivery of company products and services involves a complex mix of products and services—five types of charge cards, Travelers Cheques in nine currencies, wholesale and retail travel packages, insurance, and merchandise and data-based management services—as well as the diversity of thirty operations centers around the world, ranging in size from eighty employees to four thousand. The fulfillment of the company's mission depends on the fundamental belief that quality assurance is as vital a bottom-line function as marketing or sales. In line with that belief, quality assurance always reports directly to the top executive of each business unit or operations center.

### The Service Tracking Report

In addition, there exists an innovative, complex process and methodology for monitoring, tracking, and improving quality known as the Service Tracking Report (STR). At the simplest level, the STR is a compilation of statistics, tracked and gathered in each country of over one hundred service measures. Key service performance results based on these statistics, along with action plans for improvement, are sent for evaluation to New York headquarters, which issues a consolidated report of monthly performance to all management around the world, including the chairman. Each country's performance is measured and tracked against well-defined standards, based upon the local economic and cultural environment, as well as customer expectations.

However, the STR is much more than a measurement system. Although grounded on mountains of facts, it has become an important tool for examining and solving service problems, as well as tracking and measuring them. For example, if performance is not up to par, explanations and positive recommendations to turn the situation around are provided by each country's management. And each country's management knows that the STR, like a monthly report card, is closely read. For example, TRS president Aldo Papone reviews the STR findings and regularly communicates to worldwide management his pleasure at service improvements or concern over potential problems.

Finally, the STR communicates and disseminates information so that solutions to problems in one location can be applied to similar problems in another. In short, it is a unique, interactive QA method. In fact, a top management consultant quoted in *Fortune*'s article on service (December 1987) called it "the best feedback on service quality I have ever come across."

## The Business Review

The second major tool for implementing and overseeing QA at American Express is the on-site review. Headquarters and division staff take a holistic view of what is going on at divisional operations around the world. That is why the process is called a business review, not simply a QA review. These two groups team up with local line management and form a review team. Each team looks at the region's competition, operations, and systems, then comes up with action programs to support the company's strategy for superior service delivery. It is as if a review team evaluating a local car manufacturing plant looked beyond the assembly line and examined the entire process of acquiring materials, assembling them and so forth, to come up with more cost-effective ways of turning out higher-quality cars.

Business reviews exemplify the practice preached by quality experts such as Tom Peters that good quality is obtained through "management by wandering around." During a business review, which may take between two and four weeks, a great deal of time is spent monitoring customer letters and phone calls, as well as talking to employees. The review team rolls up its sleeves and helps local management solve problems, especially those which are interfunctional. In the process, new opportunities for improving service, profitability, and productivity are uncovered.

The on-site time is both a training process which enhances the skills and insights of local managers, and a recruiting opportunity. While in the field, high-potential line management—usually with five or six years' experience—may be offered a year or two of QA training at headquarters. When these managers return to local environments, they are more tuned into the overall business and how the role of quality in improving and developing the business are related. In fact, they are better equipped to assume the duties of general managers.

## Monitoring Quality Assurance: External Methodology

To complement its internal measurement methods, the company recently developed a new, highly sophisticated external measurement methodology. It is a transaction-based system that puts card member satisfaction and loyalty on the bottom-line.

As everyone in the service business knows, the most difficult element to measure is how a customer *feels*. Through unique, transaction-based surveys, focus is placed on how customers feel about a single contact with the company as well as the impact of this contact on their opinion of the credit card product; on their overall opinion of the company; on their renewal intentions; on their future American Express Card usage; and on their word-of-mouth recommendations. In sum, this transforms an area of so-called *soft* information into a documented measurement tool. Finally, the company continues to invest heavily in systems and technology so that employees have available all the information required for accurate and quick decision making at their fingertips.

## Overall Quality Assurance Benefits

In retrospect, quality assurance at American Express began modestly as a way to ensure consistent delivery of its products and services. However, during the past ten years its benefits have far exceeded the original expectations. It has:

- More sharply focused the attention of the entire company where it belongs—on the customer;
- Improved productivity—not an easy trick in a highly personalized service business that is international in scope;
- Contributed millions to the bottom line;
- Increased employees' morale and pride in their work, themselves, and the company;
- Proven to be an investment of time, money, and people which has paid the company back over and over again; and has
- Continued to give American Express its competitive edge. When customers see the blue box emblem, they know they are buying a first-class product from a first-class organization.

Fundamentally, the key to improving any service business is better motivating people. As chairman Jim Robinson says, "It is people, not computers, who deliver quality service one transaction at a time." In fact, of TRS' nearly 43,000 employees worldwide, about one-third have direct contact with customers handling some 21 million telephone calls, 5 million letters, 311 million charge authorizations, and 650 million transactions per year.

## The Information Revolution and Quality

It has been said that American Express is at the forefront of today's information revolution because it employs thousands of knowledgable workers, whose jobs require them to make a variety of decisions with each transaction they handle. Management believes their quality assurance methodology, which has been continually fine-tuned over the last ten years gives employees the right tools and philosophy to take the right action. Often, as the Great Performers Awards demonstrate, doing the right thing for customers is not always in a manual or procedure book. But, if employees have the flexibility to take appropriate actions and demonstrate a customer-first attitude, then the results are amazingly inventive and appropriate.

That is why, for example, four card authorizers responded with sensitivity to the plight of customers whose cards were confiscated by hijackers: they not only replaced their cards overnight, but also hand-delivered them to their Paris hotel. Likewise, that is why a credit authorizer in Greensboro, North Carolina, worked night and day, on his own initiative, to assist the stranded husband of a card member. Finally, when a card member was seriously injured in an auto accident, another authorizer assisted the card member's wife by arranging for an extension for a late payment, and also recommended a physician whose surgery eventually resulted in the card member's return to mobility, instead of paralysis.

In conclusion, quality assurance at American Express is a complicated, sophisticated, and flexible process for carrying out a simple, old-fashioned promise to the customer: We care.

## Works Cited

*Fortune*. December 1987. Companies that serve you best. 98.

Naisbitt, John, and Aburdene, Patricia. 1985. *Re-inventing the corporation: transforming your job and your company for the new information society*. New York: Warner Books.

Peters, Thomas J., and Waterman, Robert H., Jr. 1982. *In search of excellence*. New York: Harper-Row.

Port, Otis. June 8, 1987. Quality-special report. *Business Week*, 134.

*Time*. February 3, 1987. Why is service so bad? 48.

# Diversified Services

Hospital Corporation of America
Thomas R. Gillem and Eugene Nelson

# Hospital Quality Trends

**Thomas R. Gillem, M.S.**
**Eugene Nelson, D.Sc.**
Hospital Corporation of America

Founded in 1968, the Hospital Corporation of America (HCA) is the world's largest health care company. It owns and/or manages nearly four-hundred hospitals worldwide.

HCA's headquarters are in Nashville, Tennessee and it employs approximately 63,000 people to run its operations within the United States.

## CUSTOMER JUDGMENTS OF QUALITY

Quality health care is a goal all hospitals profess, but few have developed a comprehensive means of asking customers in a scientific way to judge the quality of care they receive. A tremendous amount of effort has been devoted to assessing the clinical quality of hospital care. There is no shortage of books, journals, and papers on the topic. The problem, however, is that past efforts to measure hospital quality have largely ignored the perceptions of customers—the patients, physicians, and payers. Instead of formally considering customer judgments of quality, the health care industry has focused almost entirely on internal quality assessments made by the health professionals who operate the system. In effect, a system for improving health care has been created that all but ignores the voice of the customer. This traditional approach is based on measurements of structure, process, and outcomes by physicians, nurses, hospital administrators, and other health care experts. Such a system may be a fairly effective way for providers to inspect the quality of a health delivery organization—the manpower, facilities, equipment, and supplies. But it is doubtful that this internal system alone—without patient views—can adequately assess both the process, which concerns how well services are delivered, and the outcomes, which are the consequences of health care as viewed by patients.

The leadership of Hospital Corporation of America believes hospitals need to make the transformation from the current practice of attempting to *assure* quality to actually measuring and improving the quality of care from both the external, customer perspective *and* the internal, provider perspective; hospitals that successfully make the changeover, will be the survivors in a new age of health care ahead. This new age represents a shift in the medical paradigm away from the traditional perception that the accepted standard is to deliver health care in just a scientific and caring manner.

Now, fueled by concerns in recent years about costs and medical practice variation and by the demand for greater social accountability, there is an emerging demand by patients and payers that quality health care be provided at best value. Quality of services will be the way one hospital differentiates itself from another in the new age of health care, according to the leaders of HCA. As the prices people pay in the future for given levels of service become more similar, hospitals will be distinguished largely on the basis of their quality and value as assessed by customers.

## PATIENT SATISFACTION SURVEYS

This increased importance of quality change will mean a significant reorientation for hospital leaders. To meet the challenge, the leaders must have accurate information about how their customers, not just the health care professionals who work there, judge the quality of care in their institutions. Many hospitals already have some methods for measuring patient satisfaction. A recent survey of more than two hundred hospitals showed that two-thirds routinely conduct patient satisfaction surveys. Typically, the surveys are distributed at discharge to patients who are free to respond or not. The main value of such surveys is to gain quick knowledge of problems experienced by patients, many of whom often fill out questionnaires because they are disgruntled about some specific aspect of the care they received.

## Scientific Survey Standards

The problem, however, is that most current strategies for measuring patient satisfaction are not based on questionnaires that have been proven to be valid and reliable according to standard statistical techniques. Responses are not received from a representative sample of patients and are not used as part of a process for improvement that is supported by the hospital leadership. Satisfaction surveys often can be successfully used to extinguish brush fires, but if hospital leaders are serious about improving the quality of care, they must have more valid and reliable data on which to act. *Validity* is the degree to which a particular indicator measures what it is supposed to measure, rather than reflecting some other phenomenon. *Reliability* concerns the extent to which any measuring procedure yields the same results on repeated trials.

If hospital leaders decide to redesign their hospitals to improve quality, they must have answers to specific, quality-related questions about activities in areas that affect patients—admissions, nursing, medical staff, daily care, and ancillary staff. A sufficient rate of surveyed patients must respond, and the information must be available on a continuing basis for the leaders to evaluate and act upon over time. With this data, the leaders will be better able to make the decisions necessary to improve the many processes that occur in their hospitals.

## Hospital Quality Trends Survey

HCA is developing four customer judgment systems to generate trend reports on hospital quality from its major external customer groups—patients, physicians, payers, *and* its employees. The first system, called the Hospital Quality Trends: Patient Judgments System (HQT: Patients), went into widespread use within the corporation in late 1987. This system samples a representative group of discharged patients, gathers their reports about hospital services, measures their rating of quality using a data collection instrument with demonstrated measurement properties, and generates quality trend reports. A hospital's leaders can use this data as part of its quality improvement process to recognize areas of excellence, spot opportunities for improvement, monitor the impact of quality improvement efforts over time, and track trends in patient ratings of quality. The system is based on the premise that customers' judgments about quality of services form an essential phase of the continuous improvement cycle.

The HQT: Patients survey required more than a year to plan, pilot, and implement. It was developed by a design team that included hospital administrators, nurses, physicians, and specialists in health services research from HCA, the Rand Corporation, and the Harvard School of Public Health. The HQT: Patients survey will be placed in the public domain.

The pilot test, using a questionnaire containing just over one hundred items, was conducted in the spring of 1987 at ten hospitals in Texas, Kansas, and Massachusetts. The hospitals ranged in size from less than one hundred beds to more than six hundred beds, and the communities covered the spectrum from rural to metropolitan. The goal of the pilot was to develop a valid and reliable questionnaire that could be administered efficiently to a representative sample of patients and whose results could be used to produce trend reports for hospital leaders to recognize excellence and improve quality. Adjusted response rates in the pilot averaged more than 70% after patients were excluded for such reasons as death, severe illness, and inability to read.

From the pilot, the designers pared the number of questions to sixty-nine, divided into four categories of information—structure, process, outcomes, and open-ended comments. The questionnaire requires fifteen minutes on the average to complete; it is designed to be self-administered by patients. A goal of HQT: Patients is to obtain a survey response rate of greater than 70%, which is several times better than the typical response rates hospital administrators now experience with patient satisfaction surveys.

## HQT: Two Case Studies

HCA Medical Center of Plano, a 230-bed medical-surgical hospital in Texas, was one of the pilot sites. Plano administrator Allyn Harris said HQT: Patients caused him to reflect on the truism that "perception is reality:"

The patient is the key reason for our existence, and I refocused my thinking on how the patient perceives his or her hospital experience. I decided to recommit our total organizational focus to quality improvement and excellence.

This isn't to say that we didn't think about this in the past, but I think we tend to get bogged down from time to time with details, processes, and putting out fires. As a result of the patient judgments report, I decided to adopt quality improvement and excellence as a major thrust of our total organization.

In this market-driven environment, it is my belief that we can use the quality improvement process as a means of differentiating ourselves from our competition. Thus, I believe quality measurement and improvement will lead to a stronger organization which better serves our customers.

Harris said he considered the information he received from the survey as an important quality measurement tool and did not attempt to rationalize why results in some areas were lower than he had hoped. "I tried to avoid being defensive and, instead, considered the results as good, reliable information upon which to base an overall quality improvement process throughout the hospital."

Department directors at Medical Center of Plano were presented elements of the data and asked to focus on how patients rate the quality of the different departments, such as admissions, nursing, housekeeping, and food services. The hospital also reviewed how patients perceived various aspects of their hospital care, such as caring and courteous service, information given, skill, coordination and access, and patient orientation. The hospital considered this information as its report card from patients on how it was doing in the area of quality and customer satisfaction.

Mike Spurlock had just arrived as administrator at HCA South Arlington Medical Center, when the pilot results became available. The valid information about how patients perceived the quality of care at South Arlington helped him deal with several problems he faced. "The physicians had one perception of what the patients were saying, and what I found was that the physicians were focusing on the negative," Spurlock said. "Nobody ever says the positive, and that's the only thing the physicians thought." Because the survey was a scientifically valid sampling of patients' judgments, most doctors at South Arlington Medical Center accepted the results as indicating the situation was better than they had perceived. According to Spurlock,

Being new in the hospital and coming into a facility with many competing demands and priorities, it allowed me to say that HCA is interested in quality and then have something to show for it and something on which to base the measurement of quality improvement. It started some accountability. People are now aware that they are going to know how the service they provide is perceived by patients.

Everybody tinkers with the term 'quality', and the patient survey has helped us because we just keep emphasizing it over and over. Employees are now starting to define what quality is in their departments. They are expanding it beyond the technical expertise into the consumer way of looking at it. That's something brand new for this hospital.

## CONCLUSION

In the short term, trend reports can validate management inclinations to act — to take the steps necessary to diagnose the root cause of problems and subsequently to implement durable solutions that will result in measurable improvements in the quality and efficiency of services. But the key to the HQT: Patients system is using the data over time to systematically refocus and redesign the myriad processes of a hospital to better serve the needs of the patient. A similar Hospital Quality Trends survey was piloted in early 1988 by the HCA Psychiatric Company, which owns or manages fifty-one psychiatric hospitals in the United States.

If hospitals mean to strive for quality care, their employees must know how their leaders define quality. The HCA Quality Improvement Council, chaired by chairman and chief executive officer Thomas F. Frist, Jr., formally established the corporation's definition of quality: *At HCA, achieving quality means the continuous improvement of services to meet the needs and expectations of the patients, the physicians, the payers, the employees, and the communities we serve.*

Other surveys in the Hospital Quality Trends series will measure how physicians, payers, and employees judge the quality of care in a hospital. As those surveys are installed, hospital leaders will add both breadth and depth to their picture of how all customers view the quality of hospital services. Ultimately, the key to effective quality management in hospitals will be the ability to integrate the judgments of customers with information from the providers for the design and delivery of hospital services that specifically address the needs of all customers.

## Works Cited

Albrecht, K. and R. Zemke. 1985 *Service America! Doing Business in the New Economy*, Homewood: Dow Jones-Irwin, 96.

Marr, Jeffrey W. October 1986. Letting the Customer be the Judge of Quality. *Quality Progress*, 46.

# Electronics, Appliances

AT&T
Roberta J. Coleman

TRW, Inc.
Jack Smith

Westinghouse Electric Corporation
Kenneth W. Kilderry

# AT&T: Building on a Quality Tradition to Ensure Quality Service Delivery

**Roberta J. Coleman**
AT&T

American Telephone and Telegraph Company was established in 1885 as a subsidiary of the American Bell Telephone Company, and became the parent company when management relocated its headquarters to New York City in 1899. Currently, headquarters activities are spread among several locations in New Jersey and New York City.

AT&T provides its customers worldwide with products, services and systems for the movement and management of information. The company designs, manufactures, markets, and services telecommunications equipment and systems; engineers and installs telecommunications networks for domestic and international customers.

# INTRODUCTION

Market share and profitability in a highly competitive marketplace are directly related to two customer-based judgments: Does this product or service offer high value compared with cost? Will I be satisfied with the delivery?

The importance of these two customer judgments can even be quantified by a research study. The validity of a corporate strategy that couples the goals of high customer satisfaction and relatively low internal costs have been repeatedly demonstrated by those companies, frequently Japanese, that have achieved significant growth in market share and "best-in-class" reputations in a global marketplace. The simple lesson learned or rediscovered by American industry in this decade is that quality pays, where quality is defined by the customer.

AT&T has a longstanding reputation for high-quality products and services. Its history is rich in contributions to quality technology. In fact, many of today's quality fundamentals were laid down in the first fifty years of AT&T. To name a few, these include:

- Quality assurance acceptance inspection of "telephonic appliances" that began in 1882;
- Walter Shewhart's development of the statistical quality control chart in Bell Laboratories in 1925;
- The development and subsequent publication of Inspection Sampling Tables by Harold Dodge and Harry Romig of AT&T Bell Laboratories in 1944; and
- The publication in 1956 of the *Western Electric Statistical Quality Control Handbook* that was developed by a team of manufacturing engineers led by Bonnie Small. Some thirty years after the first printing, it is still recognized as the book on statistical process control methods.

While AT&T, like many other American businesses, is justly proud of this quality heritage, its traditional focus has been on quality control in manufacturing operations. This focus on the technical quality of products and the reliability of a network has sustained its reputation as a provider of high-quality telecommunications products and services. However, with more parity in technology than ever before, service and product support are being judged.

AT&T now recognizes that quality of service that is, attention to the customer, and technical product quality are essential for movement toward a market-based system; in fact, the first provides the competitive advantage. To appreciate the strategic value of quality, one must recognize that quality is more than a product: it is intrinsic to planning, design and development, service, installation, repair and maintenance, and post-sales customer services. Service, product delivery, and support function as key factors in the customer's decision to purchase a company's product or services.

This is not to ignore the fact that AT&T is a company that traditionally has focused on customer service. Its service ethic is best represented by a painting of a lineman working to repair a fallen telephone line during a blizzard. The painting is appropriately entitled Spirit of Service. On an annual basis, Spirit of Service awards are given to employees who best exemplify this service heritage. However, the attitude in the past was one of "service at any cost," a strategy that is clearly not well-suited for a business operating in a competitive marketplace. According to one senior manager at AT&T, the company's "service heritage goes back more than a century," but "the system, processes, and management approaches that had allowed us to provide high quality service so well for so many decades were too costly, cumbersome, and fragmented for long-term success in a competitive environment." In other words, for the company to sustain a competitive advantage in the marketplace, it not only has to focus attention on services to the end-customer, but also must pay strict attention to the quality and efficiency of all internal processes and customer support systems. Experience has taught the company that quality and process are inextricably intertwined. Every business process must be viewed and managed within the context of the whole, in order to deliver quality products and services to end-customers.

## MODERN VIEW OF QUALITY
### AT&T Policy on Quality

Successful companies have long realized that the customer is the reason that the company exists, and a foolproof way of guaranteeing customer loyalty is to provide high quality service. The AT&T policy on quality establishes for each employee a set of responsibilities and a course of action that contribute to the realization of AT&T's overarching goal of customer satisfaction. Specifically, it states that "quality excellence is the foundation for the management of our business and the keystone of our goal of customer satisfaction. It is, therefore, our policy to consistently provide products and services that meet the quality expectations of our customers and actively pursue ever-improving quality through programs that enable each employee to do his or her job right the first time."

The intent of the policy is to reinforce quality. Its underlying goal of customer satisfaction represents a major, strategic thrust that lies at the heart of everything AT&T does. It enjoins every employee to be dedicated to continually improving quality of products and services. Inherent in the policy statement is the recognition that the quality of actual customer service rests largely with the individual employee—every employee—not only those with direct responsibility for customer service. By focusing on the processes by which the employee performs his or her job, identifying and eliminating the sources of problems that have an impact on their ability to do a quality job, and striving for continuous improvement in these processes, each employee ensures high quality service delivery. This focus on the quality of internal work processes, that is, the quality of the product and services delivered to a series of "internal" customers is critical.

## Surveys of Quality

The level of customer satisfaction with AT&T's products and services has been tracked for a number of years using formal surveys such as those conducted by Telephone Service Attitude Measurement (TELSAM) centers. Different types of measurement vehicles are used by the various business units. Basically, they all query end users of telecommunications products and services, as well as business decision-makers about everything: From installation (How well was the order taken? Was the work completed on time? Were records complete and accurate? Was the installer knowledgeable?); to repair and maintenance (Was the work completed when promised? Was the original trouble corrected? Was the repair person courteous? Were you updated on the repair status?); to the technical quality of products and services, post-sales service and billing, and the overall customer's satisfaction with AT&T.

However, to achieve a consistent level of customer perception of a high quality of service, AT&T has begun to focus aggressively on those service and administrative processes traditionally thought of as being in the "soft" area of customer needs and expectations. The service quality focus is both internally and externally directed. To facilitate the implementation of this new service quality strategy, AT&T has developed a set of process-quality guidelines to help employees routinely focus on delivering to their customers what the customer needs and wants.

These Process Quality Management and Improvement guidelines (PQMI) are designed to help managers increase the effectiveness and efficiency of their work processes and, consequently, achieve a higher level of customer satisfaction while reducing internal operating costs.

## PROCESS MANAGEMENT AND IMPROVEMENT

Why a focus on processes? The capacity to serve a customer effectively and efficiently is an issue that every organization that wishes to remain competitive must face. Operating under the premise that all work is part of a systematic process, a proactive approach to understanding and managing the process seems to make good business sense. Effective process quality management demands that customer requirements guide day-to-day work activities. Using a customer-driven approach to quality management ensures that the outputs of one's work satisfy the customer and that the process is responsive to changes in customer requirements.

## The Customer-Supplier Model

The PQMI methodology is based on a customer-supplier model (figure 1) which presupposes that everyone has a) customers, either inside or outside

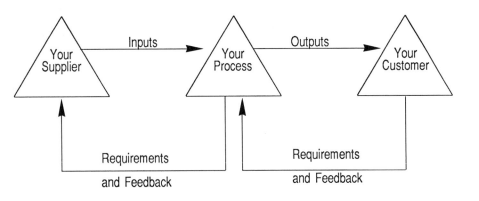

FIG. 1. CUSTOMER/SUPPLIER MODEL

the company, who use the outputs of their job and b) suppliers who provide inputs to their job. This model provides a framework for establishing and maintaining effective relationships with customers and suppliers.

The model begins with customer requirements and stresses the active measurement of customer satisfaction in order to provide on-going feedback for improvement of the specific operation or work function. Any business can be thought of as consisting of hundreds of interdependent customer/supplier links. Successful final service delivery is dependent upon the extent to which each link in the business chain contributes to satisfying customer needs.

## Four Stages of the Work Process

The PQMI methodology consists of seven steps that operate as a cycle: you *manage* the process and *improve* the process, and continuously repeat the cycle. The seven steps of the methodology include tasks to be performed at each of four distinct stages within the management and improvement phases. Each stage addresses different goals.

Stage 1. *Ownership*. The purposes of the ownership stage are to ensure that someone is in charge of the process and that a team exists to carry out day-to-day management activities. The key activities of this stage are

- To identify an "owner" who is ultimately accountable for the overall process and who can manage the process across functional or organizational boundaries (step 1).
- To define roles and responsibilities and to ensure that everyone involved in process quality management and improvement works as a team under the direction of an owner (step 1).

Stage 2. *Assessment*. The purpose of assessment is to assure that the process is clearly defined, that customer expectations are clearly understood, and that measures are in place to determine how well the process satisfies customer requirements and internal business objectives. At this stage the employee needs

- To understand how his or her work process operates (step 2).
- To identify customers' needs in measurable terms (step 2).
- To determine what elements of the process should be measured and controlled to meet customer requirements (step 3).
- To test and then implement appropriate new measures, or to validate existing measures on a wide scale (step 3).
- To gather data on process performance (step 4).
- To control and stabilize process performance (step 4).
- To assess process performance against customers' requirements (step 4).

Stage 3. *Opportunity selection*. The purposes of the opportunity selection stage are to understand how internal process problems affect customer satisfaction and cost, and to identify and compare various opportunities for process improvement. In carrying out the key activities of this stage, the employee needs

- To identify critical internal process problems that are affecting customer satisfaction and cost (step 5).
- To identify process simplification opportunities (step 5).
- To rank improvement opportunities, based on customer satisfaction and business objectives (step 6).
- To set appropriate quality-improvement and performance targets (step 6).
- To identify quality improvement projects to pursue (step 6).

Stage 4. *Improvement*. The goal of the improvement stage is to achieve and sustain a new level of process performance. That means implementing an action plan for realizing the opportunities identified in the previous stage. Essentially, the stage requires the employee

- To organize a team that will develop an action plan to address opportunities for the improvement of process quality (step 7).
- To identify and remove root causes of problems (step 7).
- To control and monitor the process at the improved level of performance (step 7).
- To monitor and assess process performance on an on-going basis (step 7).

Figure 2 provides a graphic illustration of the mapping of the seven steps within the ownership, assessment, opportunity selection, and improvement stages. Also provided is a detailed listing of the objectives and key activities for each of the steps. These process improvement guidelines have

| STAGES | STEPS | OBJECTIVES | KEY ACTIVITIES |
|---|---|---|---|
| Ownership | 1. Establish process management responsibilities. all process members. | • Identify the owner in charge of the end-to-end process. • Identify responsibility of • Establish review | • Review owner selection criteria. • Identify owner and process members. responsibilities of owner and process members. |
| | 2. Define process and identify customer requirements. | • Understand how the process operates at a high level and what is required of it. | • Define process boundaries and major groups, outputs and customers, inputs and suppliers, and subprocesses and flows. • Conduct customer needs analysis. • Define customer requirements and communicate your own requirements to suppliers. |
| Assessment | 3. Define and establish measures. | • Determine what needs to be measured and controlled to meet customer requirements. | • Decide on effective measures. • Review existing measures. • Install new measures and reporting system. • Establish customer satisfaction feedback system. |
| | 4. Assess conformance to customer requirements. | • Find out how well you are doing against customer requirements and how well suppliers are doing against your requirements. | • Collect and review data on process operations. • Identify and remove causes of abnormal variation. • Compare performance of stable process to requirements and determine chronic problem areas. |
| Opportunity Selection | 5. Investigate process to identify improvement opportunities. | • Identify internal process problems affecting customer satisfaction and costs. • Identify process simplification opportunities. | • Gather data on process problems. • Identify potential process problem areas to pursue. • Document potential problem area. • Gather data on subprocess problems. • Identify potential subprocess problems to pursue. |
| | 6. Rank improvement opportunities and set objectives. | • Decide on order of fixing problems. • Set targets for improvement. | • Review improvement opportunities. • Establish priorities. • Negotiate objectives. • Decide on improvement projects. |
| Improvement | 7. Improve process quality. | • Achieve new level of process performance. | • Develop action plan. • Identify root causes. • Test and implement solution. • Follow through. • Perform periodic process review. |

FIG. 2. PROCESS QUALITY MANAGEMENT AND IMPROVEMENT STEPS

been tested successfully, and the practice is now being disseminated throughout AT&T.

## SUMMARY

A major impetus for the development of the PQMI guidelines was the recognition of the need for a disciplined approach to managing and improving the quality of service provided to AT&T customers. Traditionally, services have been viewed as different from manufacturing, since service is consumed as it is produced.

However, experience has taught AT&T that the principles of quality management apply equally to manufacturing and service businesses. By using the basic operating principles inherent in the customer/supplier model to design internal and external systems that meet customer service needs, companies will be able to create and sustain a competitive service-quality advantage. The environment where multiple vendors compete on the basis of price is changing to where the customers' decision to purchase is based on the price in concert with various non-price attributes of the product or service: delivery, repair and maintenance, sales service, complaint handling, customer support, and billing. In developing the PQMI guidelines as a tool to implement its customer-focused service strategy, AT&T has provided its employees with a blueprint for action. It will take focused and committed leadership, supported by effective performance measurement systems, to make this goal a reality. AT&T has started on this journey toward continuous quality improvement.

# Quality in Computer Services: Maintenance, Repair, and Support Services

**Jack Smith**
TRW Inc.

The customer service division of TRW is an independent supplier of maintenance, repair, and customer support services for computers and other information-handling systems. The division has a wide range of customers who use information-handling systems in a variety of ways. This division has built customer support capabilities for over fourteen hundred different equipment models built by seventy different manufacturers. TRW employs approximately 78,000 people worldwide and through its network of 150 service centers in the United States, TRW employs approximately 2400 service professionals.

## INTRODUCTION

As the world grows more dependent on information in order to manufacture products and deliver services, the demand for quality in information systems is felt with increasing strength. Huge opportunities have emerged for suppliers of information itself, hardware, software, and related support services. Handling information efficiently, quickly, reliably, and cost-effectively determine quality as the world copes with the information explosion.

TRW Inc., has built a group of businesses providing information systems to meet these challenges. As part of this commitment to the Information Age, TRW has built one of the world's largest independent service organizations.

## THIRD PARTY MAINTENANCE

TRW is part of the growing third-party maintenance industry. Third-party maintenance service firms are different from manufacturer service organizations. The third-party suppliers do not, as a rule, sell hardware or software products, except as a product-life extension service when the original manufacturer has discontinued support of such products. They serve customers by providing maintenance, repair, and related support services alone. As such, these third-party maintenance service companies compete with manufacturers such as IBM and DEC.

At the same time, much of the third-party maintenance service business is developed in response to manufacturer and customer need. Some smaller manufacturers do not have the resources to build nationwide service operations for their customers. Some manufacturers have gone out of business or discontinued product lines. Many customers have elected to purchase different types of hardware and software products to enable them to take full advantage of available technology and to minimize costs. Many manufacturers have refused to support such mixed-vendor systems. Still, some other customers simply have not been satisfied with a manufacturer's service program, its personnel, or its cost. All of these causes have contributed to the growth of the third-party maintenance services industry during the last decade.

## SERVICE AS A QUALITY ENHANCEMENT

Service itself has long been recognized as a key differentiator among manufacturers of information-handling systems. Delivering a high-quality package of support services is part of the formula for long-term success for many major manufacturers.

Ever since computer systems and automated office equipment were introduced to the business world, there has been a need for organizations to repair equipment. Part of the fear involved in automating business operations has been that office operations would get out of control when data was kept on magnetic storage devices rather than in file drawers. There was the fear of computerization—that business could not be conducted efficiently because information would be lost.

As manufacturers of automatic data processing equipment encountered this customer fear, their strongest ally was their service organization, the people who would be on-call at any hour of the day or night to fix problems with the computer. They were the save-the-day heroes who would straighten out confusion caused by automatic data processing systems and automated offices. A strong customer-support program overcame the fear of computerizing a business operation. Early adapters of computer systems had to have the assurance that they would not be risking their business operations to the computer. They had to have a comfort factor; they had to know that service people were available to find lost information, restore system operations, and keep the productivity high. To ensure this safety factor, they would gladly sign maintenance contracts even if they were not included as part of the system purchase.

## TRADITIONAL MEASURES OF QUALITY: THE CUSTOMER'S CRITERIA

Customers learned quickly how to recognize a quality service operation. They had only a few things to count among the criteria for a quality-oriented service operation.

The first was *response time*. When a customer had a problem, how long did it take a service representative to get to the customer site? If the time was low—let's say one hour, the service company earned a high score for quality. The service person was responsive; he or she came when it was necessary. That the service person came quickly demonstrated concern for the customer.

The second criterion was *repair time*. If the service representative came to the customer's site quickly and fixed the problem immediately, the service organization was considered a quality provider. If a service representative did not have the knowledge to fix the problem or if the service person did not have the necessary replacement parts, the points won for a quick response would be lost. Since the customer's operation was not restored to a complete degree, the service organization was viewed as inferior to the standard that was expected. Having to order parts and wait for them to arrive made the situation worse for the customer. Downtime would be measured in terms of lost productivity, and the customer would feel that his hardware or software was of inferior quality. Unless the customer's system was restored to full operational status, the service organization had failed. In addition, the manufacturer suffered an unrecognized wound to the product's reputation. Basically, this is how quality standards were established as computerized equipment found its way into American business, government, and manufacturing.

## TRADITIONAL MEASURES OF QUALITY: THE SERVICER'S CRITERIA

Service organizations have always recognized that response time and repair time were the prime indicators of quality. Both were the cause of customer satisfaction and customer complaint. Therefore, service organizations work hard to ensure that their service personnel are well-trained and that they have an ample supply of spare parts to do their jobs. In addition, service personnel are trained in customer relations so that the image they leave with customers is a positive one. The traditional quality principle is simple: respond quickly, fix the equipment as fast as possible, and do it with a smile.

## WHY THE FUTURE CANNOT BE LIKE THE PAST

There have been many changes during the past decade that have made it more difficult for service providers to meet their customers' expectations for *quality* as defined by traditional measurement standards. New expectations and measurement standards have emerged.

First, customers and equipment operators have changed. Older systems used to be installed in large businesses or data centers with proper electrical power and environmental controls. Operators were highly trained and fully experienced. Today there is a computer on almost every business desk, and it is connected to the nearest wall outlet. There are no special environmental controls. Operators of these systems often receive little or no formal training and are far less experienced. Still, these are customers who expect prompt resolution to any and all problems. Whatever the cause, it is up to the successful servicer to correct the situation and get the customer back on-line. This may mean doing much more than fixing the equipment. It might include preparing a customized preventive maintenance program or a recommendation to minimize the problem situation that a customer site is experiencing. It may include recommendations for new software or a totally new environment. It may require spare parts and training so that the customer can service his or her own equipment. Whatever it takes to fix the customer's predicament is what is necessary for the successful, quality-oriented servicer to supply.

Adding to this complexity of servicing tasks is the tremendous increase in the number of different hardware and software providers and products that customers can select from. Customers are more apt to purchase mixed hardware and software products from various suppliers to enable them to take full advantage of available technology and cost savings. But they do not want to work with a wide number of service suppliers and their many different programs. They prefer to have one service provider for all products. To further complicate the servicer's task, these same customers are installing these products across local and wide-area networks. This often results in lower density of a given product in a specific location—making it more difficult for the service provider to support the investments required to ensure the availability of technical expertise and materials for all products in all locations.

Regardless of size, any business that has automated for productivity and better business control becomes dependent on the fast, uninterrupted flow of information. The size of a business has little to do with the quality standards that are established. The criticalness of the application in the business is what determines need and standards. Quality servicers are learning that they have to know the intimate details of a business operation, to understand how technology is applied and how system interactions are vital to making a business run efficiently and profitably. By recognizing these features, a service organization can tailor a total service program that addresses uptime, convenience, operational disturbance, and costs. Tailoring services to specific needs can add significant value to the offerings of a service provider. The fact is that customers do not think about maintenance or repair services. They think about uptime and their businesses. To get onto this important wavelength with a customer can mean the success or failure of a quality service program.

With the advancements in technology comes an increased reliability of information-handling systems. As a result, some customers are less quick to insure their systems investment with maintenance contracts. This is true especially when system downtime does not seriously impact the operation of a business. Instead, customers often are willing to risk a failure and secure service on an as-needed basis. Others are interested in a self-service approach. Still, because they are paying for service on a time-and-materials basis, they are not tolerant with extended repair times, repeat service calls, or unnecessary replacement of parts. Even though they may not have a maintenance contract, these customers expect a reasonable response time when they do have a problem. Customers want a simple service program tailored to their needs.

Providing traditional service quality to customers would be easy if costs did not enter into the picture. However, with the costs of service rising—due to the high *people costs* of the service business and the reduction of price in software and hardware—services are becoming a more significant portion of the costs of ownership. Over the useful life of the product, the cost of service may be greater than the original purchase price of the product. As a result, customers are not only more sensitive to the cost of service, they expect more from it.

Even if servicers could afford to supply the traditional type of quality, it would not mean that customers would be more satisfied. We have to examine a new definition of quality as it relates to maintenance and repair services because expectations and situations are different from what they were.

## DEFINING NEW QUALITY STANDARDS IN THE COMPUTER SERVICES INDUSTRY

Fast response time and fast repair time will always lead the list of quality standards within the computer services industry. Equally important, however, are a number of *communication* standards that ae becoming increasingly important. John Naisbett, in his bestseller *Megatrends*, foresaw that a *high-tech* society will be balanced by *high-touch* human interactions. This has become fact in the computer services area. Customers want the person-to-person interaction that assures answers, builds confidence, and reduces worry. Current customers judge their service programs and service providers on the amount and quality of communications that take place when problems occur and after they are resolved. Customers are expecting complete and timely communications with their service suppliers—at least, that is what the people at TRW have concluded. All of these people-oriented services are costly for the service provider; but, since they are key determinants of quality, they cannot be understated and definitely cannot be ignored.

An important component in a quality service program is a steady focus on the customer's business, not on the customer's equipment. Understanding how a customer has applied technology to a business operation will provide the focus necessary to develop a quality service program. Treating each customer as having a unique situation helps the servicer focus on quality standards. One size does not fit everyone, especially in the service business. Service organizations that understand this get in touch with specific customer requirements and determine standards of quality based on those requirements and expectations.

With the new technology now available to service organizations, customizing service programs will continue to become easier and more effective. Whatever services make up the program, customer and servicer must agree on preestablished performance standards so there is no ambiguity in measurement methods. In the case of on-site maintenance services, exact standards should be developed for the following components and should be part of the service program:

- Response time
- Repair time
- System availability or uptime
- Protocols for calling the servicer
- Protocols for communicating with the customer
- Emergency repairs
- Preventive maintenance activities
- Protocols for reporting service activities to the customer
- Calendar to review service program with the customer
- Problem-escalation procedures
- Customer responsibilities

Regardless of the scope or type of a support service program, exact standards should be established with—and for—each customer.

TRW, as a leader in third-party maintenance and repair services, has probably the most visible quality program in the industry. This program addresses the new definitions of quality, including the expectations for a high degree of customer communications. In addition, it is a program built on the principle of applying technology to the service business in the most advanced ways possible. Quality will be determined largely by the extent to which there is a balanced program of applied technology and personal interaction that demonstrates concern for the customer.

## APPLYING TECHNOLOGY

In response to the many changes that continue to unfold in the marketplace, TRW has placed increasing emphasis on the application of technology in its service delivery systems. This is needed not only to maintain and improve quality, but also to address increasing costs of people and materials.

One of TRW's early applications, driven by the need to support complex nationwide data communications networks, was the development of a centralized data communications test center. This center is used to assist both customer personnel and TRW service engineers in diagnosing data communications problems. It has all but eliminated the delays, frustration, and expense that often result when the customer attempts to work with telephone companies, data centers, and service providers to resolve data communication problems. The real proof is that problems are often resolved without even having to dispatch a service engineer to a customer's location.

A later application, driven by the rapid growth in the microcomputer systems market, was the development of a multipurpose system and assembly tester called *SLEUTH*. Equipped with this highly versatile tester and proprietary operating system and diagnostic software, TRW service engineers can service a wide variety of mixed-vendor systems without the difficulties and costs associated with carrying vast amounts of technical documentation and specialized test equipment. The same tester is used to service equipment that is carried into TRW service centers. In either case, it enables prompt, accurate fault diagnosis without the costly *shotgunning* approach of swapping assemblies, a method used by many other service providers. In addition, the tester is used to test and screen assemblies received at TRW service centers, prior to adding them to local spare parts inventories. This screening of received parts and assemblies detects any possible damage resulting from shipping and handling.

While the SLEUTH tester is an intelligent device, it is also a freestanding unit. That is, its intelligence must be updated or supplemented if the complexity of the problems exceeds its capabilities. To address this feature, TRW has undertaken the development of two additional technology applications. The first is an on-line technical information system called

*SLATE.* This system provides all TRW service engineers access to the latest technical information pertaining to products they are servicing, and it updates the SLEUTH testers with current diagnostics and support software. The system consists of central database and a communications controller that allows access via dial-up telephone lines. Contained in the database is the latest product information received from hardware and software providers as well as technical information developed by TRW's own engineering department.

In addition, the SLATE database contains a file of problems and related solutions for the products serviced by TRW. Based on analyses of the thousands of service activities completed by TRW daily and the input received from service engineers, who enter their data directly to SLATE via the dial-up communications link, an extensive file of product problems, symptoms, causes, and solutions is maintained and made available to all TRW's service engineers.

In addition to the information SLATE provides, it also serves as a terminal tester. Any data terminal that is serviced by TRW can be connected to SLATE via dial-up telephone lines. Extensive testing is performed by SLATE to assist the service engineer in diagnosing the failure, verifying the repairs, and detecting other potential failures. All the information and capabilities of SLATE are available to all TRW service engineers and authorized customers twenty-four hours a day, seven days a week. Although the information and intelligence provided in SLEUTH and SLATE have greatly enhanced TRW's ability to deliver consistently high quality services across a wide range of products, further enhancements are underway.

In 1988, TRW began its *BETA* test of a newly developed system of integrated hardware and software intended to streamline the service and maintenance of computers and computer-based equipment. This system incorporates state-of-the-art artificial intelligence technology, specifically in the area of artificial intelligence known as expert systems. Similar to SLEUTH and SLATE, but far more advanced in its level of intelligence and reasoning, this expert system has the ability to guide TRW service engineers through the troubleshooting procedures: recommending tests, initiating them automatically, interpreting their results, and then using these results to determine the next step or a final diagnosis. This is accomplished through the use of a portable computer linked to a central knowledge base via dial-up telephone lines. The knowledge base is an accumulation of product knowledge and service expertise that has been obtained from both the product manufacturers and from TRW's most experienced service engineers. The system combines the knowledge and rules derived from human experts with a computerized *inference engine* that can deduce new facts and arrive at conclusions based on the accumulated knowledge. This expert-systems technology will have the same effect as sending the best trained technical expert on every service call.

# SOFTWARE TO MANAGE A NATIONAL SERVICE ORGANIZATION

Further enhancing its own ability to deliver consistently high quality across a wide range of products, TRW is installing new systems that promise gains in quality and efficiency.

## Fieldwatch

*Fieldwatch*, an integrated software package developed by the DATA Group, is the fundamental tool to manage and ensure quality. TRW is installing this software package to manage its complete service operation. The package includes six modules—all of which help the service organization deliver its services faster and better than it could with non-integrated software systems. These modules are titled as follows: *dispatch, technical assistance center (TAC), billing, logistics, repair center,* and *scheduling.*

The *dispatch* module contains customer records pertaining to the site, equipment, contract provisions, and the complete service history. It also includes information on the training and locations of technicians and service engineers. The system allows information to be stored and given to a service engineer when service calls are required. The package also contains an easy *report-writer* so that any number of reports can be derived from the information in the database.

The TAC module allows for product-line technical experts to screen calls for service. TAC experts are able to define the customer's problems and, in many cases, to solve the problem without having to send a technician to the customer's location. When this is not possible, the product-line expert is at least better able to provide the technician with important information on what is required to fix the equipment before the technician travels to the customer's location. In this way, the call can be completed on the first trip and in the shortest time. The TAC also runs remote diagnostics and provides technical assistance to service engineers at customer locations.

The *billing* module handles all billing and recordkeeping to ensure that invoices are filled out accurately and are based either on contract terms or actual expenses for time and material.

The *logistics* module handles the spare parts inventory. All information on spare parts is easily available to anyone involved in the delivery of services to a customer. Instant access to part numbers, prices, and stocking locations makes the service call faster and more productive.

The *repair center* module contains information to track repairable assemblies by part number and serial number. With repair time and parts standards built in, the system can report performance against standards. The repair center module works in concert with the *scheduling* module, so that repaired parts are available when and where they are needed. Applying information technology to the computer service business has already brought quality enhancements; adding to current applications of technology promises even greater gains in quality, efficiency, and customer satisfaction.

## Quality as Management's Commitment

Management leadership is the most important feature of the quality-oriented service organization. Along with the entire management's commitment to quality, TRW has established a vice-presidential-level executive with the sole responsibility to ensure that quality is a major ingredient in every service product. In addition, quality-oriented leadership sets the tone for all customer relations programs. This leadership ensures that quality is addressed in everything from call-handling to spare parts procurement.

## Continual Research for Higher Quality

TRW's Fieldwatch system gathers the information from every single service call as they are taking place so that problem areas can be identified and corrected much faster than with traditional reporting systems. In addition to this minute-by-minute research, TRW routinely conducts studies with customers and prospective customers to determine satisfaction levels. These studies help TRW plan new service products that address performance issues, quality, and price.

## THE INDUSTRIALIZATION OF SERVICES

In his book *The Marketing Imagination*, Theodore Levitt provides a lengthy discussion on the importance of industrializing the entire scope of service industries. To become more cost efficient, the service industries will have to augment the expensive *people costs* with highly automated information and logistics to make quantum leaps in quality and profitability. Service professionals will have to become more productive by having better information available to them while they perform services.

Levitt's principle applies absolutely to the computer services industry. Travel time will be reduced significantly by employing better remote diagnostics. Spare parts will have to be on customer sites so that no time is lost in procuring them. It may be that the quality standard in the near future will be an almost *invisible* service program from the customer perspective. Advancements in diagnostic software will become so responsive that they will be able to detect hardware and software failures before they emerge at the customer's site; this means that corrective action can be taken before any downtime results. Real quality then will be far removed from the response time and repair time that are now dominant.

With these invisible service programs, it will become more important to communicate with customers. They will need to know all the details to see what they are paying for. With enhanced diagnostics and overall advancements in service delivery technology, customers will need to understand these services and the benefits they bring before they will be willing to pay for them. The visibility of the service representative will have to be replaced with some other tangible evidence that quality services are being provided.

Quality in the computer services industry will always be determined by the satisfaction of customers over problems being avoided or solved. As technology is applied to our industry, we must not lose sight of the emotional needs of the customer when it comes to resolving problems with sophisticated information-handling technology. Servicers are in the world to serve—to keep their customers happy—a fact that should never be forgotten.

# Quality Improvement In the Service Sector

**K. W. Kilderry**
Westinghouse Electric Corporation

Westinghouse Electric Corporation was founded in 1886. Its principal business is the manufacture of electrical equipment for generation, transmission, and distribution of electricity. Westinghouse is headquartered in Pittsburgh and employs over 100,000.

## THE CONCEPT OF TOTAL QUALITY

Westinghouse Electric Corporation is a diversified technology-oriented corporation with annual sales of approximately eleven billion dollars. It has
more than one hundred thousand employees serving customers in over one
hundred countries. It is currently expanding its participation in service
market sectors such as broadcasting and financial services, and this trend
should continue.

"Total Quality" is the driving force in meeting its objective of having a
world class reputation in every aspect of its business. Total quality, as the
people at Westinghouse describe it, is a process of continuous improvement
in both the service and traditional sectors of its business. Improving business processes represents the key strategy in accomplishing the corporation's
financial and operating objectives.

At Westinghouse, *total quality* means "Performance leadership in meeting customer requirements by doing the right things right, the first time."
From another point of view, it denotes a process of continuously creating
value for all its stakeholders through excellence in all phases of business.
This value forms the cornerstone to building Westinghouse's corporate
strategy. It provides a system approach to managing the business and improving performance, instead of looking at the total business as a collection
of single functions or components. The concept of total quality is much
broader than that of conventional quality, which traditionally referred only
to the finished product or component.

In the systems approach, one analyzes the interaction of all the business
processes used and determines how each contributes to the achievement of
total quality. At Westinghouse, "Doing the right thing the first time" now
serves as a motto for a way of life for all employees. Several goals are
associated with the implementation of total quality:

- A deep-seated customer orientation and understanding, in which
  satisfying the customer's needs is the primary goal of every employee.
- A sustained advantage through habitually defining, initiating, and
  perpetuating a competitive edge.
- A positive, improvement-oriented organization that will be world
  class in the markets it serves.
- A value-creating organization for all Westinghouse stakeholders:
  customers, stockholders, employees, and the public.

By means of total quality, Westinghouse seeks to meet the challenge of
intense global competition in the future. The corporation treats it as a
business imperative for survival in present and future markets and not as a
short term, fashionable management program. As articulated by a former

chairman of Westinghouse, the corporation's mission can be summarized in brief:

- We are a diversified, technology-based corporation, operating globally.
- Our mission is to manage our resources in ways that create value for our customers, employees, and stockholders.
- We do this by managing our operations to achieve total quality in everything we do.

In other words, the corporate goals depend on applying the tools and techniques of the total quality concept.

## ELEMENTS OF TOTAL QUALITY
One can conceptualize the idea of total quality as a triangle with three main elements (figure 1).

### Requirements
The first component of the triangle is composed of requirements. These represent the basic goals set for all of the business operations. These are the targets which direct all efforts at total quality. Requirements are expressed in relation to the various stakeholders the corporation must satisfy. The

REQUIREMENTS
- Customer satisfaction
- Stockholder value
- Employee satisfaction
- Public approval

MEASURES
- Value/price ratio
- Value/cost ratio
- Error-free performance

IMPERATIVES
- Customer orientation
- Human resource excellence
- Product/process leadership
- Management leadership

FIG. 1. THE TOTAL QUALITY TRIANGLE.

customers who buy products; the investors who put their money in Westinghouse and expect a reasonable growth in value; the employees who make a commitment to the company and expect it to be a rewarding and challenging place to work; and the public, who demand that the company both coexist peacefully with the community and make a contribution to it.

## Measurements

Three basic measures can help assess the corporation's progress toward meeting those requirements. Each can be quantified by techniques developed at the Westinghouse Corporate Productivity and Quality Center.

- The *value-to-price ratio*, when compared with the competition, directly measures the customers' level of satisfaction in terms of what they are willing to pay for a product or service.
- The *value-to-cost-ratio* is a measure of how much it costs the corporation to satisfy the customer. It directly reflects financial performance. By itself, customer satisfaction is not sufficient: without good financial performance, one does not have total quality.
- *Error-free performance* is a traditional measure of product or service quality. It is a very important element in the total quality concept. Most corporations spend huge sums each year to correct poor information, mistakes, and failures. Recognizing that there are tremendous opportunities for quality improvement and cost reduction in all aspects of business operations, the corporation is energetically pursuing error free performance.

## Imperatives

The third element of the total quality triangle is the indispensable one of imperatives. This is what employees must do to make total quality happen. There are four kinds of imperatives: *customer orientation, human resource excellence, product and process leadership,* and *management leadership.* In each of these four categories the corporation has developed a variety of technologies, methods, and management tools to help implement the Total Quality concept. Here are a few brief examples.

Under the *customer orientation* imperative, *value edge* is a tool that concerns the external customer. It is a system to measure how the corporation performs in the external world when compared with competitors. One also needs to apply a similar approach to internal customers since each internal person represents a valued customer. Employees can generate total quality output only if they receive total quality as an input.

For *human resource excellence* a new and powerful process for organization improvement was developed: *organization profile.* It is used to analyze the organization and its processes (for example, Who does what? How long does it take? What does it cost? and, What is its value?). The organization profile system provides management with insights and data to improve and simplify work processes, job duties, staffing, compensation, and organizational structures. It has been used very effectively in upgrading the quality and productivity of services *and* the line manufacturing businesses.

*Product and process leadership* involves the design not only of the products, but also of the processes used throughout the corporation's businesses to deliver world-class products, hardware, or services. One of several powerful tools available to help integrate products and processes is called Operating Profit Through Time Investment Management (OPTIM). This proprietary Westinghouse technique helps to understand and analyze work processes, and points out directions for concentrating on doing the right things. It focuses on reducing costs and cycle time, in both the factory activities and the white collar service operations. It has succeeded in reducing cycle time by as much as 75 to 90% and costs by over 40% in many of our operations (see figure 2).

*Management leadership*, the final ingredient of total quality, is perhaps the most critical of all. Installing a total quality culture in the company's organizations is not a simple process. It requires a vision, a new orientation, and new ways for everyone to perform his or her job. It requires leaders, people who are driven by the obsession to create change. These are the ingredients of management leadership, itself an absolute necessity for implementing total quality.

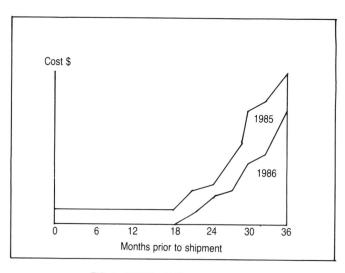

FIG. 2. COSTS—CYCLE TIME GRAPH

# TOTAL QUALITY FITNESS REVIEW (TQFR)

In the quest to achieve total quality, Westinghouse fashioned an analytical tool known as the Total Quality Fitness Review (TQFR). It has played a major role in establishing the total quality concept. It has been used with outstanding results in over two hundred organizational units.

## TQFR Procedures

As a step toward achieving world class performance, the TQFR is a customized interview process designed to examine and measure where operating units are at a point in time. It uses twelve conditions of excellence as yardsticks and, through an interviewing process conducted by senior management, identifies opportunities for improvement (see figure 3). It is

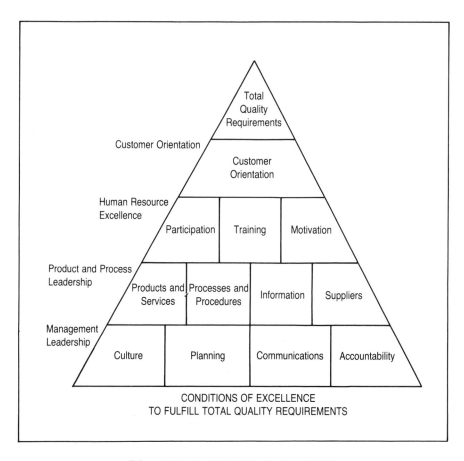

FIG. 3. TWELVE CONDITIONS OF EXCELLENCE

offered to all elements of the corporation on a voluntary basis. The results of the review are treated as confidential information and are given only to the management of the surveyed operation.

For the purposes of Westinghouse, the conditions of excellence for total quality identify long-range goals and opportunities toward which the organization should direct its resources and its efforts in order to become the best in its business.

The organization of the TQFR task force includes a team of senior managers who conduct in-depth interviews in all areas of the business-office, plant, field, and warehouse. During the review, the team, which is led by a representative of the corporate quality center, visits the location, observes its operations, and assesses its effectiveness. Discussions one-on-one in person with selected employees from all levels and functions of the business provide solid understanding of the strengths and weaknesses of the business. The TQFR provides a basis for identifying and improving the imperatives of customer orientation, human resource excellence, product and process leadership, and management leadership.

The review consists of getting answers to a series of structured questions, with scores assigned to each criterion of the twelve conditions of excellence. Detailed interview guides are used, and questions often are modified to meet the unique characteristics of a particular business. The output of the review compares current operations against a total quality operation and identifies significant improvement opportunities. A typical review lasts three to five days, and it is conducted by a team of five individuals with different functional backgrounds. Results are reviewed on the spot with the management at that site.

## Twelve Conditions of Excellence for Total Quality

Twleve conditions of excellence, together with measurable criteria, are at Westinghouse when applying the TQFR:

1. *Customer orientation.* Satisfying internal and external customers through meeting their requirements and value expectations is the primary task of every employee.

2. *Participation.* All employees participate in establishing and achieving total quality improvement goals.

3. *Training.* Training is provided to assure that each employee understands, supports, and contributes to the achievement of total quality.

4. *Motivation.* Employees are motivated through trust, respect, and recognition to achieve total quality.

5. *Products and serivces.* These are appropriately innovative. They are reviewed and verified, and are produced to meet customer requirements.

6. *Processes and procedures.* These are used to create and deliver products and services as an integrated, verified, and statistically controlled system using appropriate technology and tools.

7. *Information.* Required information is clear, complete, accurate, timely, useful, and accessible. It is integrated with products, services, processes, and procedures.

8. *Suppliers.* Suppliers are considered partners that are selected, measured, controlled, and recognized, based on their potential and actual contributions to meeting requirements for total quality.

9. *Culture.* Management has established a value system in which individual and group actions reflect a "total quality first" attitude and direction innovative enough to meet established world-class requirements.

10. *Planning.* Strategic business and financial planning recognizes total quality as a primary business objective.

11. *Communication.* Verbal and nonverbal communications are two-way, clear, consistent, and forceful.

12. *Accountability.* Accountability measures for total quality are established, reported, analyzed, and effectively used.

During the review the interviewer uses a more detailed guide to explain the conditions of excellence and to structure the interview questions.

## Scoring the TQFR

The scoring method establishes a numerical rating for each condition of excellence within the operating unit. This rating is used to evaluate present performance and to identify areas of improvement that would significantly improve future performance.

A total quality rating sheet (figure 4) is utilized so that individual and composite scoring can be developed and recorded for each condition of excellence. The score can range from zero to one hundred for each, and higher scores, of course, reflect better performance. The point scores for the twelve conditions of excellence are then added from the total quality rating sheet and recorded in the blank for total points. The total points score is divided by twelve, and this average is entered in the blank for the average score. The average score is indicative of the operating unit's rating in total quality. The total point score is generally in the range of fifty to seventy-five points. A substantial improvement in the scores occurred between 1986 and 1987 (see figure 4).

Upon completion of the TQFR, the reviewers work with each organization's management and provide an oral summary of their findings and, later, a written report. These reports reflect the findings of the team and their recommendations for actions to assure improvement. Reviews are generally repeated in intervals of twelve to eighteen months. Whenever possible, subsequent reviews are conducted by the original team.

TOTAL QUALITY RATING SHEET

Organization: Transmotor     Date: December 10, 1987     ORGANIZATION:     DATE:

| CONDITIONS OF EXCELLENCE | SCORE | TQFR POINTS |
|---|---|---|
| | 0  20  40  60  80  100 | |
| 1. CUSTOMER ORIENTATION | | |
| 2. PARTICIPATION | 1986 | |
| 3. TRAINING | | |
| 4. MOTIVATION | | |
| 5. PRODUCTS & SERVICES | | |
| 6. PROCESSES & PROCEDURES | | 1987 |
| 7. INFORMATION | | |
| 8. SUPPLIERS | | |
| 9. CULTURE | | |
| 10. PLANNING | | |
| 11. COMMUNICATIONS | | |
| 12. ACCOUNTABILITY | | |

TOTAL POINTS
12

TOTAL POINTS    790
AVERAGE SCORE    65.8

1986 •————————• 53.3
1987 •— — — — — —• 65.8

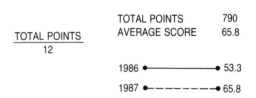

FIG. 4. RATING SHEET FOR THE TOTAL QUALITY FITNESS REVIEW

The review process has been an excellent method of identifying tremendous opportunities for improvement throughout Westinghouse. Significant gains in operating profits, increased understanding of the importance of world-class performance, more effective communication, and a closer supplier-customer partnership are but a few of the benefits experienced. Furthermore, the corporation has noted a dramatic increase in the scores for virtually all of the businesses reviewed. That seems to mean that employees are accepting the challenge of making the score of each year far better than the one of the previous year. The corporation intends for them to experience a personal sense of achievement through their participation in the total quality fitness review.

Westinghouse thinks that its approach to establishing total quality as a way of life has been very successful. It is convinced that this approach has been a major factor in increasing operating profit, generating greater value for all stakeholders, and providing world-class performance in its products and services. It is crucial to recognize that total quality is a process that involves people. Knowing how to develop and apply the tools, techniques, and technologies to achieve total quality is one thing. However, it is obvious total quality in any corporation cannot become a reality without the support, ingenuity, and enthusiasm of the most important ingredient: **PEOPLE**.

# Food

The Pillsbury Company
Anthony L. Scherber and Warren G. Malkerson

# Service Quality at Pillsbury U.S. Foods Company

**Anthony L. Scherber**
**Warren G. Malkerson**
The Pillsbury Company

The Pillsbury Company is more than just a baked goods company. Through Pillsbury U.S. Foods, it markets such brands as Green Giant, Hungry Jack, Totino's, Van de Kamp's, and of course, Pillsbury and Poppin' Fresh. It also owns several restaurant chains including Steak and Ale, Bennigan's, Burger King, and Godfather's Pizza.

Pillsbury was founded in 1869 and now employees over 95,000 people. Its headquarters are in Minneapolis, Minnesota.

## INTRODUCTION

For almost 120 years, The Pillsbury Company has been a leader in one of the most basic, stable, and essential industries in the world. From its beginning as a flour mill on the banks of the Mississippi River in Minneapolis, Pillsbury has become a major international food and restaurant company. Its products are in virtually every supermarket aisle and in thousands of restaurants worldwide. Pillsbury's reputation in both of these sectors of the food industry depends on providing premium quality products and outstanding service to consumers and customers. The test of quality for processed food is demanding because the product is eaten. Unlike garden hoses or paper cups, food has to be right every time—there are no second chances.

Two major forces present a daily challenge: increasing consumer demands for quality and convenience, and the growing sophistication of information technology in supermarkets and restaurants. For 55 million working American women and 9 million single parents, time is not only money—it often is more important than money. For this significant number of Americans, convenience is spelled t-i-m-e. Pillsbury can only remain a leader if it adds value by compressing time while delivering superb-quality food products to these consumers. Company restaurants, competing with microwave ovens, take out, supermarket delis, and home delivery, must focus more attention not only on food quality but also customer service.

## PILLSBURY U.S. FOODS

First, consider the ways in which Pillsbury serves its customers in the supermarket trade and how it measures that service. A recent *Wall Street Journal* story quoted a broker who talked of the days when a grocer "used to be an old neighborhood guy who would walk down the aisle saying, 'I'll take a case of this and a case of that,' and measured a product's turnover by the amount of dust it collected." Times have changed. Food-processing companies now introduce dozens of new products a week and yet total shelf space for many food categories grew only less than 8% in the past six years. If consumers do not make a food product move off the store shelf, then retailers surely will do it for them, by simply discontinuing the product.

Technology (for example, check-out-counter scanners) has helped shift the balance of power away from food manufacturers and toward the grocery trade. Data from the scanner, what some call the "electron microscope of marketing," reveal immediately which products and promotions are successful. Driven by this technology and more-demanding consumers, the food industry has been transformed from a somewhat stodgy, conservative enterprise into a market arena of intense competition for shelf space and brand loyalty.

The second major cause of this balance-of-power shift is the consolidation among manufacturers and wholesalers/retailers. At first, these changes were viewed as a problem: fewer customers dominating the industry and more power in the hands of customers in the retail trade. Yet the problem also offered an opportunity. How could Pillsbury U.S. Foods become more important to these fewer, larger, and more powerful companies? The company had grown rapidly through acquisition and internal development. Pillsbury U.S. Foods sales in fiscal year 1987 were double what they were four years previously. The division has twelve thousand "ship-to" locations, about seven hundred people in its direct and broker sales force; it receives about seventeen thousand orders each month and has approximately three dozen employees in sales support for customer service. These employees work in groups of three, each group being responsible for customer service from the receipt of order to the invoice in one distribution area.

## Measurement of Customer Services

Three years ago a self-examination of this huge organization uncovered many opportunities to improve efficiency, timeliness of orders, communication, and attention to detail. The company took a fresh look at itself. More importantly, employees asked customers what they thought of Pillsbury. A team of graduate students from the Harvard Business School conducted personal interviews with twenty-five of the top forty customers. Those not interviewed personally were sent a questionnairre. The response rate was an excellent 65%.

The survey found that customers considered the service just okay, generally no better or worse than that of the competition, in such critical areas as on-time delivery, completeness of orders, invoice accuracy, response to information requests, and ease of ordering. In general terms, they requested four things: deliver the goods on time; ship what was ordered; bill correctly; and keep communication channels open. It was that simple. The results of this survey galvanized the company's thinking: "If we are serious about becoming the best food company in the world, we can't settle for a reputation as 'middle of the pack' in customer service." After several meetings, the sales and materials management departments formed an alliance to create Pillsbury's Preferred Supplier program. It's really what the procurement people have known all along: the true cost of a product is never the quoted price—service adds value to the product.

The result is a way to measure service every time the product changes hands in the system, from raw materials to the plants, to distribution centers, customer warehouses, or direct-store delivery. It is a closed loop. Everyone in Pillsbury is a customer who depends on other employees and is, at the same time, a supplier who provides others with a product or service, making *everyone* responsible for service.

An important first step in the Preferred Supplier program was to measure services to the retail trade each month in four major areas: on-time shipment, orders shipped complete, on-time delivery, and invoice accuracy. The company decided to measure itself as it would measure one of its suppliers. If it was a case short on an order, it gave itself a zero. If a Pillsbury truck did not arrive when the buyer wanted it, it was counted as not being on time, even if it was a day early. If the invoice was not what the buyer expected, it was counted as inaccurate. The customer, not Pillsbury, measured service.

Those at the company were a little disappointed, though not surprised, by the results of the first measurement in 1984. Only 63% of deliveries were on time; 70% of orders were shipped complete; 78% of shipments left Pillsbury facilities on time; and only 60% of invoices were recorded accurately. There was work to be done.

Three years later, there has been progress. Deliveries are on time 83% of the time (goal: 90%); 88% of orders are shipped complete (goal: 95%); 92% of shipments leave Pillsbury on time (goal: 95%); and still only 60% of invoices are recorded accurately (goal: 90%). There is still work to be done. Based on these percentages, an average shipment from the company has only a 50% chance of being perfect: shipped and delivered on time, shipped complete and invoiced accurately.

The willingness to measure service and share the results proves to customers that a serious effort to improve is underway. Pillsbury is also determined not to hide poor performance by juggling the numbers. For instance, it has resisted the temptation to measure the "fill rate" of shipped orders. Fill rate is meaningless. It only shows a truck filled with a certain amount of product. It doesn't show if it is the right product in the right quantity in the right condition.

## Realistic Goals and Methods for Customer Services

Equally important, the people responsible for customer service in Pillsbury U.S. Foods need to know their successes along the way. To do so goals have been made realistic and achievable. Award programs for outstanding customer service have been created; a system has been developed for distribution center managers and customer service people to call the sales department when there will be exceptions to orders; formal ways to listen to customers have been established including monthly sales calls ("The Listening Post") to discuss product shortages, weight issues, and delayed shipments; a faster way to ship products to stores in support of major promotions has been found which bypasses the warehouse; invoice procedures have been simplified; a "load card" has been developed to accompany all Pillsbury shipments from the distribution centers and to invite the customer to call the company upon receipt of the order with any questions; transportation contracting has been streamlined; and report cards have been developed for customers to grade Pillsbury each month.

## Inventory Management: One Area of Improved Service

There is another important area in the product pipeline which affects the level of the customer service measured: inventory management. Maintaining adequate inventory is a delicate balance between inventory available "just in time" and inventory available "just in case."

Because food products begin to deteriorate in quality the second they are produced, customers in the supermarket trade must be assured that Pillsbury products are delivered to their stores with maximum freshness. For example, if pizza goes through two or three freeze-thaw cycles as it wanders through a poorly configured, high-inventory distribution system, it will not attract many repeat customers. Money tied up in inventory over a long period of time cannot be used in revenue-generating activities. Large inventory levels also force the company to spend more research and development money to extend the shelf life of products.

With this concern in mind, the employees tested themselves three years ago to uncover the hidden costs in the inventory system. Using package date codes, they found that they had at any one point in time, about $350 million in finished goods inventory in the distribution center pipeline, too high a level compared with the competitors. It became clear that, because the information system was designed to report financial data, not operations data, inventory information was only available two or three weeks after the end of the month or at the close of a quarter. That seemed like driving by looking in the rear view mirror; you knew where you had been but not where you were going. Immediate information was needed of the actual order flow and product movement through the pipeline, not just to improve service to the trade, but also to guarantee fresh products, more sales, better margins, and more profits.

To address this need, Pillsbury recently invested more than three million dollars to improve inventory management and customer service. It developed a new forecasting system to define specific inventory needs throughout the system; it placed the warehouse inventory control system in the hands of distribution center managers and plant managers to give them the latest, most accurate reports on current inventories; and it improved the forecasting ability of the headquarters inventory management systems by giving it better information on the status of stock levels.

Pillsbury also focuses on ways to improve its consumer services. To provide immediate answers to consumers' questions about its packaged foods, it began a nationwide, toll-free consumer response telephone service in 1981. Today, as many as fourteen hundred consumers a day call Pillsbury about food preparation, microwave oven operations, and baking ingredients.

## PILLSBURY RESTAURANTS
The way service is measured varies in each of the company's restaurant concepts but each treats customer service as a high priority. For instance, in

the fifty-two hundred Burger King restaurants worldwide, three methods are used:

- **Restaurant progress report,** a regular, in-depth study of each restaurant, based on reports from franchise and company district managers;
- **Operations audit,** performed on franchise and company-owned restaurants by an outside research team measures restaurant service (order accuracy, speed of service, cleanliness, and courtesy) from the consumer's point of view;
- **Restaurant operations consultation,** performed annually in each restaurant in the areas of product safety and preparation, service, and cleanliness (also used as an in-depth training tool).

Suggestions for improving service often become part of company programs at Burger King University in Miami which was established in 1964 as a central training center for managers. BKU trains an average of fifteen hundred students each year with such courses as "People: The Winning Edge" and "Managing the Training Function." Other Pillsbury subsidiaries also use BKU's training programs.

The company's 380 full-service restaurants (Steak and Ale, and Bennigan's) have a distinct advantage in measuring customer service: they observe and talk with their customers during service. A Steak and Ale waitperson, for example, noticing an unfinished steak, can ask the guest if the steak was cooked properly. The waitperson has the authority, without consulting the manager, to bring the customer another steak. In other situations, the manager is called to the table to decide if the meal should be complimentary. These meals are about 1% of Pillsbury's total sales in its full-service restaurants. This "trouble-shooting" service is measured by coding all of the complimentary meals into the billing process and identifying the cause of each "comp" (that is, meal cooked wrong, late service, etc.). To guarantee quality service, Steak and Ale and Bennigan's recruit only confident, outgoing waitpersons who display a strong sense of service. They are required to take part in an extensive training program to recognize and react to problems as they happen. As commissioned sales people (80% of their salary comes from gratuities), their goal is not to "turn over" a table a specific number of times each day, but to build repeat customers by providing good service.

Through the continuous measurement of service, whether in its consumer foods or its restaurants, Pillsbury seeks to manage the process of service rather than to merely correct results. By constantly focusing on the customers' expectations, and then exceeding them, the company wants to place in each employee's hands the tools for success.

# Forest Products

James River Corporation
Ernest S. Leopold

# Being Close Counts When It Comes To Customers

**Ernest S. Leopold**
James River Corporation

James River is a major integrated manufacturer and converter of pulp, paper-related products, and certain plastic products and coated film. The company and its subsidiaries process basic raw materials—wood, wood pulp, synthetic fibers, and plastic resins—into finished products such as towel and tissue papers, disposable food and beverage service items, folding cartons, and flexible packaging materials, as well as a wide variety of communication papers and specialty industrial and packaging papers.

During its nineteen year history, James River has pursued an aggressive acquisition and internal growth strategy that has significantly expanded its business and the diversity of its products. As its fiscal year ended April 24, 1988, the company (headquartered in Richmond, Virginia) had 35,455 employees and 116 manufacturing facilities located in twenty-nine states, Canada, France, Scotland, and Wales. Sales for that fiscal year totaled $5.1 billion.

## CLOSENESS TO THE CUSTOMER

In this frenetic age of computer systems, electronic mail, laser communications, overnight freight delivery, sales meetings at airports between flights, and reports written inflight, it would be easy for a business to look for shortcuts that bring the quick sell. Customer relations and quality service could be just so much business school theory. It is not just theory at James River Corporation, which has based its rapid growth on a philosophy that not only makes time for involvement with customers, but also continuously seeks opportunities for involvement.

### Strategy Statement

Since its inception, James River has been committed to a set of fundamental values and beliefs that continue to guide the company today. Employees receive copies of those values and beliefs outlined in booklet form. Central to these beliefs is providing value to customers. According to the strategy statement, "Sustaining superior financial performance in a manufacturing company requires that the primary thrust of the entire organization be directed toward providing superior value to its customers." The spirit of closeness to the customer must permeate the entire organization in order for it to achieve and sustain a preferred-supplier status with customers.

Those at James River believe that their primary competitive edge will be *performance*, defined in the strategy statement as "the development and delivery of *better performing products* and *service programs* that allow both the company and its customers to enjoy higher profitability. A customer-sensitized organization, a participative management style, and the application of the unique skills of James River people—combined with capital and cost effective products, process, and systems technology—are the primary tools that will be emphaslzed to create performance." Translating these beliefs into day-to-day practice means, for example, that sales and marketing personnel know their products well and know how their customers will use them. It means a manufacturing force that is dedicated not only to productivity, but to quality and customer service as well. And it means every member of the organization has a constant eye toward customer needs.

Another belief places the highest management priority on sustained companywide commitment to the following: the exploration of uniquely cost-effective approaches to problems and opportunities; a willingness to experiment and take calculated risks; the development and implementation of winning strategies; and excellence in individual performance.

One way in which the company fosters this environment is through a program called Finding a Better Way. It is designed to acknowledge significant individual or team achievements in ten areas, including product development, product improvement, customer service, and customer relations. The awards program initially recognizes excellence and high levels of performance at operating locations and business offices and then at the business group level. From these business group Silver Key recipients, the finalists are selected for James River's highest corporate accolade: a plaque, hung in the board room, displaying the names of the Gold Key winners. At James River, the values, beliefs, and goals outlined in the strategy statement represent the corporate lifeblood, and the Finding a Better Way program is an effective monitor of its vital signs.

## Communication Papers Business

Perhaps the real key to James River's growth from a single mill in 1969 to the largest pulp and paper company in the world in 1987 (according to *Pulp and Paper International*) is that it practices what it preaches. This chapter focuses on the Communication Papers Business, just one of the corporation's five major businesses, to see how employees have acted on these beliefs and principles in support of the company's commitment to superior service.

James River's Communication Papers Business is one of the largest in the industry. Its net sales would place it somewhere near the middle of the Fortune 500 listing if it were an independent company. Its ninety-three hundred people operate pulp and paper mills, converting operations, technical and distribution centers, sales offices, and even a barge line, in a dozen states and three countries. Its broad product line includes scores of paper grades used in everything from catalogs and magazines to brochures, advertising inserts, directories, business forms, and office copy machines.

This business focuses on three interactive elements of service quality: understanding the customer, working as a team, and executing flawlessly. It is a business that is externally focused and driven by the market, with each employee intent on getting close to their customers. Individually and collectively, employees strive to establish James River as the preferred supplier of quality products and quality service, and to consistently deliver on their promises.

The company knows that quality service as well as quality products are important to the customer, not one without the other. Both depend on employees finding better ways of doing business, thereby distinguishing the company from the competition. Crown Zellerbach Information Plus (CZIP), Quality Through Teamwork, Rainbow Express, and the Senior Merchant Advisory Council are among the programs that have been born and nurtured by this spirit of getting close to the customer.

## Senior Merchant Advisory Council

Communication Papers relies in large part on a nationwide network of paper merchants to get its paper to the end-users: printers, publishers, converters, and others. So it is essential that merchant customers are served in a way that supports their own sales and marketing efforts. To understand what those needs are, Communication Papers invited a group of its merchant customers to serve in an advisory capacity. This Senior Merchant Advisory

Council, representative of all merchant customers; meets twice a year as a forum for discussing products, service, and strategy. It is distinguished by the candor of its members.

The council, which was formed in 1981, is comprised of fifteen senior managers from among leading customers within the United States. Usually ten to fifteen James River people, including the CEO, attend the council meetings. The council represents a cross-section of customers by size, geographic area and product line.

Even the recent reorganization of the Communication Papers Business was shaped by recommendations made by the council. Because the business grew as the result of acquisitions—from the Brown Company, Curtis Paper Company, American Can Company, and most recently Crown Zellerbach Corporation—it maintained multiple sales and customer service organizations. Its overlapping sales territories and duplicated product lines resulted in confusion in the marketplace. Customers frequently had several company sales people call on them, often selling the same, or similar, products. The council's emphatic recommendation was that the company consolidate its communication papers businesses and simplify the sales force according to product line. It was a matter of becoming easier to do business with, and James River responded by forming the Communication Papers Business in mid-1987.

Another example of the respect the corporation has for its customers' opinions took place at the first advisory council meeting. They had spent a considerable amount of money on new sales promotional materials and they presented them to the council, even though the printed material was still in dummy form. The council looked at it and said in effect, we don't think you will accomplish what you want to accomplish with this promotion, because of what you are calling some of the paper grades and how you're presenting them. As a result of those opinions, the company canceled out of that advertising campaign (and probably saved money in the long run).

One year the theme was communications. They spent two days talking about ways to improve the communication links between James River and its customers. The customer representatives stated that during certain times of the day the phone system would overload. The company put a computer check on the system that confirmed the problem. Consequently, they not only changed the number of phones and lines, but also went to a computerized telephone system that eliminated many of the problems of a manual system.

These advisory council meetings represent the best of all possible worlds because both groups benefit. James River sees them as an opportunity to present ideas to, and get feedback from, a well-informed group of people who represent their customer base. At the same time, customers gain a better understanding of one of their major suppliers and the opportunity to make their needs and the needs of their customers known and acted upon.

# (CZIP)

At James River the wave of the future has reached shore and goes by the name CZIP. "Basically, CZIP is a computerized system that allows us to transact business with our customers, computer to computer," explains the project manager of electronic data interchange systems for Communication Papers. Specifically, it involves electronic data interchange (EDI), commonly called electronic or computer mail. Instead of sending shipping documents through the mail, or along with the shipment, the customer's computer receives all the information about the shipment and the product itself, like weight or lineal footage—whatever information they need to do their job—by the time the truck hits the road.

Although James River is not alone in using this technology—indeed, almost every major paper supplier has a similar system—the difference is in how the company markets it. James River lets potential customers know that it is not just paper they sell—they also sell *service*.

It was a customer's response to an earlier discussion about EDI that gave birth to CZIP in the first place. After hearing about EDI from a company representative, a customer asked how they could get on line. By using CZIP, customers receive timely, accurate information directly into their own computers, without having to rekey data. They can receive as much information about their shipments as they want, and the data they receive will automatically update whatever inventory systems they have in place.

As of now, EDI in the communication paper industry is limited mostly to processing shipping documents. But experts say invoices and purchase orders are next in line, and that's only the beginning. An educated guess is that at some point, EDI will be the way everybody does business: it is not a matter of *if*—it is a matter of *when*.

## Rainbow Express

The book, *A Passion for Excellence*, by Tom Peters and Nancy Austin, says that 80% of a company's new ideas originate from input generated by its customers. That is quite a statement. That means that if you do not listen to customers, you lose opportunities you didn't even know existed. Listening to a customer prompted James River to devise a new inventory concept called Rainbow Express.

About three years ago, some customers complained that they were being hurt by competition that could draw on a greater variety and/or quantity of colored-forms bond in less time than they could. The company responded by starting an inventory program to manufacture and store the most popular sizes and colors, and to offer customers a quick turnaround on delivery. The purposes of Rainbow Express became twofold: It allowed the mill to beef up its production with larger runs and to solidify its position in the colored-forms business. Starting with about 125 items, they are now up to around 500 items which turn over monthly.

Rainbow Express customers benefit from the program because they can buy smaller quantities of a product at one time and get it faster. Merchants who sell the product to schools, business, and other end-users, benefit because they no longer have to carry a large inventory or worry about carrying quantities of odds and ends that do not move frequently. James River makes the paper, maintains an inventory based on customer input, and fills the orders very quickly. The key to Rainbow Express is this: When its customers had a problem, the company worked with them and found a solution that would help them improve product performance.

## Quality Through Teamwork

Some people might believe the phrase "getting close to the customer" is overused and underappreciated, but participants in the Quality Through Teamwork program are not among them. This program was developed by a product manager for James River's Printing Papers Group, with the support of R.R. Donnelley & Sons Printing Company and the publishers of *Sunset Magazine*. It was designed to help the papermakers from the West Linn, Oregon mill and the pressmen who print the jumbo rolls of paper become familiar with each other's operations. Under the program, employees spend two days at each other's plant, learning about the operation and talking to their counterparts.

The people who have made the trip to Donnelley's Los Angeles plant have not necessarily become better papermakers; rather, they have become more quality conscious—and that is the main purpose of the program. The costs to the company are great when customers kick defective rolls out of their pressrooms; James River must buy back the paper and pay freight charges and, naturally, its relationship with the customer suffers. The program, which celebrated its third anniversary in July 1988, has involved over two hundred Communication Papers employees and all of the personnel from Donnelley's Los Angeles plant, with the exception of new hires. The program has cut the customer paper rejection rate by big numbers because it goes to the source and eliminates the problem with information provided by those who know best—the pressmen and the papermakers.

## Pooling Deliveries

The Premium Printing Papers Group manufacturers and sells text, cover, and cast-coated paper grades. It has a motto, "Think Like A Merchant." From that kind of thinking has sprung a delivery system that, according to their director of marketing and planning, allows them to service every region of the country *freight-free.*

Basically, it involves a system of pool routes in which trucks follow a predetermined schedule and itinerary to customers, delivering orders as they go. To make the program even more service-oriented, James River will deliver large orders directly to the paper merchant's customer, also freight-free. Like the Rainbow Express, this nationwide system of frequent, regularly scheduled deliveries promises customers speedy receipt of specified products, and eliminates their need to maintain large inventories. For example, even customers in Southern California can count on this service that originates from a central warehouse facility in Pennsylvania and reinforces the company's reputation as a customer-sensitized organization.

## CONCLUSION

These five vignettes only begin to paint the picture of James River's total orientation to customers. They believe this is a case in which the whole is greater than the sum of its parts. The company's quality service philosophy emphasizes that *customer service* depends on everything employees do— answering the phone, being able to answer a caller's question, keeping appointments, getting the product to the customer, and providing a product that will work for the customer.

The organization encourages everyone from the papermaker to the salesman to the top executives, to get into the printshops, binderies, publishing houses, advertising agencies and circulation departments where paper is being used to try to understand all aspects of their customers' business. This is what James River believes will differentiate it from the competition.

# Furniture

Herman Miller Company
Ray Pukanic and Dick Holm

# The Herman Miller Quality Audit: A Corporate Report Card

**Ray Pukanic**
**Dick Holm**
Herman Miller, Inc.

Founded in 1923, Herman Miller is a leading multinational manufacturer of furniture systems principally for offices and health-care facilities.

Headquartered in Zeeland, Michigan, the Fortune 500 company employs 5,000 people worldwide.

## INTRODUCTION

"What impresses me most about the quality audit is that it shows Herman Miller's sincerity in following up their words with action. There was no fluff in our audit, and we appreciated the way it was conducted—within a structure but very flexible and open to suggestions. The audit's purpose is to solve problems, and I think this is reinforced by the fact that the quality audit team isn't part of a department at Herman Miller that does this exclusively. Instead, the team members are from various areas and levels of their organization, and this shows the company is truly committed to the program. I think that because of this, the audit ultimately helps both the customer and Herman Miller itself." Greg Bendis, facility manager, TRW, Orange, California, where nearly 1,200 workstations were installed using Herman Miller systems, seating, and freestanding products.

Because, in the words of Peter Drucker, there are no "dumb customers," Herman Miller, Inc., makes customers the primary sources of information about customer service. Whereas internally generated corporate statistics can easily be manipulated or can otherwise be misunderstood by most members of a corporation, direct feedback from customers is a common-sense, lay-your-cards-on-the-table approach. It is credible, understandable, and appreciated by both the customer and the seller—from the CEO to the person on the plant floor who, typically, is skeptical about obtuse service quality measurements.

In fact, Herman Miller is so committed to such an approach that it is currently in the process of implementing a program by which every employee's bonus check will be heavily affected by the quality of service to the customer—as measured by the customers themselves. This change is part of the company's *Scanlon Renewal* effort, a corporatewide review to ensure the continued relevance and effectiveness of the Scanlon process in an ever-changing business environment.

## CHANGE AS AN ONGOING PROCESS

Since 1950, Herman Miller, Inc., has managed itself according to the Scanlon plan of participative management. The company adopted this system as a means to increase participation and *ownership* of problems, making every employee a member of a work team; in particular, every employee is expected to contribute to the specific goals and objectives of that work team as part of the overall goals of the corporation. By minimizing the corporate hierarchical structure, Scanlon strives to maximize communication and the understanding of crucial issues facing the company. In addition to cost-saving suggestions (in fiscal year 1986-87, employees' suggestions saved over twelve million dollars), the Scanlon process encourages any suggestions that help achieve corporate goals and improve the quality of products, services, relationships, and the corporate working environment. One of the elements of Scanlon at Herman Miller is the bonus check mentioned above, a percentage of each employee's earnings based on measurements of how well the corporation has met its objectives over a period of time. *Customer service* is *the* key category for measuring that effectiveness.

By its very nature, Scanlon promotes and solicits change. But, unlike a hierarchical structure where one person says "This is the way we're going to do it," this structure means that major change cannot happen unless informed participation has first occurred in both strategy and implementation—the collective ideas of everyone deemed greater than the singular wisdom of anyone. Herman Miller's Statement of Values, a statement of the way that the company has operated and evolved over the years, reinforces this mandate for change. It emphasizes "the responsibilities to seek and be open to new ideas; to take the risks necessary, and to encourage appropriate problem-solving designs and innovative solutions that deliver results to our customers and meet our business challenges." The statement also cites "the responsibility to constantly improve our performance and to provide the best value to our customers."

As part of this ongoing change aimed at upholding these values, the company initiated in 1986 The Herman Miller Promise[SM], a corporatewide commitment to product and service quality. The Promise includes:

- Five-year product warranties
- Quality audits after project installation
- Trade-in allowances on systems product: 20% value on Action Office® and Action Office Encore™ product; 100% value on Ethospace® wall frames
- Guaranteed move-in dates.

## THE QUALITY AUDIT

As part of The Promise, the quality audit represents the company's understanding of the long-term ramifications that a major purchase of office furniture has on a business—and on the people who chose Herman Miller products, people whose very livelihoods may hinge on the results of that purchase. Their decisions demand that they consider not only the quality of the products they purchase, but also the quality and accountability of the company that manufactures them.

Herman Miller's quality audit is, essentially, a report card measuring that accountability. The goals of product and service auditing at Herman Miller are:

- To determine if the processes, policies, and procedures in place are effectively resolving issues
- To provide solutions to 100% of unresolved customer problems.

It gives clients the opportunity to tell the manufacturer how it has performed, and with this direct contact, it gives them the means by which problems can be resolved. Instead of waiting to hear from customers, it actively solicits their opinions on all aspects of their experience with the company: Are the users really comfortable with the product? Do they feel the product will achieve the goals and objectives in the support of their work? Does it look well-designed within the context of the building? Was it installed correctly? Was it delivered correctly? Were the installers there on time—and courteous? Did Herman Miller lead them to the right decisions on the accessories to be used in supportive work? Did the dealer manage the project well? Is their total facility working, will it continue to work, and will they be able to change it easily and effectively when needed? The manufacturer assumes responsibility for that client's perception of the facility, even though Herman Miller may not have planned or installed it.

Not only does this provide the customer with the means to ensure that all their expectations are met, but it also provides the company with an accurate portrait of itself, free from any hint of self-aggrandizement. There are four stated corporate purposes for quality audits:

1. To provide the customer with a management communication link for large projects;
2. To help company management experience the office environment from the customer's viewpoint;
3. To provide company management with feedback that will help resolve problems in the areas of products, services, and relationships;
4. To ensure that customers' expectations are met.

## The Field Audit

An actual visit to an installation site is conducted for all projects involving more than one million dollars in products. These field audits generally occur two to six months following final installation, allowing territory managers, dealers, and design firms to have an opportunity to correct whatever has needed attention as part of the customary follow-up activity. At the time of this writing, thirty-three field audits had been conducted, with about forty more in the queue.

The field audit is conducted by a three-person team from headed by a company officer or director. The other two members of the audit team, from various areas of the corporation, are recommended by their supervisors; they receive special training in preparation for their involvement. To ensure a totally unbiased view of each project, the salesperson is not part of the audit team. However, salespeople do provide contact information and account information and help in the postaudit process. Salespeople are apprised of the audit results, particularly of the customer's perception of their roles and effectiveness.

"This direct contact signifies that we're really listening to the customer," asserts Gary Ten Harmsel, the senior vice president of operations. "And, importantly, it shows all those representing Herman Miller who our real customers are. A *corporation* is not a customer." In other words, the customer might be the facility manager at the site; the maintenance supervisor who's doing the installation; the administrative vice president; or the branch manager. "The customer is a different person at each location, even if it's with the same corporation. And that's something that's very important for us to understand."

The corporation's commitment to conduct the field audit is made even before an order is placed. A personal letter or telephone call from the officer or director who would lead the audit assures that the potential customer realizes this commitment. If Herman Miller wins the job, the members of the audit team, who have already taken general training in the audit process, meet to prepare for the specific audit. In addition to the officer or director to serve as chief spokesperson, the team consists of a facilitator, who makes sure the needs of the customer are clearly understood and who writes the audit report, and a technical coordinator, who ensures that all information is recorded and assists the officer or director on follow-up assignments.

At the project site, the field audit team tours the facility and discusses with the client and the end users the quality, function, and performance of the product. After the tour, the team and client discuss the findings of the tour along with other issues, such as packaging, delivery, documentation, installation, billing, and the quality of service from the company, its sales representatives, and its dealer. Based on the answers to these questions, the field audit team and the client determine which issues require further attention. The officer or director will then tell the client approximately when and from whom to expect follow-up communication.

After the audit is complete, a debriefing meeting is held at Herman Miller. At this session, the findings of the field audit team are relayed to field audit administrators and a customer service representative; follow-up work and further assignments are scheduled. Afterwards, a customer assurance team (consisting of members from manufacturing, marketing, quality, design and development, customer service, and engineering) assists in resolving the identified concerns, with high-priority issues receiving immediate attention. Each month, a summary of this team's activities, including a listing of the most important issues facing the company, is distributed to the quality review group, members of top management charged with overseeing audit results. Other concerns are documented and monitored for possible future action. The field audit team is fully informed of all follow-up activity and status reports, since the team remains the primary link to the customer in the postaudit process.

## The Survey Audit

For clients ordering between fifty thousand dollars and approximately one million dollars in products, the quality audit is conducted with a survey mailed shortly after final installation. Though determined in a less personal fashion than the field audit, the findings of this survey are treated in the same manner as those of the field audit, with the customer assurance team setting priorities and communicating needed solutions to the appropriate areas of the company.

Prior to the mailing, Herman Miller contacts the person who will be responsible for answering the survey, alerting him or her to its imminent arrival and reinforcing the importance, to them and Herman Miller, of the customer's candid appraisal. After the survey is returned, Herman Miller again telephones the contact person. This call has several purposes — to verify that the survey has been received, to ask for further clarification or amplification of any of the responses, to assure that any unresolved issues are being attended to, and to encourage a continued open line of communication. Attention to any unresolved issues is assured by the work of the customer assurance team. During the first eighteen months of implementation, nearly 50% of the quality audit surveys were returned to Herman Miller — far higher than usual for mail-in surveys.

## THE BOTTOM LINE

As stated at the beginning of this article, Herman Miller has determined that the results of these quality audits — both the survey and the field audit — will have a significant impact on the Scanlon bonus checks issued to all full-time Herman Miller employees. In addition to this, a dealer survey will also be used in the bonus calculation. Similar in form and content to the audit survey, the dealer survey will collect information from end users for all orders, including those less than fifty thousand dollars.

Such an incentive to excellence in service quality should have a positive, spiraling effect at the corporation. As individual work teams become increasingly aware of how their performance directly affects the results of quality audits, they should also become better able to contribute to superior product and service quality. According to Gary Ten Harmsel, "This puts every employee closer to the customer. We think that the more information we can get from the customer, the more effective we can be in service to that customer." Quality audits, then, become the means to both internal, corporate success and external, customer satisfaction.

# APPENDIX

## The Herman Miller Quality Audit

The Herman Miller Promise is our commitment to provide the quality products and services you expect and deserve. Our goal is your complete satisfaction, and to ensure it, we need your honest appraisal. Your answers to the following questions will tell us how well we've kept our Promise to you. In the space after each question, please provide further relevant information and explain any "No" answers. If a question does not apply to your situation, just go on to the next.

1. We promised you prompt, complete delivery of your order. Was your order:

|  | YES | NO |
|---|---|---|
| a. delivered when expected? | ☐ | ☐ |
| b. complete, with no back orders? | ☐ | ☐ |
| c. correct, as you ordered it? | ☐ | ☐ |
| d. shipped according to your special requirements? | ☐ | ☐ |

2. Have our products met your expectations for:

|  | YES | NO |
|---|---|---|
| a. quality manufacturing? | ☐ | ☐ |
| b. performance? | ☐ | ☐ |
| c. consistency of finishes, fabrics, and detailing? | ☐ | ☐ |
| d. ease of installation? | ☐ | ☐ |

3. If you had to return any products, was our return process:

|  | YES | NO |
|---|---|---|
| a. prompt? | ☐ | ☐ |
| b. simple? | ☐ | ☐ |
| c. fair? | ☐ | ☐ |

4. Were our invoices, acknowledgements, packing slips, and other documentation materials:

|  | YES | NO |
|---|---|---|
| a. understandable? | ☐ | ☐ |
| b. timely? | ☐ | ☐ |
| c. accurate? | ☐ | ☐ |

5. Was our packaging:

|  | YES | NO |
|---|---|---|
| a. labeled correctly? | ☐ | ☐ |
| b. easy to manage? | ☐ | ☐ |
| c. protective of the products? | ☐ | ☐ |

6. Did the customer service you received:

|  | YES | NO |
|---|---|---|
| a. resolve problems satisfactorily? | ☐ | ☐ |
| b. occur promptly? | ☐ | ☐ |
| c. remain courteous at all times? | ☐ | ☐ |

7. If you worked with a Herman Miller sales representative, did you find that person to be:

|  | YES | NO |
|---|---|---|
| a. available when needed? | ☐ | ☐ |
| b. knowledgeable of our products and their application? | ☐ | ☐ |
| c. courteous? | ☐ | ☐ |

8. Did your Herman Miller dealer:

|  | YES | NO |
|---|---|---|
| a. provide the services you needed? | ☐ | ☐ |
| b. demonstrate knowledge of our products and their application? | ☐ | ☐ |
| c. keep you informed of the status of your order? | ☐ | ☐ |
| d. act courteously? | ☐ | ☐ |

9. If you did not use your own installation crew, was the outside crew:

|  | YES | NO |
|---|---|---|
| a. knowledgeable of our products and their application? | ☐ | ☐ |
| b. successful in completing your project on time? | ☐ | ☐ |
| c. considerate? | ☐ | ☐ |

10. Overall, how do you rate our:

|  | Excellent | Good | Average | Poor | Unacceptable |
|---|---|---|---|---|---|
| a. product quality? | ☐ | ☐ | ☐ | ☐ | ☐ |
| b. service quality? | ☐ | ☐ | ☐ | ☐ | ☐ |
| c. business relationship with you? | ☐ | ☐ | ☐ | ☐ | ☐ |
| d. Herman Miller sales representative? | ☐ | ☐ | ☐ | ☐ | ☐ |
| e. dealer? | ☐ | ☐ | ☐ | ☐ | ☐ |

11. Are there any problems with your project that are still unresolved? If so, please explain.

12. Did you receive the following product-related literature:

|   |   | YES | NO |
|---|---|:---:|:---:|
| a. | specification guide? | ☐ | ☐ |
| b. | planning guide? | ☐ | ☐ |
| c. | installation manual? | ☐ | ☐ |
| d. | product service manual? | ☐ | ☐ |
| e. | product care and maintenance guide? | ☐ | ☐ |

13. How would you rate our Leasing programs?

| Excellent | Good | Average | Poor | Unacceptable |
|:---:|:---:|:---:|:---:|:---:|
| ☐ | ☐ | ☐ | ☐ | ☐ |

---

\* *Below each question in the Herman Miller Quality Audit is a space for comments and explanations.*

# Glass, Building Materials

Owens-Illinois
Bernard L. Keating

# Owens-Illinois
# The Best at What We Do

**Bernard L. Keating**
Owens-Illinois Glass Container Inc.

In 1929, the Owens Bottle Machine Company merged with the Illinois Glass Company to form the Owens Illinois Glass Company. (The word "glass" was later dropped from the company's name.) Owens-Illinois is in the packaging business, including glass and plastic containers, glass tableware, and specialty glass products. Today, it also runs health care facilities and financial services.

Owens Illinois was a public corporation until 1987 when it became a unit of Kohlberg, Kravis, Roberts and Co., New York. With 100 plants in the U.S. and others worldwide, Owens-Illinois employs 44,000 people and is headquartered in Toledo, Ohio.

## THE CONTEMPORARY EMPHASIS ON QUALITY

Glass containers have been around for a long time. Their uses have addressed varying needs during the course of history. In response to the ongoing challenges to adapt glass containers to modern needs, Owens-Illinois, the world's leading glass producer, has subscribed to a strategy of technical innovation in development and manufacturing.

As we move into the decade of the 1990s, the image of the glass container is healthy and upbeat. In particular, the local supermarket is a showcase for attractive and innovative glass container packages. Makers of glass containers have reacted positively to the needs of the consumer and have brought excellence into their new product lines. It would be an over-simplification to say that management set new goals for high quality and low cost, and then used a strategic approach to reach those goals. These things did, in fact, happen, but such a simple tag line fails to adequately describe all the difficult decisions and hardships involved: that is, closing obsolete factories, gutting and modernizing others, trimming work forces as high-production machining came on stream, pulling in new technical talent, and changing plant and corporate structures. Such gut-wrenching steps are needed to survive and compete in today's environment.

This author remembers well a key moment at the start of the upward climb in the late 1970s. After eighteen years as a quality manager of several factories, I had just arrived in Toledo as part of a new division quality team. The company was reorganizing, moving away from geographic decentralization to a new functional organization with strong central controls. Our manufacturing manager gave us the new direction in a speech from which I vividly recall two basic points. First, the objective was to be the high-quality and low-cost producer of glass containers. Secondly, it was a myth that there was a conflict between high quality and low costs; in fact, if the job is done correctly, both come together without compromise by either.

Maintaining the top-quality standard for the product was absolutely the first priority. The company could not yet look at costs or productivity. Quality was front and center. Management believed that if they approached the quality job correctly, the rest would ultimately fall into place. They then redefined *quality* as a different concept: *quality is excellence*, that is, *as perceived by the customer*.

## FOUR QUALITY ASSURANCE SYSTEMS

*Satisfy the needs of the customer*—everyone gives at least lip service to this motto, but how can it really be accomplished with substance? The company decided early on to establish quality assurance systems that incorporate actual customer input and, wherever possible, to use attributes that could be measured. Specific examples can illustrate four such inputs that are used.

The first is the frequency of customer complaints. What counts as a customer complaint is any occasion in which a customer registers with the account manager a significant dissatisfaction concerning the quality or performance of a product. Then starts a process that involves factory reaction, account manager follow-up, etc., in response to the customer. This is perhaps an over-simplification because there are elements of quality that go beyond what customers may see, but defining excellence in terms of the customer is a new and significant experience.

Having established this point of view, where did it lead Owens-Illinois? It was a complex scenario. Many different elements began to gestate in the new, dynamic organization. Later they found that many of the activities and programs that developed through an unplanned, natural, reactive process did in fact fit into well-defined strategies (but that recognition sometimes came after-the-fact when looking over their shoulder). At the beginning, the picture was not that clear. For some period of time they were fire fighters reacting to problems and to the market, rather than strategists following a well-conceived game plan. But their gut instincts were correct in regard to priorities. Of highest priority was satisfying the needs of the customer. From the beginning through today, that has been the hallmark of the quality program.

A second system involves measuring the severity of complaints and responding to the monetary claims submitted by customers for commercial loss. This was an activity formerly handled by accountants in sales administration. The responsibility for investigating and resolving all such financial claims was reassigned to the quality assurance department. The results were remarkable: under the fact-finding logic of quality-trained professionals and a simpler decision-making process, the settlements became more sensible, timely, and fair to all parties.

A third system deals with problems related to customer deliveries, service, or billings. In some instances these problems created the highest degree of customer dissatisfaction. No one could afford to hear the customer say, "You make a fine bottle, but what good does it do me if the truck is two hours late or has the wrong product?" Again, the company has seen the numerical results for over a decade; it is in a position to monitor these sensitive trends and manage the delivery programs on the basis of factual information.

A fourth system is a ranking of the company's overall competitive quality in cooperation with the customer. Does the customer consider Owens-Illinois his number one quality supplier, or something less? In former times they had to develop these ratings with the customer by using a variety of internal inputs. In more recent years most of their major customers have developed vendor rating systems and now routinely supply vendors with this input. The company finds vendor rating systems very useful because being rated number one is beneficial to both the customer and the vendor. Also, finding out that the service provided is rated as being less than number one provides for the opportunity to work on inefficiencies. Without customer input, a supplier may not know that its service is inadequate compared to the competition.

These are four of the indices that are measured and reviewed routinely for all operating units of the glass container operations. Using these objective measures of quality places constant emphasis on maintaining the degree of excellence required to differentiate Owens-Illinois from the competition.

## GOAL: QUALITY AND PRODUCTIVITY

This customer feedback must be seen as only one part of the quality program. It measures the results at the back end of the process. If the system were to start and end there, then it might develop into little more than a reactive fire fighting program. A number of management systems must also exist in the latter stages of the manufacturing process.

What is the overall program? By the early 1980s goals to be the high-quality producer were achieved, so they began to rededicate themselves to production cost control. That meant readdressing how to do a better job within the manufacturing process and to obtain quality and productivity together.

### Fine Quality Strategies

One remaining issue was the fragmented organizational structure of the various technical groups. These were now all pulled together into a new packaging organization. All product-related functions such as quality assurance, design, and customer technical services were now coordinated by this new department; such coordination made possible a new level of effectiveness.

It was at this time that Owens-Illinois formalized the use of quality strategies that fit their style of management and that realistically addressed their new priorities. The company then understood its manufacturing process well enough and knew where it wanted to go so that it could move beyond the reactionary process and truly manage its destiny. The academicians helped put needed programs together. American Management Association (AMA) seminars and consultants were utilized. At the end of this process Owens-Illinois defined five principal quality strategies to address each major element in their operation: the product, the materials, the people, the customer, and the manufacturing process itself.

A simple statement for each strategy suffices:
- Start with excellence in product design.
- Assure the excellence of all incoming materials.
- Make every employee a contributing member of the quality team.
- Place great importance on the needs of your customers.
- Identify the critical points in the manufacturing process that must be monitored and controlled, and then effectively manage these key parameters.

In their simplest form, these strategies appear to be only superficial statements. Much substance must be added to each and the tactics developed that would bring the strategies to life.

## The Influence of Outside Factors

The simple road maps these strategies provide turned out to be particularly useful to plant managers and quality managers to keep a proper perspective as they went about their business and struggled with day-to-day issues. Surprisingly, the strategies were also useful for some external factors that developed. Three are worth citing.

First was the need for managers to stay on course and maintain high morale as the industry went through the difficult times of plant closings, work force reductions, reorganizations, and the other restructuring measures dictated by the economics of the times. Owens-Illinois itself became a private company early in 1987. More recently it has expanded with new growth. Its quality strategies were a *given* that set a course for product excellence regardless of the corporate form of operation. If the change in the company's status had any effect on quality programs, it was only to make employees more committed: good quality is good business.

A second factor was the seeming rediscovery in America of ality. It became an issue that dominated the media, including cover stories in magazines, newspapers, and trade journals. It was a welcome, long overdue breeze. The company's quality strategies had helped prepare them for this development.

A second factor was the seeming rediscovery in America of quality. It became an issue that dominated the media, including cover stories in magazines, newspapers, and trade journals. It was a welcome, long overdue breeze. The company's quality strategies had helped prepare them for this development.

A third factor was the large international community of worldwide glass companies with which Owens-Illinois is affiliated and to which it provides technical assistance. In addition to the traditional cost and productivity issues, Owens-Illinois developed international quality programs with many of its licensees and affiliates. It is now engaged in an ongoing consulting relationship with twenty-five worldwide affiliated companies. The quality strategies it developed are now being used by the major glass container companies around the world. One of the things that São Paulo (Brazil), Sydney (Australia), Madrid (Spain), and Streator (Illinois), all have in common is a glass plant where the management team is well-schooled in OI's quality strategies.

To operate successfully within this contemporary quality climate, the company uses clear objectives to tell where it is heading and quality strategies to outline how it will get there. This basic management approach does work. It worked for Owens-Illinois. The company became a high-quality and low-cost producer. With these strengths it has been able to successfully navigate the rough waters of the past several years; it expects these basic quality strategies to serve it well in the future as more options for materials become available to customers.

## MANAGEMENT SUPPORT FOR QUALITY PROGRAMS

There is one other critical ingredient for a successful quality program: genuine, visible, and active support from the highest levels of management. It takes more than speeches. The decisions that are made and implemented tell the real story and send a message throughout the organization. Within the glass container operations, this kind of support was supplied by the general manager (now Owens-Illinois president) Joe Lemieux and chairman of the board, Bob Lanigan. Within Owens-Illinois the commitment of top management to quality is now taken for granted.

When Mr. Lemieux became the Owens-Illinois president, other divisions and subsidiaries were beginning to travel down parallel paths. Similar quality programs now exist at Libbey, Kimble, TV Products, Plastics, Closures, and other operations of Owens-Illinois. Most of these units are already leaders as high-quality and low-cost producers. Others are close, with goals clearly in focus.

This author recently visited one plant where the production manager plays a dominant role. Having worked his way up from a machine operator over a thirty-five year career, he carries high respect from his peers. His plant had just been honored Owens-Illinois Packaging Plant of the Year.

This production manager believes that quality and excellence as perceived by the customer is a minimum starting place. The idea is to go beyond the minimum customer expectation and make the best bottle there is.

# Industrial and Farm Equipment

Caterpillar
James E. Redpath, Jr.

Cummins Engine Company
Marianna Grossman

# Delivering Quality Service To the Caterpillar Earthmoving Customer

**James E. Redpath, Jr.**
Caterpillar, Inc.

Headquartered in Peoria, Illinois, Caterpillar Inc. is a multinational company which designs, manufactures, and markets engines and machinery for earthmoving, construction, and material handling. Caterpillar manufactures its products in the United States and abroad. It has fifteen plants in the U.S. with an equal number spread throughout the rest of the world.

Caterpillar began in the late 1800s as a developer and manufacturer of plowing and harvesting machinery. These efforts were driven by advancing technology and the needs of two world wars. The company was incorporated as Caterpillar Tractor Co. in 1925, the result of a merger between The Holt Manufacturing Company and the C.L. Best Tractor Co., and changed its name in 1986 to Caterpillar Inc. to better reflect its growing diversity. Caterpillar employs more than 72,000 people worldwide.

## BUSINESS PHILOSOPHY

Imagine a construction site, a mine or perhaps a highway project. It could be in any country. This morning at this particular site, work has just started, and a Caterpillar wheel loader is busily loading a fleet of six trucks. Suddenly, the machine stops; the transmission appears to have failed. The equipment superintendent learns of the problem and becomes upset. He is thinking of the lost production, which is of course lost revenue, and then he focuses on the overhead expenses for six trucks, one wheel loader and seven operators that will still have to be paid. Next, his attention turns to the failed transmission. He wants it repaired or replaced quickly, and he wants it done at a reasonable price. But most importantly, he wants it done properly the first time. He picks up the phone and calls his Caterpillar dealer. He wants service—quality service—and he wants it immediately.

The hypothetical situation depicted above is quite realistic. Users of Caterpillar products rely on Caterpillar dealers for the majority of their repair work. Caterpillar's basic business philosophy is to build quality products and back them with quality service. Caterpillar realizes that its reputation is dependent on the lifetime performance of its products which are measured in years and thousands of operating hours. Because of this, product support, or service, is an integral part of Caterpillar's corporate quality program which extends from product concept through product completion. Service is accomplished through the factory as well as through independent Caterpillar dealers. A customer's ultimate measure of Caterpillar's products and services should be his owning and operating costs per hour of operation or unit of production basis over the life of the product. Caterpillar has incorporated into its marketing effort a computer program called Equipment/ Investment Analysis (EIA) which provides such a comparison between Caterpillar and its competitors while allowing the user to enter his own cost figures. Cost of availability and downtime is also figured in the analysis in terms of lost net profit. Consequently, providing quality service is critical to the customer and therefore to the success of Caterpillar.

Product support is an integral part of Caterpillar's Corporate Quality Program, which "takes the quality process from the evaluation of customer needs through the design setting process, the manufacturing process, the supplier network, through the finished product stage, and into the product support stage." The product support point is to provide "a product support service to the customer from factory and dealer which maximizes his return on investment in Caterpillar product."

## DEALER ORGANIZATION

Caterpillar, Inc. has several marketing units each of which is responsible for a specific geographic territory which sells the earthmoving products to independent dealers who in turn sell them to customers. These dealers are also responsible for product service. It is important to Caterpillar that each dealership adheres to the corporate standard of business philosophy.

A Sales and Service Agreement, which must be signed by every dealer and Caterpillar, places the responsibility on the dealer for providing service at a level satisfactory to Caterpillar.

Corporate philosophy is communicated to dealers in a number of ways. In 1926, *Across the Table* (Jones, Gardner, and Mee) was written especially for dealers by three senior Caterpillar executives. This book provided information concerning Caterpillar policies and procedures relating to all phases of dealer operations, and as such, proved to be a valuable resource for dealer managers. Such communication is now often handled in one-on-one discussions by local representatives or the district manager. Also, regularly scheduled dealer meetings are held so that Caterpillar representatives or district managers can convey these policies and procedures.

The relationship between the corporation and its dealers is based on mutual trust and understanding and dealers are often referred to as "business partners." It has always been Caterpillar's objective to develop long-term business relationships with its dealers, and the average tenure of the eighty-four dealers in North America is over forty years.

## Management Training

To enable a good relationship to exist between the corporation and the dealer, business strategies and philosophies must be compatible as well as complementary. To assist in this process, a new program was announced in early 1987 to dealers in the United States and Canada—the Caterpillar Dealer Executive Program (CDEP). It was developed by Caterpillar in conjunction with several dealers and faculty from leading universities. The CDEP is an intensive week-long conference for dealer principals and their senior managers. Using the case study method of a fictional but representative Caterpillar dealer, the program challenges dealer management to critically examine their style and beliefs and to adjust to the changing needs of the marketplace. Improved effectiveness in dealer management and marketing of products are its primary goals. Responses from dealer participants have been extremely positive.

Complementing this program is a four-day Owner-Managed Business (OMB) session held separately for the dealership owner, and any probable heirs to the business; the dealer's spouse is also welcome to attend. Each dealer is challenged to address the integration of business and family issues as the principal considers the company's strategic future and the plans for his succession.

The CDEP and OMB programs help assure that the organization and philosophies which have made dealerships successful will be carried forward to assure the highest possible level of customer satisfaction.

Throughout the years, orientation programs have been conducted for the sons and daughters of dealers to familiarize them with products and Caterpillar business philosophy. Participants have suggested a more appropriate title might have been "Caterpillar Indoctrination Program," which may be true, but the programs have been very beneficial. Several past participants in these programs currently serve as chairman or president of their dealerships.

## A QUALITY APPROACH

Another important factor in the communications process between the corporation and the dealer is the example set for the dealers by the products themselves. Quality is truly an important objective at Caterpillar, and the corporation continually points this out to dealers in product discussions and during factory tours. The attitude generated is pervasive and helps to develop a similar attitude in dealership organizations regarding the services they provide. The quality of each dealer's service must match the product quality in order to achieve the desired level of customer acceptance and sales. Of course, the machines must first be designed with quality.

To ensure that quality is designed into every product made by Caterpillar, a set of references to guide engineers in the design of all new products has been installed. For example, the maintenance functions for a piece of machinery are assigned point values. A point value is a reflection of the frequency with which the task must be performed and the degree of difficulty. This system gives design engineers target points for maintenance for all new products. Their objective then becomes designing machines that require less maintenance than allowed by the target without reducing the reliability of the machines. The targets are developed by comparing the proposed new model to existing Caterpillar and competitive models. The results have been very noteworthy. For example, the D9N Tractor, which weighs over 76,000 pounds, has a maintenance cost of $1,514 per 2,000 hours of operation. This cost includes materials and labor for oils, wet and dry filters, engine coolant and lubrication by following factory recommendations. By comparison, a competitor's two models nearest in size, one smaller and one larger, have similar costs of $2,395 and $3,114, respectively, following that manufacturer's recommendations for 2,000 hours of operation.

Another design reference which has a significant impact on the quality of service is the repairability index that assigns point values to the removal and installation of components. Use of this process has contributed to the development of a modular design concept for all product lines. Major components are designed in such a way that they can be easily removed or installed. The repairability indices of our new products have continually been lowered, and our machines are far more repairable today than in previous years. These improvements mean far less downtime for our customers.

The diagnosis of mechanical problems has also been made easier with the help of the design reference system. Fluid level check points and the introduction of a new transmission have been developed because of research in this area. These innovations enable repairs to be made faster and more safely.

## Dealer Support

Once a machine has been designed and built to a standard that will allow service to be performed in a quality manner, attention is focused on continuing that quality to the dealer in the form of product support. Dealers are kept abreast of production schedules and notified of shipment dates for machinery, service literature, training materials, training schools, tools, and parts.

In providing dealer support, the first item of importance is to ensure that parts are available. Once the customer buys a machine and begins to use it, his first need will be for spare parts. Therefore, parts availability is the most important element of service. Since Caterpillar products are used in every country of the world and sold in countries where politics and governments allow it, parts distribution requirements are substantial. Caterpillar has fourteen domestic and eight foreign parts facilities comprising nearly 10 million square feet of warehouse storage area. Worldwide parts inventory value is about four billion dollars, and the primary parts facility stocks about 250,000 part numbers. Considering the investment and volume of inventory, a great deal of effort and attention has been placed on inventory control techniques and has resulted in a highly sophisticated system. To ensure that dealer requirements are met, availability and internal performance are measured in several different ways. Emphasis is placed on stock order service and emergency order service for dealer orders.

Parts availability to the customer is a function of the local dealer. Currently Caterpillar has 201 dealers worldwide and these dealers have 1,239 main and branch stores providing customers with parts service. Dealers are provided with inventory control training and on-site assistance and are encouraged to use procedures similar to the corporation's for measuring and monitoring their performance. Standard percentages have been established for dealer parts service in over-the-counter service, twenty-four-hour service, and forty-eight hour service.

In addition to the parts support that Caterpillar provides to dealers, it also attempts to make available everything that is necessary for prompt repair of all equipment that they sell. For instance in the hypothetical situation at the beginning, the service mechanic and the truck he drove to the job site were carefully selected by the dealer field service dispatcher. The dispatcher was able to learn from the troubled equipment supervisor enough about the problem to make an educated decision on what would be needed to correct it. When the mechanic arrived at the job site, he was able to quickly determine the problem by using diagnostic tools. Then by comparing his findings with service literature he was able to determine the steps necessary to repair the problem. In this case, the dispatcher had correctly recommended the parts needed to repair the machine at the job site.

## Training

With over two-hundred different product models, training repairmen is a great challenge. Training was previously done at the company's Peoria headquarters; however, as the product line expanded, the number of mechanics increased and the training demand exceeded capacity at that location. Today Caterpillar conducts factory schools primarily for dealer training instructors and senior mechanics to introduce new or improved products. Most of these schools are certification schools where the student is required to perform or demonstrate predetermined skills to obtain a certificate of qualification on the subject. Half are conducted regionally with the remaining half held at the corporate headquarters. Training is also done via slide presentations, videotapes, wall charts, and cut-aways of actual parts which are supplied to dealers by Caterpillar. Using these materials, dealers can conduct the bulk of their technical training themselves via their own personnel. Of course, Caterpillar supplies service mechanics with technical specifications, service manuals, parts books, and any other necessary information.

An important link between Caterpillar and its dealerships is the service representative. Service representatives provide assistance and advice to dealers on all matters from technical problems to shop operations. They act as specialized business consultants whose objectives are to ensure that the dealer is efficient, productive, and profitable, while providing quality service to the customer.

## Improved Dealer Efficiency

Since Caterpillar products are distributed through independent dealers only, the corporation must maintain sound and profitable dealerships. This calls for an objective measure of dealer service quality. The company has tried various ways of evaluating dealer performance over the years including evaluation teams, questionnaires, and statistical analysis. None of these proved effective.

In 1981, Caterpillar enlisted the help of Dr. J. M. Juran and his program "Juran on Quality Improvement." The company-wide involvement with this program has produced an effective method of measuring dealer service quality which is still in its completion stage today. The first step, according to this program, was to determine service quality "as was seen by the customer." This was done by customer focus groups and telephone surveys. Customers were asked open-ended questions about their opinions on service quality. From their responses, several service characteristics were developed and ranked in order of importance. A mail survey was developed from this and sent to customers in a dealer's territory. The results from this survey will be used to objectively measure dealer service levels so that standardized methods of performance can be developed for each service characteristic. This will allow for market-driven improvement plans that will improve the quality of Caterpillar's service.

## SUMMARY

Caterpillar strives to produce quality products and follow up with quality service to dealers who in turn give quality service to their customers. Caterpillar defines in writing their responsibilities for dealers and then follows up with an extensive communication effort to ensure understanding and agreement. Products are designed to be serviceable, and product support is provided to dealers for parts, training, literature, tools, and equipment. Controls on product development and an objective method of measuring dealer service quality will enable Caterpillar to make further improvements in its service.

## Works Cited

Caterpillar Tractor Co. 1982. *Caterpillar Corporate Quality Program*. Peoria: Caterpillar Tractor Co.

Jones, I. E., Gardner, W. H., and H. P. Mee. 1926. *Across the Table: Caterpiller Tractor Co. and its Dealers in the United States and Canada*. San Leandro: Caterpiller Tractor Co.

# Process Improvement In Customer Service: An Example

**Marianna Grossman**
Cummins Engine Company

Cummins Engine Company, Inc., is a worldwide designer and manufacturer of diesel engines and related components and services. The company was founded in 1919 at Columbus, Indiana, which remains the site of its corporate headquarters. In 1987, Cummins reported net sales of $2.8 billion and currently employs approximately 24,500 persons worldwide.

Principal market for the Cummins Engine Company is the U.S. heavy-duty truck industry. Customers include Ford, Freightliner, Volvo/GM, Navistar, Kenworth, Mack, Peterbilt and Western Star. Approximately 55 percent of the heavy-duty, on-highway trucks produced today are powered by Cummins.

Major off-highway customers are the construction, mining, agricultural, oil and gas, logging, marine, industrial locomotive, electrical generator, compressor pump and other special-purpose machinery industries.

Cummins sells directly to original equipment manufacturers and through 30 distributors in North America and 145 distributors internationally. In addition, there are approximately 3,900 locations in North America, at which Cummins-trained service personnel and parts are available to repair and maintain Cummins' engines.

In 1956, Cummins became an international business. Today, Cummins' operations have expanded to include plants, joint ventures or license agreements in the United Kingdom, India, Mexico, Canada, Brazil, South Korea, China, France, Indonesia and Turkey.

# INTRODUCTION

In the late 1970s, Cummins management recognized the need to improve their warranty system. Warranty costs were high. Distributors and customers were dissatisfied. A task force was formed to investigate the problems with the system and to implement solutions. In the course of this effort, the capability of the warranty system was improved. The task force streamlined the documentation requirements and converted forms from paper to an electronic claims management system. Once it had made the system more efficient, it introduced changes in order to install process controls that would foster continuous improvement.

# CUMMINS TOTAL QUALITY SYSTEM

In 1985, Cummins adopted a company-wide Total Quality System (TQS) with the help of Dr. Armand V. Feigenbaum and General Systems Company. TQS provides an integrated network of work processes centered on a new product planning, development, and introduction procedure. This procedure enables departments within Cummins to work more effectively together to understand and serve customer needs, and to provide products and services of the lowest cost and highest quality. A fundamental principle of TQS is the use of data for problem solving. Data is used to identify areas requiring attention and to diagnose root causes of problems. There are five key measures of effectiveness in the Cummins TQS: 1) quality costs, 2) internal quality levels, 3) internal audits, 4) customer quality attitudes, and 5) field performance data.

The warranty system is the primary method of gathering field performance data. Data from the warranty claims system are automatically compiled into a reliability database. This information is analyzed and regularly reported to engineering, manufacturing, and product teams so that it can be used to solve field problems, prevent future problems from occurring, and improve product design. Distributors now receive reports of warranty information for use in managing the work in their own facilities. This article describes how Cummins changed the traditional warranty system to a new system based on the principles of process control.

# THE QUALITY FRAMEWORK

## Inspection-Based Quality Control

Before the introduction of process control, management in a manufacturing setting relied on inspection to achieve quality standards. When inspection detected poor quality, action would be taken to fix the problem. Each department tended to work independently. People spent their time responding to problems and breakdowns, and a culture of "firefighting" and "heroism" developed. People were encouraged to respond rapidly and decisively to crises. The focus was on short-term results, and less attention was paid to the consequences of expediting orders or of compressing product development schedules. Management's attention was caught by anecdotes, and actions were generally after the fact.

Traditional U.S. manufacturing companies are often characterized by a failure-driven system; the cost of inspection is high both within manufacturing and in the delivery of associated services, such as marketing. Late detection of errors or poor quality leads to even higher costs associated with failure, particularly when defective products reach customers in the field. Information cannot be captured systematically and used effectively for improvement purposes. This costly style of management was not competitive in the global marketplace.

## Improvement-Based Quality Control

Cummins management recognized the imperative to improve quality and lower costs. The TQS is one of the means Cummins is using to identify areas that were primarily inspection- or failure-driven, and to shift to a way of operating based on improvement and prevention. An improvement-based culture strives to control all work processes and then to improve the capability of both people and systems on a continuous basis. Problem solving is driven by data, not anecdotes, although anecdotes are still used to bring the data to life. Problem solvers do not stop at identification of symptoms, but work through to root causes. The emphasis is on prevention of future problems through improving the design of both products and work processes. Designs are based on a thorough understanding of customer needs and are constructed so as to reduce or eliminate the possibility of errors and failure.

In a prevention-driven system, data is friendly. The goal of inquiry is to improve the way work is done or the way the product is designed. The goal is not to find out who the "culprits" are or to assign blame in the event that a failure has occurred. Quality is designed-in from the beginning. In a prevention system, the purpose of inspection is to find ways of improving the process.

An improvement-based system relies on key measures of effectiveness rather than on inspection which sorts good from bad. The customers' attitude about quality, and field performance data are external measures. Cost of quality, quality levels, and an audit process ensure that work processes are in control, and help to identify problem areas for further improvement. Performance reports are used as control charts to identify the patterns of results and to track normal and special variances.

Successful implementation of an improvement-based system requires extensive ongoing training so that people know how to use data to make improvements. To make a cultural shift from a "hero"-based way of life to a systems orientation requires leadership. Management must value and recognize quiet, steady contributions to improvement as well as the extraordinary efforts required to meet customer demands and solve immediate problems.

One objective is to achieve continuous improvement. Once the work processes are well understood, attention can be focused on improving people's skills and refining the capability of the processes. In these ways, customer needs can be better understood and reflected in product design, and the quality of service rendered will continually improve. The goal is to have enthusiastic, satisfied customers (see Table 1).

## QUALITY APPLIED TO THE WARRANTY SYSTEM

### Traditional Warranty System

As the Total Quality System was being developed, management of the service department began to consider how to apply the concepts of process control to improving Cummins delivery of aftermarket services. The traditional warranty system was similar to traditional manufacturing in its reliance on inspection for after-the-fact detection of poor quality. Work had been done between 1979 and 1985 to improve the basic warranty system at Cummins; what was needed now was a means for generating continuous improvement.

Before 1979 the warranty system was expensive to run but both customers and distributors were dissatisfied. A number of problems contributed to this. Everyone had to wait too long to get reimbursed. There was uncertainty about what types of failures were covered, and distributors sometimes billed customers for work that was later proven to be covered under the warranty. Forms were long and complicated. The system was characterized by too many checks and too little trust. There were many manual operations in the processing of warranty claims which introduced errors and delay. The extensive backup documentation required resulted in an unmanageable volume of paper to handle. The returned-goods policy resulted in high shipping and handling costs for distributors and in additional delays for Canadian claims due to slow through-put time at customs. In addition, there was ineffective use of warranty data.

From 1979 through 1985, basic improvements were made in the warranty process. The claims system was automated so that claims could be filed electronically, and a reliability database was established. The claim form was simplified and shortened to one page for claims below five hundred dollars (about 85% of the total). A second page was required only for claims above that amount. Manuals of standard repair times were updated for new products and installations so that payment for warrantable repairs would be consistent across all distributors and dealers.

### Current Process Control Techniques

In the spirit of process control, Cummins took a new approach to managing warranty after basic improvements had been accomplished. In 1985, Cummins instituted on-the-spot/hassle-free warranty decision making. Responsibility and accountability for decision making were given to people at

TABLE 1
KEY ELEMENTS OF FAILURE VS. PREVENTION-BASED SYSTEMS

| FAILURE-DRIVEN | PREVENTION-BASED |
|---|---|
| – After the fact | – Before the fact |
| – Event-focused | – Process-focused |
| – Judgmental/critical | – Curious/investigative |
| – Right/wrong-based | – Data-based |
| – Non-systemic/narrow | – Systemic/broad |
| – Short-term fix | – Long-term change |
| – Expedite out-of-control operation | – Upgrade of in-control operation |
| – Immediate, direct reward | – Long-term, indirect reward |
| – Problem fix | – System/operation improvement |
| – Minimum diagnosis | – Continuous diagnosis |
| – Work/problems come to you | – You go to the system |
| – Hero-oriented | – Customer-oriented |
| – Narrowing of thinking scope | – Widening of thinking scope |
| – Time to re-do | – Time to do it right |
| – Progress is only tangible | – Progress is often intangible |
| – Working harder | – Working smarter |
| – Varying from standard | – Upgrading standard |
| – Fragmented jobs/tasks | – Unified flow of work |
| – Disconnected individual effort | – Connected joint effort |
| – Things always break | – Never be surprised |
| – "If it ain't broke, don't fix it" | – It can always be improved |
| – Give me simple answers now | – How does this work? |
| – Don't ask questions—get it done | – Good questions help us understand what to do |
| – Job security is in getting them to depend on my fix | – Job security results from increasing our capability |
| – Learning takes too long | – Learning is continuous |
| – Learning means you are inadequate | – Learning is necessary to deal with change |
| – Learning is for the other guy | – Learning is for all of us |
| – Getting by for now is good enough | – Fixing it permanently is the only solution |
| – Quality is passing inspection | – Quality is zero defects |
| – Quality is not as important as quantity | – Quality is all there is |
| – Quality is in the hardware | – Quality is in everything we do and think |
| – Don't challenge the system | – Everything can be improved |
| – Success is individual | – Success is of the whole |
| – Work manages me | – I manage my work |
| – Customer reactions drive improvement | – Customer input blends with technology input and capability input |
| – I get paid to react | – I get paid to think, then do |
| – Who is at fault is important | – What went wrong is important |
| – Targets are to be hit | – Trends of improvements are tracked |
| – Don't worry about the big issues | – Work on seeing how large issues affect the small |
| – Mistakes mean failure | – Mistakes show where we need improvement |

*Adapted from T.R. Lane, unpublished manuscript. The Way of Quality.*

the place where service is rendered, just as shop floor workers have responsibility for decision making in an improvement-based manufacturing system. Personnel at the repair location determine whether or not a failure is warrantable. There is a handbook that describes various failures and the conditions that are to be met in making the determination. Each type of failure is coded, and each has a standard repair time associated with it. There are provisions for the difficulty of repair, depending on the type of vehicle or equipment the engine is installed in and the engine's accessibility. Failed parts are no longer required to be sent in. Backup documentation is kept on file at the distributor.

Warranty specialists in Columbus used to act as inspectors determining the cause of failure from the parts and paperwork sent in. They now act more as coaches and trainers. They review all warranty claims above five hundred dollars and any claims that are rejected by the computer system due to errors. They determine the cause of the error, if any, and evaluate how well the claim form has been filled out. If they disagree with the conclusion a repair location has reached, that information is added to a monthly report sent to each repair location.

The monthly report informs distributors of the performance of each branch, dealer, and distributor repair shop, compared to the national (or international) average. Detailed information on how well their claims were filled out is provided so that warranty managers can improve their performance. When the warranty specialists at the factory disagree with a diagnosis, they will code the claim accordingly. Based on this information, warranty managers can improve their diagnostic skills, but the long arguments between field and factory have been eliminated.

The warranty reports are analogous to statistical process control charts in a factory setting. Repair shop managers can monitor their performance over time and identify normal and special causes of variance. The warranty system management in Columbus can give special attention to those areas whose performance is substandard. The reports also help to identify good performers so that insights about what makes some locations more effective than others can be shared. Distributors can also use this information in the management of their service shops (see Figure 1 and Table 2).

The concept behind the on-the-spot decision-making policy is that the honest majority should not be burdened by a system designed to thwart opportunists. People who want to get around the system will always find a way. It is very expensive to construct a system designed to protect the company's interest. The goal of a system should be to serve customers efficiently. Many people were concerned that allowing distributors and dealers to determine whether a failure was warrantable would result in the filing of unjustified claims. In fact, Cummins has seen a reduction in warranty costs of about 50% since 1979, due primarily to improvement in

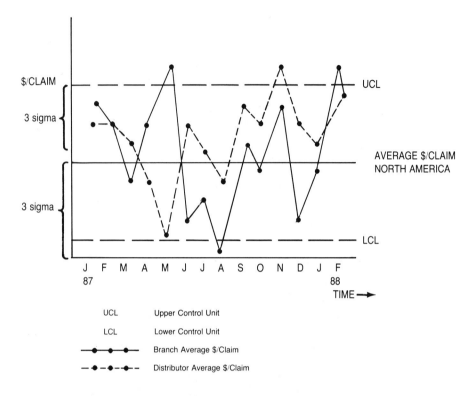

FIG. 1. SAMPLE CHART

The sample chart shows that most of the variation in dollars per claim ($/claim) is normal. Investigating repair practices should only be considered in May and August, 1987, and in January, 1988. If management would prefer to see less variability overall, then work can be done to improve the service system. Service management can use this chart to discover trends of deterioration or improvement. This chart is not meant to be the sole source of information; when trends are unsatisfactory, further investigation and corrective action are needed. If trends are favorable, management can analyze the causes of extraordinary performance so those gains can be applied elsewhere.

product quality. No increases have been seen that could be attributed to dishonest claims filing.

The new system has resulted in increased clarity in what types of engine failures are warrantable. Increased certainty benefits both distributors and customers. Now distributors are better off because they can file forms electronically and receive payment immediately if the forms are filled

## CUMMINS ENGINE COMPANY

TABLE 2
COMPUTER PRINT-OUT OF SAMPLE/CHART (FIG. 1)

★★★★★★★★★★★★★★★★ PERFORMANCE SUMMARY ★★★★★★★★★★★★★★★★★★★★★★★★
FUEL SYSTEM CALIBRATION
★★★★★★★★★★★★★★ DISTRIBUTOR CLAIMS COMPLETED ★★★★★★★★★★★★★★★★★★★★★
DISTRIBUTOR: XXYYZZ
DISTRIBUTOR BRANCH: LLMMNN
BAR CHART OF AVERAGE $/CLAIM

```
        +-----+-----+-----+-----+-----+-----+-----+-----+     # CLAIMS   AVG $
JAN87                   ★   N   ★
   B    $$$$$$$$$$$$$$★$  N    ★
   D    ddddddddddddd★dddN    ★
FEB87                   ★ N   ★
   B    $$$$$$$$$$$$$   ★   N   ★
   D    ddddddddddddddd★d   N   ★
MAR87                   ★   N   ★
   B    $$$$$$$$$$$$$$$$★$$$N$$$★$$$$$$$$
   D    ddddddddddddddd★ddddddd★dd
APR87                   ★   N   ★
   B    $$$$$$$$$$$$$$$★$$$N   ★
   D    ddddddddddddddd★ddddddd★
MAY87                   ★   N  ★
   B    $$$$$$$$$$$$$$$$★$$$N$$$★
   D    ddddddddddddddd★ddddddd★
JUN87                   ★  N   ★
   B    $$$$$$$$$$$$$$$★$$$N$$$★
   D    ddddddddddddd★dddN★
JUL87                   ★   N   ★
   B    $$$$$$$$$$$$$$$  ★   N   ★
   D    dddddddddddddddd★   N   ★
AUG87                    ★  N   ★
   B    $$$$$$$$$$$$$$$$$$$★$$$N   ★
   D    ddddddddddddddddddd★ddddddd★ddddd
SEP87                   ★   N   ★
   B    $$$$$$$$$$$$$$$$$$$★N  N   ★
   D    dddddddddddddddddd★dddNd   ★
OCT87                   ★  N   ★
   B    $$$$$$$$$$$$$$★$$$N$$$★$$$$$$$$$
   D    ddddddddddd★ddddddd★ddddd
NOV87                   ★  N   ★
   B    $$$$$$$$$$$$$$★$$  N   ★
   D    ddddddddddddd★dddNdd   ★
DEC87                   ★  N   ★
   B    $$$$$$$$$$$$$★$$$N$$$★
   D    ddddddddddd★dd  N   ★
```

KEY:  B = branch
      D = distributor average
      $ = average $/claim for branch
      d = average $/claim for distributor
      N = average $/claim for all N. American distributors
      * = band of normal variation (any result below or above this level should be investigated for special
          causes)

NOTE:  This chart is an example that is not based on actual data.

This type of chart is used by Cummins to show distributor and
branch performance because it can be easily transmitted over a
non-graphics computer system. It is meant to be used and interpreted in the same manner as the chart in figure 1.

out correctly. Customers are receiving better service and are not caught in the battle that used to be waged between the factory and the distribution network in the determination of claims settlement.

## THE SECOND GENERATION:
### The National Overhaul Warranty (NOW) Program
Due to the success of warranty system changes, the service organization decided to apply the approach of process management to post-warranty service. A program was devised to monitor and improve the quality of parts and labor provided by the distribution network. Through this program the benefits of a national warranty could be extended beyond the period covered by a new engine warranty.

The National Overhaul Warranty (NOW) program warrants parts and workmanship on overhauls performed by authorized Cummins repair shops. If, after receiving a NOW overhaul, a customer's engine has a failure related to the overhaul, he or she can have it fixed free in any authorized location in North America. In the event of a failure, a claim is filed with Cummins so that it can compile information on the performance of each dealer and distributor location. In the same way that reports are generated from new engine warranty data, monthly reports are issued on NOW performance. Patterns of unusually high failure rates alert Cummins field personnel to determine the cause of failures and to work with the distributor to identify needed improvements.

Causes of poor performance vary, ranging from lack of mechanic training, or inadequate tooling for specific operations, to problems with parts quality. Data from the NOW program have enabled a considerable upgrading of the quality of service provided by Cummins distribution network. Another benefit of the NOW program is the customer information recorded on NOW certificates. Using this information, customer satisfaction surveys can be conducted to determine the quality of the customer's overall experience in dealing with Cummins. Also, the NOW program is popular with customers who put many miles on their trucks each year, because it extends the benefit of nationwide coverage beyond the initial engine warranty period for customers.

### Results of NOW Implementation
**Savings: Reduced Overhead and Expenditures.** The first series of improvements in warranty systems (1979-1985) resulted in considerable reduction in the corporate staff required. The warranty department has been reduced by two-thirds since 1979. Now that backup documentation is no longer required, reliance on central services such as micrographics and data entry has decreased significantly. Overall warranty costs have not increased with the introduction of on-the-spot decision making for warranties.

**Increased Responsiveness to Customers.** Claims-processing time has been reduced from an average of ninety days (with some claims being held six to nine months) to an average of ten days or less. Because claims under five hundred dollars are paid electronically, the only waiting time is the time it takes the distributor to process the claim.

The customer perceives greater responsiveness when decisions are made at repair locations. Customers do not have to wait for a factory determination and can have the repair performed immediately. The warranty manager at the repair location has more data available on which to base a decision than a factory-based claims adjuster would. When the cause of failure is indeterminate, the warranty manager can call the factory for advice. Another benefit of improved claims management is that the claims system can be used to administer additional marketing programs such as NOW, various programs of extended coverage and preventive maintenance, and so forth.

**Improved Use of Data.** Data from each warranty claim automatically enters the reliability database. Various reports based on this data are compiled and used to forecast warranty accrual levels and to identify product problems. Product development engineers and the manufacturing organization use this information for identification of problems and improvement purposes. The next generation of data is derived from the National Overhaul Warranty data. NOW data allows the service and distribution organizations to monitor the quality of repair work, to identify system weaknesses, and to upgrade overall service.

## The Challenges of NOW Implementation

**Culture Change.** Logically, improvement-based management makes sense. On a day-to-day basis, operating in a new way requires a new way of thinking. Firefighting, heroism, and excitement are replaced by constant, incremental improvement. Improvement is achieved by steady, detail-oriented work. To people accustomed to a relatively unstructured organization, the prospect of proceeding in an orderly manner seems stifling. How can one be creative if one has to follow procedures? How can one maintain control if the people one used to control (the distributors and dealers) are allowed to make warranty determinations themselves? As with learning any new skill, at first one feels awkward but with practice the new thinking patterns produce superior results.

A cardinal rule of an improvement orientation is that data may be used as a tool and not a weapon. For example, reports are used as control charts, to monitor a process and to identify normal and special variances in warranty claims activity. Reports are not used to punish poor performers or to reward stars. Reports provide data and help focus management attention most productively.

Another challenge of adopting a new way of working is to create new roles for old pros. Warranty specialists have developed considerable expertise in problem diagnosis. They have also perfected a balance between the roles of adversary and advocate. They know when to resist distributors and dealers who are trying to take advantage of the factory and when to act as champions for the distribution network and for customers. Their presence ensures that people in the field are taken care of by knowledgeable, caring factory personnel. The new role of coach requires warranty specialists to drop their policing function. They are being asked to exercise their expertise as helpers. It is important that a mechanism be established to enable them actually to spend time coaching, and that training be available to equip the old pros with new skills, so they can be comfortable operating differently.

**Logistics.** There are many logistical considerations in the implementation of a new system. Are reports getting to the people who need them? Do people know how to use the reports once they receive them? An effective training program and clear documentation are necessary in order to code and process claims correctly. An audit program is needed to make sure that the system patterns that seem normal are in fact acceptable and to uncover any irregularities that may be occurring.

Finally, it is crucial to have a means of addressing the improvement needs that are uncovered. If the reports and audits of the process for warranty claims uncover the need for upgraded tooling, training, or other intervention, then resources must be allocated to address those needs. Otherwise, people begin to lose faith in the system. Why catalog problems if they are not going to be resolved?

**Checks and Balances.** As stated earlier, the new warranty system at Cummins assumes that the majority of people, both customers and distributors, are honest. Everyone recognizes that some are not. There must be policies for dealing with variance from the norm, such as dishonesty, incompetence, or lack of knowledge. Cummins has determined that a trust-based system is less difficult and expensive to administer. There is a value in the good will generated by not hassling customers and dealers that compensates for some minimum level of inappropriate activity. However, at times it becomes necessary to be tough.

Sometimes distributors and dealers welcome the factory playing the role of the bad guy. It may be that an engine failed due to a customer's neglect, but the truck dealer does not want to alienate a customer; so he authorizes a repair as warrantable that should actually be paid by the customer. In another case, the cause of the failure may be indeterminate, and the expert factory warranty specialist, who sees multitudes of types of claims, may be better able to determine whether a repair is warrantable or not. In these cases, the factory may have something to contribute by intervening. However, the repair location has the authority to make the decision: the factory will not second-guess them. Along with the privilege of autonomy comes the responsibility to make difficult decisions. The factory has determined that trust, rather than mistrust, is a better basis on which to do business and has willingly given up a certain amount of perceived control and power over the warranty process. So far it seems to be working well.

**Making It Stick.** Process control and improvement require time for extensive ongoing coaching and training. For people raised in a firefighting environment this may seem like an excessive requirement. Successful implementation requires constant follow-up and management attention to keep from sliding back into the default, firefighting mode. While the data from control charts are useful, it takes time and self-discipline actually to study, analyze, and take action based on what the data indicate.

The greatest challenge of all results when customers become accustomed to improvements. Customer satisfaction is an ephemeral target. At one time, customers would put up with sixty- or ninety-day delays in warranty settlements. Soon, ten days will seem too long. Customer expectations continually rise, as does the performance of competitors. There is always opportunity to learn, to improve, and to discover new and better ways to serve customers.

# Life Insurance

Metropolitan Life Insurance Company
John J. Falzon

The Prudential Insurance Company of America
Ethan I. Davis

The Travelers
Len Sparks

# Met Life's Quest for Quality

**John J. Falzon**
Metropolitan Life Insurance Company

Metropolitan Life and its affiliated companies provide a range of insurance, investment, real estate and other financial products and services. The parent company, Metropolitan Life Insurance Company, insures or administers coverage for 42 million people in the United States and Canada. In addition to the operations in the U.S. and Canada, Met Life has an office in Japan and a joint corporate venture in Spain.

Headquartered in New York City, Metropolitan Life has 33,000 employees including a 10,000 person sales network and 1,250 offices.

# INTRODUCTION

After being given the assignment as the Metropolitan corporate quality officer, this author did what presumably most quality management professional would do: visited people in other companies who had a similar assignment. Almost universally, they offered a similar piece of advice, make sure you enlist the cooperation of your CEO; otherwise, you are doomed to failure.

At Met Life this was not a problem. It was the CEO who enlisted *my* support. The president and CEO, John J. Creedon, has been the driving force behind Met Life's quest for quality. For example, be coined the phrase, Quality is more a journey than a destination—which has proven to be a truism. It is certainly definitive of what has happened at Met Life so far. The programmatic features of the quality process have been enhanced, and the company has recognized that improvement is always possible. Fortunately, each improvement and record of change has been consistent with its overall concepts about quality; each has been introduced in a way that reflects continuity with the past.

# QUALITY IMPROVEMENT PROCESS (QIP)

Just like many other companies, Met Life during the initial phases of quality awareness formed a quality steering committee made up of the heads of major departments throughout the company. After a good deal of discussion and deliberation the committee provided a series of directives that became the foundation elements in the (QIP) Quality Improvement Process. They said that any program for quality must have a strong customer orientation; that all people in the company must be involved. In fact, they emphasized the fact that each employee should identify with the customer. They went on to say that the quality process should not be seen as an academic exercise, but should be viewed as something that provides a significant business advantage to the company. They were emphatic about the need to have the entire process administered through the line organization with minimal staff support; in general, any process should be implemented in a unified way throughout the entire company.

Using these directives as guidelines, a process was introduced to the company that was designed to alter both the way things were being managed and the way the work was being done. The new process required every organization to identify the major services being rendered and the customers to whom they were being directed. This was accomplished through *identification meetings* conducted by each organization. These meetings were generally presided over by a quality officer, a senior-level person in the organization who had the responsibility for implementing the Quality Improvement Process within the organization.

## Quality Improvement Teams (QITs)

The identification meeting resulted in eight major products or services being identified; for example, loans, surrenders, claims, and policy issue were among those identified. A member of middle management agreed to serve as product champion for each of the eight products, and each of them assembled a quality improvement team (QIT) with a representative from each team to help create the final product or service. For instance, policy issue represented several units in the organization: the mail team, the underwriting team, and the issue team. Thus, one or more representative from each of these units joined the Product Champion to become part of the Policy Issue Quality Improvement Team.

To provide direction at the outset, there were three major challenge areas identified for all quality improvement teams to address: effectiveness measures, customer dialogue, and extra processing. The primary task of the QIT was to address these challenge areas, respectively.

Customarily performance standards for major transactions were set. The basic performance standards for policy issue was that 80% of all policies should be issued within three days of their approval, 90% within four days, and all policies issued within five working days. The product champions and the quality improvement team agreed to shoot for a 5% improvement in service, that is, 85% issued within three days and 95% within four days. Work-group meetings were held to develop ways to reduce processing time. Each work group (mail, underwriting, and issue) met separately to discuss ways to meet the objective; then the larger QIT met to examine and approve the work-group team suggestions for implementation.

Quality improvements resulted from the application of group problem solving techniques to the various challenge areas already mentioned. All members of the organization participated in quality improvement teams after they had been trained in quality improvement concepts and techniques as well as group problem-solving techniques. These techniques were then used to address challenges identified by the team. A similar process was followed by the quality improvement teams for each of the seven other products established in the identification meeting.

## DEVELOPMENT OF QUALITY MEASUREMENTS

In the process, through structured problem-solving techniques, teams were encouraged to isolate both problems and opportunities and to develop solutions that represented improvements within those factors being measured. They were encouraged to establish challenging goals, especially through an open dialogue with customers; by such dialogue they might well obtain the most precise evaluation of their performance.

These initial steps appeared to meet the criteria established by the steering committee. However, there were some open ends that still needed attention. The first of these was that, although customer dialogue was encouraged, they did not say how to conduct this dialogue or how to evaluate the results of the dialogue and define new opportunities for improvement. A second aspect of the design requiring attention was a need to forge a link between the quality management process that was being introduced at the operational levels of the company and the strategic planning conducted at the higher levels of the organization.

## Four Characteristics of Services (versus Goods)

Define and measure the customers' view of service. Management benefitted from research completed by a group of professors from Texas A&M. (Their research was conducted under the auspices of the Marketing Science Institute of Cambridge, Massachusetts.) The objectives of the research were to understand the nature of services and to define quality in the service sector. The findings were very interesting. It was the first research this author had come across that specifically addressed the issue of quality in a service work environment. The reader may agree that most of the literature addresses the manufacturing sector, and although many of the principles can be applied to companies in the service environment, there are still many gaps left unfilled, and many differences left unexplained.

Some of the more significant findings in the Texas A&M research are worth summarizing. There are four main distinctions that set services apart from goods or products. First of all, services are intangible: they cannot be measured, tested, or verified in advance of sales to assure quality. Second, services are heterogeneous because they generally have a high labor content. Service personnel are intrinsic to the service, and therefore, the performance of the service or the evaluation of the service can vary, depending on the individual providing the service and the customer who receives the service; it can also vary from one delivery of the service to the next. Third, the production and consumption of many services are inseparable. In many situations the customer participates in the process, providing input that affects the outcome, for example, getting a haircut. These situations in which the customer is directly involved in the production become critical to the quality of service performance. Finally, services are perishable; they cannot be saved or inventoried. Once the opportunity is missed, there is no second chance to sell a service to a customer.

Obviously these four characteristics of service pose problems to firms who desire to deliver high quality services. They also lead to the conclusion that because of the interpersonal involvement, the *process* of delivering a service is as important as the *outcome*. In other words, the way a customer is treated in a service transaction can be as important an influence on customer attitude as the actual outcome of the experience. Additionally, it was found that as much attention must be paid to the *nonroutine* transactions as to the *routine* because nonroutine transactions, although less frequent than routine ones, can have a disproportionately larger impact on customer impressions of a firm's services.

## Five Dimensions of Quality

As a basis for measurement, the research was able to identify the most significant factors that influenced the overall evaluation. These factors were grouped within five generic classifications or dimensions of quality: *reliability*, the ability to perform the promised service dependably and accurately; *responsiveness*, the willingness to help customers and provide prompt service; *tangibles*, physical facilities, equipment and appearance of personnel; *assurance*, the knowledge and courtesy of employees and their ability to convey trust and confidence and finally, *empathy*, the caring, individualized attention paid to customers. For each organization, these five generic dimensions of service quality need to be translated into performance specifics. Naturally these will vary from industry to industry and, to a lesser degree, from company to company within an industry.

Met Life has developed its own version of performance specifics for the five dimensions. The company's view of *reliability* is that customers expect notices to be sent out on schedule and the information to be correct (that is, name, address, amount premium, and due date). Customers expect that all transactions (loans and policy surrenders) are calculated accurately. At Met Life, *responsiveness* means paying or at least processing all claims within five days of receipt in the home office. When a customer calls, if a call back is necessary, a response on the same working day is required. *Tangibles* means that customers expect insurance companies to use modern systems and computer technology to service them. In addition, the company is intent to provide offices that are conveniently accessible to customers, and are adequately equipped so that their business can be conducted easily. *Assurance* leads customers to feel confident that personal data disclosed to an insurance company are always kept confidential. *Empathy* is shown by writing letters to customers in terms they understand and by avoiding jargon in dealings with them. Employees are encouraged to recognize that insurance is a complex business and to reflect this understanding in dealings with customers. In summary, each of these five dimensions, responsiveness, reliability, assurance, tangibles and empathy can be translated into a series of expectation statements that further define each.

Based upon the foregoing factors, the researchers developed a survey instrument that could quantify service performance by comparing customer expectation levels with how well the service provider meets them. Moreover, the instrument was designed within a system that assists management to identify and isolate problem areas. One of the most significant findings of the research was the ability to apply a rather precise definition to the measurement of quality in the service sector. Namely, one can measure the quality of services by the difference between the expectation levels of the customer on the one hand, and the perceived levels of service delivery on the other.

An interesting aspect of this research was that the researchers originally presumed that among the better companies the perceived level of delivery would consistently exceed the level of expectations. In reality this was rare, even among the better companies. What they found was that the better companies merely had a smaller gap between the customer's expectations of service quality and the perceived level of service quality provided.

It is interesting to speculate that providing excellent service may be one way of *raising* customer expectation levels. That idea provides a rationale for the theory that the pursuit of quality is a never-ending process. Also, it makes a great deal of sense out of the statement that quality is more a journey than a destination.

## COMPANYWIDE PLANNING

With the assistance of one of the Texas A&M professors, the company structured a special seminar that was delivered to principal officers from all parts of the company, with the expectation that each department would proceed with the construction of appropriate survey instruments and use them to quantify customer satisfaction.

To address the second problem of the gap between higher level strategic planning and the quality planning process instituted at the operational level, the company looked to the academic community for help. Specifically, it is now adopting a unique approach to planning developed by Dr. Russell Ackoff (formerly of the Wharton School of Business). It is an interactive planning process that has many of the characteristics associated with the company's quality improvement process. There is a great deal of consistency and continuity between the two. In particular, it provides the means to bring all levels of planning from the very top of the company to the bottom. Its introduction to the company is not being viewed as a replacement, but as an add-on and enhancement to existing systems.

Met Life is currently engaged in the task of introducing the new planning method at the top layers of management in the company. They expect this to percolate throughout lower levels of the organization as an enhancement to the quality network. A phrase one hears repeatedly is *achieving quality through planning*.

The use of the new survey technology from Texas A&M is being encouraged. All organizations are being requested to provide (as part of their annual planning objectives) an assessment of the gap that exists between customer expectation and perceived levels of service, and an expectation of how to reduce these gaps. Enthusiastically, the company is continuing to participate in further research being conducted by the Texas A&M group. Such research can provide additional understanding of how and where management behavior can influence the quality of service delivered.

## CONCLUSION

As the research continues, and as more customer survey instruments are developed, the future should bring significant insights into the needs of Met Life customers. Met Life aspires to continually provide an enhanced level of service with the goal of exceeding customer expectation levels. This can be accomplished by improving the skills of management personnel and more importantly, by improving the skills of the people with the responsibility of directly servicing a customer. Customer-contact people need to have broader and more demanding responsibilities in order to respond independently to a broader range of customer service requests. By the same token, the company should strive to develop an environment that does not limit personal growth.

# Quality Service at The Prudential

**Ethan I. Davis**
The Prudential Insurance Company of America

The Prudential Insurance Company of America is a multiline financial services organization providing a full range of services to a primarily North American customer base. Some form of coverage is provided to an estimated fifty million individuals through individual and group insurance. Prudential insurance products protect against the financial consequences of dying, becoming ill or disabled, or suffering an accidental loss. The Prudential owns over two hundred subsidiaries, employs over ninety-three thousand people, and manages and invests assets of over $130 billion. Its corporate headquarters are in Newark, New Jersey, where the company was founded in 1875 as The Prudential Friendly Society.

## INDIVIDUAL INSURANCE AREA

This paper describes the philosophy of The Prudential's Individual Insurance operations for delivering high quality customer service. Many of the strategies, tactics, tools, and management actions designed to meet the commitment to providing superior customer service to its customers and its field force are identified.

The Prudential's Individual Insurance area employs close to fifty-four thousand people, 60% of whom are associated with over seven hundred sales and service offices located in each of the fifty states and most of Canada's twelve provinces. It has a customer base of some fifteen million individuals and small business owners. Delivering service that exceeds the customers' expectation is its goal.

The Prudential was established to make it possible for working people to avoid a pauper's grave by providing life insurance for as little as three cents a week. While it stopped selling weekly premium (industrial) insurance in 1968, there are still two million contracts in force providing four billion dollars of insurance coverage. The payment of remaining premiums due was waived beginning January 1981.

### Individual Insurance Area Service Philosophy

Since the company's founding, it has consistently believed that personal service-face-to-face whenever possible—produces the highest degree of customer satisfaction.

The individual insurance area's commitment to customer service was summarized in an ad in the January 1988 edition of *Fortune* magazine:

> Our most important policy isn't life insurance. It's our service policy. The kind of personal service that goes above and beyond. Because we're not just looking for customers…we're looking for long-term relationships. Whether you're interested in insurance, savings, or investments, our commitment is to your future. And that takes more than just knowing what we're doing. It takes caring about what you're doing. Keeping in touch with your wants, your needs. It's everyone at The Prudential making that important extra effort. Going above and beyond…for you.

It is an explicit organizational goal to provide service that exceeds customers' expectations. The Prudential's national advertising theme *Going Above and Beyond* is being backed up by many new measures.

### KEYS TO SUPERIOR CUSTOMER SERVICE

The Prudential has identified five critical success factors that must consistently implement extremely well in order to widen its lead over competitors. Superior service to its customers and field force is one of them; moreover, it is on a par with the other four.

The ability to consistently deliver value-added service requires superior performance in the following eight areas, which are key to becoming customer- and market-driven: people recruitment and retention; training; continuing education creative use of information technologies; accessibility to customers; performance measurement and monitoring; recognition for superior performance; and customer satisfaction monitoring.

The key elements of Prudential's approach to these eight areas focuses on those features that may be different in emphasis or unique, and on their connection with customer satisfaction.

## People Recruitment and Retention

Discovering and satisfying the individual needs of current and prospective customers is the focus of activity for most of their representatives and employees. Selecting individuals who will be successful is a continuing challenge, particularly the selection of field sales representatives.

In addition to standard preemployment testing, other selection tools (some in consultation with the Life Insurance Management Research Association), were developed. Since The Prudential is a Federal subcontractor, these selection methods had to be acceptable to the Federal Equal Employment Opportunity Commission. The Prudential now requires that a prospective sales representative pass the required state licensing examinations prior to appointment. Starting April 1, 1988, new representatives will be required to pass the National Association of Securities Dealers (NASD) examination, since so many life insurance products have investment elements regulated by the Securities and Exchange Commission.

These steps help ensure that customers will have a representative who understands current products, who has demonstrated the ability to provide reliable financial advice, and who can therefore be trusted to propose appropriate solutions to a customer's financial service needs.

## Training

Training material is internally developed and is directed to the new employee and to teaching existing employees about new Prudential products and services. Extensive use is made of audio-visual material; every one of the seven hundred sales and service offices, as well as all operations centers, are equipped to use AV material for training and role playing.

Some of the more interesting applications are: (1) a trademarked financial security selling system, which includes sales presentation materials for customers and prospects; (2) precontract product training for prospective representatives, often including observer participation in the prospecting and sales process; and (3) a commitment to providing training material about new products and services in a timely manner to keep employees and representatives knowledgeable and able to assist customers.

Customers expect to deal with Prudential people who are familiar with company products and services, or who can quickly refer them to someone who is, if they are not. The training programs are designed to eliminate any gap between customer expectation and employee performance.

## Continuing Education

For at least the past forty years, the company has acted on the belief that it must encourage and help employees and representatives to understand the nature of financial services, not just to be knowledgeable about their particular current duties. Employees and representatives are reimbursed for the successful completion of undergraduate and graduate study related to the business in particular or management skills in general.

Employees throughout the organization are encouraged to complete specialty insurance-related examinations (actuarial, chartered life underwriter, chartered financial consultant, chartered property/casualty underwriter, claim theory, data processing, Life Management Institute, life underwriting, etc.) irrespective of the nature of an employee's assignment. They are reimbursed for the cost of examination fees and study materials for successfully completed examinations. In addition, they receive supplementary cash awards for completing specified series of examinations. There are annual education achievement recognition events held throughout The Prudential to which successful employees and their managers are invited.

The percentage of Prudential employees who are studying or have completed one or more of these courses has been significantly above the industry average. The Prudential's customers benefit from dealing with an organization in which a higher percentage of employees are voluntarily maintaining and improving their understanding of financial services products.

## Creative Use of Information Technologies

The strategic use of new information technologies is another key link in service delivery system. The strategic use of new technologies is a Prudential enterprise goal. Every major subsidiary, operating center, and corporate department has a designated Information Systems Executive (ISE) who reports dually to the regional or subsidiary president or corporate department head and the senior vice president in charge of information systems research and support. Annual reviews are conducted on how such tools can be used for competitive purposes and how competitors are adapting them.

The uniform automation of customer records was completed by the late 1960s. Status information can be obtained for all product lines via the Field Office Communication System (FOCUS); and virtually all of these are accessible by field office service assistants. Most common transactions can be entered via terminals in local offices for nightly batch processing by separate product-line support systems.

Field representatives are encouraged to buy point-of-sale computers; 60% of the representatives have already done so. These computer's enable representatives to prepare sales illustrations in a customer's home or place of business, thanks to Prudential-developed applications and proprietary software. This has significantly reduced the time it takes to answer a client's questions while greatly increasing the accuracy and reliability of the answers given.

Premium quotations for the full range of products are computerized. This benefits clients by reduced error rates that are inevitable when depending on manual calculations and an extensive line of products. This also avoids the unpleasant surprise for customers should a representative happen to understate the cost of a product or service.

A client database system that interconnects all individual insurance contract records at the client and family level is in the implementation stage. This will enable representatives to deliver comprehensive, and current client reviews when they choose to or when a client requests it.

Over sixty million computer-prepared communications annually from a dozen separate systems are produced. There are about three hundred different outputs in five generic designs, ranging in volume from the twelve million nonmonthly life insurance premium notices produced annually to letters produced only three times a day. In order to make them customer-friendly, all these communications are being systematically redesigned and reworded to avoid words requiring more than an eighth-grade reading-comprehension level.

Recent customer satisfaction surveys indicate at least a ten-point increase in the percentage who find the redesigned communications very easy to understand. As of the end of 1987, half of the communications have been redesigned.

## Accessibility to Customers

As stated earlier, local representatives and his or her local office form the heart of the service delivery system. That office's address and telephone number appear on virtually all computer-prepared documents, so that the customer has a telephone number to call or an address to write to or visit. If a service center is the one to contact, then its address and telephone number are substituted. An agency database system is also being installed that will incorporate the name and telephone number of the customer's personal servicing representative on computer-prepared outputs.

Seven hundred sales and service offices are interconnected electronically. Each can obtain limited information about the current status of contracts being serviced by another office and, so, can be of assistance to customers who contact them instead. Each can also forward service requests electronically to the appropriate service office for action.

Eight-hundred numbers are available for specific purposes, such as the transfer of funds between investment accounts; for reporting property and casualty claims; and in conjunction with certain targeted direct mail sales campaigns. These toll free numbers will continue to be used selectively, since questions should be answered by a customer's personal representative. Collect calls are accepted without question.

## Service and Quality Measurement

Systems are designed first and foremost to enable supervision and management to help improve employee performance and to spot potential bottlenecks or problems. Secondarily, systems are designed to detect possible financial manipulation or fraud.

Time service on specific transactions (such as new issues, claim payments, cash surrenders, dividend withdrawals, etc.) has been measured on a calendar day basis for twenty-five years. Within each business line (life, health, auto, home, etc.), the number of calendar days it takes to complete specific transactions are measured. Single-handling (transactions which can be answered upon initial receipt of the request) and multiple-handling transactions (which require additional contact with the customer or the representative) are monitored. Quarterly service performance goals are established one year at a time in advance, and the performances of major organizations, divisions, and offices are measured and reported monthly. (Service results are never averaged over a period of more than three months.)

To avoid unproductive and economically unjustified interoffice competition, a standard of excellence for single-handling measures was established and does not show the actual numerical performance level once the standard is achieved. Service performance versus objectives is considered in management compensation decisions.

Another important element of service measurement is an aging feature built into the product line support systems. Transactions that are blocked (because something else must happen first) are held mechanically and aged. The responsible processing area is alerted so that the requested service is not overlooked.

## Service Quality

The sales representatives are compensated for service as well as sales activities. They receive a percentage of the premiums and considerations paid on contracts for which they have servicing responsibility. They are also able to earn additional compensation based upon the longevity of new sales, an excellent measure of customer satisfaction. A representative's eligibility to attend a sales conference is also linked to the longevity of his business as compared to the standard for his area or region. Salespersons receive commissions or replacement sales subject to standard rules.

A continuous desk quality review system administered by supervisors is in place at the regional and specialized service centers. A valid sample of completed work is selected and reviewed. The employee is assisted and counseled when the handling of a particular service request was incomplete or incorrect, or when a written explanation was inadequate. Valid customer complaints involving that employee are also part of this desk quality approach. Periodic organizational reviews are conducted by the internal auditing or corporate systems staff to verify compliance with financial and document control guidelines as well as the rules for resolving disputes and misunderstandings. The real purpose is to ensure consistency of decision making.

A companywide system for recording and analyzing complaints is in place. Briefs are prepared for all closed cases based on the model Unfair Trade Practice bill enacted by the National Association of Insurance Commissioners. Monthly service performance reports with hierarchical summary data are produced at the division and field office levels. The coding system separately identifies executive, formal, media, and regulatory complaints and indicates whether the complaint was valid or invalid (people did exactly what they should have, and the contract language or operating policy caused the complaint). The analysis of invalid complaints has helped modify policies and improve contractual language.

Some state insurance commissioners develop complaint ratios (generally the number per million dollars of premium income) as one tool in monitoring market conduct. The Prudential calculates its own ratios (by state and line of business) in accordance with the NAIC model bill; and monitors their movement to further improve performance and identify localized problems that might not otherwise have surfaced. There are also built-in verification routines to monitor combinations of events where financial manipulation can occur. The selection criteria are changed from time to time by the internal auditors, and reports of results are made to the board of directors' audit committee. The customer service purpose of this is clear: to make sure that insurance proceeds are in fact received by the contract owner or claimant.

## Recognition for Superior Performance

Superior performance by individual sales representatives and sales management has been recognized for many years. While qualification requirements are based primarily on sales results, policy longevity is also a qualification factor. Leading sales offices are also recognized at special evening events, to which the entire sales and service staffs are invited together with spouses or friends. The competition to qualify for this recognition is intense.

In January 1988, a quality service leaders program was introduced for the forty thousand or so nonmanagement staff of the individual insurance area. The program will select and honor those individuals who take the time to understand customer needs and respond in a knowledgeable, caring way to let people know they are important. This plan has five major features.

First, the nomination process is open. Second, nominees must be endorsed by their immediate manager as models of giving above-and-beyond service. They must meet all job requirements and have an absence of valid complaints. Third, first-time nominees receive a small gift that has recognition and utility. Fourth, up to 7% of an area's staff is eligible for a monthly award. Winners will be recognized in company publications and have a choice of a gift from a catalog. Fifth, twenty-one of the monthly winners will be selected quarterly to travel to the corporate office, meet with the president and key officers, and attend a Broadway play. This program will help motivate employees to exceed customers' service expectations.

Late in 1987, a new program—*Prudential Partners in Community Service Awards*—was announced to recognize sales representatives who have provided outstanding volunteer service in their communities. Grants of up to $1,875 (Prudential's founding year) can be made to individual organizations designated by the representative. This, too, represents an important element of quality service.

## Customer Satisfaction Monitoring

The baseline public attitude studies conducted annually since 1968 by the American Council of Life Insurance have provided very useful data. Employees regularly use that data as part of customer satisfaction monitoring.

Prudential began conducting its own general attitude studies in 1975 and have repeated them every three to five years. Questions having to do with the quality of service and communications, as well as accessibility, are included. The movement of those measures is closely monitored.

Prudential also participates in national surveys conducted by outside organizations to measure customers' satisfaction with service, as well as the satisfaction of the customers of key competitors.

Surveys are conducted among new and recent buyers of new products and periodically Prudential surveys customers who dropped their policies to pinpoint causes and develop remedies.

Claim satisfaction surveys began soon after the inception of the Property Casualty division in 1970. The claim satisfaction surveys now also measure results based on *Consumer Report's* measurement methodology. Surveys of satisfaction with back office activity (endorsements, relocations, etc.) were begun about ten years ago.

## SUMMARY

The Prudential's individual insurance area is committed to delivering quality and personal service and to fulfilling the promise of making the customers' experience of service exceed their expectations. To that end, Prudential is working with an outside consultant to review and sharpen their tools and measures. They expect by 1990 to have in place an integrated service measurement system that is actually driven by customer satisfaction. It is their expectation that individual offices and service units will know how well they are doing in exceeding customer service expectations in the areas of greatest importance to them. The goal is consistently to do the best job in the industry of succeeding in those daily moments of truth—when they have the opportunity to excel.

# Service Quality: Nothing New Under the Sun

**Len Sparks**
The Travelers Corporation

James G. Batterson introduced the British concept of accident insurance to America on April 1, 1864 when The Travelers officially opened for business. Today, The Travelers Corporation is one of the world's largest multiline insurance, financial, and health service institutions with 37,000 employees. Its headquarters are in Hartford, Connecticut.

## INTRODUCTION

The maxim from Ecclesiastes "There is nothing new under the sun" carries a message that is related to the issue of quality service: the *basics* have been with us since the beginning and will not change. There remains, however, the challenge to be innovative and creative in applying those basic principles. For example, close customer contact is not new. The *way* organizations enhance customer relationships, however, can be something new under the sun. In this chapter, service quality at The Travelers will be examined from this perspective.

Traditionally, like most major multiline insurance companies, Travelers organized its operations according to product-line markets. With advancements in technology and new multiple-line marketing concepts, the opportunity for change presented itself. In February 1985, chairman Edward H. Budd launched a significant companywide reorganization to focus on customer markets. The main objective was to group product lines according to targeted purchasers of products.

This realignment resulted in the formation of three major business groups: agency marketing, national accounts, and business diversification. Each business group is responsible for marketing and service strategy according to the customer base it serves. In addition to the major business groups, there are corporate infrastructures: the finance, communication, and information processing group, the investment group, corporate personnel administration, and the law department. Before turning to concentrate on the service organizations within the different groups, one needs a brief look at the customer service philosophy of The Travelers.

## TRAVELERS SERVICE PHILOSOPHY

In the financial service industry there are no patents. A unique and innovative product successfully brought to market is easily and swiftly imitated by competitors. It is a competitive environment where companies have little product difference and limited price variation. The customer with a fistful of dollars has a choice of where to do business. Clearly, the differentiation must come from superior service. No question about it, customer satisfaction is the bottom-line measure of success (or failure). The reverse is also true: profitability and business success are the best measures of customer satisfaction. The Travelers has always placed great emphasis on quality service.

In April 1987, chairman Budd commissioned a customer service planning team composed of six people representing a cross section of the company's businesses. The team was charged with assessing the current competitive environment, developing a mission and vision, and recommending specific actions. With Ecclesiastes' message in mind, the intent was not to change basic principles but to suggest a direction or methodology that would enhance service quality. The mission statement developed by the team and expressed by chairman Budd issues the challenge to all Travelers people to "execute throughout The Travelers a level of service which is competitively superior in meeting our customers' expectations as we strive to be a profitable market leader in each of our businesses."

The most critical (and challenging) task for Travelers people is defining their *customer*. In applying concepts of quality service, they could easily think of the customer only as a purchaser of a product. While this is true in defining ultimate or external customer, a broader scope is needed to fulfill their mission challenge. A definition of the *customer* at The Travelers is *the beneficiary of effort expended by any individual or group*.

This definition incorporates an internal customer concept that includes two relationships. The first is the relationship to an employee as a purchaser of company products. The second is the interaction between individuals and departments within the company. The company's executive vice president and chief financial officer summed it up: "We have to treat ourselves like customers. There's not a single person at The Travelers who doesn't have a *customer* relationship."

The basic principle of customer contact has always been and will continue to be an integral part of the company's quality service. Most service companies have creative ways of "putting a face" on the corporation by establishing a closer relationship with their customers. One of the more widely used innovations is the toll-free 800-number phone system. The Travelers has various 800 numbers available for specific customer groups, products, and claims.

In a large and diverse company such as The Travelers, different business groups operate somewhat independently. The following discussion reviews a cross section of the quality service efforts within each of its business groups.

## AGENCY MARKETING GROUP

The ultimate customers of the agency marketing group are individuals and small business owners. Products target-marketed to these groups include financial services (life, accident, health insurance; annuity and retirement plans; financial planning) and property-casualty (auto, homeowners, and property insurance) for personal and commercial coverage.

Sales and service for these products are provided by a nationwide network of independent agents who represent different companies. Since they can place business with a company of choice, independent agents represent another species of Travelers customer. A number of field locations support the agents within a geographic region. At the home office in Hartford, Connecticut various departments within the agency marketing group provide service to the tri-level customer base: the agent, the field office, and the purchaser or the purchaser's representative.

## Financial Services

A second vice-president serves as the quality service officer in the financial services department. His bottom-line responsibility is to make sure that service efforts are in line with customer expectations. According to him, the key areas in which financial services units aim to deliver quality service are customer contact, the measurement of internal transactions, and the tracking of performance standards.

A centralized service unit utilizing the toll-free 800-number concept was recently established in the financial services department for life and health insurance customers (agents and purchasers). The primary purpose was to give customers easy access to a central home-office service area that would provide consistency and timeliness of response. The end result will be improved quality of service.

Customer service management are intent to go beyond *providing* quality service to *insuring* quality service. How does one insure quality service? In the customer service unit, the answer involves performance standards, internal monitoring, customer feedback, training, and communication. Various report items generated by the phone system are used by management to establish standards or benchmarks for the evaluation of customer service representative performance. There are benchmarks associated with the average number of phone calls per day that can reasonably be handled by each representative; the speed of answering, with an average of no more than thirty seconds on hold; the length of each call; an evaluation of phone lines and equipment; and the assessment of specific training needs by reviewing the types of calls. A mechanism to monitor actual calls provides essential feedback on the quality of their content. Random observations by supervisors permit immediate informative and/or corrective contacts with representatives as necessary.

As a team, the customer service representatives have decided to do some monitoring of their own. With appropriate agreement from the customer, they record certain phone conversations for use in group discussion meetings. Also, supervisors share customer feedback letters, both positive and negative, in a group discussion session. This self-evaluation process provides the critical feedback essential for quality improvement. In addition to internal feedback, representatives will periodically call recent users of the 800 number and solicit their input on service quality.

The issue of training is taken very seriously. All new customer service representatives go through two months of training before getting on the phone. During this period, they are exposed to the financial services organization, products, and the transaction process, as well as to telephone skills and procedures. The feedback items described above, coupled with monthly reviews with allied process units, are the main determinants of content for ongoing training. A daily bulletin keeps representatives informed of changes and timely topics while more in-depth needs are addressed by classroom training. With all these elements in place and working properly, the customer service unit can insure quality service.

An important phase of the sales process is life and health insurance underwriting. Quality service to the sales force is essential for building a strong customer relationship. The promptness, accuracy, and professionalism of the underwriting of insurance applications are constantly scrutinized. A secretary in the financial services underwriting division is responsible for new business and the measurement of service quality. A number of service standards have been established for the time it takes to underwrite and issue life insurance, hospital and disability insurance contracts.

Several computer-produced reports have been developed to help achieve and monitor quality service goals. Together, these reports provide detailed information on time service results, production figures, and backlog statistics. The Time Service Study—New Business report provides complete data on the processing of all applications for insurance; it is essential for the measurement of service levels. Produced monthly, it contains the numbers, percentages, and average days for applications processed in various time frames. The report displays five time categories: set-up time, underwriting time, system time issue time and total time. Total time is measured from the date when the application is received to the date when the policy is mailed to the agent for delivery to the purchaser. Each of the five time categories has specific goals associated with it and contributes directly to the achievement of total processing goals. The total time is the primary measurement of the service goals for underwriting.

In addition to the time service reports, information is gathered and maintained on the production by underwriters and policy-issue support staff. Reports enable management to assess production expectations and to manage shifts in business. A daily backlog report helps determine how much business is coming in and what the workload status is in each processing area.

The amount of data produced is done so with minimal input; consequently, service times are not hindered by excessive number-crunching efforts. Weak links in the processing flow are easily identified, and corrective actions taken immediately. The measurement process has enabled the financial services underwriting division to meet and exceed service quality goals consistently, identify training needs better, and recognize individual production and achievement.

## Property-Casualty Department

The property-casualty department of the agency marketing group provides property insurance for personal (individual) and commercial (small-business owner) customers. The products for personal and commercial lines include automobile, homeowners, and business property coverage. These products are marketed and serviced through the independent-agent network (mentioned earlier). By the very nature of the business, there are a large number of transactions per policy, in contrast with those associated with life and health insurance products. To accommodate the processing volume associated with this activity, fifteen service centers are located in various parts of the country. In 1985, customer service units were established in each center to provide a central easy-access location for the independent agent as customer. Each unit has a toll-free 800-number system for agents in their geographic region.

As with all 800-number systems, various reports with different degrees of information are produced to measure phone activity in the customer service unit network. Certain standards have been set to maintain consistency for all units. A manager of the field operations in Hartford oversees the service quality of the network. This manager compiles and analyzes the statistics weekly, then provides customer service management with feedback on quality.

The property-casualty department defines *quality* as *the sum of Teamwork, Expediency, Accuracy and Motivation, supported by People and multiplied by Customer Commitment*—expressed in the graphic formula:

$$Q = \frac{\Sigma\ T + E + A + M \quad C^2}{P}$$

According to the network manager, "Quality service is not *part* of our business, it *is* our business." Property-casualty customer service representatives, since they interact with agents who are technically familiar with the business, must have a high degree of technical competence as well as good interpersonal skills. Each service team must be strong, self-policing units where peer pressure sets and maintains quality standards for the group.

The supervisor of a customer service unit in the Richmond, Virginia service center keeps tracks of specific data from phone system reports. This, coupled with *monitoring* calls (by walking around), help this supervisor keep the team at the top of the quality scale. Are the methods new? No, they are creative extensions of basic principles. To generate an acceptable level of confidence in their service, all individuals must share their knowledge and experience with the whole team. Communication is an essential basic. The supervisor challenges the team members to educate each other through informal training and motivation.

The result has been a true team effort in producing training material, *homegrown* posters, inspirational sayings, and an overall turning of negatives into positives. Through all this the supervisor sees her role as that of a coach who keeps the team upbeat, reduces stress, promotes interaction, and provides direction and constructive feedback. Customer service representatives survey agents informally and periodically to determine how satisfied the agents are with responses to specific service requests. The agents' answers help the team to evaluate practices and to align their service delivery with the expectations of the agents as customers. The team is in control: service quality is up to them.

If you were to play word association using *insurance*, a typical response would be *claim*. So, claim departments signify much more to an insurance company than cost centers alone. A reputation for quality of claim service goes a long way in retaining customers and generating new business. The agency marketing group's property-casualty claim department looks inward, asking *Why* and *What if* questions to make an honest assessment of how it is (or is not) meeting customer needs. The goal of closing the gap between customer expectations and practical reality was instituted under the banner of *Achieving Claim Excellence* or (ACE). The basic premises of ACE are to view quality service from the customer's perspective and to act on meeting the customer's needs.

Over the years, rapid advances have been made in the auto industry with new sophisticated products. When you add concurrent advances in medical technology and federal and state legislation, you have the basic factors impacting claim operations and service. Changes in auto-damage claim service became a necessity for survival. The assistant director, in the auto-damage claim unit has seen a "shift from serving only our needs to serving the needs of our customer-who may be the insured, the agent, marketing, or ourselves."

Many of the fifty-five claim offices located throughout the country have established customer service units. Their purpose is to handle initial claim contact in such a way that the individual insured knows what to expect. They are, in essence, removing the unknown and also making sure the customer does not get bogged down in a lot of the behind-the-scenes detail. After all, bottom-line concerns of the customer are When? and How much? Each claim office looks at its own particular service situation and allocates its resources according to customer convenience.

In the area of technology, innovations to improve quality are beginning to take hold. Some claim locations are using an auto appraisal system that assists the expert in making routine damage-estimate decisions. Another advancement is *tele-estimating*, a system that electronically links an appraiser with a claim office, and eliminates the back-and-forth mailing of appraisals and approvals.

Measurement is essential to ACE. Claim experts in each office physically review the closed claim files to determine whether the handling met, exceeded, or fell below standards for customer satisfaction and cost containment. If the processing is identified as substandard, it will be noted as a *missed opportunity*. After the countrywide review of closed claims is complete, claim managers draft proposals on ways to improve handling in their offices. Since opportunities for improvement vary by claim, they try to find solutions tailored to the particular needs in each office. Individual performance is measured through an employee appraisal review process that assesses actuality against espoused service goals. In addition, questionnaires are periodically sent to customers (claimants, agents) to solicit their input on the quality of service for specific claims.

If people say that Travelers property-casualty claim unit is the best in the business, the unit's assistant director asks, "By whose standard or perception? The assessment is gratifying only if it comes from our customer." In the land of poor quality, mediocrity is king. By viewing each claim as an opportunity to help, to remove fear, or to project a positive company image, the property-casualty claim department aspires to go beyond mediocrity and to achieve claim excellence.

In agency marketing, quality service efforts are never ending. Program becomes process; training becomes learning; a group becomes a team; and customer dedication becomes a standard value in action.

## NATIONAL ACCOUNTS GROUP

The customers of the national accounts group are small- to large-sized businesses and organizations. They might be purchasers of insurance to cover business liabilities or sponsors of benefits for people having a defined relationship with the business or organization. A typical example would be employer-employee groups. The national accounts group meets customer needs with products and services for property-casualty coverage, employee benefits, and pension management.

### Employee Benefits Division: Claims

In the employee benefits division, quality service can mean prompt, accurate life and health insurance claim processing. A critical front-end element is the determination of eligibility for coverage. Group sponsors or contract holders provide The Travelers with initial-participant census data at the time of sale and with periodic updates. The employee benefits division have been servicing about fifteen hundred contract holders who have anywhere from fifty to fifty thousand employees, so they have to be flexible in their format requirements; their rule is to make it easy for the customer. As a result, the eligibility data systems unit receives participant information in a variety of formats.

The basic submission will usually be hard-copy output for small-to-large group customers and magnetic tape for some larger group customers. Hard-copy data are input to the claim payment system on-line. A quality assurance unit audits a random sample of input by each operator and produces an accuracy report. The acceptable error-rate standard, based on volume input, is 5%. When the error rate rises above the standard, management reviews such items as group case complexity, volumes, and the newness of the operator to determine staffing or training needs. The current level of accuracy is 98%.

When a customer provides magnetic-tape information files, *translation rules* are applied to conform data for input to claim systems. Then the tapes are run against a nonproduction look-alike claim system to determine acceptability. Any errors from the *scrub-run* are evaluated as critical or noncritical. Critical items are defined as those detrimental to the establishment of eligibility and are addressed immediately. All others are passed over to the claim system and are corrected later. The main emphasis is on getting a large volume of information processed quickly and with a high degree of accuracy.

Quality control does not end here. Listings of employee data are referred back to the customer-employers for their review. This is important feedback for making sure the company's interpretation of their information is correct. Also, any input errors not detected earlier may surface. Massive amounts of information are turned over and updated constantly to maintain a process-ready claim system. Sometimes claim processing is hindered by insufficient employee data. Field claim representatives file discrepancy reports. Each report is researched; discrepancies are corrected; and an appropriate response is made to the field. All reports are tracked to identify trends or any unusual number of problems associated with one particular customer.

Finally, home office employee benefits analysts plan face-to-face visits with their customers throughout the year. This interaction provides personal-touch feedback to let them know how they are doing. It does not take long to find out, to accept the praise or to correct any problems swiftly, and to maintain good customer relations.

The employee benefits claim department looks at functions in terms of *customer deliverables*. A recently developed manual on standards of performance identifies elements associated with the delivery of quality service. Each deliverable is defined in terms of the end-service result, the customer or recipient, the related internal-process steps, and the overall standard of measurement. In practice, applying standards of performance makes each task goal-oriented in terms of timeliness and accuracy.

Of course, the standards for delivery must meet or exceed customer expectations. In addition to detailed internal productivity reports, home office claim people continually communicate with claim field staff as well as employers and benefit recipients to assess customer satisfaction. The director of product support echoes the thought that, although they go to great lengths to audit their performance, it is the customer who really determines how well (or poorly) they do. If they feel it necessary, a customer-employer can conduct an independent audit of claim processing.

One of the new innovations in recent years has been the *performance guarantee*. With the employee benefit claim unit, some employers have negotiated performance guarantee arrangements. These contractual agreements guarantee a specified dollar accuracy rate for claim payments. The rate is determined by dividing the dollar amount paid accurately by the total dollars paid over a designated period of time. The terms of the performance guarantee contract usually provide for monetary adjustments and/or incentives based on the actual claim performance in relation to the dollar accuracy rate. Striking a critical balance between timeliness and accuracy is a key goal for claim processing. The customer must be confident in The Travelers ability to act swiftly and decisively.

### Employee Benefits Division: Accounting

The billing and collection of customer deposits present an equally visible service contact with employee benefits group customers. Specialized premium accounting units work closely with group plan underwriters in establishing new business, updates and rate changes. They also deal with customers on billing matters. It becomes a complex process of coordinating and balancing customer inquiries; problem solving; and updating data on employee census statements, rates, and products. While they keep a watchful eye on quality, timeliness is their prime concern.

Since the function involves money deposits, regular audits of procedures are conducted by independent auditors. The auditors, along with departmental management, develop practical performance standards that meet legal and business requirements. To make sure that actual performance aligns with standards and goals, status reports are prepared and analyzed weekly. Items in the unit more than a certain number of days are scrutinized to find out why, and every attempt is made to resolve the cause of the problem immediately. With all the benefits and implications associated with the heavy dependence on technology of on-line systems and a paperless environment, data processing downtime is kept to a minimum. Needless to say, this is a priority performance measure.

Service areas within accounting provide contact points for customers, (contract holders, agents, and field office staff). Any discrepancy brought out through customer contact is researched and responded to promptly. Training in the areas of telephone and letter-writing skills is ongoing. For written responses, automated selective paragraphs are used to assure standard wording without sacrificing personalization. Outgoing letters are spot checked for quality.

Employee involvement is very important to quality service. The company cannot afford to overlook processors in their automation and procedure efforts, because everyone must be involved in job improvement.

### Asset Management and Pension Services

As with other departments in the national accounts group, asset management and pension services has a written manual on standards of performance. General communication standards are outlined in the beginning for telephone contacts, written inquiries, complaints and internal processing. Each section then addresses timeliness standards for functional organizations, including new business and marketing, field operations, financial reporting, support, and client services.

In client services, accuracy is also essential for such varied activities as the actuarial valuation of pension plans, contract drafting, and benefit payments. A series of checks and balances assures that a quality *product* is delivered to the customer. They place strong emphasis on *zero defects*: although the concept has been around for some time, there is no clearer, simpler message in the world of quality than zero defects.

Balancing accuracy, timeliness, and productivity requires strict standards for quality; everyone knows what is expected of them. Client services staff use feedback from customers and field staff, peer review of work, and complaint analysis in order to assist in quality improvements. The open and honest exchange of information is important to this effort. Individual performance is reviewed against standards and job descriptions on a monthly basis.

Training is a recognized need in the pension business. New people in client services go through a stringent orientation to the business and their specialty (underwriting, actuarial, etc.). There is also constant activity to upgrade and retrain people as they progress through their careers. In summary, the national accounts group's quality efforts hinge on standards of performance for every function, whether that function involves external or internal customers. Publication is only the first step; follow-through and action make the difference in putting together a winning team.

## BUSINESS DIVERSIFICATION GROUP

One of the fastest-growing markets for financial services is the middle-income customer. A primary objective of the business diversification group is the innovative mass marketing of Travelers products. The group's strategy is the distribution of financial services to middle-income customers at the workplace and through association memberships. Consequently, customers include corporate sponsors and their employees.

A new initiative of the business diversification group is the delivery of a uniquely integrated financial services package to customers at their workplace through an employer-sponsored plan called MoneyTrac. MoneyTrac offers a full range of banking, investment, credit, mortgage, insurance, and financial-planning products. The key to MoneyTrac's success is the ability to provide customers with convenient and superior one-stop customer service for a wide range of financial service products. Continually striving to be a world-class customer service provider, The Travelers expect, by these efforts, to rise above the competition.

A MoneyTrac customer service center was established to provide a central and easily accessible customer-contact area for transactions and inquiries relating to any of the wide range of financial service products provided. The center is staffed by customer service representatives hooked up to a single 800-number system. Customers have the option of dialing into an automated response unit (ARU) for computer voice-generated information on current banking products, interest rates, account balances, and recent transaction status—twenty-four hours a day, seven days a week. They can switch out of the ARU to a person on duty or they can call the center directly.

Since the MoneyTrac staff operate in a highly competitive service environment, their customers must feel confident in the way their business is handled. It all begins with the selection of service people who will be in direct contact with the customer. High selection standards help recruit the right people for the job. An in-depth training effort begins to shape their interpersonal and technical skills.

The phone standards set for the customer service representatives include answering every call in two rings, leaving no call on hold longer than thirty seconds, and making a minimum number of calls per representative. If a situation requires a call-back, that should be accomplished within two hours. The suggested standard for the average length of call is four minutes. This is separate from definitive standards; it is suggested as a guide so that necessary service needs are not impeded. All phone standards are measured against performance by using daily reports from the telephone system.

In the MoneyTrac service center, there exists another dimension of quality customer service: referral calls and tracking. They cannot entirely avoid the need to transfer a customer's request to another organization for response or as a part of the process. When doing this, they must maintain a vital link between the customer and themselves. The Customer Analysis and Tracking System (CATS) captures and maintains the information input by service representatives. Besides trend and request analysis, the system will track customer transactions or inquiries referred to another area for banking, insurance, or mortgage services. Valuable information is provided for open requests and response time. In this way, management can effectively measure service levels from receipt to resolution.

MoneyTrac service presents a real challenge. Customers are offered a centralized point of contact for all financial services, presenting the need for a creative unity of people and technology. For the most part, it is a behavioral change for the customer in the way of doing business. A customer must feel confident when using an automatic teller machine, Automated Response Unit, 800—service number or other methods. The personalization of service, with the customer service representative as focal point becomes even more important. The selection and training of these people must be in line with high service quality objectives. It is essential that performance be measured against the objectives. MoneyTrac has specific service-task job descriptions that, along with defined standards, provide measurement tools to assure a level of competence that meets customer expectations.

# CONCLUSION

## Corporate Infrastructures

As stated earlier, a number of corporate infrastructures support the business operations of the company. These structures include finance, communication, information processing, investments, law, and personnel administration. Each organization has adopted the concept that the people it supports throughout the corporation are its customers. This becomes evident in information processing (technology systems) where the term *user*, to denote people for whom a computer system is designed and/or maintained, has been changed to *customer*. Once you say you have *customers*, everything changes. All associated quality measurements and concepts must be applied to the service provided.

This chapter, has attempted to show how different organizations within The Travelers approach quality service by means of enhancing the basics and of creating something new under the sun. When you look at the company as a whole, certain common elements of quality service become evident: customer service strategy, training and communication, the use of technology, teamwork and involvement, the selection of people, leadership, and standards and measurement. These major efforts within The Travelers are making a new impact on quality service.

Travelers *innovation through involvement* process is a quality-circle concept that gives people the opportunity to have a say about how their work is to be accomplished. There are many such groups in the different areas of the company, and they are resolving quality issues with a great deal of success. The process brings leaders and workers closer together in solving business problems. Training programs underway at the business group and corporate levels contain a service focus. Specific training efforts address key interpersonal and technical skills. A new employee appraisal system closely links individual performance with organizational goals and objectives. Defined strategies for service and technology have been developed and are being communicated across company lines. There is a lot left to do at the Travelers, but commitment to quality service for *customers* stands at the forefront of the corporate mission.

The need to meet and exceed customer expectations cannot be overemphasized. In a competitive financial service market, how do consumers make a choice? You can be sure that a primary factor in customer loyalty is satisfaction with service. New customers consider the reputation of a company and the service experiences of others. The measure of The Travelers success is the *customer's* perception of quality in the service they receive. The final measure of customer perception depends on the votes that they make in the marketplace to continue and to expand the business they do with The Travelers.

# Metals

Reynolds Metals Company
R. J. Hickerson, Jr.

# Service Quality at Reynolds Metals Company

**R. J. Hickerson, Jr.**
Reynolds Metals Company

Reynolds Metals Company was founded in 1919 as U.S. Foil Incorporated and changed its name to the present in 1928. It is involved in the development of mineral and real estate properties, is a leader in aluminum recycling, and produces base materials which it sells as well as fabricates into products. Reynolds' 25,000 employees are headquartered in Richmond, Virginia.

## CORPORATE QUALITY ASSURANCE DEPARTMENT

In these very competitive times the company that can deliver products to customers on time and within specification will be the company that succeeds in the marketplace. Top quality and customer service are the factors that differentiate the superior company from the merely ordinary one. Quality is hardly a new fad at Reynolds: a corporate quality assurance department was formed in 1970 when the company established operating divisions along functional product lines and staff service units. Personnel for the new quality department were drawn from distinct backgrounds in manufacturing, sales and marketing, accounting, and product development.

The first order of business was to establish a working policy to govern all future activities. Over the years this policy has changed very little, and today it remains the foundation for the company's quality activities. It reads:

Every Reynolds employee has a responsibility to produce products or render services that meet our customers' expectations. No one has the right to accept or ship an unsatisfactory product.

Our products and services must conform to their requirements, as expressed in a specification with measurable characteristics, and exemplify pride in workmanship. They must be reliable, offered at a reasonable cost and delivered on time. Reynolds' objective is to be the quality leader in everything we do.

The company realized, of course, that a policy was not a program and that good intentions were not a substitute for good results. To get started, it developed a charter of responsibilities for the corporate quality assurance department and a number of quality procedures. It identified eighteen key areas, such as records maintenance, purchasing, control and acceptance, process control, quality auditing and similar functions. It published a corporate manual that outlines the guidelines in each area. This manual defines *what* must be done. The operating divisions and service groups must then define *how* they will carry out the policy and *who* will do the work.

When management began to work with the operating divisions and staff departments to establish these new procedures, they met a certain amount of resistance. There were hundreds of quality control inspectors and this new group was preaching, make it right the first time and you don't have to worry at the end of the line. Management found that they were not making much of an impression. What was lacking was a total understanding on the part of the operations people about the degree of commitment from top management. Also, they found that the audit program did not take into consideration the finer points of production operation. Management knew that they were not on the right track, but were not precisely sure what the right track was.

About 1980 or so, America woke up to the question of *quality*, and the media were full of reports on how this country was falling behind foreign competitors in the ability to manufacture reliable and satisfactory products.

Reynolds management decided that, while their quality assurance programs were adequate, they did not bring forth the kind of total commitment necessary to be a superior company in a very competitive industry. Consequently, a program was established to bring the weight of the entire organization to bear on quality performance in every area of the company.

The senior management determined that Reynolds would be *the* quality company in the aluminum industry. The position of vice president of corporate quality assurance was created to get top management involved in quality programs on a regular basis. The corporate quality assurance charter was rewritten to give the corporate quality assurance department not only the *responsibility* for quality improvement programs but also the *authority* to make the programs work.

## CORPORATE COMMUNICATIONS PROGRAM

A dynamic corporate communications program was established to ensure that every employee in the company was aware that improved quality was a top priority. Management was determined to train people and to make sure that people knew what their responsibilities were.

The need for statistical quality control and statistical process control was determined, and plans were developed to install these procedures. The quality assurance department was directed to develop quality objectives that would measure results. At the same time, sufficient funds were allocated to make sure that the new programs could be accomplished. It was obvious that there was much work to be done. The 200-page corporate quality assurance manual was completely rewritten in terms that anyone with the proper training could understand. Division support manuals were rewritten along the same lines. With this strong management structure and appropriate tools in place, the companywide communications program was launched to deepen the involvement and participation of everyone in the company, from senior management to the newest employee. A concomitant program directed at Reynolds' suppliers was also developed to make sure that those who sold goods and services to the company were part of the program. The programs continue today with three major objectives:

1. To create awareness and understanding of quality as a priority corporate trust.
2. To motivate people to provide the highest quality products.
3. To encourage and recognize the highest quality from our suppliers.

The communications program was launched by top executives with the introduction of the company's new quality logo and the slogan *our quality shines through*. This program is still in effect today.

## THE GRID SYSTEM OF PERFORMANCE MEASUREMENT

As the enhanced quality procedures evolved, the position of vice president of corporate quality assurance was expanded to include responsibility for the company's technological operations. This synergistic approach blends the research, development, and engineering functions to support the company's renewed focus on quality, and adds an important degree of credibility to company efforts.

An annual quality awards competition was inaugurated to maintain employee interest and involvement. The Chairman's Award for Quality is presented to a plant in each of three categories, based on the size of the plants; also to one service department, and to the operating division that has achieved the most outstanding quality performance for the previous year. Initially, each division, plant, and participating service department has specific quality objectives. A grid system is used for setting objectives and measuring performance, with each criterion or objective assigned a numerical value. Total points for all objectives must be one hundred, although all are not weighed evenly, since some objectives are necessarily more valuable than others.

The grid defines specific levels of performance and has a built-in method for evaluating and measuring performance. Each objective is quantified, and a minimum acceptable level, as well as an ultimate goal, is established using current performance as a benchmark. The grid can be used to measure future performance against objectives, and the highest total number of points on the grid is one thousand. Points are calculated by multiplying the weight of the objectives by the rating level earned, and the sum of the list provides the total points. The objectives, when established, are approved at the vice president level. In this company, quality is everyone's business: it is not applied just to manufacturing and operations environments; rather, Reynolds service departments have also been included in the quality programs.

## QUALITY COMPLIANCE AUDITS

To help educate company service departments, management asked some basic questions, such as, How do you know the temperature indicator on your home oven is correct? How can we assure customers that they get 25-plus feet in a roll of Reynolds Wrap aluminum foil? The answers come from statistical process control techniques.

As an increased emphasis on quality on the part of employees was developed, the corporate quality assurance staff was developing and introducing new statistical process control techniques throughout the company. The staff was required to establish additional quality policies, identify processes and activities to be monitored, develop measuring systems, train both division and plant personnel, and initiate auditing and monitoring systems to evaluate results and performance.

Today, the corporate quality assurance staff of fifteen, which includes compliance, technology directors and engineering standards specialists, and division-assigned quality assurance managers, has in place a system of production checks and balances that effectively control the risks of making errors. The quality assurance managers became proficient in the auditing process through the development of quality compliance audits performed twice a year at virtually every facility. Each audit requires forty hours of advance work before the audit is begun; it is then conducted by a corporate compliance director and a division quality assurance manager. The two- or three-day audit, which covers every shift in the plant, uses a checklist developed from plant and division quality assurance manuals. Significant findings, both positive and negative, are summarized and submitted in a final report to management. Follow-up audits are performed until the corrective action is completed. Review audits are performed to make sure that the systems and procedures are doing what they are supposed to do. The company demands that products be traceable completely through the production process. Product audits are performed to make sure that this traceability is present.

The company audits incoming items from suppliers to ensure that the items meet specifications and that they have SQC traceability. As is the case with internal top-quality performers, there are awards for suppliers who consistently meet their quality objectives. For our suppliers, price is very low on the company's evaluation scale.

## CONCLUSION

Reynolds corporate quality assurance department's activities involve other areas. Members of the department review and approve all product claims in advertising, public relations releases, and other external communications for technical accuracy. The department is an active participant in the investigation of product liability claims, and it approves all new products introduced by Reynolds to assure that proper testing, evaluation, patent considerations, and product claims have been addressed prior to manufacturing.

The quality assurance department coordinates plant practices and procedures with those of the corporate division through the development of interdivisional specifications for products transferred among divisions and procured through outside sources. The department furnishes technical assistance to divisions-quite a valuable service since the department members have actual production experience in various plants and divisions and across several product lines. Members of the department represent Reynolds through their active participation and membership in quality assurance and technical associations; consequently, they maintain high skill levels and expertise in the most current quality assurance techniques.

Because of Reynolds' rededication to quality five years ago, all employees now realize that quality is central to their day-to-day activities. They know that quality demands a total commitment and that ultimately, quality is what the customer says it is.

# Motor Vehicles and Parts

Ford Motor Company
Lee R. Miskowski

General Motors Corporation
R. J. Bugno

Mack Trucks, Inc.
R. A. Raiue

Navistar International Transportation Corporation
Merrell J. Fischer and Paul R. Roseland

Winnebago Industries, Inc.
Ronald W. Post and Randal L. Fingarson

# Ford: The Quest for Quality

**Lee R. Miskowski**
Ford Motor Company

The Ford Motor Company, founded in 1903, is primarily a manufacturer of passenger cars, commercial vehicles and parts. Headquartered in Dearborn, Michigan, Ford employs 180,000 in the United States alone. The company also is represented in the aerospace, communications, and financial services industries.

# INTRODUCTION

In the decade of the seventies the American automobile market entered a period of great historical significance. For years a huge wall of protection provided by natural geography and cheap fuel yielded industry conditions that determined, in effect, the nature and character of vehicles the American people would drive. This is not to say that there was no competition; but the competition was an inbred sort, conducted within the oligopoly that ruled out dramatic changes in products or operating philosophy. Then, prompted by double-barreled fuel crises, world economics and global marketing became realities. Under conditions of rapidly escalating gasoline prices, relatively free trade provisions, and an expansion-minded free-world automobile industry, the lush United States market became fair game. And the American automobile market, previously dominated by just three corporations, was enveloped by a world-wide competitive environment that would bring about unprecedented and permanent change.

In this new arena American car and truck manufacturers responded, in time, with very substantial changes in product direction and business philosophy. Their philosophy began to incorporate a new emphasis on listening to the customer better. In terms of vehicles produced, they responded with new standards in design and features and, most importantly, in quality. As a logical outcome of this vast transformation of the American market and the not-so-coincidental escalation of the expectations and demands of the public, service quality became the next major frontier to be conquered.

At Ford Motor Company this meant development of a quality service process to meet the needs of the market while exploiting the opportunity to intensify the focus on the customer. It was necessary to go back to the fundamental support level of the business and acknowledge that, indeed, the customer had not been uppermost in the minds of the planners and producers. This quality service philosophy can best be described by five key terms which designate the remaining themes of this chapter: *define, commit, design, measure,* and *improve.* The result of this process is the emergence of a new business culture at Ford, bolstered by tangible progress in customer approval (and market share) as well as by quantum leaps in satisfaction for the corporation and its employees throughout the distribution system. In addition, it has signalled the need at Ford to commit itself to ongoing improvement.

DEFINE: *Find out first-hand clearly what customers want.*

Consumer research input, much of it qualitative in the form of "focus groups," made a large contribution to the new direction for products at Ford. In the process other factors beyond concern over products were revealed about the mindset of consumers. This, in turn, stimulated extensive research into all aspects of customer satisfaction. Ford learned that only the customer can define, in his terms, what it would take to win him over after years of indifferent and rejectful treatment by the manufacturers.

The research results were clear and consistent, cutting across differences in ownership preference, service outlet and gender. The problems with automotive service quality were four-fold:

- treatment-"No one seems to care about my problem."
- price-"It's too expensive; where is the value?"
- convenience-"I want a repair when I need it, where I need it."
- technical competence-"Please! Fix it right the first time."

In summary, the manufacturer should deliver service competently and courteously on a convenient basis at a reasonable cost.

Following the first round of extensive focus research, every study-qualitative and quantitative, ranging from product design tests to advertising tests-has confirmed the significance of these factors. The public responded dramatically to questions, and customer "vignettes" became notable and quotable. It was important for Ford to record many of these customers on video in order to carry the message about the demand for quality service back to Detroit.

COMMIT: *Develop a mission, a purpose. Commit yourself to a focus on the customer. Show you care.*

In November 1984, Mr. Henry Ford II addressed the top five hundred managers at Ford from around the world in a forum where everyone was expecting to hear his views on the economy, products, or prospects for the future. Instead, Mr. Ford dedicated his entire talk to the establishment of a statement of "Mission, Values and Guiding Principles" which were intended to become the future hallmarks for Ford Motor Company. In effect, it was a parting message in terms of Mr. Ford's direct involvement in the operating aspects of the company. Given what many at Ford already considered a bold new direction in its products, the world-wide management group seemed enthusiastic in responding to the need for a change in business culture at Ford.

In the mission statement the customer focus appears throughout, with specific applications to service quality covered in the guiding principles:

- Quality comes first.
- Customers are the focus of everything we do.
- Dealers and suppliers are our partners.

Service quality is also addressed in the section on values. People are the source of our strength. They provide our corporate intelligence and determine our reputation and vitality. Involvement and teamwork are our core human values.

The company was in the early stages of a dramatic corporate recovery and the chemistry was right. Ford managers soon found out that from then on their performance would be measured by specific quality contributions; for example, the demonstrated abilities to be a team player and a long-range thinker. Changes in business culture do not come easy, particularly in a large corporation, but Ford began to run its business on the simple premise that its main purpose is to satisfy customers. Amid constant internal reminders, the nature and direction of decision making changed dramatically. The process now included the need to answer the question, "What is the impact on customer satisfaction?"

The word quality expanded in meaning to encompass customers' entire ownership experience with their automobiles. It also came to imply the development of relationships with dealers and the millions of owners. The meaning of "Quality is job #1" was extended to "Quality *care* is job #1." With fifty-five hundred independently-owned-and-operated dealerships in the U.S., and more in Canada, it would take time for needed communication, motivation, and change in service quality to occur. Over the last forty years some very bad habits had developed, so it would take more than a magic wand to make a justifiably skeptical public notice a difference. Despite the numerous tasks and resources required, the stage was set for the introduction of new concepts and programs that would address the all-too-familiar customer issues.

DESIGN: *Develop and implement supporting concepts, programs, and new approaches that respond to customer expectations.*

Change in attitudes and sincere commitment to a new purpose are prerequisites to innovations in service, but the substance lies in doing business very differently and convincing the customer that you care. Examples of change, of new customer benefits, include the following:

- *Goodwill toward the customer.* Recognize that some corporate responsibility exists to fix the vehicles beyond the warranty period. Allocate new funding to cover reasonable customer expectations. Customers will tell you what is fair and most will be reasonable in their demands.
- *Customer assistance programs.* Guarantee repairs better than anyone else through the Lifetime Service Guarantee and provide dealers the opportunity to give customers alternative transportation with a free service loaner program.
- *Dealer quality commitment.* Work with dealers to show more consideration for the needs of the individual when he shops for or buys a new car. Explain the warranty provisions and new car features. Fill the gas tank on all new cars. Demonstrate that the customer's business is appreciated and tell him what to do if problems are encountered.

Make the buying process the beginning of a relationship, not the end of a transaction.

- *Owner notification programs.* Upon detection of a product's problem that clearly is built-in develop a solution, voluntarily contact all buyers of that type of unit, and fix the product free. This focus on the customer becomes necessary as product engineers, manufacturing organizations, and suppliers acknowledge and pay for past mistakes.
- *Communication.* Set up a system to make yourself accessible to customers; listen to them, solve their problems, and try their suggestions. This takes a vast network of telephones, computer systems, and people who are well-trained and courteous. In the auto industry the logistics in terms of the great number of owners make the task of communication sometimes overwhelming.
- *New training techniques and technical support.* Provide interpersonal skills training for Ford and dealership personnel. Completely revise traditional technical assistance by means of instant electronic communication with dealerships, of diagnostics by remote control, and of a person-to-person technical hotline to solve tough problems. Develop partnerships with community colleges around the country in order to provide consistently new supply of entry-level dealership technicians with two-year associate degrees.

The intent of designing new programs to meet customer demands is to respond to the strong feelings of the American public about the experiences of shopping for, buying, and owning an automobile. The solutions are a combination of "high touch" and "high tech" designed to make a substantial improvement over conventional ways of doing business. This process is still developing and is subject to the complexity of the distribution system. Dealers are independent business people, Ford's first customers, and they must be convinced, collectively and individually, that *customer satisfaction* is key in creating future business success.

How does one know if progress is being made? Does anybody among the public know Ford is dedicated to changing its old ways of doing business? The answers can be found in a measurement system that establishes a relationship with customers.

MEASUREMENT: *Stay in touch with the customer and develop effective yardsticks to measure progress at all levels.*

At Ford Motor Company the greatest catalyst for positive change at the dealer level has been the successful implementation of a customer survey system. Perhaps its success was due to a very special appeal to the entrepreneurial spirit of the retail organization, or for the timeliness of the whole idea of customer satisfaction; in any case, it was a near-magical experience.

The most important lesson gleaned involved the essential notion that a customer survey should inspire motivation in company and dealer personnel and a genuine feeling of partnership to addressing a fundamental problem whose solution promises significant mutual rewards.

The survey must be primarily a tool to enable effective follow-up with customers. Second, it must be detailed enough to provide corporate self-analysis in determining the causes of problems. Third, and very importantly, it must measure performance in order to generate a competitive index or value. Commitment to the concept of a customer survey system on the parts of both corporate and dealer personnel, as well as complete integrity in survey standards, are necessary.

The Ford survey system consists of an initial questionnaire thirty days after the purchase of a new car or truck, and a nine-months' questionnaire, following sufficient driving experience. The initial survey is designed to evaluate the selling process but it also includes evaluation of the product itself. Product information is important also as supplemental feedback that helps separate product considerations from customer opinions of the dealership experience. The nine-months' survey reports on customers' judgement of service, since by then any owners have had an occasion to return for maintenance or warranty work. While the surveys yield a variety of information, only the key summary questions are used to develop an index. Market research professionals must authenticate the process and use techniques that will assure an adequate response rate from customers. In order to satisfy the basic goal of measurement—that is, enabling individual follow-up—*every* customer must be surveyed. Thus, integrity of survey standards is preserved within the corporation and throughout the retail organization. For the longer term, supplemental customer surveys and other quality indicators are necessary to gain more detailed product and customer information.

Following full acceptance of the survey, as well as adequate experience with the process, Ford took the opportunity to reward dealers. The company announced the "President's Award" as its most prestigious dealer recognition (among numerous awards, trips, and banquets for sales accomplishments). Presentation of the award by the president of Ford to those dealers with the highest customer ratings at a black-tie affair in a first-class resort sent a strong message to dealers. In addition, it was obvious that this group of dealers deserved and received peer recognition: along with being customer-focused, they achieved sales and profit success. Ford learned quickly that this was not a coincidence. Just one year after the inception of the President's Award, winning it seemed to be the ultimate experience a dealer could achieve and statements such as "I would kill to win" became prevalent. This notion became so successful that care was taken to maintain the emphasis on customer satisfaction, not on some "numbers" achievement.

It should be pointed out that unless the product itself can hold up under the scrutiny of the selling organization, integrity is seriously jeapordized. Earlier attempts in the 1970s to institute customer focus by means of numerous programs with proper-sounding themes failed because dealers did not have confidence in the product. In other words, dealers seemed to say, "Do your job right before you check up on me."

IMPROVE: *Never relax. Adopt the philosophy and develop the environment that builds in continuous improvement.*

When a corporation has the good fortune to achieve outstanding results that stand the test of time, there are countless factors that contribute to that success. Development of products that gain acceptance and credibility with the public is, of course, paramount. But it is not enough. A corporate commitment to a mission that includes a sharp customer focus is an absolutely critical ingredient. Care for the customer after his or her purchase and even beyond warranty is necessary to sustain any success. Resources must be committed for a longer-range payoff and the dedication to human needs, both internal and external, must be continually encouraged among suppliers, dealers and employees. Mutual trust is essential.

There is a normal inclination to assess quantitatively the specific contribution of service quality to business success. While the analysts can busily examine surveys and extensive research, such examination cannot yield definitive answers. Faith, trust, and belief in what is right—principles previously not thought to be common in the corporate world—must be adopted and applied in day-to-day business operations. There is a way, however, to add a quantitative dimension to these virtues: it is called *continuous improvement.* Simply, you know what you are doing is right but you don't know how right, so your objective becomes doing a little better than you did before. The surveys noted earlier are good examples: the index or value is important primarily as a numerical base by which to judge performance gains in each subsequent increment of time. The compounding effect of doing better through each cycle is amazing.

The auto business is a cyclical business. The promise of overcapacity·in the next five to ten years is certain to intensify competition in the United States. The philosophy must be to "run scared" in terms of keeping up with product innovations while controlling costs—all with a global perspective. In this competitive process the commitment to the customer must not suffer: it has proven to be fundamentally sound, if not critical, in carrying out the mission of prosperous survival. Conscious recognition of market conditions plus effective communication with the retail organization are essential. "Running scared" also means that you are never quite satisfied. At Ford the precept is to assume that whatever has been done up to that point is not enough. Automotive products and services are so visible that critics and customers with problems will always require attention. The corporation must remember this and must try to perform better all the time.

Much has been written and speeches delivered about the lack of service quality and genuine concern for customers in today's world. The needs and demands of the "yuppies" and other contemporary groups have been described in great detail and various responses to their needs have been recommended. The bandwagon of companies that want to recognize their past sins and repent in the direction of customer service reform is indeed becoming very crowded. As a result, it is important to delineate between those that talk and those that act. Making a fresh commitment and living it out daily are very difficult, particularly in a traditional industry that some observers believe to be at its peak or on the decline.

Very few large companies so far have made such a commitment. Although simple in concept, it takes a serious commitment at the highest level of management. Ford Motor Company's chairman, as described in Adweek (August 3, 1987), makes a good example:

Petersen believes so strongly in the team Ford concept that when *Motor Trend* magazine wanted to name him man of the year, he flatly refused the honor. Instead, he put together a symbolic team with a member representing each department, from design to the production line, to accept the award. And, when the same magazine picked Taurus car of the year, award certificates were presented to everyone who worked on the assembly line.

It takes time for positive changes to transform a business culture. To be proven genuine, commitment must also stand the test of time, through peaks and valleys, and must arouse enthusiasm at every level of the core business and throughout the distribution system.

The philosophy of continuous improvement begins with the quality of the product itself and broadens to include all related services for the life of the product. The rewards comprise the tremendous satisfaction of all concerned, the enhancement of one's public image beyond expectation, and the customer's repurchase and after-market loyalty. The latter ensures the resources for accelerated, continuous improvements in the future.

Ford wants to be one of those transformed companies. It has launched a strong, solid beginning. It has made competitive gains in a United States market that has become a global battleground for world manufacturers. Its customer-driven philosophy and its management style, both as outlined in the company's statement of mission, values, and guiding principles, represent the conviction that it takes to sustain these gains and to make new ones. If the commitment to the customer and the day-to-day dedication to high quality in products and services prevail, Ford's contributions to American business and American society can be historic.

# General Motors Service Quality

**R. J. Bugno**

General Motors Corporation

General Motors Corporation, founded in 1908, manufactures cars and trucks. GM products are sold and serviced through a network of ten thousand dealers employing over 125,000 service technicians. The average number of employees throughout the entire General Motors Corporation in 1987 was 813,000.

The headquarters facilities for General Motors Corporation are located in Detroit, Michigan.

## INTRODUCTION

In the automobile industry, quality service results when you listen to your customers, support your dealer sales and service organization, and provide a safety net for complaints. Listening to customers is not simply providing a complaint department; it involves continued communications with your customers during the buying experience, at the time of delivery, and when the product requires service. Once you have made the commitment to listen to your customers, you must be willing to hear what they are saying and to respond positively.

General Motors products are sold and serviced through a network of ten thousand dealers employing over 125,000 service technicians. To insure superior quality service, GM must provide that network with the best parts, training, and tools available, based on the needs of customers and dealers. Finally, if, at the dealer level, they are unable to satisfy customers, then it is incumbent on General Motors to provide a complaint mechanism that allows a last opportunity to talk. That mechanism must be responsive; also, it must be perceived by the customer to be both fair and objective.

General Motors has been a customer-service oriented organization for many years. In the past the focus of customer service activities was more reactive than proactive. In the 1980s they reoriented their approach by building systems to identify and quantify specific customer needs, reshaping the organization; and, as necessary, building new systems to satisfy those needs. An additional focus was on developing procedures to insure that customer complaints are heard and given a substantive response. What follows are some actions taken by GM to provide high quality customer service satisfaction.

## LISTENING TO THE CUSTOMER

In addition to the many systems that provide information on product quality and reliability, styling, and so on, GM has established survey programs with the primary purpose of providing customer service experience data. To understand customer satisfaction, one must concentrate on the causes of dissatisfaction. Invaluable knowledge has been gained from the many day-to-day contacts between the field organization and dealers, and from the more formal dealer forums (councils) established to communicate with the company. In addition, General Motors has developed and put into place programs to collect information on problem areas; thus, necessary changes can be incorporated into the design, distribution, manufacturing, and dealer systems. In recent years General Motors has taken several innovative steps in customer communications with programs such as the Dealer Satisfaction Survey, the Customer Satisfaction Index, and the Dialog Survey.

### Dealership Satisfaction Survey

GM's Dealership Satisfaction Survey is designed to monitor the long-term satisfaction of dealership managers with divisional and corporate policies and practices. It serves as an impetus to change those policies and practices. Questionnaires are mailed under divisional sponsorship to dealers, sales managers, and service managers in all dealerships.

The questionnaires solicit management's views on their respective areas of responsibility. For example, dealers are asked to respond on the policies and services affecting the short- and long-range health of their business. Sales and service managers are asked to evaluate: (1) the sales, service, and product information, (2) the training programs; (3) their district or area manager; and (4) merchandising programs. All questionnaires contain a question measuring the overall satisfaction with the division and a section for general comments. Each quarter, GM issues reports showing scores on all questions to the corporation, the divisions, and the zones and branches within the divisions. These reports are used to improve the quality of service provided to the dealer organization.

## Customer Satisfaction Index (CSI)

Over two hundred thousand retail purchasers of GM cars and light-duty trucks are surveyed each month from the dealerships who sell over 90% of GM's products. The primary purpose of the survey is to provide dealer-level reporting. This provides dealers and factory service development specialists with specific directions on where meaningful improvements can be made and customer satisfaction improved. Results of this questionnaire are also tabulated by zone or branch, division, car line, and assembly plant.

Reflecting the importance that is placed on this survey, each vehicle division has incorporated specific CSI performance criteria into their dealer program. Dealers are no longer judged merely by sales; rather, equal emphasis is placed on sales and customer satisfaction performance. For example, dealer CSI performance is a criterion for judging dealers for additional dealership investment eligibility. Further, every vehicle division has a program to identify dealers with low CSI scores and work with them to improve customer satisfaction.

In addition, all vehicle marketing units utilize the CSI together with sales performance for various dealer recognition programs. In this regard, dealers and their employees are eligible for trip and merchandise awards in sales contests and recognition events. Each division also has contests for dealer service personnel, based on the CSI performance.

## Dialog Survey

The Dialog Survey measures customer satisfaction using a four-page questionnaire mailed to current owners of one- to five-year-old vehicles. The study includes all models of GM cars and light-duty trucks as well as selected competitive models.

The questionnaire covers both the vehicle and dealership service, and contains a checklist of over one hundred possible vehicle problems. Respondents are asked to identify those problems that developed during the previous twelve months. Additional questions gauge the customer satisfaction with various aspects of the ownership experience. Finally, the survey questions the customer's future purchase intentions, assessing the consequences of problems described in other sections of the questionnaire. These data are then summarized in a series of annual reports that address aspects of performance, such as service reliability. In addition to these standard reports, the data are also available on a computer-inquiry system for analysis by members of the GM corporate staff as well as by other divisional central office personnel.

This system can also be used to generate lists of customers who have specific problems with their automobiles. These customers, or their dealerships, may be contacted to obtain more detailed information to correct product and service problems. Most respondents provide their phone numbers and names of their dealerships in order to facilitate this process. Dialog gives a longer perspective (five years), which allows GM to monitor customer satisfaction with nonwarranty, non-GM service. They can access where consumers choose to have service work performed and why.

## SUPPORT FOR THE DEALER SERVICE ORGANIZATION

All data concerning service-related problems are of little value without the commitment to change. As a result of the ongoing dialog with dealers, customers, and field organization, they have taken positive steps to improve service.

### People Training

General Motors offers, on a regular basis, training programs for GM dealership personnel. The programs, available in major cities across the U.S., are designed to develop the managerial knowledge and skills of key dealership personnel and to improve customer satisfaction.

In addition to courses tailored to dealer development and sales management, GM offers service department managers the GM Service College. Participants use concepts of personnel, financial, and operations management to improve departmental operations. Courses are also available for the professional service advisor. Participants learn systems and procedures for correctly analyzing the customer's service problems the first time. The course recognizes that the service advisor is the employee most often in contact with the customer; therefore, the advisor is most responsible for assuring satisfaction with the dealership.

## Technical Training

Recognizing that customer satisfaction is based not just on product quality but also on the entire ownership experience, GM established a network of training centers. There are a total of thirty-seven training locations at both GM facilities and the facilities of local community colleges in major U.S. metropolitan areas. The training programs conducted in the training centers and colleges are developed by a staff located at the General Motors technical center in Warren, Michigan. Using the latest techniques, programs are designed from the ground up with an eye toward providing the most comprehensive, up-to-date information in the shortest possible time.

There are approximately seventy resident instructors and a like number of contract instructors in the thirty-seven locations. Additionally, based on dealer need, these same instructors may travel to over fifty other community colleges and provide remote dealer training. Each instructor is a specialist in at least one of the eight major areas of the vehicle; most are ASE certified. In the mid-1970s, dramatic changes in technology began taking place in the automotive service field. This revolution in technology brought about an equally dramatic increase in training requirements. Not only were more sophisticated systems being introduced, but they were coming at an unprecedented pace. A need began for a qualitatively different kind of service technician. The mechanic of the past needed to be replaced by a highly skilled service technician trained in many phases of electronic and computer technology.

To deal with the challenges that this new dimension of auto service would require, GM turned to the nation's community and technical colleges. It was there that GM, like other major industries, saw a body of teaching expertise and a tradition of program excellence. Their courses, if brought to state-of-the-art levels of technology, could provide a nationwide solution to what was becoming a critical shortage: people with the skills needed to service and repair a vastly different kind of vehicle.

In 1979, General Motors launched a pilot program called the Automotive Service Education Program (ASEP) through local community colleges. It is a two-year associate degree program aimed at entry-level jobs for automotive service students working on a cooperative basis with General Motors dealers. With the success of this program it became clear that community colleges would be the key to increasing the service expertise of current GM dealer service people and the numerous independent aftermarket service technicians, all of whom were most anxious to upgrade their technical knowledge.

In the early 1980s, GM had determined that they needed to double their training capabilities. The training expansion was achieved by adding college instructors and classrooms to the existing network of training centers. Community colleges and other postsecondary schools assist GM by providing one or more instructors to each training center. The community colleges have also helped by establishing GM classrooms at a number of locations, staffed by local faculty trained by GM. Substantial amounts of General Motors equipment have been donated to the schools and the corporation has helped train instructors in the latest products. As many dealers discovered, there is a relationship between highly trained individuals and productivity. Customers are better served, and their satisfaction with products and dealership service is higher.

## GM – Computerized Automotive Maintenance System (CAMS)

Within this decade, there has been a remarkable growth in on-board automotive electronics technology. This growth has rapidly out-paced the diagnostic capabilities typically found in the automotive service environment. GM-CAMS is a service system developed and backed by GM. GM-CAMS consists of a computerized technician terminal, a nationwide electronic communications network, and an information processing center at a mainframe computer facility. The system is an interactive tool that assists technicians in servicing engine electronics, emission controls, and other vehicle electronic systems.

GM-CAMS leads the technician through appropriate repair activities and temporarily stores the results. Then, these are transmitted nightly to a host computer for analysis and distribution to the engineering and service groups. The terminal is mobile and has a user-friendly touch screen instead of a keyboard. Vehicles are connected to this terminal by a special cable that feeds data into the computer for fast and accurate diagnosis. Symptoms are entered by the technician by *touching* the appropriate choices displayed on the monitor. With complex systems the choices are chunked into easily understood portions, thus simplifying the entry process and maximizing the accuracy of the entered systems. Static tests are conducted jointly by the technician and the terminal. (As the technician moves the shift level, for example, the monitor displays the current location and validates the shift system.) The results of all the tests are combined with any other detected faults and analyzed. The analysis leads the technician through a series of tests, measurements, and diagnostic procedures.

The full benefit of GM-CAMS is realized when the two-way communications take place between the host and the numerous technician terminals throughout the nation. In addition to providing timely product-related information to the sales, service, manufacturing, design, and engineering functions within General Motors, GM-CAMS can help improve the capabilities of every technician using the technician's terminal. This help includes not only improved vehicle diagnostics, but summaries of current service bulletins, vehicle recall data, complete vehicle specifications, and a complete set of on-board instructions for using the GM-CAMS technician's terminal.

## General Motors Dealer Equipment

Over the years GM Service Research has developed a high degree of expertise in service equipment. The right service equipment can reduce labor content, reduce skill level required, increase productivity, and control quality. Service equipment purchases are most often large investments. General Motors Dealer Equipment serves as a consultant to insure that dealers buy the right tool for the right job. It aids dealers in the evaluation and selection of service equipment. Product selections are made on the basis of technical capability and the quality of equipment, along with the manufacturers' abilities to back their products and provide adequate training. An additional service provided to dealers is equipment investment planning, a program that shows the dealer how to analyze the market and select the right equipment to provide the best quality service.

## Technical Assistance System

The Technical Assistance System (TAS) was established to assist dealers with difficult-to-repair vehicles. The system includes TAS centers that are staffed and run by each division. This network of support includes vehicle and allied division service and engineering staffs and a central computer. When a dealer encounters a difficult-to-repair vehicle, he calls the divisional TAS center utilizing a toll-free 800 number. The centers are staffed by full-time service engineers with strong technical backgrounds. The service engineer records the problem in the computer database. He also uses the database to determine the fix for the problem. If the problem cannot be resolved at this first level using the expertise within the center, it can be escalated to the division's product assurance or service engineering department. If unresolved, it can be further escalated to the division responsible for design, such as Delco Electronics or Hydramatic.

## Diagnostic and Repair Centers

In major market areas of the country, General Motors Service Research operates Diagnostic and Repair Centers (DRCs). These centers have been established to repair vehicles that dealers have been unable to fix after utilizing the Technical Assistance System and other resources. Since the centers are staffed by General Motors personnel, they provide an additional level of direct technical support to dealers. In addition to the immediate customer benefit of repairing the problem vehicle, the DRC provides valuable feedback about the causes of difficult problems. Summaries of all case histories are input directly into the Technical Assistance System for ready access to all divisions, staffs, and dealers.

## PROVIDING A SAFETY NET FOR COMPLAINTS

Despite the finest efforts of GM and its dealers, they recognize that there are some problems that cannot be easily resolved; therefore, the third step in quality service is a responsive customer assistance program.

## Receiving and Responding to Complaints

To improve the ability to handle customer complaints, the vehicle marketing units continue to expand the toll-free telephone networks for complaints. In cases where the complaint cannot be resolved, the mediation and arbitration system is available to provide a satisfactory solution.

The Warranty and Owner Assistance Information booklet outlines a simple three-step procedure designed to resolve misunderstandings, which is referred to as the Customer Assistance System. The three steps are as follows: (1) discuss the problem with dealership management; (2) if the problem remains unresolved, contact the customer services department of the nearest zone office (this step is optional depending on the availability of 800-lines); and (3) contact the customer assistance advisor at the vehicle division.

GM is committed to ensuring that all complaints are resolved through the complaint resolution system. Under the existing system, which primarily involves follow-up to written correspondence, the receipt of a complaint by the vehicle division results in a customer assistance request being electronically transmitted to the dealer and to the appropriate zone or branch office. The dealer is responsible for contacting the customer within twenty-four hours and resolving the complaint within an average of twelve days. Follow-up procedures are in place to ensure that the customer assistance request is addressed.

Response time is expected to improve as a result of the installation of toll-free telephone networks. Buick has had a toll-free system since 1983, and Pontiac has had complete coverage since April 1986. GM of Canada, Chevrolet, and Cadillac are all in the process of completing the installation of a national 800 network. Using an 800 network, calls are answered by customer assistance advisors at the division's central office. As customer contacts are made, a case number is assigned, and the owner name, vehicle, date, and time are entered into a computer. Thus, the owner's complaint can be instantly recalled should a repeat contact be made. Immediate access to complete information regarding a customer's problem builds the owner's confidence.

It should be noted that Oldsmobile and GMC Truck are taking a different approach in communicating with dissatisfied customers. When the customer contacts the zone, a customer assistance advisor enters the case into a system that transmits the information to the dealer. If the customer then elects to contact a divisional central office, that representative can reference the case in the same system and electronically transmit the updated information to the dealer and zone.

## Mediation and Arbitration

General Motor's experience has shown that its customer satisfaction procedures have been very successful. However, for customers who have not been substantially satisfied GM offers a voluntary, no-charge mediation and arbitration program administered by the Better Business Bureau (BBB). The program applies to individual retail purchaser disputes involving vehicle repairs and the interpretation of the applicable new vehicle limited warranty.

The program is started by contacting the BBB and requesting access to the mediation and arbitration program. The customer provides the BBB with his or her name, address, the vehicle identification number, and a statement of the nature of the complaint. The program provides for the review of the facts by an impartial third party (arbiter) and usually includes an informal hearing before the arbiter. GM generally agrees to accept the arbiter's decision in advance, but the customer is not bound by the arbiter's decision unless he or she accepts it. The corporation has tried to design the program so that the entire dispute settlement process, from the time a customer files a complaint to the final decision, ordinarily takes about forty days.

General Motors encourages customers to try this program before or instead of resorting to the courts. This impartial program offers advantages over courts in most jurisdictions because it is fast, free of charge, and informal (lawyers are not usually present). Arbitrators in this program are instructed to base their decision on a standard of simple fairness, taking into account the circumstances of each case. Arbitrators do not try to duplicate the functions of courts and, therefore, do not apply statutes as judges in a court would do.

If a customer prefers a decision based on what they feel a law (such as a state *lemon law*) would entitle them to, they are encouraged to seek that relief in court rather than the informal program. On the other hand, many people prefer this program to courts because of its informality and greater flexibility. Regardless of his or her preference, a customer unhappy with the results of this program can still go to court because the results of the program are generally binding on GM but not on the customer unless the latter chooses to accept the arbiter's decision.

## CONCLUSION

Quality service is an integral part of the entire General Motors ownership experience. When a customer buys a GM car or truck, he or she buys a total transportation package. That package includes advertising, sales, delivery, finance and insurance, and quality service. Quality service in all its manifestations requires a commitment to talking with and listening to your employees, dealers, and most importantly, your customers.

The service system that GM has developed will not be taken for granted. It will be continually improved. Ultimately, it will succeed only to the extent that it satisfies customers. GM cannot decide whether it succeeds — the customer alone will decide if the program works.

# Quality Is the Foundation Of Our Business

**R. A. Raine**
Mack Trucks, Inc.

Mack Trucks, Inc. is one of America's largest producers of heavy-duty diesel trucks and major product components. Mack also markets a line of medium-duty diesel trucks throughout North America, parts of Central America, Australia, and New Zealand, as well as a line of intercity motorcoaches for the United States and Canada.

Founded in 1900, Mack Trucks, Inc. is a publicly held company. Its headquarters are in Allentown, Pennsylvania, and it employs approximately 9,800 people worldwide.

# INTRODUCTION

When approached to participate in providing material for this book, it became quite clear that what other companies were trying to accomplish, what authors were writing about, and consultants being hired to perform, was something that has existed at Mack Trucks for many years. A banner is visibly displayed as you enter the Mack Trucks World Headquarters Building in Allentown, PA and at the newly completed assembly facility in Winnsboro, SC. It states, "Quality is the Foundation of our Business." Some equate this statement as an inspection control process to identify performance after the fact. To the contrary, the basis of Mack's success is not in innovative systems, sophisticated marketing analysis or state of the art manufacturing process rather, the employees of Mack Trucks create the foundation for quality that ensures customers receive the maximum utilization and support of Mack products. The personal dedication to a product and its services, domestically and internationally, are what has made, and will continue to make this corporation and its products known and respected worldwide.

Products must be designed and built with inherent reliability and serviceability. Support such as spare parts, service, finance, sales, and engineering have to be made easily accessible to the customer. The key ingredient in this recipe is people—customer orientated personnel, dedicated to satisfying the customer and his needs.

Quality service is not isolated to those customers who purchase products and services. Quality service also encompasses interdepartmental encounters (sharing advice, information, and direction) with co-workers. These people are internal customers and the company cannot differentiate them from external customers.

Today and tomorrow's customers are entitled to a certain level of service and want to be recognized as being special. If their expectations are not met, they take their business elsewhere and tell everyone who will listen about their bad experience. Studies have shown that dissatisfied customers tell twice as many people about their bad experience as their good experience. In the past, Mack has not quantifiably monitored this, but with the advent of retention marketing becoming the critical issue as customer bases diminish, it is extremely important that not one customer dissatisfaction go unnoticed and unacted upon since customers are too precious to lose in an expanded sellers' environment.

The Mack Truck philosophy and strategy is to provide total service support while maintaining a competitive edge and assuring that customer satisfaction is the major element, the driving force of company strategy.

Capitalizing on the individual strengths of service professionals has enabled the company to develop an exceptional service team. This teamwork and spirit of cooperation have enabled Mack Trucks to establish a worldwide network of product support poised to meet the demands of today's customer.

Management recognizes the importance of unequivocal service support that indeed, at times, is the deciding factor in the customer's choice of purchase. In this area, the Mack Service Operations Group continually challenges competition and, conversely, is challenged by the competition. Changing products and customer needs demand and receive constant attention while improving Mack's service support.

Service Operations is comprised of interacting departments, internally and externally, positioned and prepared to address the customer's requirement of minimal response time. Each department's effective collaboration assures that management and service staff are apprised and confident to address service requirements, while thriving on the challenges and commitment to satisfy the customer's needs. This philosophy of quality service is inherent in each of our service departments as follows:

## FIELD SERVICE OPERATIONS

The Mack Domestic field service department coordinates the daily service functions for the U.S. and is divided into five regions: Northeastern, Atlantic, Southern, Central and Western. Each regional service office staff is comprised on a regional service manager and a complement of district service managers who are responsible for ensuring prompt, professional service within the regions. This organized field service group supports the hundreds of nationwide sales, parts and service facilities of the Mack Truck dealer network. Positioning service support in this manner assures and builds confidence in the customer, dealer and, ultimately, the technician charged with the responsibility of maintaining and/or servicing the customer's vehicle.

Field service managers provide the vital link between World Headquarters and the field enabling complex affairs to be routinely resolved at the regional level. It is this responsible independence and ability to work with Mack agents and customers that make the field service operations personnel such a valuable part of the Mack service team.

As regional and district service managers, they can be required, in a single day, to act as mechanic, arbitrator, consultant, engineer, salesman and instructor. Working hours and location are many times uncertain, because devotion to the customers is essential. Personal sacrifice is inevitable; being called upon or directed to investigate and satisfy customer needs can range from, possibly working through the night, to interrupting special personal occasions; such as a graduation, the kids' football game, their daughter's school play, that birthday or anniversary. Yes, it does take a special person to be dedicated to the service profession, but it is equally important that the sacrifices a family makes in the name of customer satisfaction not go unnoticed, and are to be praised for their patience and understanding. The position does not go without its rewards. The satisfaction derived from being able to continually help those who count on you is undeniable achievement.

## SERVICE ENGINEERING

The Service Engineering Department comprises professional technicians (service engineers) which links the field organization to home office expertise in product, policy and procedure. Each one of these individuals possesses years of product knowledge and practical experience to broaden their service expertise.

It is essential for this group of professionals to maintain current information on product changes, improvements; engineering releases and updates, new product development, warranty policy, service part releases and updates, plus company policy and procedure. Mack Truck service engineers are of two distinctions; fleet specialists and component specialists. Fleet service engineers are assigned and concentrate their activity to fleet accounts to assure that overall product performance and customer satisfaction are realized by its customers.

The component service engineers are assigned specific components of the product; i.e., cab, chassis, engine, transmission, etc. They constantly develop and maintain their expertise in these specific areas to afford other service support groups immediate, up-to-date information vital to informing others and resolving product problems.

Mack distributors, factory branches, customers and field service operations do not have to settle for alternatives when seeking advice on uncommon product problems. They can rely on the expertise of the service engineering department to get the truck back on the road with minimum downtime.

## INTERNATIONAL SERVICE OPERATIONS

International Service Operations is comprised of a manager and supervisor located at Mack World Headquarters in Allentown, PA, plus four regional service managers responsible for service expertise in the international marketplace. These individuals are strategically located around the globe providing after-sale support.

Does -50°F and a 30 MPH wind sound inviting? Though this may sound like an extreme, it is not the unusual. For the personnel of the International Service Operations Department, this is only one in a long list of challenges. One similar occasion was when an urgent request came from an oil company experiencing problems on the southern tip of South America. A Mack service engineer was dispatched from the sunny Caribbean to assist the customer. Little did the representative know that the repairs would have to be made out of doors, plus the fact that the majority of the local inhabitants were penguins, who thought it was amusing to pick up shinny nuts and bolts in their beaks and waddle off unbeknownst, or another incident when our Service representative utilized the services of a "local taxi" (camel) to eliminate the need to spend hours in rush hour traffic. These are a few of the memorable events, but are not to be overshadowed by the daily experiences encountered by the International Service Department.

They are a dedicated group, primarily foreign nationals, who have come to be a part of the Mack family and who know no real differences in language, culture or environments. They do not look upon these elements as barriers, but merely challenges to be met and overcome in the course of doing business globally and their dedication to customer satisfaction.

When making a commitment to being a global company, it does not only mean selling a product worldwide, it means providing the support services required to assure the customer the maximum utility of his vehicle.

## CUSTOMER SERVICES

Management at Mack Trucks has traditionally looked at the customer service group as being complaint receptive. Through a recommitment and dedication to increasing customer satisfaction, this department will be expanding and is envisioned that, ultimately, it will become the true "switchboard of customer satisfaction."

Presently, the staff is involved in receiving not only complaint telephone calls and correspondence, but also complimentary messages, plus providing assistance to individuals seeking information for technical or promotional literature. As a point of interest, on average, two to three times as many telephone calls are made by this department as received to expedite and respond to customer's questions, plus additional follow-up communications are made to insure that the customer has been satisfied.

Just providing a customer service group is not enough. There is constant need for improvement. Properly managing such a department is one way of providing a quality service to internal as well as external customers: Externally to the customers who have purchased Mack Truck products and services, plus access to those customers who require additional information about Mack products or services. What better target marketing tool—customers calling you, rather than an expensive shotgunning the universe approach. Internally, by providing specific information, good and bad. The service department must be made readily available to other departments directly responsible for taking action on a timely basis.

To understand and then solve a problem requires listening to the customer. The time spent listening to the customer is ultimately of the greatest value to both Mack Trucks and its customers. Conversely, for listening to be effective, it must produce results. This is where the Mack customer service department excels. The employees advise customers as to how their problem can be resolved at the local level as well as through factory branch or distributor organization. If difficulty persists, customer service representatives are urged to request that the sales facility involved contact the Mack regional office responsible for their geographic area. Historically, the majority of all situations can be and are remedied at this level.

After sale-support is where the true measure of service quality and where perceived values are formulated. The company works diligently to be first class at all levels, but in the actual end of this process, it is the customer who leads the way down the road to true excellence—"the customer is the boss."

## SERVICE PUBLICATIONS

Mack Trucks, Inc. builds and markets an astonishing variety of custom-built vehicles, all of which require the creation of technical publications to effectively and efficiently operate, maintain and service the vehicle. It is this formidable task which employs the ability and expertise of the Service Publications Department. Constant technological advances of products guarantee an endless supply of new assignments, while previously published material is continually updated.

Throughout the life of a product, Mack service publications personnel continually update and write publications in the following areas: operation, maintenance, emission, and warranty. Handbooks are delivered with each new truck, plus individual component and service manuals are made available to the customer for a nominal fee. A constant flow of service bulletins announce the latest advancements in product and service technique, along with master service manuals, wall charts, warranty and service standards manuals.

As Mack continues to maintain its leadership role in the marketplace, the contributions and resourcefulness of the service publications department becomes more apparent as being essential, rather than a routine activity in the customer satisfaction process.

## SERVICE PARTS

Reliability is a standard part of the business of making medium and heavy duty diesel trucks which require low maintenance and have a high resale value just as manufacturing and marketing replacement products (service parts) which meet stringent Mack OEM specifications and federal performance standards. Mack approved service products are Mack Trucks specified, Mack Trucks engineered and Mack Trucks tested. No substitutes will be accepted.

There are more than 250,000 Mack trucks currently in operation around the world, of which many thousands have logged in excess of one million miles of service. Mack Trucks Parts Operation unit maintains complete vehicle chassis records dating back 87 years when the first truck was produced.

The Service Parts Division provides continuous support to customers and their products through a worldwide spare parts distribution system containing inventories in excess of 160 million dollars.

The U.S. is serviced through five regional parts distribution centers, while Canada is served by one parts distribution center. Globally, Australia is serviced by Mack Australia located in Brisbane, Australia, while the remainder of the world is supplied by drawing upon domestic inventories. These distribution centers are linked together via an electronic communications system to expedite parts requirement, search inventory levels, order filling, and shipping thereby reducing parts demand to an absolute minimum for the customer. To ensure that customer demands are met expeditiously at the local level there is a complete network of factory branches, distributors and service dealers.

An additional affirmation of Mack's commitment to offer and support its products at a reasonable cost is by direct operation of two component and spare parts remanufacturing centers; products are remanufactured to exact Mack and original equipment specifications and are supported with a replacement warranty.

In the event of an untimely breakdown Mack also provides and maintains a 24 hour, 7 day a week toll-free (800) telephone number that provides customers with the name, location, phone number, and hours of operation of the nearest authorized Mack dealer. A customer service department is also available capable of locating parts required specifically for emergency situations.

## RELIABILITY ENGINEERING

A liaison group exists between Product Engineering and Service Operations whose sole purpose it is to analyze reports of product problems and to ensure that future designs are void of repetitive problems. It is this department which implements the design criteria of, "Do it right the first time", but is also poised to assist should the initial design prove to be unsuccessful. Reliability and serviceability are the two main elements which this department is responsible for assuring that the customer will receive maximum utilization of product by design.

## MANAGEMENT RESOURCE PLANNING (MRPII)

Management Resource Planning is a methodology assuring that Mack employees are "Planning together into the Future". Recognizing and understanding the essential success of this policy of total employee involvement has resulted in a major corporate commitment to develop a complete education program for Mack's employees. MRPII concepts education program has been developed and implemented as part of an ongoing vertical education effort. This method of education in Management Resource Planning/MRPII includes order management, configuration management, materials management and process management.

### MRPII Corporate Mission Statements

- Build a 21st Century corporation.
- Eliminate disconnected, uncoordinated, competitive systems.

- Establish an integrated, coordinated decision-making way of functioning which comprehends business plans, budgets, product programs and relevant functions that support our business—a total systems approach.
- Create the ability to review all parts of the business, as well as the linkages holding them together to allow for more informed, more timely and more shrewd business decisions.
- Develop a company computer-integrated paperless operation, to the most practical extent possible.

In the 1960's, the material and inventory control management in American manufacturing looked to electronic technology as a better tool to schedule and order materials. The program is known as the *Materials Requirements Planning (MRP)* system.

A decade later the MRP system grew to involve all operations and computer software was improved to support the planning and manufacturing processes. The term *Manufacturing Resource Planning (MRP)* is used to describe this process. The whole concept developed into a *Closed Loop MRP System* and the term MRPII was coined

At Mack, MRPII means the tools, the plans and, most importantly, the People planning and working together to close the *loop* in formulating and executing one game plan. The corporate mission statements show *what and when* must be done. The MRPII closed loop system shows how it is to be done.

In closing, an ongoing internal and external measurement system determines areas that are weak allowing for a solution to be developed and implemented with the end result being a better quality product or service.

Employees are given extensive training in MRP and MRPII processes and why quality products and services are so important to the success of Mack Trucks. Emphasis is placed on the important role each and every employee plays in providing quality products and services. Employees and quality go hand-in-hand because employees are the producers and providers of quality products and service. Employees are the foundation for a quality program and at Mack Trucks quality is the foundation of its business.

# Quality Customer Service

**Merrell J. Fischer**
**Paul R. Roseland**
Navistar International Transportation Corporation

Navistar International Transportation Corporation, a wholly owned subsidiary of Navistar International Corporation, is a manufacturer of medium and heavy duty trucks and diesel engines.

Founded in 1902, International Harvester changed its name to Navistar International Corporation on February 20, 1986. On April 1, 1987 Navistar International Corporation combined its truck division and engine division to form Navistar International Transportation Corporation.

Now headquarterd in Chicago, Illinois, the company employs more than 13,500 persons.

# INTRODUCTION

At Navistar *quality* is defined by saying, "Quality is what our customers say it is, not what we say it should be." This basic principle is the foundation of the company's permanent commitment to serve its customers with quality products and support that meet *their* expectations of performance and value. So just how do Navistar employees fulfill this commitment? How do they specify, measure, manage, and evaluate quality service to their customers? The company's basic approach is to divide quality service into two dimensions: the *system* dimension and the *individual* dimension. Each is equally crucial to the delivery of quality service. The *system* dimension consists of all the established policies and procedures needed to deliver products and/or services. The *individual* dimension concerns how employees interact with customers— such things as the appearance, attitude, knowledge, and communication skills of individual workers.

## SYSTEM DIMENSION

Simplicity in design has to be the primary goal in system planning. A strong, well-trained distribution organization is paramount to user confidence and acceptance. Knowing that the distribution team has competent company-trained technical support (as needed) enhances quality service to the customer. The easier it is for customers to seek resolution and support for product concerns, the more appreciative they are of your system. Therefore, Navistar delegates the responsibility and authority for decision making to the level that interfaces with the customer, in order to provide on-the-spot settlement.

### Technical Service Support

Technical service problems are primarily handled by Navistar's dealer organization across North America. Dealers are supported by geographically located area Technical Service Managers (TSMs). Depending on the vehicle concentration, each TSM supports approximately ten dealer locations and their customers, plus national fleet accounts sold directly by the company (see figure 1).

Technical service problems that are immediate or chronic, or that appear to be a customer sensitive issue are referred by the TSM directly to the truck reliability center located in Fort Wayne, Indiana, for reliability engineering assistance. The controlling region receives copies of all such correspondence for their information and management needs. Technical problems requiring long-term resolution are communicated via a Truck Field Service Report (TFSR) directly to the regional office for advice and, if necessary, are forwarded to the Fort Wayne reliability engineering center for evaluation and resolution. Administrative concerns are similarly handled.

Technical service problems from customers can also be received by mail or phone by the customer relations department at the company's world

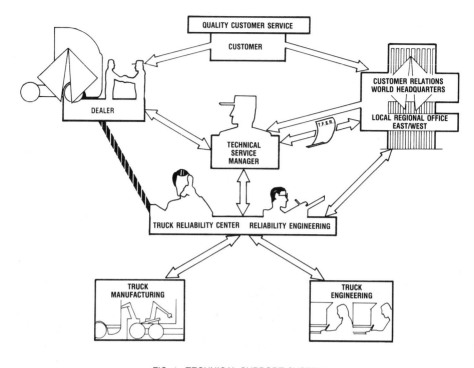

FIG. 1. TECHNICAL SUPPORT SYSTEM

headquarters in Chicago. The issues are immediately referred to the controlling regional office (east or west) and to the TSM whose territory is involved. If a Navistar dealer is involved directly or indirectly, the dealer is requested to make customer contact within twenty-four hours to initiate resolution of the complaint. The area TSM schedules a follow-up to resolve all such complaints within a ten day period.

Fort Wayne reliability center personnel communicate daily with the company's departments of engineering and manufacturing. This makes the entire field service organization a single call away from the manufacturing and engineering sources responsible for the design and assembly of company products.

## Warranty Administration

All that customers want is what they have been promised. When warranty coverage is properly explained at the time of sale and delivery of the product, the user knows exactly what to expect from the manufacturer and the seller. Warranty administration thereafter is simplified for all. Misunderstood coverage is the primary cause of warranty disputes.

Optional service contracts are offered as advertised options on the company's international product line; they are available to customers who wish to purchase extended warranty coverage on the total components of the vehicle. Such service contracts are modestly priced from reliability and warranty history data to enhance our product's value to the user. Service contracts are administered through a standard warranty system. (See figure 2).

At Navistar, warranty responsibility and accountability rest with the field service organization. The area TSM has final authority for warranty

## WARRANTY ADMINISTRATION SUPPORT SYSTEM

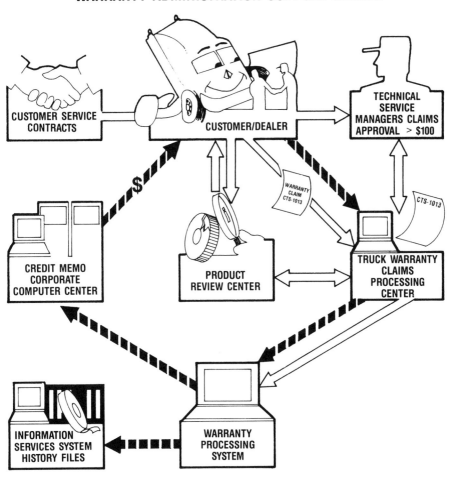

FIG. 2. WARRANTY ADMINISTRATION SUPPORT SYSTEM

administration in his or her assigned territory. Dealer warranty claims under one hundred dollars are submitted directly to the Truck Warranty Claims Center (TWCC) in Naperville, Illinois, for processing. Claims over one hundred dollars are reviewed and approved by the TSM, who returns them to the dealer for mailing to the TWCC. The data processing system then electronically stores the information for reliability management and credits the dealer account by the appropriate amount.

Via a random sampling program, failed material is requested for review by the engineering and reliability analysts, and by the supplier. The TSM or TWCC instructs the dealer to return specified material to the Fort Wayne product review center. The center shares information on its analysis with the dealer and the TSM in order to improve service techniques and support to the customer. The company's dealer organization has responded well to this system which has been in effect since 1982. Currently the company is converting its paper system to an electronic (paperless) system that will further improve efficiency, speed, the communication of information, and remuneration to the dealer organization.

## INDIVIDUAL DIMENSION

Understandably, the *individual* dimension at Navistar forms the backbone of its quality service delivery. As resident field service personnel, TSMs are assigned strategically throughout North America to serve our customers (see figure 3). Navistar has 83 field service TSMs supporting 500 major fleets and 776 medium- and heavy-duty truck dealer outlets. This group of professionals possess a broad base of technical experience, interpersonal skills, and business management expertise. The company's continuous training programs dedicate several weeks each year to honing their skills and introducing them to new information about products.

While many other companies chose to start all employees in their service departments and to promote from within, Navistar has developed its field service organization into a professional team with a distinct identity, as with other career paths within the company. The field service organization is an intricate part of the company's reliability and quality department. The vice president of that department occupies a position on the same organizational plane as those of other vice presidents who report to the company president. It follows that when a company treats quality and service with the same importance as sales, engineering, manufacturing, and finance, it builds an organization of professionals with a common purpose—that of quality service—and with pride and team spirit. Per person, this group averages almost twenty years of international product-line experience at their specialty.

## CUSTOMER FEEDBACK

The final judgment of authentic quality service must come from the customer. After all, he or she is really the only one who receives the service and can

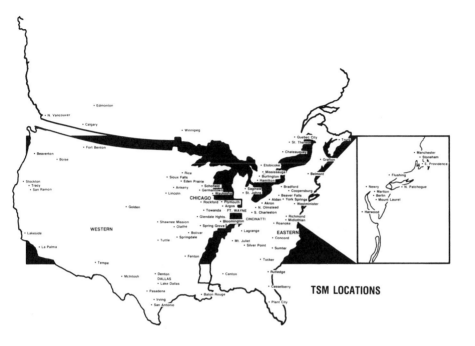

FIG. 3. TSM LOCATIONS

speak from experience. It is the customer's perception which determines whether or not the company offers quality service. To understand that perception, one can listen to two types of customer feedback: solicited and unsolicited.

## Solicited Feedback

The truck assembly plants randomly send out comment cards to the customer and dealer on record. Users' comments are shared with plant assembly-line personnel who rarely get firsthand contact with the buyer. Everyone wants to know if he or she is doing a good job.

The majority of Navistar products are "drive-away" delivered, by independent carriers, transporting up to four units at a time via piggyback. Their drivers are the first professional drivers to test "off-line" quality. Information from drive-away drivers provides an invaluable tool in assessing the company's systems of quality in manufacturing.

Dealer service technicians utilize "new vehicle quality inspection report forms" to report product deficiencies that require repair or adjustment beyond the normal pre-delivery inspection guide. Their comments serve, for the assembly plant and the engineering department, as another source of early warning of potential product problems.

Fleet customers ordering multiple unit quantities are invited to participate in a pilot review of the first off-line unit of their order. This type of
review affords both the customer and Navistar the opportunity to inspect
the vehicle in the plant, along with the customer's maintenance director to
ensure that the order will be built according to *his* expectations. Additionally,
it gives the plant personnel the opportunity to review any problems on this
order; this might be problems the maintenance director has experienced
with either Navistar's or a competitor's product. Any changes required to
satisfy the customer's expectations can be made prior to "build" of the
remaining order.

Quarterly quality feedback sessions are held with dealers in different
locations across North America. These meetings, which are chaired by the
vice president of reliability and quality are designed to provide the company
with an ongoing assessment of the dealer's perception of company quality
and to elicit specific recommendations for improvement.

The Truck Maintenance Council (TMC) of the American Trucking
Association is a member organization of more than fourteen hundred members;
approximately half are users and half are suppliers or manufacturers. They
meet three times annually at different geographic locations. The themes of
"technical interchange" and "partners in progress" between users and Original Equipment Manufacturers/suppliers allow for a timely round-table session
where users can challenge the quality or reliability or service support of
anyone's products. This meeting continues to be a valuable tool to measure
the industry's perception of Navistar's service support organization.

Periodically (approximately four times per year), Navistar reliability
personnel host a meeting to update a major user about product quality.
Vice presidents and directors of maintenance, and regional warranty and
maintenance management personnel represent the user. Navistar has key
reliability, field service, and engineering personnel available to discuss any
current product problems, recent product improvements, and plans to address known problems.

## Unsolicited Feedback

As you might suspect, this is the sweet-and-sour of any feedback program.
Customer complaints and compliments are the most immediate sources of
customer evaluation of products. Navistar publishes two toll-free "800"
numbers for this purpose and encourages their use. One number is a direct
line to the customer relations department in the world headquarters, and the
other number is linked to the reliability center in Fort Wayne to respond to
specific technical questions from dealers. This line enables dealer personnel
to have access to the reliability engineering department who can assist them
with pressing technical problems when their TSM is in transit or is otherwise unavailable. The TSM remains the primary source of technical support
for day-to-day advice.

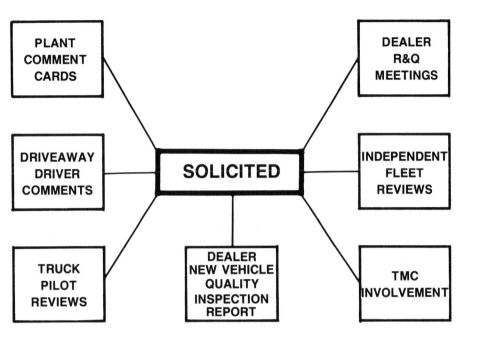

FIG. 4. SOLICITED CUSTOMER FEEDBACK

Any type of feedback is an opportunity to better understand the customer's views of a company's ability to respond to and support their needs. A company's responsiveness to customer feedback is readily visible to the user. The customer's opinion and perceptions are measures of the company's quality service; therefore, one seizes the opportunity to demonstrate the importance of the user's concerns to the company.

## IMPLEMENTATION of BETTER CUSTOMER SERVICE
Quality service cannot be assigned to any one department or individual. Quality service is considered to be everyone's job at Navistar. In moving toward the 1990' s, the company has mapped out an action plan for the near future in order to improve customer services. In particular, to improve its current level of support, the company set goals to have service people *more available* to customers and to *speed its resolution* of problems.

### More Available Time
Field service personnel will spend more time with customers by
- Reducing the amount of time spent in warranty administration.
- Handling their administrative duties more efficiently.

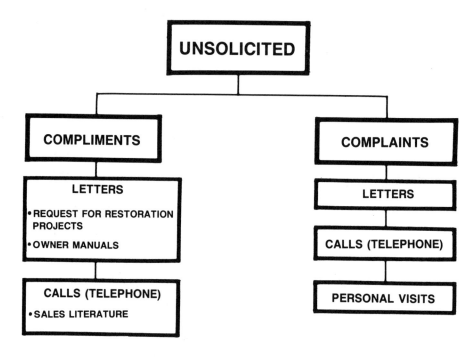

FIG. 5. UNSOLICITED CUSTOMER FEEDBACK

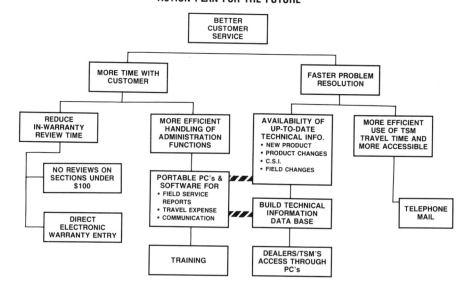

FIG. 6. ACTION PLAN FOR THE FUTURE

Warranty administration time has been reduced by authorizing dealers to submit all claims under one hundred dollars directly to the TWCC for processing without prior TSM review and approval. The company has confirmed a 30% reduction in warranty administration effort by TSMs as a result of this change. Direct electronic warranty entry, currently in place at 33 dealer and 7 fleet locations, is expected to expand to approximately 150 locations by the end of FY88. When completed, the electronic warranty system will further reduce the TSM involvement with the processing of claims and will increase the TSM availability to focus on customer needs.

Administrative duties are being done more efficiently by means of high-tech, state-of-the-art electronics. The company in the process of providing all TSMs with portable PCs and appropriate software to communicate reports, technical information, and training aids electronically.

A new technical data collection system (figure 7) demonstrates how company personnel equipped with PCs and related software can access a bulletin board program. This programs allows any TSM to communicate via a modem with a dedicated computer programmed with the bulletin board system. He may ask a question, make a statement, or request specific information from any individual. The reliability engineer responsible for the component or product involved can respond on the same bulletin board; any other TSM receiving the same message on "call-up" can answer the problem or simply become informed about the problem and solution. Complete training programs can also be transmitted through this system: the latter will enable TSMs to conduct specific on-the-spot training.

## Faster Problem Resolution

Truck Field Service Reports can be submitted via the same system, thus eliminating the delay of mailing and routing information. New product information, product changes, customer sensitive issues, and field change information can also be transmitted by this system so as to speed problem resolution for our customers.

While all this speedy, electronic communication is transpiring, a technical database is being created for future use and training. Additionally, the company can foresee that failure analysis results (from failed material reviews) can also be incorporated daily into this communication system. This will permit the immediate opportunity to share with the entire organization failure analysis data in a timely fashion.

"Windshield" (travel time) amounts to 25% of the field service organization's time, often leaving the TSMs inaccessible by their various constituencies. To improve their accessibility, the company introduced a telephone mail system that allows dealers and customers to call an individual TSM's number and receive daily or hourly information on the travel itinerary of each. They can also leave messages on the system for periodic

## TECHNICAL DATA COLLECTION SYSTEM

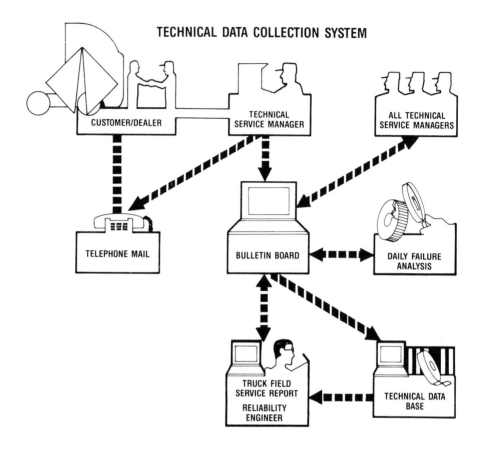

FIG. 7. TECHNICAL DATA COLLECTION SYSTEM

call-up by the TSM during the day. All of these actions mean *more available time* with our customers and *faster problem resolution*.

## CORPORATE COMMITMENT

The commitments described will guide Navistar to its goal of offering quality service and products that are clearly superior to those of its competitors. It will improve Navistar's position as a leading producer of medium- and heavy-duty trucks in North America and progressively improve its profitability and shareowner value.

We believe our people are the source of our competitive advantage which is created by:

- Making "Service to the Customer" the primary goal of all Navistar people.
- Continuously improving the quality of our efforts and thereby the overall productivity of the organization.
- Working together in the spirit of teamwork and cooperation to achieve our common goals.

Only by continually focusing on creating value for our customers can we create value for our shareowners, and reward our employees, who are the source of competitiveness.

There are many accepted definitions of quality. Webster defines "quality" as "that which makes something what it is." Quality Engineering departments preach that "quality is conforming to requirements" . . . "that there is no such thing as good quality or bad quality, because a product or service either conforms to specific requirements or it doesn't. If a product meets its specific requirements, then it is a quality product." David Garvin in the Fall, 1984 issue of *Sloan Management Review* defines the philosophic approach as "innate excellence", which like beauty can be understood only through exposure to objects that display its characteristics." However, at Navistar we define it by saying, "Quality is what our customers say it is, not what we say it should be."

Any company unable to promote increased employee involvement, productivity, teamwork and knowledge will not survive in a mature market. Quality customer service has to be recognized as the foundation of repeat business. Navistar intends quality service to be a reality, not simply a slogan.

# Quality Service Program

**Ronald W. Post**
**Randal L. Fingarson**
Winnebago Industries, Inc.

Winnebago Industries, Inc. is a leading U.S. manufacturer of motor homes used for leisure travel and recreation activities. The vehicles are sold through dealer organizations under the Winnebago and Itasca brand names. Subsidiaries of Winnebago Industries include Winnebago Acceptance Corporation, a financial subsidiary; Cycle-Sat, Inc., a satellite courier service used by television advertisers; and North Iowa Electronics, an electronic equipment assembly firm.

Winnebago Industries was incorporated in 1958 and assumed its present name in 1961. It employs approximately 2,800 individuals and is headquartered in the rural community of Forest City, Iowa.

## CORPORATE QUALITY STATEMENT

It is Winnebago Industries' policy to provide products and services of a quality that fully and consistently meets the initial and continuing needs of its customers. Quality is no longer defined as conformance to manufacturing standards and specifications, but rather as a measure of performance excellence in every aspect of the company's business. Products and services must incorporate features of performance, durability, reliability, safety, and appearance that consistently reflect favorably on the company and its employees. It is not possible to create quality by inspection. It must be designed and manufactured right the first time. The success of Winnebago Industries begins and ends with its people. Every individual must do everything possible to satisfy customer needs. Delivering products and services that consistently meet customer requirements will ensure a satisfactory relationship and a continuing and thriving business in the future. To achieve this goal, Winnebago Industries has made a corporate commitment to "a total quality process."

## Dealer Selection

Given the method of product distribution, Winnebago Industries has two customers to satisfy: the Winnebago or Itasca dealer and the retail buyer. Both must be satisfied for the company to be successful.

The company's primary customer service support is through its dealer network, so it makes sense that dealers are carefully selected with consideration toward providing customer satisfaction. Dealers are selected and approved only after compliance with corporate standards in areas such as commitment to customer satisfaction; plant, property, and equipment knowledge; manpower; financing; and desire, experience and market penetration.

## Dealer Training

Having met the selection requirements, the dealer and sales staff are trained by the sales district manager in product features and benefits. Training is by means of video tape, brochures, and detailed product books.

The first service a customer encounters with Winnebago Industries is the product knowledge of the sales staff. Since this first encounter is so important, the company hires independent people, "mystery shoppers," in each area of the country to pose as retail buyers and test dealerships on their product knowledge. If the salesperson accurately presents key features, he or she is financially rewarded on the spot. Good dealers are identified and rewarded. The program also identifies those dealers in need of additional training. Based upon these results, special on-site training programs are started for dealers needing improvement.

Service district managers train the dealership in proper service administration. Winnebago Industries was the first in the RV business to have a service district manager (DM) team and the company still has the largest in the industry. Each of the service DMs are trained in Winnebago Industries' systems and techniques before they go on the road representing the firm. They know the priority the company places on satisfying customers and they are in a position to assure that each dealer places a similar priority on satisfying their customers. These service DMs train the dealership in policies and procedures necessary to their everyday business and in the proper methods of dealing with customers to assure that quality services are provided.

Technical training of the dealership service staff is ongoing twelve months a year. Winnebago Industries has its own staff providing constant training regionally throughout the country. The training program focuses not only on updating technicians on new products and technology, but also on helping the dealers train new people in RV service. All class participants evaluate the course content to assure that Winnebago Industries meets their service training needs. Also, the instructor evaluates the students' participation and performance. This information is provided to the dealer and student. Twice a year, questionnaires are mailed to dealerships to determine their future training needs. The responses to these questionnaires directly drive the curriculum development.

New to Winnebago Industries in 1987 was WSTV, the Winnebago Service Training Video program. Having met with outstanding initial response, this video training program is becoming an integral part of the dealer training program. While currently focusing on high tech components and skills necessary to service RVs, plans are being developed to expand training films into handling customer complaints, service administration, warranty submission, and service management.

As a first in the RV industry, the company pioneered WIDDI, Winnebago Industries Dealership Development Institute. With its development costs funded by the corporation, this institute has completed the first significant survey of the industries' dealers and their needs. The goal of the program is to bring top professional management ability to the industry.

In the relatively young recreational vehicle industry it is common to find entrepreneurs who have successfully brought a small business up to a current $2 to $10 million-a-year business. These entrepreneurs are successful because of long hours, hard work, and risk-taking. On the other hand, these are not the keys to maintaining customer satisfaction, maximizing profits, and developing employees in an already successful business. WIDDI helps develop the dealers' awareness and ability in achieving precisely those goals in all facets of their operation. Programs are conducted for dealership principals, sales managers, service managers, and parts managers.

The final measure in dealer training is Cycle-Sat. Acquired in 1987 as a subsidiary of Winnebago Industries, Cycle-Sat is a satellite uplink and courier service. A direct uplink with Winnebago and Itasca dealers is planned for 1989. This opens up such possibilities as instantaneous nationwide product training for salespeople on new models, nationwide multiple-dealer service training and seminars and conferences with top corporate management. All can be broadcast directly from our offices in Iowa.

## PRODUCT SUPPORT SERVICES

Obtaining and training quality dealers is only the first step in Winnebago Industries' thrust to supply quality service to customers. It is followed by a corporate commitment to supplying quality services to dealers. The company's product support services area does just that. By maintaining a staff of technical service consultants and a toll-free telephone line, dealers have free access to consult with factory experts as the need arises. The company tracks any calls that were not received because the line was busy and makes adjustments to meet these needs.

With product changes and innovations occurring throughout the year, dealer support is needed constantly. The Service Publications Department supplies information to dealers on new products and service techniques as changes take place in production. After all, the quality of service given by dealers is dependent on the quality of service they receive.

Quality service must be supported by quality parts and parts availability. In addition to the parts sales division at the home location, parts warehouses are located in the same area as production facilities. In this way the entire manufacturing operation can support the parts needs of dealers. Winnebago Industries maintains a parts warehousing facility in Nevada for the West Coast and in Delaware for the East Coast. These parts warehouses supply 24-hour to 48-hour service. This allows dealers to better serve their customers.

Parts distribution is a multi-million dollar segment of Winnebago Industries' business. It is computerized so that reports can be published on the following key areas:

- Same day fill rate of daily, stock, and expedited orders
- Next day fill rate of daily, stock, and expedited orders
- Back-ordered inventory
- Line fill percentages
- New items filled first time
- Comparisons of order points and inventory turns to projections
- Items picked, packed, and shipped per employee
- Sales per employee, and
- Individual dealer sales compared to last year and current year projections.

But while technology is useful, the truly indispensable part of any success equation is people. Each area of the country is assigned a special parts representative who insures that dealers' needs are met. Also parts departments have toll-free phone numbers for dealers. The company recognizes the need for fast, easy, and cost-free access for dealers, and by lowering barriers that could inhibit dealers from calling, they are encouraged to assist the retail customer.

## RETAIL OWNER SUPPORT

Although the dealer supplies the primary support to the customer, Winnebago Industries also offers them direct support. Recognizing that recreational vehicles are purchased by people for leisure, travel, and group companionship, Winnebago Industries organized a special club for Winnebago owners in 1969. Its purpose is to enhance the ownership experience for those that wish to participate.

WIT, Winnebago-Itasca Travelers Club, organizes national activities and supports local chapter activities throughout the United States and Canada. The WIT Club currently serves 11,000 owners, 6 international clubs, 45 state clubs, and 171 local chapters.

The WIT Club provides owners with such services as a monthly club newspaper, regional rallies, international excursions, trip routing service, special campground and part purchase discounts, and a mail forwarding service.

Highlighting the WIT Club activities each year is the Grand National Rally held in Forest City, Iowa. Each August, approximately 1,700 Winnebago and Itasca vehicles carrying 4,300 people converge to take part in this company-sponsored event. The Grand National Rally is an event for everyone. Suppliers are on hand to answer questions and provide services. Winnebago Industries service employees also hold several seminars on principles of operation and maintenance of the motor home. A bazaar-type atmosphere exists, comradery is easy, and new acquaintances are formed while old friendships are renewed. Each year's activities include nationally known entertainment for the final evening of the rally.

Careful not to lose the opportunity of gathering knowledge during the Grand National Rally, Winnebago Industries holds meetings each day with owners. These meetings focus on details such as dealer service, product quality, factory support, and product development. They are structured in a manner to solicit criticism and new ideas to improve our products and services. The company places great importance on those meetings and the information derived from them. They provide two important outcomes: first, owners feel closer to Winnebago Industries and the product, thereby furthering their product loyalty; second, the information gained is incorporated in new products, programs, and services allowing the corporation to stay close to the customer.

### Owner Relations

The Owner Relations Department is staffed by customer-oriented professionals trained in the arts of communication and negotiation. A procedural manual has been epecially developed for representatives in this department because of the demanding nature of the job. These men and women answer thousands of calls and letters each year ranging from requests for information by an owner who just purchased a used motor home to dissatisfied owners of new vehicles who cannot control their temper or language. The number of calls, type of product and inquiry are monitored and measured in order to adjust manpower and measure performance.

Dealing with the customer in a fair and equitable manner is the prime reason the owner relations department began. But over recent years, it has evolved into an information gathering service that helps the company monitor the quality of its products, dealers, and services. Now all complaints are categorized by product, service, sales, or parts, and all pertinent vehicle information is gathered to properly reflect exactly why the problem exists. This information is fed into a computer which gives reports on the following:

- The dealer with most service complaints
- The dealer with most parts complaints
- The dealer with most sales complaints
- The complaints in each service district
- The model of vehicle with most complaints
- Each dealer's percent of complaints as related to retail sales activity
- Product areas in need of improvement.

These reports are distributed to the appropriate departments so that action can be taken to reduce complaints. Weekly meetings are held to communicate any existing problem, initiate corrective action, and assure that the problem stays resolved. This information is important because it relies upon information given directly by the customer. It is immediate and identifies problems within the entire range of the product cycle: sales, service, and distribution network.

## WARRANTY

Winnebago Industries' warranty system provides another means of obtaining valuable information. Data is taken from every warranty claim submitted by dealers for vehicle repair. Because warranty data is considered to be an important problem identification source for products, a Technical Information Code (TIC) for accurate defect reporting and warranty claim processing has been developed. This TIC is used by the dealer as a method of identifying the part that failed and its mode of failure.

Warranty data can be submitted by the dealer by filling out a Warranty Repair Order (WRO) or via computer link. This makes all warranty feedback immediate, and avoids unnecessary delays from paperwork processing. Whether the claim is sent through the mail or entered via a modem link direct from the dealer, all claims are audited for accuracy through a series of computer edits. Once claims are accepted into the database, they become a part of the Quality Department's ongoing product review system. The warranty product review system identifies quality problem areas. The database provides the following information: product model, failed component, cause of failure, frequency of occurrence, and cost of repair. Information is statistically analyzed and restructured by quality assurance personnel to establish a priority ranking. The major variables used in establishing the priority ranking include safety, inconvenience to the customer, frequency of occurrence, and cost. This system insures that quality problems are identified and prioritized from the customer's perspective.

Once quality problem areas have been identified, effort is then focused on investigating the cause of the problem and implementing the corrective action to resolve the problem. The final step is measuring and monitoring the results to assure that the quality problem has been eliminated. Special reports monitor units by build date to assure that the corrective action was made and remains successful.

Input from the warranty system has resulted in significant improvement in product quality and a dramatic reduction in warranty expense. Warranty information also gives significant data for the Service Department to use in accessing its internal needs and the needs of its dealers. For example, claims submitted that contain errors or misinformation are returned to the dealer for correction. If a dealer has many claims returned for correction or denied, the service district manager will educate the responsible personnel on proper claim submission. This is not done with the intent of denying payment, but rather to assure accurate information so that problem areas are identified. The importance of this step cannot be overstated. Business relationships have been won and lost through warranty payments. Lack of corporate action means improper payments to the dealer and improper defect reporting. Real problems go unidentified, ultimately affecting the success of Winnebago Industries.

Dealer warranty expenses that reflect significantly out-of-norm conditions are reviewed according to average warranty expense per wholesale vehicle, average warranty expense per retail vehicle, percent of warranty expense prior to retail, labor to parts ratios and transient warranty expense. All statistics are weighted to provide each dealer within a district with the same labor rate. This is a must to achieve accurate expense comparisons.

Low, as well as high, dealer warranty expenses are checked for possible problem areas. Low expense normally means one of two problems. Either the dealer is not providing service to the customer, or the dealer is providing services but is not properly submitting or being credited for the work. High expense normally means either the dealer is improperly requesting the warranty, or the dealer's service personnel is improperly trained and needs more time to repair a customer vehicle.

When a dealer is not providing service to the customer, customer dissatisfaction and loss of market share will ultimately result. When a dealer is not properly collecting for services provided, profits are lost and business success is jeopardized, as is the manufacturer/dealer relationship. This, as well, will result in customer dissatisfaction and loss of market share.

Service district managers review those dealerships requiring attention. Sometimes a consultant from the home office service department will be called in.

When such consultations are performed, the following procedure is carried out:

- Advanced planning
- Preliminary dealer contact
- Dealer service analysis
  - work efficiency analysis
  - diagram actual repair order flow
  - review shop time control
  - review dealer recording and scheduling practices
  - review warranty claim ledger
  - perform warranty claim analysis
  - assure vehicle predelivery inspection procedure
  - review parts department ordering, inventory, and disbursement practices
- Findings and recommendations to the dealer
- Report to home office
- Dealer follow-up.

Winnebago Industries has had great success with this consultation program. Management has been able to see positive results from these efforts as have the company's dealers. By performing the program in an atmosphere of cooperation and completing it a professional analysis and follow-up, dealers and Winnebago Industries have been brought closer together.

## CIRCLE OF EXCELLENCE

The Circle of Excellence is made up of dealers who excel in providing quality service to their customers. It is also a program that rewards the excellent dealer regardless of the size of the dealership or market area. Based upon a perfect score of one hundred points (forty available in sales, sixty available in parts and service), Winnebago Industries' personnel rate every dealer using qualitative and quantitative measurements. The criteria for this evaluation can be found in Table 1.

TABLE 1.
CIRCLE OF EXCELLENCE CRITERIA

Sales

| | |
|---|---|
| Dealer-Manufacturer Relationship | • Willingness to participate in Winnebago Industries programs, constructive product input (competitive and Winnebago & Itasca product)<br>• Forecasting and maintenance of required inventory levels<br>• Market penetration<br>• Advertising, merchandising, shows and open houses, use of Winnebago Industries' co-op advertising and public relations programs<br>• WIT activity support—rallies, show-and-tells, encouraging customer membership |
| Sales Personnel | • Appearance, politeness<br>• Product knowledge<br>• Effective salesmanship (qualifying buyer, closing techniques, follow-up, etc.) |
| Product Presentation and Buyer Satisfaction | • Features and benefits<br>• Demonstration<br>• Review warranty coverage |
| Facility | • Signage<br>• Vehicle display (inside and outside)<br>• General appearance |

Parts and Service

| | |
|---|---|
| Owner Care | • Customer relations<br>• Transient care<br>• Dealer personnel, attitude, cooperation<br>• Facility, equipment, cleanliness |
| Warranty | • Familiarity with policy and procedure<br>• Network system<br>• Submission of warranty claim—flat rate and TIC codes<br>• Warranty expense<br>• Turnarounds, denials, adjustments |
| Technical Service | • Service—quality, promptness, courteousness<br>• Product knowledge—information<br>• Communication—organization |
| Training | • Utilization of available training<br>• Maintain trained technicians |
| Parts Sales | • Personnel—professional and knowledgeable<br>• Familiarity with policy and procedure<br>• Credit submission—shortages, damages, etc.<br>• Percentage of stock orders<br>• Use of parts sales materials—microfiche, catalogs, accessories, etc.<br>• Inventory control |

## Customer Satisfaction Index

In 1988, Winnebago Industries will begin a Customer Satisfaction Index (CSI) to measure its success and make changes in its products and services. The CSI will be an analysis of two buyer surveys. The first will be conducted thirty days after the purchase and will focus on sales and products; the second will be six months after the purchase and will focus on service and product reliability.

Correlating with the CSI is a dealer survey conducted each year by Winnebago Industries. The surveys are conducted anonymously to find out how dealers compare Winnebago Industries with other manufacturers and with the dealer and customer needs.

## SUMMARY

In closing, Winnebago Industries is proud of its commitment to quality service. That pride and that commitment flow from the founder and chairman of the board, John K. Hanson, through the president and CEO, Gerald Gilbert, to every employee in the company. Quality *statistics* mean nothing without quality *action* and our charge is clear: the action taken must respond to the *customer's* perception of what is needed. Only then does real quality exist.

# Office Equipment, Computers

Control Data Corporation
Neil C. Lien

Digital Equipment Corporation
Will O'Brien

Hewlett-Packard
Phil Carter and Thom Edmonds

IBM Corporation
Johnson A. Edosomwan

Wang Laboratories
Joseph Lester III

# Service Quality at Control Data Corporation

**Neil C. Lien**
Control Data Corporation

Control Data Corporation provides computer products and services for scientific, engineering, and business applications. Founded in 1957, it was one of the first major computer companies in the country. In that same year its first computer, the 1604, was introduced and delivered to the U.S. Navy Bureau of Ships. Today, the company generates annual revenues of $3.4 billion from five major business groups:

The Computer Systems and Services Group which provides complex computing solutions and information management for companies worldwide. A complete range of maintenance and support services, for both Control Data and other manufacturers products are also provided.

The Data Storage Products Group supplies high-performance, high-capacity magnetic data storage products.

The Business Services Group provides marketing information, business administration and financial information services through a combination of in-depth industry knowledge and information processing technologies.

The Government Systems Group supplies standard military computers and peripherals and is also a prime contractor in electronics system integration.

The Training and Education Group supplies training and education products to business and industry as well as the kindergarten through junior college academic market.

Headquartered in Minneapolis, Minnesota, the company employs more than 34,000 employees and conducts business in more than 40 countries worldwide.

## SERVICE QUALITY CONCEPTS

Service quality as perceived by customers has meaning only when viewed with a full understanding of the definition of the term *quality*. At Control Data, quality is defined as *meeting customers' needs and expectations*.

To fully appreciate this definition, the word *customer* needs further explanation. What customers are and are not should always be clear, especially to a service organization. Mistaken notions of this can create devastating results.

Customers are *not* dependent on employees; rather, the reverse is true. Instead of being interruptions to employees' work, they are the purpose of it. Customers are not outsiders to the business; they are the most important part of it. Finally, customers are *not* cold statistics; they are human beings with problems and feelings. You must treat them as you expect to be treated.

On the other hand, customers are affected by the way each employee does his or her work. Anything done to improve customers' opinions of employees is important. That is why a customer-conscious employee is always a better employee: he or she recognizes what the business is all about. Customers are people who rely on workers.

An organization that is committed to serving its customers by meeting their needs and expectations has positioned itself for success. But commitment is not enough. A process is also necessary, through which a service provider can continuously gain understanding of its customers—a process through which the company can actively and routinely strive to improve its quality image in the eyes of its customers.

### Service Quality Model

Technical services at Control Data has patterned its quality improvement efforts around a service quality model developed by A. Parasuraman, V. A. Zeithaml, and L. L. Berry, professor at Texas A&M (see figure 1). As the model indicates, customers develop a set of expectations against which they judge the service delivered. Those expectations result from things such as word-of-mouth communications, a set of personal needs, and certainly, past experience. The job of a service supplier is to understand clearly any gaps between what the customer expects and what the customer perceives they are receiving. (This is noted as gap 5 on the model in figure 1.) Thus, if the objective is to measure the effectiveness of the service delivered, the company needs to measure gap 5. The mechanism for measuring this gap is Control Data's customer satisfaction survey process.

Measurement, however, is not enough. The company needs to recognize that things happen on the supplier side of this model that cause gap 5 to be larger than it needs to be. First, a gap may exist between what the customer expects and what management perceives the customer expects (gap 1). Second, even if management's perceptions of the customers' expectations are

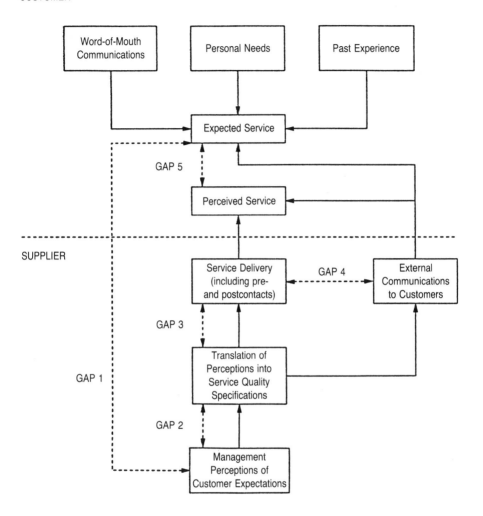

CUSTOMER

SUPPLIER

FIG 1.   SERVICE QUALITY MODEL

accurate, those perceptions may not get completely translated into service quality specifications (gap 2). Third, there are always some implementation problems, differences between specification and actual service delivery (gap 3). Last, if communications with the customer either oversell or undersell the true service delivery capability, yet another gap which alters customers' expectations and perceptions can be created (gap 4).

## SERVICE MANAGEMENT PROCESS

This service quality model clearly illustrates that to minimize the gap between customer expectations and the perceived level of service, the service provider needs to have *a defined process by which it internally converts customer and marketplace needs and expectations into the actual delivery of the product — effective service.*

### Functional Service Organizations

Figure 2 is an illustration of how this occurs. The marketing organization is responsible for understanding customer needs and expectations. Those needs and expectations establish market requirements which drive the sales, administration, support, and customer service organizations. Figure 2 highlights the key cross-functional processes required to drive Control Data's service business. It links those requirements together into an overall process by which the total service organization operates. Here, then, is how Control Data's service business actually operates and is managed.

**Marketing.** Marketing is responsible for the front end and the back end of the process. At the front end, they convert customer and marketplace needs and expectations into a set of market requirements that drive the functional line organizations. *Market-driven* is one of three key values at Control Data. At the back end of the process, marketing is responsible for managing the customer satisfaction assessment process. As figure 2 indicates, the assessment results (perceived levels of service) are fed back to all functions within the organization for appropriate visibility and corrective action.

**Sales.** Sales is responsible for selling in concert with the marketing plan, managing attrition, and forecasting future business and sales activities.

**Administration.** Three administrative processes are key to overall customer satisfaction with service the customer order process, invoicing process, and the collections process.

**Support operations.** Activities here are vital to Control Data's quality-of-service efforts. Many different processes are used to ensure that proper support elements are in place and functioning. An overall support planning process ensures efficiency and effectiveness of the spare parts, asset management, training, and technical support functions. Deficiencies in, or late delivery of, any of these support elements will cause hardships for customers.

**Customer service operations.** This is the field service organization which consists of two thousand-plus employees who service the products that Control Data sells as well as provide maintenance services for selected products by other manufacturers. All the planning in the world will not do any good unless the field organization prepares and executes according to

ENGINEERING SERVICES

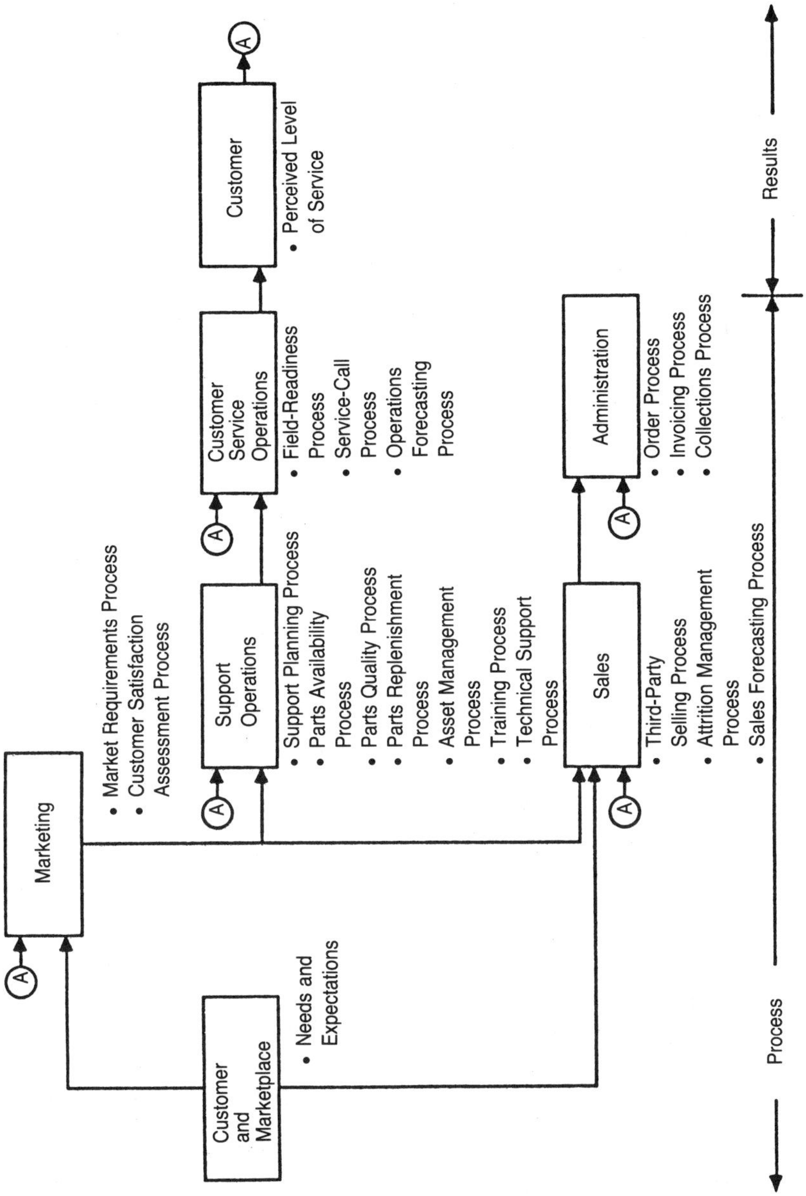


FIG 2. SERVICE MANAGEMENT PROCESS

documented plans. Thus, the company holds customer service operations accountable for the field-readiness process and the actual service-call process. The internal measurements for these processes are supportive of the customer satisfaction survey results in terms of what is important to customers. Three measures are key to customer satisfaction: (1) response time—how fast Control Data responds to the request for service; (2) repair time—how long it takes to resolve the problem, and 3) first-call effectiveness whether the problem is resolved on the first attempt.

## Seven Levels of Service Progress

The *basic* service management process at Control Data, stripped to its essentials, is illustrated by figure 3. (Obviously, additional measures of success exist which will be discussed as part of the customer satisfaction assessment process.) There is an overall model to follow and a set of service management processes that define organizational responsibilities. These cross-functional processes drive the service business. In addition, internal measurements that indicate the health of the service business have been established. Ultimately however, it is not only the data that counts. What really counts are *customers' perceptions* of service delivery versus their expectations. Here is where the customer satisfaction assessment process becomes important.

Control Data has defined seven levels of progress which are used to gauge how a given functional area is progressing in measuring its customers' satisfaction. Level one requires that there be a documented customer satisfaction assessment process in place. Level two certifies an area for being in the process of implementing the assessment. At level three, assessment data are being used to drive improvements. Level four means that a baseline has been established relative to past performance (or, for level five, relative to the competition). At level six, an area can show statistically valid improvement in baseline performance. When it can show statistically valid improvement in baseline performance *relative to the competition*, level seven is reached. Technical Services has been assessing its service and striving to improve customer satisfaction for several years. It is currently at level seven for 1988.

## CUSTOMER SATISFACTION ASSESSMENT PROCESS

A key element in accomplishing all of this is the customer satisfaction assessment process. Through this process Control Data learns whether prior efforts have hit the mark and areas in need of improvement are identified. Historically, engineering services has surveyed customers once a year. Random samples from the customer base provide statistically representative data at the U.S., district, and Kind of Business (KOB) levels. Kinds of businesses distinguish types of Control Data product maintenance, such as third-party maintenance. A pilot methodology is currently under test in which Technical Services surveys one-twelfth of its customers each month, rather than all customers at once. This methodology provides more current

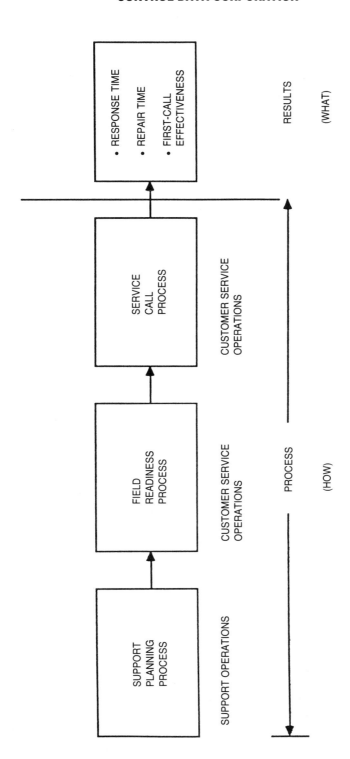

FIG 3. SERVICE MANAGEMENT

data; it is more supportive of the continuous improvement objectives than single annual surveys.

## Survey Process Categories

Even though repair time, response time, and first-call effectiveness have already been mentioned as three key measures of Control Data's service success, there are several more which also deserve close attention. By conducting focus group sessions with customers, six survey categories have been developed with several questions assigned to each: response time, human relations competence, technical competence, sales, administration, and customer comments. As the survey categories indicate, there is much more to customer satisfaction than simply fixing the problem at hand. Human relations skills are key. Included in this category are questions relative to problem follow-up activity, listening skills, and general responsiveness to customers' needs.

The sales category deals with such items as the sales representative's performance in answering customers' questions, keeping customers informed, and knowledge of the services offered. The administration category focuses on billing timeliness and accuracy, contract clarity, and proper handling of general administrative issues and concerns. The customer comments section is free-form. Any customer's comment, positive or negative, helps to better understand and improve service strategies, planning, and delivery.

## Measurement of Performance

The design of the survey instrument itself enables all categories to be measured. Looking at overall averages is not enough. Every average (regardless of the data) has a distribution associated with it. The data may be distributed by geography, kind of business, and the like.

Additionally, Technical Services needs to know how important a given item is to its customers, how satisfied customers are with that item, whether services are improving or declining over time, and how Control Data compares to the competition. For these reasons, satisfaction is measured via six different cuts of the data: overall satisfaction, satisfaction by geography, satisfaction by kind of business, importance versus satisfaction, satisfaction change from previous year, and satisfaction compared to competition. The importance-versus-satisfaction picture enables priorities to be set and focuses on areas that will have the biggest return to customer satisfaction. The same is true for the comparison-to-competition information.

## Timetable of Survey-Related Actions

The survey methodology, the survey categories, and the measurement methodologies discussed above are important, but they are ineffectual without a process or system to facilitate action.

The process begins about mid-year when marketing begins to work with an outside survey vendor to prepare for the next survey. A sampling plan is developed. The vendor mails the survey to customers in August; the surveys come back in September and during October, the data from the survey are processed and the survey vendor returns reports to Control Data. During November, Control Data does some additional internal analysis. Organizational executives receive a briefing in December.

During the first quarter of the following year, the line organizations act upon the data and put improvement strategies and plans in place. Meanwhile, survey results are communicated to all of the employees because each worker has the ability to affect the overall customer satisfaction with service. The remainder of the year, in parallel for getting ready to do the next survey, is spent on implementing the required improvements. In June, they also prepare a customer response brochure which highlights the findings, action plans, and any results from actions taken.

As illustrated in figure 2, the Technical Services service management process is a closed-loop system. It starts with understanding customers' needs and expectations. Those needs and expectations translate into service requirements which feed the planning processes that produce spare parts, training, and technical support.

The support plans developed drive the customer service (field) organization. Customer service takes the plans that have been developed and converts them into field readiness and service delivery processes. Service delivery is measured by three key indicators: response time, repair time, and first-call effectiveness. The customer satisfaction assessment process measures the gap between what customers expect and what they perceive they are receiving. This feedback is used to identify and drive improvement in all parts of the organization.

## RECENT IMPROVEMENTS IN SERVICES

The following represents a sample of some recent improvements in service delivery made as a result of listening to customers and taking action to improve the way the business is managed.

First, one of the key measures of effective service delivery is first-call effectiveness, the ability to fix the customers' problems on the first attempt. In the past two years, Control Data's performance has improved more than six percentage points. This is a big plus to the company's customers; it also saves Control Data in excess of one million dollars a year in revisit labor (rework).

Second, average service call response time has improved one half of one hour in the past year. Third, human relations skills, as perceived by Control Data's customers, is among the highest in the industry. Fourth, the response time to ship a part (if unavailable locally) to a customer engineer has improved by 100% in the past year-and-a-half. Finally, order processing response time has improved by 20%.

Control Data has seen much improvement; it continues to occur every day as part of the organization's commitment to serving its customers. It is a process that had a beginning, but has no end. Customers' needs and expectations continue to change; so, to be successful, Control Data too, must change. Control Data intends to be an advocate of change rather than its victim.

# Digital and Service Quality

**Will O'Brien**
Digital Equipment Corporation

Digital Equipment Corporation, headquartered in Maynard, Massachusetts, is the world's leading manufacturer of networked computer systems and associated peripheral equipment. Founded in 1957, the company provided real-time multi-user systems, primarily to scientific and technical users. Today, Digital offers a wide range of computer products and services through 650 sales and services facilities in more than sixty countries throughout the world.

Since the mid-1970s, Digital has grown dramatically, with its customer base expanding into every major industry and its revenues increasing an average of 20% annually. Service has grown to become a critical part of Digital's overall business. In fact, service and support now account for roughly one-third of the corporation's $9 billion-plus in annual revenues and one-third of its 114,000-person work force.

## INTRODUCTION

Digital Equipment Corporation wants to be number one. Not in size. Not in revenues. Not in profits. Digital wants to be number one in the eyes of its customers. Clearly articulated by top management, customer satisfaction has to be the company's foremost chief goal. Digital wants to be perceived as number one in every aspect of its business: the products it designs and manufactures, the solutions and services it provides, the people it employs, and the way it conducts its business with customers. Digital believes that by aggressively pursuing customer satisfaction in all these dimensions, industry leadership in the form of technological innovation, new markets, increased market share and higher profit margins will follow.

A company wide quality improvement drive plays a major role in Digital's determined pursuit of customer satisfaction. The program focuses on customers and on fully meeting their requirements 100% of the time. The company has made significant strategic investments in dollars, technology, education and human resources to incorporate quality into every operation at Digital, and into the very fabric of corporate culture.

The push for quality represents a refocusing on and a formalization of values and attitudes that have long been part of the company's business philosophy. Today, Digital sees itself as making the transition from being a quality-conscious company to being a quality-driven company.

Quality efforts at Digital are spearheaded by a corporate staff organization. Led by a quality manager with senior status and high visibility, the small cross-functional group does not serve as a "quality cop," but rather in a leadership role providing direction for the quality managers and helping management to integrate quality improvement into operational plans.

The corporate quality group has established a senior policy group, a leadership committee comprised of senior operating managers and a board of directors in engineering, manufacturing and field organization. The staff also works directly with line management and other functional groups— finance and administration, sales, field service, personnel—to implement quality improvement practices into each business.

The ultimate responsibility for quality lies not with the corporate quality group but with each individual function and operation. Each organization must identify its own quality goals, develop measurement criteria, invest in quality-related training and determine what human and financial resources are to be allocated for quality improvement efforts.

## THE CHALLENGE OF SERVICE QUALITY

To fully appreciate the challenge of pursuing service quality in this context, one must understand the complexity of Digital's service business. The company's customer support organization employs nearly 37,000 people worldwide in field service, software services, and educational services. Digital maintains more than 450 service locations, including fourteen Customer

Support Centers (CSCs) which operate 24-hours-a-day, 7-days-a-week; and twenty-seven Application Centers for Technology (ACTs) that provide industry-specific software applications support. In a competitive service environment, these centers provide a large portfolio of service offerings: field service programs to support hardware and software; computer-facilities planning services; services for computer networks; round-the-clock, onsite support for high-priority computer facilities; service on multi-vendor systems that are based on Digital central processing units (CPUs); data-security and disaster-recovery services; consulting services, and educational services.

The service organization makes extensive use of computer technology and artificial intelligence to expand the scope of services and shorten the time for service delivery. These tools include telephone call-handling software, computer-based learning materials, and diagnostic systems to analyze error data from computers at the customer site in order to repair predicted hardware failures before they occur.

Most importantly, in keeping with Digital's nonhierarchical form of management, the service organization works closely with virtually every other major function of the corporation. This occurs not just in day-to-day business operations but in strategic activities as well. For example, service works with sales and marketing to design products that are tailored to the customers' needs; with engineering to see that "serviceability" is designed into every product; and with manufacturing to ensure that system problems discovered by service personnel are quickly corrected.

This matrix structure—which stresses teamwork, communication, cross-functional interaction and interdependency—is derived from the very nature of Digital products and services, which are themselves designed for ease of interaction and are highly interdependent. Digital's company wide quality efforts also rely on cross-functional teamwork. With the emphasis on continual quality improvement and prevention, collaboration across company lines is essential if quality is to impact the way business is conducted with customers, suppliers, and internal groups.

## CHANGING ATTITUDES AND BEHAVIOR

The quest for total quality is closely linked to attitudes and behavior, as well as to technical skills and management leadership. Senior managers are important "stakeholders" in the program. Their visibility and support is critical to incorporating quality ethics into the organization.

Making the transition to total quality requires managers and employees to behave differently and to participate in new, more effective ways of planning, analyzing and restructuring processes for simplicity and smooth, continuous flow. The investment in quality improvement requires managers and employees to learn and apply new skills, tools and quality methodologies in their day-to-day operations. Education, therefore, is the cornerstone of Digital's drive for quality.

A cross-functional team of educational sponsors has produced an education curriculum to be delivered to all levels of Digital's workforce. Topics addressed range from quality awareness and statistical tools to process management and customer/vendor relationships. Using a "train the trainer" approach, each organization is learning to conduct its own training, with a resident expert driving the process.

By the end of 1988, nearly 30,000 people—one fourth of Digital's worldwide work force—will have received some form of quality training.

## DEVELOPING MEASUREMENTS AND GOALS

One of the most critical and difficult quality-improvement tasks is to develop a well-defined set of criteria for measuring customer satisfaction within major functions. Once these criteria have been identified, an effective set of tools for measuring those criteria and a feedback mechanism must be developed so the data can be used to improve products, services, and processes. The company must commit resources to resolving problems that are identified by the quality process. Lastly, each internal group must set goals and periodically measure progress made against those goals.

This is a time-consuming and costly process, yet a very necessary one. Digital has developed a set of corporate goals for quality and customer satisfaction to measure the performance of the engineering, manufacturing and field functions. These goals—for predictability, reliability and ease of doing business—are defined by the customer.

More specific goals are then defined and assigned for functions to work on collaboratively to meet commitment dates of new systems; to identify—to the week—the expected delivery of an ordered system, and to coordinate delivery and installation of complete systems. These quality goals must then be translated into actual programs and activities. For example, in keeping with the goal for "ease of doing business," Digital is redesigning its Order Transaction Processing System (OTP), the administrative system which tracks a sale from the first customer quote through the sale, shipping, delivery, installation, and invoicing. The previous system is being replaced by an automated system that will provide manufacturing with more timely information, thus impacting inventory control. When combined with other quality improvement efforts, issuing invoices in a timely manner helps reduce "days sales outstanding" and contributes to the corporation's cash flow.

### High-Tech, High-Touch

Digital's DECdirect Service provides a good example of how the company often combines high-tech and high-touch approaches to achieve quality-improvement. Through DECdirect Service, customers can call a toll-free number and order hardware, software, peripherals, supplies, and accessories from a catalog. The process is fast and convenient for the customer and a cost-effective sales channel for Digital. In recent years the number of calls and orders placed through DECdirect has skyrocketed. Rapid growth can be difficult to manage and is often characterized by overworked and harried staff, overtaxed administrative systems, and runaway costs resulting in very high "hidden" costs: customer dissatisfaction and lost business opportunities.

Yet during this period of growth, DECdirect has not only managed to maintain customer satisfaction but has dramatically improved it. Every DECdirect employee, from telemarketing representatives to the group manager, has undergone quality training, including customer services training and listening skills. In addition, DECdirect has invested in automated tools that make it possible to measure the average number of rings before a customer's call is answered, the average amount of time spent placing an order, the average length of time between placing an order and shipment of that order. The group also measures the time required to generate an invoice and send it to the customer.

DECdirect uses these measurements to identify trends such as peak calling periods, to plan for future staffing and equipment needs, to improve administrative systems, to target potential trouble spots, and to set new customer satisfaction/quality goals such as increasing the percentage of transactions completed on the first phone call. For Digital, savings reflected in higher profit margins and repeat business from satisfied customers are enormous.

## DELIVERY AND INSTALLATION

As part of the quality-improvement effort, Digital has also established the following closely linked goals for the delivery-and-installation phase: on-time shipments; order completeness; and trouble-free installation. Because Digital's products are so highly integrated—even a mid-size system may include dozens of separate components manufactured at several different sites. These three goals require an extremely high level of interaction, information exchange, and responsiveness among a number of internal groups: sales, which makes time-sensitive shipment commitments; manufacturing, which must schedule materials and produce the equipment; field service which must schedule engineers to install the system; and administrative groups that manage the flow of paperwork.

The quality installation program provides another example of how Digital combines automated tools with human resources to establish a system for detecting installation issues. When a field service engineer encounters an installation problem relating to design or manufacturing, he or she can report these issues electronically via the PRISM system, a feedback/reporting system which routes messages directly to the appropriate manufacturing facility. The PRISM contact at their plant determines and assigns the responsibility for corrective action to the right technical resource and communicates the solution back to the field engineer. The objective is to trace the problem to its origin and invest in preventive measures so it does not recur.

## WHEN THE CUSTOMER TALKS...

Although automated tools play a critical role in Digital's efforts to measure, report, and improve quality, the company uses two other important measurement methods: customer surveys and good old-fashioned person-to-person communication. Digital pays close attention to the quantitative data and the qualitative comments that are collected through independent industrywide surveys on service quality.

Every year Digital also conducts its own series of surveys asking customers to rate the performance of the company in key areas such as system availability, product capability, professional attitude, responsiveness and technical competence. Using this information; management can evaluate customer satisfaction on an industry-by-industry basis, or look at satisfaction levels of different groups within a major account. The data can also be broken down by service function—field service, software service, and educational service—or by geography at the national, area, district, or local level.

Customer survey results are one of the tools used to measure management performance in the service arena and to determine nonsalaried recognition and rewards, such as annual the "excellence awards week" for top performers. The data is also used to fine-tune existing service products; develop new products; identify areas that need improvement; and set new customer satisfaction goals.

## THE HUMAN FACTOR

When all is said and done, Digital still believes that the human ear is one of the most sensitive tools available for measuring service quality. Digital encourages all employees to listen carefully to its customers: their concerns, their complaints, their wish lists. Over the years, the company has developed numerous formal channels for feeding that information back into the loop so it can be used to improve existing products, services, and processes or to develop new ones.

Especially in the field organization—which has the highest level of customer interface—managers at every level are expected to maintain ongoing, personal contact with their counterparts in the customer's organization. Every Digital corporate officer is assigned an "Executive Partner" within a customer account. This kind of communication ensures that Digital is always attuned to the customer's needs and thus better able to meet its customer satisfaction goals.

Digital's Field Service organization provides a final example of how the company's approach to service is customer-driven. A number of Digital's service products—network-level services, guaranteed service response times for large systems, disaster-recovery services—evolved from "the ground up."

They came into being because customers expressed a need, and Digital listened.

For example, up to and during the mid-1970s, Digital had a policy of providing maintenance service only on its own products. Yet many customers had developed multi-vendor systems that were based on Digital CPUs and incorporated other vendors' peripherals. These customers wanted to deal with a single service vendor, and they were constantly asking local field service representatives to service the third-party equipment. To keep their customers happy, a number of local offices were quietly providing the requested support.

Digital's Field Service organization saw this as both a customer-satisfaction issue and a business opportunity. The group brought in a number of field service employees to develop the service capability, including training and support materials needed to provide such a service. Within two years, surveys showed that the original customer satisfaction goals regarding third-party equipment had been achieved. Soon after that, DECompatible Service was turning a profit, as well.

In Digital's view, the equation works: an investment in quality is synonymous with customer satisfaction. The company sees a direct correlation between quality and financial success, for as quality improves, costs go down and opportunities arise to increase profits, productivity and market share. Improving quality is the key to improving performance and gaining the competitive advantage in the industry.

# Service Quality at the Hewlett-Packard Company

**Phil Carter**
**Thom Edmonds**
Hewlett-Packard Company

The Hewlett-Packard Company, headquartered in Palo Alto, California, designs, manufactures, and services electronic products and systems for measurement and computation. Technology has come a long way since the company was founded in 1939. Today, HP's 81,000 employees provide the tools necessary to harness the power of the information age. They produce a range of computer and peripheral products to help analyze, manage and store information; graphics and printing capabilities to make it visible; plus networking and software to link it all together.

## HEWLETT-PACKARD'S SERVICE ORGANIZATION

Within Hewlett-Packard, the responsibility for delivering services resides with the Worldwide Customer Support Organization. This group has the following mission: to provide services of the highest possible quality and the greatest possible value to customers, thereby gaining and holding their respect and loyalty.

This mission is accomplished through an organization which includes, a headquarters located in Mountain View, California, and a worldwide field team of customer engineers, application engineers, customer education instructors, response center engineers, and management in over 275 offices around the globe. These field teams work in conjunction with sales representatives to focus on achieving a high level of customer satisfaction. The departments at the headquarters provide support strategies, implementation plans, and marketing for the services delivered by the field teams. Hewlett-Packard support services have long been considered *products*, and while the headquarters divisions provide the traditional product-development and marketing functions, the field teams manufacture the service product. This approach has proven to be extremely effective. In fact, some industry surveys show that Hewlett-Packard has been rated the best in support in the computer industry.

This product approach to services has also aided measurably in the application of quality improvements to Hewlett-Packard services. The authors of this paper, as quality managers located at the headquarters, have provided guidance to the customer support organization for the development and use of quality improvement methods. Quality managers are members of the functional staff who provide overall strategic and operational direction for the organization. As a department, they have the authority, responsibility, and freedom of action to plan, develop and implement programs, to improve service quality. Within the last few years, the company has begun to add quality managers to the field locations as one means of ensuring the quality of the products and processes close to the customer. While these quality managers are focused today on the sales process, they are also of help in rolling out the quality programs for support.

## CRITERIA FOR QUALITY

The horizons of quality in Hewlett-Packard extend far beyond the manufacturing function into all aspects of the operations. This broadening of quality as an issue for the company began in 1978 in Yokogawa-Hewlett-Packard (YHP), a joint venture in Japan. In 1983, it spread to that portion of the company involved in providing customer support for products. YHP, which had in 1982 won the coveted Deming Prize for Quality, utilized the concept of Total Quality Control (TQC) as the methodology for driving quality throughout the organization. The TQC methodology focuses on the process, involves everyone, and employs statistical methods. Since the delivery of service is a process, it lends itself well to the TQC methodology and makes it possible to define and measure the quality of the services.

Identifying the criteria for service quality begins with a few basic questions that stem from the TQC methodology, including the following:

- Who are my customers?
- What are my customer's needs?
- What is my product and/or service?
- What are their measures/expectations?
- What is my process for delivering these products and/or services?
- Does my product and/or service meet their needs?
- What action is required to improve my process?

These may seem like simple, straightforward questions that one ought to be able to answer quite easily. In asking these questions of various people, you often get very different answers. That suggests that the answers are not so obvious. Still, such questions put to employees represent one indispensable way of measuring service quality.

A second criterion for measuring quality is the customer's definition of quality. Since quality is defined ultimately by the customer, Hewlett-Packard seeks to develop solid mechanisms for learning from the customer. These include customer focus groups, customer visits, worldwide and third-party surveys, and user groups. By doing a good job of identifying the customer and listening to the customer, it becomes easier to define quality from the perspective of the customer.

A third criterion is to separate those quality attributes of the product from those quality attributes of the relationship with the customer. Tom Peters's book, *In Search of Excellence* addresses the issue of relationships: after a store clerk dropped a nickel piece of candy into the bag because Tom had to wait for the clerk to verify his American Express account, Tom was so impressed that he was sold on being a customer for life.

How has Hewlett-Packard used the seven TQC questions to identify its customers and their needs? Whenever quality managers from the support organization visit customers, they always start with a discussion those seven questions in order to verify the customer's definition of quality. The quality attributes may be separated into two broad categories. The acronym for the first of these is FURPS and refers to the quality of the product. The support organization has just begun to use these categories but, as yet, it does not have much experience in applying this concept to **support products**. The product divisions are further along, especially in the area of $R$. The letters in FURPS have the following definitions:

- $F$ = Functionaiity: The feature set, capabilities, compatibility, and security.
- $U$ = Usability: The human factors, consistency, and documentation of the product.

- $R$ = Reliability: The frequency and severity of failures; the predictability and accuracy of the product.
- $P$ = Performance: The speed and efficiency of the product as well as the resource consumption.
- $S$ = Supportability: Maintainability and serviceability of the product along with its ability to be installed.

The second broad category of quality attributes, or AART, refers to the quality of the relationship with the customer. The letters in AART have the following definitions:

- $A$ = Anticipation: The ability to identify, understand, and help solve customer needs before they become problems.
- $A$ = Availability: The degree to which our products and services provide for uninterrupted usage at full functionality.
- $R$ = Responsiveness: The ability to provide timely, accurate, and complete information and/or solutions to customer initiated requests for help.
- $T$ = Transitions: The ease of initial start-up and of ongoing changes as individual products and services evolve and conform to new needs and technologies.

In an optimal setting, you would like to measure the relevant customer metric for the quality This is not always possible since this could interfere with the customer's operation. Thus, you often substitute an internal measure in the place of the actual customer measure. The other important characteristic of the metric is that, from the customer's viewpoint, it is event-driven, while for Hewlett-Packard, it is process-driven. This means converting the event measure into a process measure and ensuring that the process correction will prevent the event from recurring. Some of the process measures currently being used in customer support are as follows:

- On-site maintenance:
  1. Response time: the time from the first customer call to the arrival of the customer engineer at the customer's site.
  2. Repair time: the time it takes the customer engineer to repair the customer unit.
  3. System downtime: the total elapsed time from the customer call to the unit being repaired.
- Customer service centers:
  Turn-around time: the elapsed time from the unit arriving at the service center to the time it is repaired and shipped.
- Customer escalation centers:
  1. Mean time to solve problem.
  2. Mean time to install work around (a temporary solution) on those that don't have an immediate permanent correction.

- Customer education:
  1. Student exit evaluations of instructor quality, course content, and facilities.
- 2. Student achievement of learning objectives.
- Remote support:
  1. Number of downtime hours moved from emergency to scheduled maintenance.
- 2. Percent of solutions correctly diagnosed by the remote process.

There are other measures currently being used for other products, such as software maintenance, but this should give the reader some ideas. All of these measures are contained in management reports on a periodic basis (usually monthly).

## MIS SYSTEMS AND THE IMPORTANCE OF INTEGRATION

There is a vital need for information with which to evaluate continuously the quality of service delivery. Without this basic need for data being met, quality improvement activities are doomed to fail from the beginning. The best places to collect this information are at the points of customer contact: those "thousand moments of truth" where a company has the opportunity to deliver excellent service or something less.

The methods used to collect this information are crucial to its accuracy and timeliness (that is, the quality of the information about the transaction). At the points of customer contact, there are two potential strategies availabie. The first is to ask the participants, either the customer or the employee, to manually record their perceptions. The second is to collect the information in a system which allows for data processing, analysis, and electronic distribution. The advantages of the latter approach are obvious: a high-volume of data collection, standardization, rapid dissemination, programmatic editing for out-of-limit conditions, and programmatic analysis for exceptional conditions.

Due to the need to collect information on the relationship (AART) components of service quality as well as the attributes of service quality (FURPS), it is necessary actually to implement a hybrid version of the two available strategies. That is, there is some information which only the participant can record since it is not present in any data file. This includes such factors as repair verification or observations of behavior of the customer's system. A second key factor which greatly affects the quality of the information which employees are requested to supply is the degree of need for the information by the employee or by his or her operational management. If the information is used by either to make decisions as a routine part of the operation's activities, the quality of the information is far better than if the information seems to be of no use to the employee, who then feels burdened by entering data. It is this operational need for information then which must drive the implementation of the appropriate MIS system and tools. The properly set linkage is the key to success.

There are several examples of this type of MIS implementation currently used in the Hewlett-Packard service environment:

- The field customer engineers (CEs) who provide on-site hardware maintenance are equipped with hand-held portable terminals. Through these terminals, they receive notification of service calls they need to fulfill. At the completion of the repair, the CE enters the repair details: for example, revised failure symptoms; parts and labor hours needed; information about whether this was a repeat call and, if so, the reason. This information is used for operational needs such as parts stocking, capacity planning, training needs, and financial analysis. This hand-held terminal is also used to collect the information required to produce the on-site measures previously mentioned.

- Response center engineers, who provide telephone assistance to customers on software or documentation problems and questions, utilize on-line data access terminals to record their activities and the resolution of the problem. The response center management uses this information to perform capacity planning, training needs analysis, and analysis of problems and causes. These direct access terminals also collect the information required to produce response center process quality measures.

In both of the above cases, the vital "moment of truth" information is supplied by the employee; it represents his or her account of the attributes of the transaction. In other words, the employee records objective data concerning the delivery of the service. The MIS implementation provides consistent recording, editing, reporting, analysis, and distribution of the information.

An example within Hewlett-Packard of the systematic collection of data on the customer's perception of service delivery occurs in the area of customer education. At the completion of each class for customers, the students are requested to complete a questionnaire on the learning experience including their opinion of the instructor's ability, the course content, the appropriateness of the laboratory or exercises, and the facility, as well as their overall satisfaction. These questionnaires are completed on a machine-readable form and transferred to a central processing point. Detailed operational reports are produced for the educational center management team; such reports lead to improvements in the processes used to develop and deliver educational programs.

## MANAGEMENT PROCESS FOR MAKING QUALITY HAPPEN

As was mentioned earlier, the TQC methodology was introduced into Hewlett-Packard several years ago. The initial application of this methodology was in manufacturing since this was the area where the processes were more clearly defined and understood. Over time, TQC was adopted in other areas, including customer support. All during this time, TQC had the support of management, but it was support more in voice than in deed, since TQC was not thought to have application to as-yet undocumented processes, including the process of management.

In recent years, YHP has developed a planning process which they refer to as *Hoshin Kanri*. Literally translated, this means "shiny metal pointing direction." *Hoshin* applies the *plan, do, check, act* (PDCA) components of TQC to the management planning process. Figure 1 shows the process flow of the planning cycle. The process is followed at each level of management and results in linked objectives, goals, strategies, and measures. Utilizing Hoshin has resulted in several tangible benefits: (1) it creates a superior planning process which stresses the importance of goals and measures; (2) it improves (documents) the process of annual and intermediate-range planning, implementation, and review; (3) it provides management with direction for TQC; and (4) it shows management's use of TQC. Within the customer support organization, responsibility for quality is in the hands of the operational management team, not the quality department. The service quality department is there to educate, facilitate, develop tools, and help in the identification and measurement of the process. The implementation of the Hoshin planning process has been an immense help in getting plans linked across the organization and has provided renewed emphases on planning and the use of TQC.

According to the maxim, that which is measured gets better; but that which is measured and reported gets better faster. So, in addition to having a standard planning process for quality improvement, HP also has reviews and reports on the various products and the processes for delivering support to them. These reports and reviews are available to all levels of management, thus permitting them to ask questions about the quality of service performance. As is often the case, the initial reaction from employees is that unfavorable data is suspect. As soon as they realize that management will continue to question, employees begin to focus on the issues, and in fact, the performance does improve.

Management's visible interest in quality, both for the product and for the relationships, goes a long way in making quality happen. This is particularly true when management sets *stretch objectives*. Employees will accept the extra measure because they realize that when managers talk about quality, they are talking from a secure knowledge base about the quality of products and services; employees will be supportive of improving quality, thus improving customer satisfaction.

## MEASUREMENT OF CUSTOMER PERCEPTION OF SERVICE

As discussed earlier, there are two distinct methods of measuring service quality. The first is internally to collect performance information which

HOSHIN MANAGEMENT PROCESS

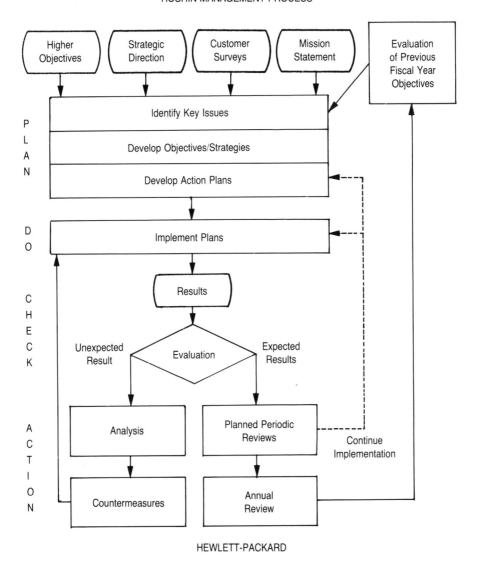

HEWLETT-PACKARD

FIG. 1. HOSHIN KANRI PLANNING PROCESS

measures both the event and process performance against the desired service attributes. The second is to collect the customer's perceptions of the service quality level, including the very important perception of the relationship between the customer and the employees in the act of delivering the service. Both views are important, but of course, the customer perception is the more important. To be successful, a company must have both measurement systems and must establish a linkage between the two.

The first kind of information, supplied by the company's internal resources, can be a real-time measure of service quality with regard to the service attributes. The second, since it depends on *imposing* on the customer, must be used sparingly and less frequently (that is, it is limited in real-time application). Customer perception is vital and precious and is not to be abused. The challenge, therefore, is to build on the functional linkage between the infrequent, but systematic, customer perception data and the day-to-day internally available service attribute data. Within Hewlett-Packard the customer relationship data are collected over several methods. A service satisfaction survey is conducted annually. This survey identifies customer perceptions of both importance and satisfaction with the attributes of service. Armed with both importance and satisfaction ratings, Hewlett-Packard operational management develops plans which lead to improvements in those service attributes indicated by customers as being important and needing improvements in order to meet their needs.

This technique, borrowed from Jeffrey W. Marr, (1984) involves the availability and the active use of both internal and external service quality data which is vital to the success of improving service quality. The internal data is available and can be used continuously to monitor service performance and to indicate success in improvements in the processes which deliver service. The customer perception is used to correlate these internal measures to the "real world" and to monitor behavioral aspects of service which cannot be reliably collected internally.

## CONCLUSION

At the Hewlett-Packard Company, employees feel they have made good progress in establishing a customer focus for their service programs and building a shared vision of service quality among all parts of the company. That focus on the customer has been extended in the support and service organization, as illustrated by some of the programs discussed in this paper.

The need for criteria for service quality is fairly pervasive throughout the organization. The company has a management philosophy and structure which place service quality and customer satisfaction at the forefront of what employees do. It has systems which help to track quality measures and there are more on the drawing board. Surveys, such as Data Pro place HP at the top in customer satisfaction. Yet, employees still feel that they have just begun to make inroads.

Through emphasis on the *Hoshin* planning process, the company hopes to get additional customer inputs and to do a better job of evaluating the previous years' performances from a customer's perspective. The *Hoshin* focus permits the company to strengthen its TQC efforts and to provide the necessary visibility to those programs. The addition of field quality managers will help bring programs and processes closer to the customer and to take yet another step in listening to the customer.

Perfection in service quality and customer satisfaction are Hewlett-Packard's ultimate goals. Its own assessment is that it has a sound foundation for reaching those goals: the right team, the right management commitment, and the right value system in place.

# A Program For Managing Service Quality

**Johnson Aimie Edosomwan**
IBM Corporation

IBM (International Business Machines Corporation) produces computers and other business machines to customer order. Headquartered in Armonk, New York, it employees over 400,000 people. IBM has demonstrated leadership in high technology through excellent service to its customers. Service quality is of utmost importance in every facet of IBM's business.

# INTRODUCTION

The following approach presents a formal definition of service quality and the major requirements of a service quality program based on the author's work experience at IBM. The program outlines the key customer, task boundaries, organizational, and process control requirements for service quality management. Emphasis is placed on the requirements for measurement, improvement and monitoring, customer partnership, education, and training. A step-by-step approach for designing and implementing a service quality program is presented.

# SERVICE QUALITY DEFINED

Service quality can be defined as the total satisfaction of the requirements and expectations of the internal or external customer receiving a service in a timely fashion, at minimum cost and price. The measure pertains to both the tangible and intangible elements of service offered by individuals, operational units, and the total organization.

## Customer Requirements

Unlike product quality, which focuses on the level of relevance, uniformity, and dependability, service quality is a function of the production, delivery, and consumption processes. Most services have more intangible input and output elements than tangible elements. Improving service quality at the source requires commitment and training of both management and other employees as well as empathy for delivering the right service to the customer.

Significant improvements in service quality can be achieved if an adequate program is in place to continuously manage and improve the various requirements specified in figure 1.

# MEASUREMENT SYSTEM FOR SERVICE QUALITY

There is need for service quality measurement at the various levels in the organization. A formal service quality measurement system can have the following benefits:

- Service quality measurement creates a basis for assessing the degree of customer satisfaction, so that necessary actions to improve the process through which the services are offered can be made.
- Service quality measurement provides an important motivation for better performance by suppliers, vendors, departments and organizational units.

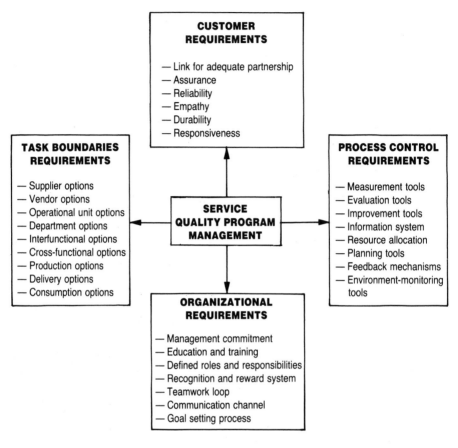

FIG. 1. SERVICE QUALITY PROGRAM REQUIREMENTS

The service quality measurement concept can be designed and applied at five levels as specified in Table 1:

TABLE 1
FIVE LEVELS OF THE SERVICE QUALITY MEASUREMENT CONCEPT

| Level of Service Quality Measurement Concept | Potential Areas of Impact |
|---|---|
| Fitness for use | Customer and total organization |
| Fitness for standard | Processes and operational units |
| Fitness for demand | Seasonal, random, or cycle demand for a specific service |
| Fitness for planning requirements | Planning service quality variables and parameters; future impact assessment of service quality |
| Fitness for control | Protecting the customer requirements |

*Designing the right service quality measurement system.* The following two suggestions are offered to aid decision makers, system analysts, and quality improvement facilitators in designing the right measurement system for service quality: believe that everyone has a customer and create the right awareness about the need for measures.

*Believe that everyone has a customer.* Often, people perceive service quality to be important only to the final customer receiving service outside the organization. It is important to accept the fact that everyone within an organization has both internal and external customers. Internally, each individual is a customer of people working in different tasks in various departments and units; in turn, each has customers of his or her own services. Reducing the service quality errors at the level of individual operations also ensures that good quality service is delivered to the end customer. Appropriate service quality data should enable individuals to access their own work and to control and correct errors at the source of service. For example, the author has used the types of data shown in Table 2 for analyzing service quality as it pertains to large operating systems.

*Create the right awareness about the need for measures.* In order to control the production, delivery, and consumption processes involved in offering a service, adequate measures for both tangible and intangible elements are needed. Control charts for variables and attributes are used for the tangible elements. Figure 2 shows an example of a rate control chart of service quality failure for controlling the quality error rate at the plant level.

TABLE 2
EXAMPLES OF DATA ON QUALITY

| Types of Data | Sources |
|---|---|
| System in-house performance data | Manufacturing, engineering, and quality assurance departments |
| System field performance data | Customer service departments and marketing representative office |
| Field replacement due to failure in service | Spare parts sales log and marketing representative sales data |
| Competitive quality ratings | "Reliability plus" (A quality report that evaluates IBM systems against competitors) |
| Updates on engineering changes | Manufacturing, engineering, and development quality reports |
| Service error rates in plant | Individual control charts and system control charts |
| Field service error rates | System performance control charts |

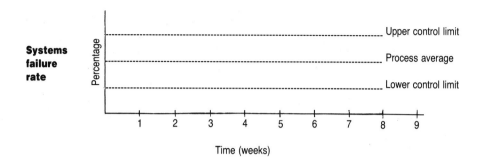

FIG 2. RATE CONTROL CHART OF SERVICE

Intangible elements such as customer satisfaction level and degree of assurance are measured by using surveys and questionnaires. For example, a customer survey included questions and response analysis in the following areas: system reliability, response rate to service calls, mean time to resolve a problem, system availability, mean time for installation of spare parts, service representative support, and down time due to scheduled maintenance.

Everyone within the organization is trained to use the various measures for control, improvement, and planning. For the measures to be meaningful and useful, there is a need to collect accurate data that truly represent the current state of the service process.

## IMPROVING THE SERVICE QUALITY

Excellence in service quality cannot be achieved through a one-time action. Improving the service quality process, therefore, involves the organized use of techniques, tools, intellectual capabilities, and teamwork to deliver high quality service at the source.

### Guiding Principles

Based on the author's work experience in quality management, the following guiding principles are recommended:

- The *approach* to improving the process requires that management take the leadership role, create the right awareness, and set priorities for the various improvement projects.
- The *theme* that should be communicated to everyone in the organization is that continuous improvement is needed in the process.
- The *scope* of the improvement effort should cover all activities and tasks performed in the organization.
- The *scale* of the improvement activities should specify that everyone is responsible.

- The *style* should focus on a prevention system for defects. Inspection and other non-value-added operations used for detecting defects should be discouraged.
- The *standard* that is set should require everyone at the source to do the job right the first time.
- The *measures* used for service quality should include indexes of customer satisfaction, the defect percentage, the cost of quality, and the error rate.
- The *rewards* for improved service should be given to both management and the other employees.

The following process improvement methodology is also recommended:
- Create an awareness or a vision of the improved service process.
- Understand the current service process thoroughly.
- Specify opportunities for improvement by key process parameters and areas.
- Specify the scope of the involvement effort in each process at the operational unit level.
- Test the proposed improvement in the process. Start small with a pilot project.
- Evaluate the results and verify that the proposed improvement occurred. Obtain feedback from both management and other employees on the proposed improvement.
- Ensure that action plans are in place to control the utilization of resources.
- Implement the new improvement techniques, tools, and methods. Institutionalize the new ideas into the service quality process.
- Monitor results from the new mix of resources to ensure that expected outcomes are obtained.
- Follow up periodically and repeat the steps to discover new opportunities.

The process of improving service quality at the source should be based on adequate data and the total involvement of the key personnel involved in delivering service to the internal or external customer.

## EDUCATION AND TRAINING

Table 3 summarizes the types of service quality training required by different levels in a typical medium size company. One way to reduce training expenses is through the use of an interactive video system. Other methods such as training specific in-house instructors, (who in turn train others) are also very affordable. In order for the education and training program to be effective, adequate resources must be provided for support; trained personnel must be given the immediate opportunity to apply the new concepts and

TABLE 3
SERVICE QUALITY TRAINING REQUIREMENTS BY LEVELS

| Level | Training Highlights | Training Time Required | Training Budget Allocation (cents per dollar spent) |
|---|---|---|---|
| Upper management | Customer partnership Customer requirements Goal-setting process Key service quality programs | 1-week initial training followed by 3-hour periodic training | 10 cents |
| Middle management | Resource allocation Program development Program maintenance Customer partnership | 1-1/2 weeks initial training followed by 5 hours periodic training | 25 cents |
| Supervisors and first-line managers | Program maintenance Tools and techniques for managing quality program Feedback mechanisms | 2-weeks initial training followed by 1-day periodic training | 25 cents |
| Technical personnel and workers | Tools for measurement control, planning and improvement Tools for reliability, assurance, durability, and customer satisfaction | 3-weeks initial training followed by 2-days periodic training | 50 cents |

ideas learned; a feedback mechanism must be in place to access the effectiveness of the training received; and there must be an ongoing retraining program in place to update experts on new techniques and breakthroughs in service quality.

## ENHANCING CUSTOMER PARTNERSHIP
Both the internal and external customers are crucial to the success of any business. Service quality errors can be detected if the following provisions are made to enhance the input from customers and to form a partnership with them:
- On-line communication channel between service process owner(s) and customer(s);
- Periodic survey conducted to access the degree of customer satisfaction;
- Customer participation in new service strategies

- Feedback mechanism to customer(s) on improvements achieved in the production, delivery, and consumption processes;
- Encouragement of the suppliers to participate in implementing a service quality program. This can be very useful in situations where the supplier's commodities are essential to the services delivered.

Adequate customer partnership comes from the willingness of management and other employees to take ownership for results, to be accountable for all actions, and to provide assurance to satisfy the customer requirements. For example, IBM's chief executive officer declared the year 1987 as "the year of customers." Several meetings were held with IBM customers to enhance both the overall business relationship and service quality.

## STARTING A SERVICE QUALITY PROGRAM
The following steps are recommended for starting a service quality program:

1. Top management's support for quality improvement through policies and practices must exist. For example at IBM Americas Group Corporation, the following are the fundaments of quality: management commitment, training, teamwork, measurement cost, error cause removal, awareness, corrective action, goal-setting, and recognition. Programs such as quality-plus, designed to provide quality by all employees, are fully supported by the management team.

2. Understand the business environment thoroughly and define the specific service quality goals and objectives.

3. Find out what programs, techniques, and tools are already available for use, and design your own program. The program should contain measurement, planning, training requirements, and reward mechanisms.

4. Sell the content of a service quality program to management and other employees by showing the benefits and costs of specific quality improvement projects.

5. Train everyone and implement program components for each operational unit.

6. Evaluate the effectiveness of the service quality program periodically, and make adjustments as required.

7. Be sure the expected results from the program are obtained.

8. Establish mechanisms for quality audits, process control techniques, training, weekly status meetings, and quality update sessions for ongoing program maintenance.

## CONCLUSIONS
Delivering excellent service for both internal and external customers does not happen by accident. It requires commitment from both management, and other workers to organize the use of common sense, tools, and techniques;

to constantly manage the production, delivery, and consumption processes involved in providing services. Based on personal work experience at IBM, this author believes that the quest for excellence in service quality is achievable. Improvement comes from the appropriate implementation of the fundamentals of quality presented in this paper. The degree of success in improving service is bound to vary from one organization to another. The level of motivation, commitment, enthusiasm, and practice of management and other employees will make a big difference.

# Striving for Customer Satisfaction and Quality

**Joseph Lester, III**
Wang Laboratories, Inc.

Founded in 1951, Wang Laboratories, Inc. is a worldwide supplier of computer-based information processing systems including data, text, image and voice processing, as well as telecommunications and networking products.

An employer of more than thirty thousand individuals worldwide, Wang Laboratories' headquarters is located in Lowell, Massachusetts. For the fiscal year ended June 30, 1987, the company reported revenues of $2.83 billion.

## INTRODUCTION

The goals of quality and customer satisfaction at Wang Laboratories do not represent just a grass roots program. They go across all levels of the corporation beginning at the top. Fred Wang, the president of Wang Laboratories, puts quality and customer satisfaction at the top of his list of corporate goals: "We want to become the number one company in our industry for customer satisfaction in three to five years. Not just by our own measurement but also by the various independent industry analysts who rate this subject."

Viewing customer satisfaction from a broad perspective, one can assess its impact on all employees and customers. As customer satisfaction increases, selling becomes easier; employees feel better about themselves, productivity goes up, and attrition goes down—neither customer nor employee wants to leave a winner. Generally stated, customer satisfaction derives from quality.

The company's approach to customer satisfaction through quality is structured around four corporate quality objectives:

1. Conduct independent product reviews or IPRs in order to ensure that all organizations are prepared and working together.
2. Establish a corporate awareness program.
3. Establish a senior management committee on customer satisfaction and product quality to monitor the company's progress and develop a preventive action program. It is better to do it right the first time rather than fix it later.
4. Establish product line quality teams so as to ensure that all organizations understand what is needed and are working as a team.

The strategic worldwide movement regarding customer satisfaction and quality is known as *total quality*. As part of Wang's customer satisfaction or total quality program, preventive action programs will help to stop problems before they get started. Quality is not free, but is cheaper than correcting mistakes. For a typical company without a total quality program, costs related to correcting mistakes are between 20 and 30% of total sales dollars.

To accomplish the goal of being number one in customer satisfaction, the company has adopted seven basic principles:

1. Quality must be led by management.
2. Quality has to be company-wide.
3. Everyone is responsible for quality.
4. Prevention, not detection, is the rule.
5. Do things right the first time.
6. Quality is a continuous process.
7. Lack of quality lowers customer satisfaction and profit.

Wang is undertaking a number of programs to increase customer satisfaction through enhanced quality. While the activities discussed below are accurately described, not all aspects are in place at the time of this writing.

## CUSTOMER SATISFACTION SURVEY

In support of Wang's goal to become the industry leader in customer satisfaction, marketing has taken steps over the past year to strengthen its customer satisfaction survey and to make survey data more useful to both corporate management and field representatives.

Wang's domestic customer satisfaction research program consists of interviewing eight thousand customers per year within the United States. An additional eight thousand customers are interviewed each year internationally. Customers are asked to evaluate Wang on a broad range of product sales and service areas.

Two major changes in the research have characterized Wang's determination for improvement: the method has changed from a self-administered survey to a telephone survey of Wang's entire customer base; and the survey will be conducted on a quarterly rather than annual basis as of the third quarter of fiscal year 1988, to provide more frequent readings on levels of satisfaction.

Wang has moved away from a mail survey method to telephone interviewing because it has several advantages. Unlike mail, telephoning allows Wang to:

- Obtain a sample that is truly representative of its customer base. Wang now designs a plan for contacting different *types* of customers by telephone and no longer relies on the customer to take the initiative to respond by mail.
- Have greater knowledge of who the respondent is and to ensure that, in fact, the most appropriate person is interviewed.
- Probe to clarify respondents' answers while these individuals are still on the telephone.
- Reduce biases associated with mail surveys. (People who go to the trouble of filling out a mail survey tend to be much *more* satisfied or much *less* satisfied than the general population.)
- Obtain results faster.

All telephone interviewing is conducted by an outside research firm to provide objectivity. Of course, the benefit of conducting the survey every quarter is that corporate management and field representatives receive feedback on a more timely basis and are able to address customer issues as they arise.

The interview itself investigates the customer's satisfaction with a comprehensive list of Wang offerings. The person in the customer organization who is most knowledgeable about the organization's relationship with Wang as a vendor is located and asked to rate Wang on a scale from *1* to *10* (*10* being the highest) in each of the following areas (among others):

- Hardware
- Software

- Applications software
- Competence of the sales and service staffs
- Presale and post sale consulting services
- Hardware service
- Telephone software support
- On-site software support
- Documentation and education
- Administrative services

Other information includes the customer's likelihood of recommending Wang, suggestions for ways in which Wang could improve its service to the customer, and the type of system the customer has and what it is used for.

Scores for customer satisfaction with Wang are evaluated within a competitive framework wherever possible. At customer sites where more than one computer vendor is reported, the customer is asked to rate competing vendors on five key measures of satisfaction. In this way, Wang gains information on its performance in light of what its competition is providing. Results from the customer satisfaction study serve a dual purpose in that they are an aid to top management in strategic decision making and to field personnel in servicing their accounts. Verbatim responses from interviews are shared with the field so that representatives can be aware of and address customer issues.

While many important changes have already been made in the customer satisfaction program, this is a project that is still evolving. Wang's plans for making the study even more meaningful include making results available for distribution as quickly as possible; gaining greater understanding of what determines satisfaction; and conducting more detailed analysis of the subgroups in the customer population. Some possible subgroups include those with particular system types, new customers versus longstanding customers, and very satisfied customers versus the very dissatisfied.

## FIELD SERVICE

Translating Wang's goal to secure a consensus rating by independent analysts as the leader of customer service within its industry into a more tangible set of operational aims requires the field service division to consistently provide 1) quality management and services, 2) timely response to queries, 3) timely and effective problem resolution, and 4) a well-trained and efficient work force that can effectively implement solutions using state-of-the-art systems.

Focus is placed on those essential factors that ensure a consistent level of high quality service of the products marketed by Wang. Wang's internal service measures, of which there are over 140, are used by line managers to monitor and enhance the service quality delivered to customers. The

internal measurements vital to the delivery of quality service fall into the following categories:
- Employee satisfaction
- Customer satisfaction
- Service response
- Operations
- Logistics
- Productivity

## Employee Satisfaction
Employee satisfaction is measured by an annual employee opinion survey administered to all field service personnel along with the entire staff of the company. Wang recognizes that satisfied personnel have the motivation to deliver quality service to the customer.

## Customer Satisfaction
Every week, each customer will average from a field service employee at least one visit or telephone call about software. The results of the internal customer survey (described earlier) in the areas of field service are used as an objective measure of customer satisfaction with service.

Line managers strive to meet or exceed goals for the customer survey score as a method for increasing customer satisfaction with service. The scores are based on key survey questions which reflect perceptions of quality within the categories of hardware service, on-site software support, and telephone software support. Performance against the goal is monitored; this, along with employee satisfaction scores, is an integral part of the line management review process. As an additional motivation to strive for excellence, recognition awards are given to the line managers who earn the highest satisfaction scores from their customers and employees.

## Service Response
The customer places requests to the support center for both hardware and software services. The service response achieved through the centers is critical to the customer's perceptions of quality. The service response is measured in several ways, including how quickly calls are answered when customers use the 800 number, the percentage of calls immediately answered, and the average waiting time for calls placed on hold.

Hardware calls from customers cause the dispatch of a branch customer engineer (C.E.) to the system site. C.E. activity reports are data entered into a hardware service database, with the error rate tracked to maintain data quality. The hardware engineer's arrival on-site after the call-in is called *response time*; it is measured not only overall, but also for strategic products, such as CPU families and peripherals, and for customer groupings, such as select national accounts.

Customer software calls, answered by the support center operator, are channeled to a qualified analyst with the product expertise for solving the problem. Responsive service regarding contact with the analyst is reflected by the percentage of calls resulting in immediate contact, the average response on all calls, and the percentage of software calls which are returned by an analyst within various time periods.

## Operations

Operational performance measurements are used to ensure that customer problems are resolved quickly after the service response, in other words, to minimize customer downtime. On-site hardware repair time, when inclusive of response time, is referred to as *on-site completion time* and is correlated strongly with customer satisfaction with hardware service. Average completion time, as well as response time, is tracked at the product and customer level, and the technique of measuring the percentage of calls within certain hourly thresholds is also applied. A special report listing detailed data for calls with exceptionally long completion times is used by line management to get underneath the numbers so that action plans for improving repair quality can be effectively developed.

Quality of service goes beyond on-site repair time; it is monitored by several internal measures which reflect the customer perspective. Repeat calls, (the number of repair calls on one product within five days of each other) is monitored both overall and for components critical to the customer's system. A low repeat-call rate indicates that quality repairs are being made. Return calls (where the C.E. had to leave the site and return later to complete the repair) are tracked both overall and for those due to lack of a part. Completion time is driven down primarily by managing the reduction of return calls through processes such as call screening and better provision of parts.

Call preparation helps the C.E., in conjunction with the customer, identify the device for repair. The success rate of determining the correct device for repair is an indicator of quality. Customer system uptime is increased by the regular delivery of preventative maintenance (PM). Completion rates of scheduled PMs to critical devices and the percentage of field time spent performing PMs are used to encourage field staff's contribution to maintaining the reliability of the system. Other operational measurements that reflect the customer perspective include calls where an assisting C.E. aids the primary C.E.; the frequency of repair with the required part available; calls that rollover into the next day; customer installations, site audits, and facility inspections; and field change orders completed to improve reliability, safety, and potential performance.

Remote maintenance is an offering which gives Wang the ability to diagnose hardware and software problems remotely via telecommunications, thus increasing customer uptime and satisfaction, while furnishing the C.E.

with the information necessary to correct the problem. The number of customer sites certified to use remote maintenance diagnostics, along with effectiveness measures of remote sessions, are tracked to realize the full potential of this tool for increasing service quality.

Increasing hardware reliability leads to better repair times for the customer and higher customer satisfaction. Measurements such as the following are trended to gauge the effectiveness of product reliability improvement programs developed for the field:

- Hours spent servicing the top candidates for C.E. attention.
- Overall C.E. field hours engaged in repair activities.
- Failures per year of CPUs critical to customer system performance.
- Failures per year of individual peripheral devices.

Techniques similar to those used for measuring the operational performance for hardware service are also applied to software service. Resolution of software calls entering the support centers is tracked, including groupings by *elapsed time to resolve*, with breakouts by strategic software products. Typically, software calls that exceed long resolution thresholds are difficult to assimilate or reproduce, or they require code design correction. In some cases the customer wants Wang to customize the software for unique requirements, necessitating design change requests. The percentage of calls that are resolved by the support center with the customer, by the field with the customer, and with home office technical support operations or R&D are measured along with the respective resolution times. The number of software problems are trended to verify enhanced resilience and other software improvements.

## Logistics

On-site repair times are greatly reduced by parts availability, and hence logistics measurements are used to provide an important control mechanism vital to hardware service quality. Quality in logistics means the ability to provide, on a consistent basis, a desired level of service (LOS) at minimum cost. Eleven second-level centers have been established which will receive material from the home office and will subsequently allocate material to the field stockrooms twice daily (previously weekly). Level-of-service measurements include:

- *Demand LOS*, that is, the percentage of time the C.E. is provided with requested spare parts at the stockroom window
- *Cluster LOS*, that is, the percentage of time the demand is filled by the stockroom, the second level center, and the stockrooms supported by the second level center
- The percentage of time that the C.E. is within one hour's transit time of receiving a core system part that is critical to customer satisfaction.

Several factors influence the quality or level of service such as, inventory levels, inventory accuracy, number of stocking locations, transportation capabilities, systems, and packaging and handling techniques.

In the past few years, several enhancements were made which have dramatically improved the level of service. The second-level centers coupled with more frequent replenishment will provide the desired demand LOS and cluster LOS without an unnecessary increase in the field inventory. Further, the core system sparing strategy will be accomplished with little incremental investment. Additionally, significant strides have been made above and below the stockroom shelf to improve inventory accuracy. By standardizing cycle counting with stockrooms and developing trunk models, the company expects to improve accuracy dramatically. This will, in turn, improve the accuracy of replenishment from the second level centers and result in a higher level of service.

Another key program aimed at improving the quality in logistics involved the handling and packaging of parts. Improvements are currently being made to the packaging of printed circuit boards for better protection from shock and electrostatic discharge. This new packaging will reduce dead-on-arrivals, the spares that do not function when first installed, and the space required to store parts. It will also allow the C.E. to keep parts within their protective housing.

Other measurements of quality in logistics include:
- Number of priority orders
- Level of service for peripheral and secure product spares
- Inventory balance on hand and minimum/maximum stocking levels
- Dead-on-arrivals
- No-fault-found, spares sent to repair but subsequently found not to be defective.

## Productivity

The internal service measurement categories discussed so far are used by Wang both to support an efficient field work force dedicated to the delivery of high quality service and to gauge the resultant increase in customer satisfaction. This work force must also make productive use of its time so that the quality service provided is also cost-effective to the customer. Several internal measurements are used to maintain service productivity.

Field attrition rates are tracked to ensure that the need to rehire and retrain personnel is kept low. The utilization of paid and available hours is measured by comparing payroll records with field hours (customer site and travel time) from direct labor activity reports. Overtime is also compared with paid and available hours to meet overtime goals. The utilization and overtime levels are maintained at planned levels to ensure that the most productive mix of customer, administrative, and training time is achieved.

Internal measurements are communicated all the way down the line to the individual employee. In this way, individual accountability and responsibility are achieved; the issues involving skills, training, and motivation are identified and quickly resolved.

Wang's systems are bought by customers to increase their operating efficiency and, ultimately, their profitability. Wang realizes that downtime of a system or a device can have a major effect on the customer's business. At Wang, quality of customer service is synonymous with customer satisfaction; it thus forms an ongoing commitment to a customer's continued success. Internal measurement systems provide field service with the information needed to develop and execute successful strategies and tactics for increasing customer satisfaction through the delivery of high quality service.

## FINANCE AND ADMINISTRATION

In recognition of the importance of billing accuracy to customer satisfaction, organizational changes were made to enhance sales order integrity. Customer assurance and quality assurance groups were put in place to expand the scope of order processing. Calls are now taken from the field on sales order problems, and problem resolution with a turnaround of twenty-four hours (or less) is provided. The complaint is recorded; the paperwork is pulled to verify the complaint; the problem is identified and then solved.

The customer expects a low error rate on sales orders. Errors from sales order audits go back to the individual, and good performers are recognized in order to reinforce their performance. As needed, training is provided on reading a bill of material, interpreting documentation, matching paperwork to the database, and understanding Wang's products. The yardstick used to measure sales order integrity is generated through data from customer assurance and quality assurance audits in the distribution department.

The company is developing a training package to be delivered shortly to the field to heighten the awareness of potential problems by sales bookings. The programs already implemented to improve sales order integrity have resulted in markedly improved error rates, which further enhance customer satisfaction.

## MANUFACTURING

The time had come in the manufacturing division whereby it was not good enough to inspect quality "into" products. The quality organization could no longer be held responsible for the quality of the finished product. From an economic point of view, manufacturing could not justify either the costs involved with all the extra quality inspectors needed as product rates increased, or the extra capital equipment expense to fully test and inspect suppliers' products at the incoming inspection area. Adding to that the manufacturing just-in-time philosophy, the company found that it could not afford to manufacture with defects. It needed to change its philosophy to one more focused on prevention.

Manufacturing has expanded its definition of who their customers and vendors are. Included in this new definition are the various internal vendors and internal customers. This is a new way of looking at internal processes; it adds the missing checks and balances from operation to operation, whereas in the past inspectors reviewed the quality from area to area. The release of pilot or new products to manufacturing is measured by *its* customer, the final assembly and test group. In the specific categories of bill of materials, documentation, diagnostics, product configuration, shipping package, and environment testing: the performance is measured by established transfer criteria. The involvement of the manufacturing division's representatives in the early stages of process development insures that the process is designed to meet the production specifications of the particular site that will eventually assume production responsibility.

The quality organization has begun an evolution from inspecting quality by sorting out defects and reworking them, to an audit function concentrating on product and process control. Measurements have become easier due to the elimination of anything less than 100% as the goal. The primary goal for the quality organization is to change the mind-set of production from acceptable quality levels to that of zero defects and conformance to customer requirements.

Wang manufacturing is moving away from the traditional measurement system based on percentage acceptance toward one that measures the dollar impact. Cost-of-quality reporting has been established at the site level to measure and report on product and process repair activity. This directly aligns the product performance yields with product nonconformance and highlights the associated costs.

The integration of quality inspection and test procedures into the process documentation provides the operator with specific product criteria and responsibilities in building the product. The requirements are very specific; they are intended to achieve operator accountability, and reduce redundant documentation maintenance, while insuring that everyone will be working from one set of criteria. Production personnel now are directly responsible for the quality of the product. A training package has been developed that addresses quality assurance as a profession having a unique language and science associated with it. This core curriculum represents "boot camp," beginning at the site level, for all quality assurance personnel. The areas covered are the language of quality, the tools used in the quality assurance profession, policies and procedures, problem-solving methods and tools, auditor training, and basic statistics.

Spare parts quality assurance has several systems in place to help maintain and improve quality of Wang products. These programs have several highlights. There is a source inspection at repair vendors to verify and ensure that repaired items conform to Wang requirements.

If repair vendors maintain a specified level of performance over a period of time, the vendor is eligible for the ship-to-stock program. This vendor qualification program is in concert with the overall supplier ship-to-stock program. Under this program the vendor is allowed to deliver repaired products to Wang without prior source inspection; this results in saving inspection costs for both the vendor and Wang.

A customer satisfaction reporting system has been implemented that tracks spare parts quality (called Plug & Play). A report is issued monthly to all field locations.

The supplier quality program is based upon a strong, lasting cost-effective partnership. This includes Wang's ship-to-stock program, which is designed to assure long-term conformance to specifications. An incoming quality information system provides the database control and information to produce a vendor performance rating and the timely identification and resolution of problems. Vendors receive monthly report cards containing ratings on quality, completeness, and delivery, with details as back-up.

Satisfaction of the customer is the number one goal while manufacturing products. The customer receives a product from various Wang distribution sites around the world. Dramatic improvements in the distribution arena have taken place over the past two years. A fully defined, automated process, including bar coding, has been implemented; it has resulted in a substantial decrease in customer complaints associated with the distribution process.

As Wang increased its distribution in the international marketplace, the need for monitoring product handling became apparent. Customer satisfaction was being impacted by transit damages. The use of mishandling identifiers, such as ShockWatch and TiltWatch labels, was instituted because of Wang's commitment to the customer. The ShockWatch program offers extended product care by avoiding potential handling damage. Extensive training serves as the foundation of a continuous control program spanning from manufacturing, through the carriers, to the customer site. The ShockWatch program comes complete with a tracking and reporting system that isolates areas of mishandling. The activation of a ShockWatch or TiltWatch label triggers a response from receiving sites, carriers, distribution sites, and quality organizations. The program results in the prevention of transit damage and assures that the customer receives the product in the best possible condition.

The quality assurance audit group conducts customer site visits to observe the installation of the computer systems. Issues identified during the visits are researched and reported, corrective actions are initiated. An individual is assigned responsibility for correcting the deficiency within a specified time frame. Action items are tracked and reported until the cause of the problem has been satisfactorily corrected. Even when the reported issue turns out to be one-of-a-kind, the investigation still serves a useful purpose. Open discussion of the issue brings it to the attention of all concerned, right down to the lowest echelon. Once informed, personnel become attuned to ensuring this particular discrepancy is not repeated in future assemblies.

A Key Customer Account Program assigns a manufacturing director to certain market-specific customer accounts. From Wang's perspective, this program achieves increased customer sensitivity, while from the customer's perspective, it affords increased satisfaction. These manufacturing representatives are expected to report on virtually all aspects of the interface between Wang manufacturing and the customer, including open orders, scheduled deliveries, installation quality, and ongoing reliability. Field trips to installation sites to assist the customer engineer are included as program requirements.

The ultimate yardstick utilized by Wang manufacturing as a measure of customer satisfaction and manufacturing quality is based on the installation and reliability performance data reported from three worldwide regions: the Americas, Europe, and Asia-Pacific. This data is combined to form a worldwide management report on producer quality, with the final measurement being the system level Plug & Play. Each subsystem product is reflected by its contribution to the system level performance. Products with the greatest margin for improvement are highlighted, along with trend data, and targeted for investigation, problem identification, and corrective action. The effectiveness of these actions is measured by future performance.

## RESEARCH AND DEVELOPMENT

### Wang Performance Architecture

Wang drew upon extensive market research to develop and implement a comprehensive and achievable program to address the full range of performance-related issues. It developed a fresh perspective on customer performance needs that in turn led to the Wang Performance Architecture.

The key goal of the Wang Performance Architecture is to deliver a methodology that allows Wang to address the system performance issue on the customer's terms, rather than to force the customer to translate poorly understood measures into his own work and productivity expectations; assures a cohesive, integrated program that meets customers' needs efficiently and effectively; and insures that performance is treated as a key design criterion and as a measurable feature of a product prior to its introduction.

The Wang Performance Architecture draws upon a clear understanding of customer needs to identify the truly meaningful indicators of power and speed. The Wang methodology provides for broad coverage, eliminating both overlaps in performance measurements and gaps, and puts responsibility for measurements where it is most effective in shaping the corporate attitude towards performance. It also develops the maximum insight into the real-world performance characteristics of company products.

The computer industry has tended to ignore the complex equation that determines the effective capacity and responsiveness of a computer system or network. Instead, the customer is asked to rely on a few technical measures as indicators of the relative value.

The industry's common measures include millions of instructions per second, transactions per minute, various throughput and response-time criteria, bandwidths, and so on. All of these measures (and many others) are useful, but only as elements in the total picture of performance as it pertains to customers. Individually, they are too technical, or too narrowly defined, to be very useful as a measure of the true value to a broad range of customers or as a measure of the ability to meet needs and expectations. Such measures do not lend themselves to translation into the work that the system will do for the customer. Thus, there is frequently a demand to conduct a benchmark demonstration. Unfortunately, only the largest contracts can justify the time and expense of a full benchmark, and even then, only the most sophisticated customer can design benchmark specifications that reflect his real requirements. More significantly in the long run, a dependence on narrowly defined, technical measures can distort the design process and lead to products that score well on standard tests (as defined by the customer), instead of supporting high productivity.

## The Three Issues: Sizing, Tuning, Planning

The customer must get the maximum business value from his investment. His performance issues may be simplified into the following three questions:

1. What size system do I need? The measures listed above do not readily translate into work and productivity requirements.
2. How can I get the most out of that system, once installed? Often, the information needed to tune a system for maximum performance is not available. The lack of insight into the true nature of either the system capacity or the application resource requirements may turn the tuning exercise into a game of trial and error.
3. How can I predict when I will have to upgrade or add to my current installation? Almost invariably, the load and service performance curve, be it response time or throughput, is predictably linear, until a system resource saturates and performance degrades dramatically. Effective site-planning requires tools to predict that point, the infamous knee-in-the-curve.

## Features of the Wang Performance Architecture

The core of Wang's approach is to:
- Understand and quantify the range of workloads and usage patterns.
- Maintain accurate measures of the system resource consumptions of Wang and third-party applications, on a function-by-function basis.

- Maintain accurate measures of the practical capacities of all system components.
- Understand the interrelations between system components under a wide range of workloads and develop a body of expert rules that explain and describe real-world performance.
- Centralize performance management planning, but distribute responsibility for its execution.

Wang's Performance Architecture is built around two performance databases, two models of Wang systems that draw upon those databases, and the methodologies, tools, and programs that support, enhance, maintain, and update the databases and models. The databases are the *workload and resource demand database* and the *system service capacities database*. The models are the *Wang field assistant sizing tool* and the *Wang capacity planning tool*. Both models and databases undergo constant updating and revision as the result either of the evolution of products or of the regular validation or correction from selected customer installations.

**The databases.** The *system service capacities database* contains detailed capacity information for each Wang processor and its important subsystems. Extensive, ongoing experiments determine the actual capacity to deliver work across many applications and under a variety of workloads from a single user to complete system saturation.

The *workload and resource demand database* contains workload scenarios for each major application, for the resource demand placed upon key system components by each function, and for the transaction demands placed by typical users. Normally, three scenarios of varying intensity are developed for each application through regular monitoring of work patterns at customer sites.

**The models.** The *capacity planning tool* is a queuing model that mathematically represents every component of Wang's VS 7000 series of computers. With its mathematical representation of the system service capacities database and with selected input from the workload and resource demand database, it can report the response time impact of varying the workload and the activity of each significant system resource. Not only do customers use it to plan system upgrades against workload projections, but Wang system developers use it to model the impact of changes to key system components ranging from micro-code modules to new disk controllers.

The *field assistant sizing tool* (FAST) is an expert system that draws upon both performance databases and a growing set of expert rules in order to recommend and justify the appropriate system and configuration, based upon the customer's description of his workload. The more accurate the customer's requirements, the more precisely FAST can calculate the aggregate resource demands and compare those demands against the system service capacities database and against the expert rules. While eliminating the uncertainty in system and configuration selection, FAST also clarifies the cost of uncertainty when the workload expectations are vague.

Collecting the data. The primary responsibility for the system service capacity database rests with the departments represented in the committee on performance. A growing suite of experiments and benchmarks are routinely conducted to keep the database up-to-date and to assure that the base of expert rules which is embodied in FAST, continues to grow in sophistication and accuracy. The workload scenarios of the workload and resource demand database are the joint responsibility of the corporate performance management department and the relevant product management departments. The resource demand tests and experiment designs are developed by the corporate performance management department, but the vast majority of experiments are conducted by the developers themselves. Measurements include CPU consumption, disk I/O's, workstation I/O's, paging activity, subprocessor activity, transfer rates, and response time.

Shifting responsibility for collecting measurements to the developers has had a profound effect in bringing ownership of performance implications to the development teams throughout the life of a product beginning with the design phase. This ownership, together with the entire Wang Performance Architecture methodology, has allowed development managers to set realistic performance goals for new functions and applications by budgeting the system resource demand by function. The overall effect of new designs on system performance can be predicted with the models. By allowing developers to predict the impact of new designs and design changes, tradeoffs during the development process can be more clearly highlighted and expectations set appropriately.

## CONCLUSION

Wang's Performance Architecture has had a dramatic effect on its performance management activities. The databases, mathematical representations, and expert rules deal with practical capacities, not theoretical limits. Tools, nomenclature, metrics, and benchmarks have been standardized across the corporation.

The centralized databases and their associated data collection requirements have focused the performance measurement activities and eliminated previous gaps in coverage. Since experiments are repeatable, it is possible to make quick comparisons with previous results, and rapidly update the databases and models. The prediction of system resource consumption has become an essential part of the design process. Most importantly, the company can address performance sizing and planning issues in the customer's own terms.

Wang's ability to provide tuning advice tailored to specific applications has been greatly enhanced by the knowledge gained under this program. While our activities in the tuning area are beyond the scope of this chapter, suffice it to say that Wang is now preparing to release a new generation of tools, drawing upon the expertise, methodologies, and technologies it has mastered through this program.

*The author thanks Yaakov Cohn, Cynthia Hayes, Richard Schulman, Richard Summers, and William Todd for their input, Robert Carroll and Philip Hashway for their research, and Linda Kincaid for her helpful comments.*

# Petroleum Refining

Phillips Petroleum

# Service Quality in Phillips 66 Company's Houston Chemical Complex

Phillips Petroleum Company

The Phillips brothers, Frank and L. E., founded Phillips Petroleum Company in 1917. Phillips 66 Company is its subsidiary which refines and markets petroleum and produces and distributes chemicals. Phillips 66 was incorporated in 1986, and its 10,000 employees are headquartered in Bartlesville, Oklahoma.

## INTRODUCTION

The Phillips plastics resins division is committed to cultivating long-term loyalty from their customers—companies that mold resins (raw plastics) into finished products. The plastics operations have many customers who have been with it for twenty-five or thirty years. Managers even cite customers who stopped checking Phillips shipments as part of their own quality programs because the plastic was never off-specification. In fact, for decades Phillips has been a top plastics supplier in Japan, the country that spurred America's return to a quality emphasis.

While Phillips is proud of its programs for high-quality products in other divisions such as petroleum and chemicals, the company's plastics operations are perhaps the best place to see the Phillips total quality emphasis. The plastics resins division receives raw materials from company sources, uses Phillips-developed technology to convert the materials into plastic resins, then sells the resins to manufacturers that make film, fibers, packaging, automotive parts, appliance parts, and other products.

Besides being a plastics producer, Phillips also knows the customer's role. Plastics resins division provides polypropylene resin to Phillips Fibers Corporation, which makes nonwoven fabrics for textile and civil engineering markets, and supplies high-density polyethylene to Phillips Driscopipe, Inc., which makes pipe for the oil and gas industry, city water and sewer networks, and fiber optics businesses.

Another reason Phillips plastics operations are worthy of attention is the company's heritage in the plastics business. Phillips scientists invented Marlex® crystalline polypropylene and polyethylene in the early 1950s. Most plastics of the era were either brittle or too easily softened by heat. But crystalline polypropylene and polyethylene were tough, heat-resistant, and relatively inexpensive to produce. They were the plastics that chemical companies around the world needed in order to meet the growing postwar demand for consumer products. Before Phillips had sold an ounce of Marlex® resins, its management decided to license the manufacturing process to other companies both in the United States and abroad. One of the reasons was that market projections showed demand for Marlex® resins would be more than Phillips could supply. The result: today Phillips plastics manufacturing processes are the most widely used in the world. That means Phillips's reputation as a plastics supplier is largely based not on manufacturing secrets but on overall quality performance. Since many competitors built their plants from its drawings, Phillips has to outperform them in other ways.

One of those ways is through a reputation for technical support. Because Phillips pioneered modern plastics, it also invested much effort in developing plastics molding technology. For decades the company has supported its customers with one of the finest plastics technology centers in the industry at Phillips headquarters in Bartlesville, Oklahoma. The center established Phillips's reputation for working with customers. A number of company engineers and technicians have been honored by groups in the plastics industry for their contributions. The company is committed to provide sales people who not only are at home in the customer's front office, but also are knowledgeable about the technical aspect of operations in the customer's back shops.

## THE HOUSTON CHEMICAL COMPLEX

An excellent case study of the Phillips 66 Company plastics division's quality effort is the company's Houston Chemical Complex (HCC) in Pasadena, Texas. To be sure, not all of Phillips plastics are manufactured at HCC; for example, Ryton® polyphenylene sulfide, the company's high-performance engineering plastic, is made in the Texas Panhandle and Japan. But HCC is the industry's largest single plastics manufacturing facility, producing six million pounds of pellets daily. In addition to Marlex® polyethylene and polypropylene, HCC also produces K-Resin®, a clear plastic used in disposable containers and packaging.

Besides HCC's size, another asset is its simplicity of centralization. Managers of every phase of Phillips polyethylene, polypropylene, and K-Resin plastics are under one roof in the office building at HCC. Since, for example, manufacturing and marketing and lab testing are not in different locations, the key people can meet together every day. That helps keep the quality control efforts consistent. As an aspect of centralization, even the complex's primary raw materials—ethylene and propylene—come via pipeline from the Phillips Sweeny refinery only seventy-five miles away.

Generally, HCC's efforts toward plastics quality can be categorized into three areas: operations, quality programs, and employee commitment.

## OPERATIONS

Although Phillips's basic technology is used by many other companies, the plastics division has continued to improve processing techniques through the years. One result is that the division makes many different grades of polyethylene and polypropylene to suit specific needs of customers. HCC's size and broad range of products represent, in the eyes of customers, the capability to support products in very large markets.

Phillips also specializes in computer control of its manufacturing processes. All reactors at HCC are equipped with on-line control equipment, much of it made by Applied Automation, Inc., a former subsidiary of Phillips Petroleum Company. HCC operators control processes through keyboards attached to color consoles that show a representation of the reactor. Process functions such as temperature, pressure, and flow rates are instantaneously updated, thus enabling operators to fine tune operating conditions.

A fully equipped, on-site laboratory supports the manufacturing process. Having testing equipment, scientists, and technicians at the plant (instead of a remote research center) offers several advantages: an immediate response to problems; a direct access to information, like manufacturing conditions at the time a problem occurred; and consistent testing procedures, in other words, more accurate quality comparisons. The high caliber of equipment at the plant site improves reaction time.

One of HCC's priorities is to install even better analytical equipment in the lab. Advances in rheology—the science of polymers or chemical compounds in long molecular chains—are making possible equipment which goes beyond the measurement of traditional variables (such as temperature and flow rates) in that it is able to characterize polymers in such terms as molecular weight and the distribution of molecular weight. Likely, rheological measurements will have sweeping effects in the plastics industry, enabling producers to modify polymers at the molecular level and to make the product even more uniform. If so, the traditional means of measuring products will give way to new rheology techniques. That is one reason why HCC has already begun installing new equipment.

High technology is also evident in other HCC operations. Its storage and transportation employees, for example, developed a computer bar coding system to track product inventory. In the administrative area, HCC is tied to a computer-based management information system that links Phillips executives in refining, marketing, chemicals, and plastics. Executives use the system daily to monitor economic news, and internal supply and marketing data, and to send electronic mail. In addition, new computer control systems are being installed to control polypropylene production from the tank farm to hopper car shipments.

## QUALITY PROGRAMS

Phillips has emphasized quality in its plastics from the time production began on Marlex® 50 resin, the first modern plastic, more than thirty years ago. When America's modern quality movement began in the auto industry in the early 1980s, Phillips began to consolidate its quality effort under a common program. Today, Phillips's entire refining, marketing, chemicals, and plastics operation share a corporate quality program under the theme, "Our customers buy quality."

### Plastics Resins Quality Policy

The plastics resins division also has its own quality policy:

- Our fundamental policy is to be a responsible supplier of quality resins and services to our worldwide customers.
- Quality is a strategic business principle for plastics resins.
- Our commitment to quality assures our customers of products and services that meet their expectations.
- Quality is the responsibility of every employee.

A policy statement is important because it focuses the efforts of many operations and employees. A quality policy keeps the plastics division from making quality solely a manufacturing function. Instead of trying to institute a quality program on one or two parts of the organization, the idea is to address it everywhere.

## Quality Management Council

To put policy into practice, the plastics resins division has a quality management council composed of its top level managers. It has several subcommittees to address specific needs and carry out needed procedures:

- An analytical test committee charged with testing procedures that monitor production quality.
- A raw materials subcommittee assigned to create specifications and ensure that suppliers of raw materials have quality programs that conform with Phillips's requirements.
- A procedures subcommittee that reviews quality exceptions or concerns, audits action plans to determine if they are effective, and determines if sufficient quality control procedures are in place.
- A process capability subcommittee that oversees statistical process control (SPC) and other quality improvement programs in the manufacturing process.

## Statistical Process Control

The centerpiece of the quality program for the plastics resins division is the use of statistical process control (SPC) in the manufacturing process. The complex began using the technique in 1985. Before SPC, operators were mainly concerned about whether the resin produced was on or off specification. Production of an off-spec or nearly off-spec product sometimes caused operators to overreact in making reactor adjustments. That resulted in plastic that was within specifications but that sometimes varied widely enough inside the specification boundaries to cause problems in molding.

Adoption of SPC raised production quality to a new level. Using SPC, operators chart reactor variables, such as the melt index of the plastic, and follow prescribed procedures for making adjustments to the reactor when the variables change. That means product quality is monitored and improved before it reaches the end of the manufacturing cycle. By forcing people to think in terms of process control, not in terms of specifications, SPC eliminates "over control" of the process. That narrows the range of specifications during production and improves quality.

The Phillips commitment to statistical process control is also shown in its relations with its suppliers and customers. The plastics division surveys all suppliers to determine their familiarity and commitment to SPC, and offers to help them adopt SPC. For customers, the company has developed a computerized in-line rate analyzer. About the size of a portable television, the device contains a computer program that can be pre-set with allowable ranges of machine processing limits. For example, when a customer's bottle-making machine runs outside the limits, the rate analyzer alerts the operator with an alarm light and displays a coded trouble message on its display panel. The analyzer also retains the previous shift's data in its battery-backed memory for later retrieval. By using the data from SPC procedures, plant managers are able to measure the effect of any process variable and to maintain a high quality target.

SPC techniques are backed up by other quality programs. For example, quality is made a financial issue through HCC's reports on the cost of quality. Each quarter, HCC's quality assurance unit reviews various operating documents in order to detect and report on any quality-related actions or incidents that adversely affected financial performance. For example, the report may list the dollar impact of retrieving off-spec material from a customer or of losing chemicals through improper reaction. Compiling such items in one document allows managers to track the total quality effort and to focus on prevention. If those dollars could be captured, they would go directly to the bottom line.

### Systematic Response to Customer Needs and Complaints

Another key quality program is HCC's complaint system. Rather than viewing complaints from customers solely as problems to be fixed, HCC employees also see them as a source of valuable information. For example, in plastics operations it is nearly impossible to constantly monitor the level of pellet fragments—called "fines" and "angel hair"—especially at a complex producing hundreds of millions of pellets daily. Customers are one resource for such information. According to Jim Vaden, the manager of quality assurance at HCC, "We're always on the lookout for complaints. They give you important clues to what the customer's real needs are. A company that doesn't encourage complaints is a company operating at least partly in the dark."

HCC's method of resolving complaints is noteworthy. Any employee who contacts a customer may complete a complaint form documenting the customer, the complaint, and other details. The form is sent to the quality assurance staff. Instead of attempting to answer the complaint, the quality assurance staff determines which part of HCC should address the problem. The plant unit responsible not only must resolve the problem, it also must develop a permanent solution. Quality audits are performed at random to see how follow-up efforts are working. That procedure forces the entire organization, not just the quality assurance staff, to be involved with quality problems and to focus on the customer's need instead of being superficial about it. Phillips also gets feedback from customers through formal surveys and brings customers into the complex regularly to see how plastics resins are produced and transported. In addition, plant supervisors and process engineers often accompany marketers in calling on customers.

Of course, the complex keeps in close touch with customers in more traditional ways. Customer service representatives, who handle twenty-five hundred orders a month, keep each customer informed throughout the process of filling the order. For instance, unscheduled production downtime, hopper car derailments, and adverse weather conditions are reported immediately if they threaten on-time service. Each representative has the authority to change transportation arrangements to avoid production downtime by a customer. Customers also are given the home phone numbers of HCC personnel so they can call at off-hours.

Such openness pays off when things do not go right. One manager recalls that a shipment was delayed because of miscommunication on the part of both the customer and Phillips. After the company told the customer exactly why and how the problem occurred, the customer was appreciative that there was no attempt to hide the problem. That openness kept their confidence and they remained a customer.

## EMPLOYEE COMMITMENT

On any given day a visitor to Houston Chemical Complex sees small groups of employees in conference rooms discussing operations in their unit before their shift begins. Often these pre-shift meetings will include hourly workers cross-examining a supervisor or plant engineer on a proposed change in an operating procedure.

Of course, meetings of managers and workers are not new at Phillips 66 Company or any other company. But the HCC meetings are no-holds-barred discussions that include suggestions from people who turn the valves and punch the buttons. Don Kuper, manager of polyethylene, comments, "Sometimes an engineer may propose a modification to the plant and the operators will challenge the modification. Lots of times we'll go with the operators. After all, they're the ones who have to make the plant run." Such meetings are not preaching sessions or social gatherings; they focus on what the plant needs to accomplish.

The HCC meetings are an example of a total corporate effort toward participative management. The effort has produced a major change in Phillips corporate culture. The company's Participative Action Team (PAT) program, begun in the early 1980s, is the spearhead. The teams are employee groups that voluntarily solve problems in their units. Well over two hundred teams now meet regularly throughout the company; some eighteen million dollars in savings have been documented. Officials believe the PAT program succeeds because management supports it and because the program formally trains team members and leaders. Participative management at Phillips also includes other meetings where managers share information and answer questions.

In the plastics resins division, participative management is most evident in the pre-shift meetings and similar meetings of workers and supervisors in other departments. In addition, a suggestion procedure encourages employee commitment. Established by company founder Frank Phillips in the 1930s, Phillips Suggestion Plan is one of the oldest and strongest in industry. Thousands of workers submit suggestions annually, and savings run in the millions. The plan offers employees on the plant floor the chance to build financial security. As an example, two K-Resin® plant operators at HCC recently suggested a detection device that would set off an alarm if plastic began to plug up pipes that remove solvent during processing. Their award was $50,000; the savings were more than $770,000 per year.

Employee commitment to plastics quality gets reinforcement also through prizes, slogan contests, and formal recognition for employees who turn in outstanding performances. A weekly flyer and a quarterly newsletter keep employees informed of production, a quality index by plant unit, and safety statistics. The publications also honor employees and units for specific contributions to quality.

The Phillips plastics division makes an effort to keep customer awareness a part of every employee's day. "Customer of the Month" posters for each of the three major resins — polyethylene, polypropylene, and K-Resin® — are displayed in the plant and laboratory as well as the front offices. The posters include case studies of the customer company, its products, and HCC's role in meeting its needs. A recent poster featured Solo Cups, which uses K-Resin® to produce clear plastic cups for restaurants and airlines. The employee publication "Plastics News" also carries in-depth articles about customers and their use of Phillips resins. Posters help employees understand what the customers are trying to do and why customers are making certain demands on them.

The manager of plastics resins, Bob Benz, credits a major part of the company's success to the character of Phillips employees: "It goes back to people who started this business. There was no market for polyethylene. Phillips people created it. They also had to develop the applications. The inventors, the technical people, the sales people, the people who started up the first plant built a quality tradition. Our people today are following that tradition."

## FUTURE DIRECTIONS

Efforts to improve service quality at Phillips are already assuming a larger and wider scope. For example, the company completed a large polypropylene expansion in 1987; a major "debottlenecking" of polyethylene operations is set for completion in 1988. The expansions will allow the company to continue to assist customers with current applications as well as with growth into newer areas such as food packaging.

Phillips also is advancing into the next generation of plastics: advanced composites or so-called synthetic metals, made of plastics combined with strengthening materials such as carbon fibers. Some of these composites are being tested for interior panels of passenger aircraft and for such applications as "downhole" oil, gas equipment, and parts for military aircraft and vehicles.

As the company increases its output of current plastics and develops new plastics and plastic-based materials, Phillips management intends for the plastics resins division to pace the company's total quality effort. Instead of depending on any *one* thing, the company stresses the quality of a lot of little things that start at the bottom of the organization and flow all the way up.

# Pharmaceuticals

Warner-Lambert Company
Allan H. Doane

# Service Quality:
# A Warner-Lambert Priority

**Allan H. Doane**
Warner-Lambert Company

The Warner-Lambert Company is a major producer and distributor of pharmaceuticals and consumer products. Its roots are in many other smaller companies which it has acquired over the years since the mid-1800s when the original company, William R. Warner and Co., began. When that company merged with the Lambert Company in 1955, the company's name was changed to the Warner-Lambert Pharmaceutical Company. The 1970 merger with Parke-Davis reinforced the company's position in pharmaceuticals and over-the-counter drugs.

The products Warner-Lambert markets include Listerine, Chiclets chewing gum, Rolaids Antacid Mints, Schick shaving products, and a variety of drugs and other medical aids.

Warner-Lambert is headquartered in Morris Plains, New Jersey and employs 33,500 people worldwide.

## QUALITY AS A MATTER OF ATTITUDE

The tendency in the United States is to broadly categorize industries as either manufacturing or service. In this context a manufacturing industry provides a needed commodity, while a service industry provides a needed, but sometimes less tangible, service. This distinction immediately becomes clouded, however, when considering, for example, the food service industry, which provides both. That is not surprising since every business has important service components apart from its product offerings.

One immediately thinks of service quality in the context of contact between the company and its public consumers. Certainly, such things as on-time deliveries, expedient handling of emergencies, and courteous and meaningful response to complaints are critical service components. Even more important are the attitudes toward service within the company, for these help to create a culture that promotes good service wherever it is rendered. While Warner-Lambert is fundamentally a manufacturing company that places utmost importance on the quality of the products it markets, equal emphasis is also placed on the quality of service, both internal and external. Warner-Lambert believes that devotion to quality is essential to remaining competitive, and have communicated this belief as an integral part of their operating principles.

Accomplishing new goals for service quality has meant developing a new culture—a revised set of values—and then disseminating these values throughout the company. The cornerstone of this effort is the creed under which Warner-Lambert operates. The creed sets forth perceived responsibilities to several constituencies—customers, suppliers, employees, shareholders, and society. Central to the tenets of this creed is quality—of products, of service, of decision, and of overall performance. Quality is viewed more as a focus of the organization itself than as an attribute of goods or services. The ultimate goal is to imbue the entire organization with the attitude that attention to quality in every aspect of job performance is fundamental to excellence.

The efforts to heighten quality awareness began several years ago with a top-down initiative throughout the company, in manufacturing service and administrative units alike. Emphasis was placed on understanding and developing customer-supplier relationships—recognizing that every work output must satisfy someone's requirements and needs if it is to have value. Extensive effort was put forth, using interview and questionnaire techniques to better understand customers' needs and to develop measurements to test how well they were being met. Mission statements were developed to focus work units clearly on their overall objectives. Today, virtually every unit operates in this manner. In the following pages some of these service units together with the measurements employed to assess the quality of service are reviewed.

## SERVICE MEASUREMENT IN THE DISTRIBUTION FUNCTION

Warner-Lambert operates a separate distribution division that has responsibility for the receipt and processing of customer orders in a prompt, courteous, and timely manner. In view of the highly competitive markets, the quality of service in this segment of operation is absolutely essential to maintaining and expanding market shares. The personnel of this division represent a primary contact with customers, who base their opinions of the company as much on the quality of the service they receive as on the quality of the products marketed. Strict attention to many facets of service quality is therefore a hallmark of the operating philosophy of this division.

Important also is the fact that, since this is a separate division in the corporate organization, the several operating units that manufacture and market products are also its customers. If orders are not processed in a timely and efficient manner, distribution division personnel must deal with the concerns of both internal and external customers. Service quality measurements must therefore reflect performance by assuring that internal sales plans are achieved as well as by meeting external customers' delivery and service expectations.

Recognizing that it is the principal link in the supply chain, the distribution division operates with its own mission statement and strategic plan. Like similar documents developed by the manufacturing and marketing units, those of the distribution division embrace this philosophy: attention to quality results in increased productivity, and quality provides a competitive advantage. Thus, quality awareness is practiced in the distribution centers every bit as much as it is in the manufacturing plants.

Each of the distribution centers operates its own quality improvement program targeted to customer service. Strategies include the implementation of new technologies such as pick-to-light and bar code scanning to improve accuracy and optimize the flow of goods through the supply chain; the use of personal computers to provide timely feedback on delivery accuracy; and the monitoring of carrier performance. Through such things as awareness meetings and slogan contests, employees are encouraged to develop and submit ideas for improving service quality; individual recognition is given as appropriate. Here, as in all of Warner-Lambert operations, error prevention is the principal objective of the quality programs.

The transportation network is measured for consistent on-time deliveries as well as for claims as a percent of shipments. Not only is it important that shipments are delivered to customers on time; in addition, the merchandise must not have been damaged from mishandling, exposure to the elements, and so forth. Maintaining the esthetic and protective qualities of the various packaging systems is equally important to maintaining the integrity of the products themselves.

The Transportation Department utilizes a number of criteria in selecting and measuring the performance of carriers. In addition to measures of consistency and claims, other criteria include the compatibility and conformance to standard transit times, the condition of equipment, the on-time pickup and delivery in scheduled shipping lanes to coincide with plant schedules, the need for expediting, the special service response in time of emergencies, and the quality of information systems for tracing, access, etc. Volumes are leveraged among carriers, based on performance versus these criteria. With both customers and plants embracing just-in-time programs to gain productivity improvements, the need for a high-quality transportation system is essential to satisfy delivery expectations. Under this environment, missing a delivery has broad implications on both plant performance and customer satisfaction. Quality transportation is the linkage that makes reduced inventories a possibility in the supply chain.

While inventory measurements have historically been done for cost purposes, they also are necessary to assure high customer service levels. Measurement systems include total dollar variance and total unit variance. While total dollar variance is generally a business management measure, total unit variance measurement is essential to maintaining customer service levels. Anyone adept at inventory management is guided by the tenet, "beware of averages." Certainly this is critical to good customer service. Warehouse damage is also measured together with proper stock rotation, both of which affect overall service quality.

The shipping department is measured on both percent of orders without errors and percent of lines without errors. While it is important to strive for 100% of orders being filled correctly, logic suggests that when errors do occur, one must know by line what they are and what caused them. Only then can action be taken to eliminate the causes. Component performances as well as overall performance must be measured in order to assure consistency and accuracy in the quality of shipping service.

Since the performance of the shipping department is in part a function of order accuracy, a measurement of this criterion is obviously needed. The administrative department is measured on adjustments as a percent of total orders. Again, these are broken down by categories in order to facilitate corrective action and to prevent recurrence. Customer service personnel are measured not only on output but also on the matter in which they handle customer service requests. A routine service request can quickly become a major problem if it is not handled properly.

While the distribution division personnel are not responsible for *creating* the quality of the products they distribute, they recognize their responsibility to handle, store, and transport those products in a manner that will *preserve* their integrity. As a result, a close liaison with the quality assurance unit is maintained to assure adherence to appropriate procedures; for example, the latter might be storage conditions and inventory rotation to assure continued product integrity. Whether this represents a service or product quality effort is a matter of perspective; regardless, it is an essential function when products liable to deterioration are involved. This is just one more example of the inseparability of service and product quality.

It is particularly interesting to note that strategies like the implementation of new technologies and measurements like those involved in inventory management are cast in terms of their effects on service and/or product quality. Not too many years ago those would have been discussed in terms of cost reduction, profit improvement, enhanced productivity, etc., with no mention of their quality ramifications. This is a prime example of the metamorphosis that results from the understanding that quality drives productivity.

## QUALITY MEASUREMENT IN TRAVEL SERVICES

Warner-Lambert's Aviation and Travel Services department oversees a travel office, offers meeting-planning services, and is responsible for the operation of the company's private aircraft fleet. This is one of Warner-Lambert's most service-oriented departments, with a high visibility to company employees, and a prime example of the importance of internal customer service needs. When its service in the past failed to meet employee expectations, the cause was usually high-noise levels. An active program to measure performance versus expectation indices and to react to negative feedback, has reduced the noise level to virtually zero.

The travel office utilizes three principal service quality indices that are self-measured. The first, telephone answering time is measured to address the complaint that it was easier to walk to the office than try to reach them by phone. To a busy secretary who needs to make or change travel arrangements promptly, repetitive busy signals mean frustration and inefficiency. With improved telephone equipment, a measure of the percentage of calls answered within three rings is recorded. If the percentage falls below the agreed-upon criterion, appropriate action is taken.

Responding to a concern about the need for last-minute ticket pick-up, a measure of ticket availability was instituted, recording the number of days prior to a trip when tickets were ready. A target number of days was established, and exceptions to this are questioned, recognizing that last-minute changes necessitate last-minute availability. Finally, complaint and compliment incidents are recorded, and the ratio is measured. The accepted level of service is reflected through the ratio of one complaint per four thousand transactions.

Outside limousine services contract to provide transportation to and from the metropolitan airports. This service is measured by customer feedback. Each ticket envelope includes a brief questionnaire asking the traveler to rate the limousine service in terms of timeliness of pick-up and drop-off, driver courtesy, safe operation, and vehicle cleanliness, etc., in both directions. A significant portion of these are completed and returned to the travel office. The amount of business a given operator receives is in part determined by the customer feedback on the quality of the service offered by the driver.

The meeting planning section offers assistance in locating appropriate sites and planning the arrangements for outside meetings. Nothing can disrupt a meeting more than being without visual aids when needed, slow food service, poor acoustics, and so on. Good planning with appropriate follow-up is essential to flawless execution. By means of a customer feedback report, the quality of planning and preparation is measured, as well as the quality of plan execution.

Aircraft services operates both fixed-wing and helicopter transportation with a capability ranging from short hops to transoceanic flights. The passengers include management employees at all levels and board members when meetings are held at outside locations. Aircraft are also frequently made available for the emergency transportation of sick and injured persons, their families, etc. One might think that simply providing such private air transportation is service enough; however, nothing could be farther from the truth. Customer expectations of this service run high, exceeding those for commercial airlines; the staff recognizes that exceptional service, not cost, is what justifies this undertaking. With the recognition that both time conservation and comfort represent customer expectations, measures are tracked for scheduling to demand, dispatch reliability, aircraft cleanliness, pilot professionalism, on-time arrivals, food and beverage services, and cabin amenities. While these are self-measurement criteria, any voluntary comments and suggestions are certainly considered and acknowledged.

Throughout the development of quality-driven operations in these service units, productivity also improved, as expected. By eliminating unnecessary tasks and streamlining others, significant productivity gains were realized with a minimal capital expenditure for systems automation. Once again, it has been demonstrated that quality drives productivity.

## SUSTAINING THE PROCESS — NATIONAL QUALITY MONTH

While few people disagree about the importance of quality, it is a well-known fact that keeping an awareness program active in a corporate culture presents tremendous challenges. Videos can be shown and speeches can be made only so many times before attention dwindles. It is no wonder, since people are looking for tangible evidence of support for and participation in quality awareness initiatives. They also seek activities to which they can relate to, as opposed to preset, highly structured programs. With this in mind the corporate quality awareness and training manager established a Quality Awareness Committee composed of volunteers from many areas of the company, who meet periodically to exchange ideas, identify opportunities, and plan programs for both the employees and the company. One of their more significant efforts has been the planning of activities for the observance of National Quality Month.

Since National Quality Month was established by Presidential proclamation in 1984, Warner-Lambert has been a sponsor of this effort and has observed it each October. Not only have such activities taken place at corporate headquarters in Morris Plains, New Jersey, but also operating locations elsewhere in the United States and Puerto Rico have participated in their own ways. Not being content to limit the initiative to the U.S., the company included its affiliates in foreign nations in the network. Many of them have established their own programs. This has provided an excellent vehicle for reasserting the corporation's commitment to quality.

As a part of National Quality Month 1986, Warner-Lambert surveyed some three thousand employees to determine their opinions on quality, both in the work environment and outside work (as consumers). A 41% response gave the survey results unquestioned statistical significance. One question asked the respondents to rate the importance of six criteria in judging service quality for banks, hotels, airlines, etc. There were five possible ratings, ranging from not important to very important. Respondents stated that, in order of descending importance, they valued prompt and timely service, service that meets needs, courtesy and politeness, competency of staff, the right price, and the organization's reputation. Furthermore, the numerically significant responses were all in the top three ratings: average, important, and very important.

The fact that the highest importance was given to prompt and timely service (even over service that meets needs) speaks to the extreme value we Americans place on our time in this fast-moving world. Price being fifth in order of importance suggests a willingness to pay for good service. Rating as being of lowest importance, an organization's reputation seems to suggest a consumer group that is impressed by actions, not words; it also seems a testimony to the reality of a general decline in service quality.

On first examination of the results, confusion is felt because of the fact that, while promptness and timeliness together with service that meets needs were rated one and two, respectively, staff competency was rated fourth. However, the comments accompanying the questionnaire clarify the matter. The respondents seem to be saying that they are less interested in the stated technical competency of the staff than in the timeliness and substance of the service delivered. Again, this speaks to the *show me, don't tell me* attitude of today's consumers.

In 1987 the focus of National Quality Month was on service quality. The committee undertook a number of activities, including a name-the-theme contest and weekly presentations of selected videos. But the highlight was a day-long program hosting executives from many principal suppliers; they were invited to share quality concerns and experience with the company's own key executives from across the country. Included on the invitation list were representatives from Warner-Lambert's principal transporters, office automation vendors, and communications companies, in addition to those from materials and supplies vendors. Thus, the program was designed to address quality in its broadest sense and to reinforce Warner-Lambert's commitment to the importance of open customer-supplier relationships.

It is through high-visibility efforts such as these that the people at Warner-Lambert seek to sustain their quality awareness initiative. By using their employees as a source of creative ideas for programs with relevance, Warner-Lambert has been able to secure a significant degree of participation. One concern is the fact that programs are finite entities with beginnings and endings. By focusing on quality as an attitude, the preference is to call the awareness initiative a *process* rather than a *program*. A process is a way of doing something, and it can go on forever if it becomes a part of the culture. That is what is sought.

## CONCLUSIONS AND OBSERVATIONS

By concentrating on customer-supplier relationships, both within the workforce and between the company and its customers, Warner-Lambert has tried to develop quality as a prime value of its culture. An understanding that the devotion to quality in work performance creates value in the resulting goods and services is an underlying principle of the process which has been developed.

Individual operating units, both line and staff, have developed their own measurement systems for assessing the quality of products and services. Many have established quality coordinator functions to underscore the importance of the process. A flexible process that possesses a minimum of structure and that utilizes employees as resources has proven effective for the culture at Warner-Lambert.

Against the background of this awareness framework, a logical extension would be an annual quality improvement process. If properly developed and integrated, this will focus on ever-improving performance standards by eliminating waste and bureaucratic barriers that hamper efficiency. By concentrating on quality, productivity will improve. The discipline of ever-improving standards protects against complacency in the organization. If you allow yourself satisfaction with today's standards, you will never achieve excellence tomorrow. And that is a Warner-Lambert objective.

# Precision Instruments

EG&G Idaho, Inc.
Earl Fray

Eastman Kodak Company
Thomas M. Hally and John R. Bauer, Jr.

Minnesota Mining & Manufacturing – 3M
Roy W. Mayeske

Polaroid Corporation
John Lane

# Evolution of Performance Measurement

**Earl Fray**

EG&G Idaho, Inc.

EG&G Idaho, a wholly-owned subsidiary of EG&G, maintains one of three prime contracts the parent company has with the U.S. Department of Energy. This contract is for the management of a variety of research and development operations and support services at the Idaho National Engineering Laboratory (INEL) located in southeastern Idaho. At present, EG&G Idaho employs about thirty-five hundred workers and anticipates 1987 sales of about $320 million.

EG&G Idaho's initial work at the INEL began in 1976 with a five-year cost-plus-award-fee contract (CPAF). Since then, it has received two five-year extensions to the contract. The salient feature of a CPAF contract is apparent: the amount of fee or profit made from the contract is directly proportional to the customer's evaluation of performance. Conducted three times a year, this evaluation includes an assessment of the effectiveness of almost every aspect of the operation. Although this contract is with the U.S. Department of Energy (DOE), about 30% of the work is done for other government agencies, such as the Department of Defense (DOD) and the Nuclear Regulatory Commission (NRC).

EG&G research and development activities center on nuclear energy. There are extensive programs in radioactive waste management, reactor technology for space and ground-based applications, reactor safety, and materials behavior. EG&G Idaho also conducts research in chemistry, materials science, physical science, biotechnology, and environmental science.

## INTRODUCTION

Consistently strong performance in providing services and products is a key element in the maintenance and growth of a company's business. At EG&G Idaho, Inc., performance models have been developed to measure the quality, cost effectiveness, and customer responsiveness at each level within the company in order to determine the effectiveness of its strategies to support business growth. This paper describes the development, implementation, and refinement of those performance models. It also presents an overview of EG&G, Inc., a subsidiary of EG&G, that led to the development of a performance measurement program.

## COMPANY OVERVIEW

EG&G, with corporate headquarters in Wellesley, Massachusetts, is an international, multi-element organization employing more than twenty-three thousand people and maintaining facilities throughout the U.S., Western Europe, and the Far East. The company's affiliations, joint ventures, and marketing agreements extend its operations into Australia, the Middle East, South Africa, and South America—into nearly every corner of the globe. Over its forty-year history, the firm has prospered through the application of its expertise in science and technology to an ever-broadening variety of commercial, industrial, and government-related markets.

Although the corporation was established in the late 1940s, its founders—Messrs. Edgerton, Germashausen, and Grier, whose initials make up the company name—first entered into partnership in the mid-1930s. At that time, all were associated with the Massachusetts Institute of Technology and were deeply involved in research efforts in electronic circuitry, electrical measurements, and stroboscopic photography. EG&G, in 1947 incorporated and set up office and laboratory quarters in Boston, Massachusetts.

The company has evolved over the last forty years from being exclusively a government contractor to become, in addition, a commercial manufacturer of scientific instruments and of electronic and mechanical components, a facilitator of testing services for health and automotive organizations, and a manager of technology-based financial investments. EG&G is composed of 150 highly specialized business elements organized into six reporting segments: instruments, components, environmental and biomedical services, custom services and systems, department of energy support, and investments.

## MANAGEMENT STRATEGY

During the mid-to-late 1970s, EG&G Idaho experienced a period of rapid growth in which manpower increased from under three thousand to around forty-two hundred people. At that time, the company was conducting several large nuclear-safety test programs and also was heavily involved in alternate energy programs that had resulted from the oil crisis of the 1970s.

By 1982 the business environment had changed radically. The country's emphasis on developing alternate energy sources had greatly diminished with the change in presidential administrations. Also, as several of its major nuclear research and test programs were being concluded, the company could find few actual or potential replacement programs in its traditional areas of expertise. Indeed, the 1982 five-year business plan showed manpower declining to around two thousand people by 1987 unless the company were able to find and exploit new business opportunities.

Senior management at EG&G Idaho were convinced that they must find a way to compete better with other national laboratories and stabilize the work force. The first approach was simple: sell harder. This approach proved disruptive to the work force because there was no formal marketing organization. It also resulted in deteriorating customer relations because the company's activities were taking it beyond its customary program-sponsoring agencies (DOE and NRC).

In 1983, EG&G Idaho's senior management group spent two days discussing possible new approaches to solving the problems of diminishing sales and worsening customer relations. During this meeting, management defined a set of attitudes and actions they thought were necessary to ensure future success and to enhance the potential for growth into new program areas.

Generally stated, the ensuing management approaches have been guided by the following:

- The only reason the company is here is to serve customer's needs.
- A simple organization with decision making at the lowest level possible is mandatory.
- Performance is paramount. The company must be faster, better, and cheaper than the competition.

Even though these are obvious truisms, they can be difficult concepts to put in place throughout an organization. Most employees find it reasonable and logical to believe that the external customers are important. Much has been written in recent years on that subject and little needs to be added. However, senior management at EG&G Idaho, like those at many other companies, have taken the position that departments providing service to other internal departments should behave as though their internal customers are just as important as their external customers. This concept has been difficult for people to accept and managers continue to struggle to find the best way to inculcate this attitude.

EG&G Idaho has had significant success in simplifying its organization. In 1983, the company structure had five to six levels of management. Since then, management has been reduced to four levels uniformly across the company. The company did this by expanding each manager's span of control, and thus creating a flatter organization. For example, before these changes, the general manager had four or five major departments reporting to him. At present, there are twelve. This type of organizational flattening, in itself, forces delegation of authority and responsibility lower in the company, closer to where products and services are actually delivered. This action also resulted in about a 20% reduction in managerial staffing.

Against this background, the balance of this discussion describes a system EG&G Idaho has developed for defining and measuring its performance. Each department manager is required to prepare and maintain a completely current performance model. Ensuring that the models are effective has required an evolving process of careful analysis and refinements to the system.

## PERFORMANCE MODEL

A performance model is a tool to help a manager identify the actions needed to provide customers with products that are superior to the competition in terms of cost, quality and "responsiveness" (as defined below). The timeliness of the information enables the manager to set or modify goals and adjust strategies to enhance the unit's position in the market. A unit is defined as a first-line department that provides products or services to a customer. A performance model has three parts: a strategic summary, milestones, and unit measurements.

### Strategic Summary

The strategic summary (figure 1) is a concise, one-page statement of a unit's strategy. It describes a unit's products and customers, summarizes major strategic factors (e.g., unit outlook, customer options), and provides succint statements of strategy. Since framework is customer-oriented, it provides a strategy that accurately reflects the accomplishments, requirements, measures, and goals of the performance model.

A very important feature of this analysis is a definition of the standards for outstanding unit performance from the customer's perspective. EG&G Idaho requires each manager to summarize his unit's strengths and weaknesses as perceived by the customer. To do this well requires that the manager work directly with his customers to fully understand their needs and their perceptions of his unit's performance. If this evaluation is not done well, the balance of the performance measurement system will have little value since actions will be based on one's misunderstandings of the customer and the competition.

| 1. Product and/or service (specify output) | 5. Customer options (specify actual or potential) |
|---|---|
| 2. Customers and % of Unit's business | 6. Strengths/Advantages (relative to customer expectations) |
| 3. Customer's standards for outstanding performance | 7. Weaknesses/Disadvantages (relative to customer expectations) |
| 4. Outlook for Unit | 8. Summary of strategy (Detailed schedule to be on Milestone Form) |

Date: _____    Unit: _____

FIG. 1. PERFORMANCE MODEL STRATEGIC SUMMARY

## Milestone Chart

After a strategic summary is formulated, a chart (figure 2) is developed, summarizing the major milestones necessary to achieve the strategies identified. Step-by-step actions and a time frame for their implementation are identified.

| ACTION | COMPLETION MONTH (FY-  ) | | | | | | | | | | | |
|---|---|---|---|---|---|---|---|---|---|---|---|---|
| | OCT | NOV | DEC | JAN | FEB | MAR | APR | MAY | JUN | JUL | AUG | SEP |
| | | | | | | | | | | | | |
| | | | | | | | | | | | | |
| | | | | | | | | | | | | |
| | | | | | | | | | | | | |
| | | | | | | | | | | | | |
| | | | | | | | | | | | | |
| | | | | | | | | | | | | |
| | | | | | | | | | | | | |
| | | | | | | | | | | | | |
| | | | | | | | | | | | | |
| | | | | | | | | | | | | |

Date: _____  Unit: _____

FIG. 2. MILESTONE CHART

## Measurements

The heart of the performance measurement system is represented on the next chart (figure 3). For each product or service, the manager develops a set of measurements in three general areas: cost effectiveness, quality, and "responsiveness." These three elements are defined as follows:

- *Cost effectiveness*-the cost to produce a unit of product or service.
- *Quality*-product that fully conforms to the customer's requirements. Anything exceeding those requirements is an unnecessary cost and may result in added cost to the customer, and anything falling short of those requirements may, of course, result in dissatisfaction.
- *Responsiveness*-the ability of a department to respond to changes in the customer's needs or in market conditions.

The process, or series of steps, required to successfully measure unit performance provides a unit manager with the tools needed to:

- Develop a clear understanding of customer needs
- Develop a clear understanding of a unit's performance in meeting customer needs
- Develop a clear understanding of the competitor's performance in meeting customer needs
- Determine differences between actual and desired performance in meeting customer needs
- Develop unit strategies that will close performance gaps or extend advantages over the leading competitor.

A perfect set of these measures for a product seems to form a closed system. For example, if the quality requirements were to change, they would directly impact the unit cost and/or responsiveness.

| PRODUCT/ SERVICE | REQUIREMENTS | MEASURES | GOAL | CURRENT MONTH | FISCAL YTD | PRIOR FY |
|---|---|---|---|---|---|---|
| | Cost effectiveness | | | | | |
| | Responsiveness | | | | | |
| | Quality | | | | | |

Date: _____    Unit: _____

FIG. 3. UNIT PERFORMANCE MODEL MEASUREMENTS

## PERFORMANCE MODEL PROGRAM STATUS

After EG&G Idaho used the performance model system for several years, it found some general deficiencies: inadequate rigor in its application and the perception by managers that the models were not useful. Specific causes for this breakdown were identified:

1. Performance models had been top-down driven and, as a result, managers perceived no ownership of their performance models.
2. The models were not perceived as flexible enough to adequately serve the needs of a large variety of managers.
3. Direction on preparing performance models was verbal and was given inconsistently to managers company-wide.

Thus, performance models that had been generated contained several weaknesses:

1. Incomplete understanding of a customer's requirements and, as a consequence, unclear or inaccurate understanding of an organization's strengths and weaknesses.
2. Lack of a specific unit cost for some products and services. Obviously, unit cost can be very difficult to determine for functions such as research, development and consulting.
3. Lack of specific data on the unit cost competitors incur for furnishing similar products and services.

To address these deficiencies, EG&G Idaho revised the performance model system through a "performance model enhancement project" (PMEP). The goal of this project is to provide a model system that is both useful and flexible. Workshops are being held to instruct managers on the new procedures for formulating performance models. The company is providing them guidance to ensure that each unit manager within EG&G Idaho can effectively utilize a performance model.

## PERFORMANCE MODEL ENHANCEMENT PROJECT

To address the concern of top-down-driven models, the initial step in the PMEP was to dispel a prevalent attitude that only the general manager and deputy general manager were involved in performance models. Group managers who believed in the merits of performance models were selected from each department in the company to serve on a performance model committee. This committee met to revise the procedures for developing performance models and to write a handbook on these procedures. The committee members presently serve as facilitators in workshops explaining PMEP to all company managers.

The merits of the new performance model system were tested before the system was introduced company-wide. Each committee member worked with one of his or her unit managers to develop a department's prototype of a performance model for inclusion in the handbook. Customer input was solicited in developing each model's strategic summary. The committee then reviewed the prototypes critically before approving them.

In this process, it was found that the area of most revision involved a manager's understanding of his customers' requirements and the latter's perception of outstanding performance. Too often in the past, unit managers had only presumed what their customers wanted instead of actually asking their customers what they wanted in quality products and services. Obviously, without an accurate assessment of a customer's needs and *his* standards for outstanding performance, measures of a unit's strengths and weaknesses in the eyes of its customers are erroneous and result in ill-conceived strategies and misdirected resources.

In preparing new performance models, unit managers are asked to meet with their customers to obtain an accurate evaluation of their customers' needs. In those meetings, internal and external customers identify what they consider to be the characteristics of outstanding performance and define the weaknesses and strengths of a specific unit. The information obtained is then incorporated into the strategic summary of the performance model. The results of such meetings have been significant in changing the performance model strategies. No longer do strategies reflect only the unit manager's view of his service; now the manager includes specific information obtained from his internal and external customers.

Another key element in measuring performance is gathering information to help set performance goals that are realistic in the context of the competitive environment. After performance models for each company unit are developed, PMEP introduces a new concept into the performance models, that of competitive benchmarking.

## Competitive Benchmarking

Competitive benchmarking measures a unit's products or services against its toughest competitors or those companies recognized as leaders. It represents a structured approach to competition: studying other organizations and adapting the best outside practices to complement the company's internal operations. Through benchmarking, management can continuously develop the strategies that lead to a competitive advantage in the marketplace.

In this process, several companies among the competition will be visited, or consultants will be asked to contact top competitors, in order to determine a value for various measures. These values can then be retained in a data base and updated periodically. Competitors include any business that provides the same product or service in the marketplace. Industry leaders and other national laboratories that have demonstrated expertise in a particular area must be considered. Current customers may also be considered benchmark businesses.

Benchmarking involves three steps:
- Specifically identify the measures to be benchmarked, making certain they are clear and appropriate.
- Select the competitors to be studied.
- Obtain competitive information directly or through a consultant hired for this purpose. Competitors who may be reluctant to provide data directly may be willing to share the same information through a third party who would handle the results confidentially.

A central network will maintain a benchmarking data base at EG&G Idaho. Information can be then exchanged to avoid duplicate efforts and ensure consistency. Current unit performance can then be compared with that of the best competitor after performance measures derived from customer requirements have been developed and after a value for each measure has been determined for the unit and its leading competitor or leader in the field. On the basis of comparison, a list of unit performance gaps and advantages can be developed. This listing will help redefine the strategies, milestones, and possibly the measures themselves. Such a process is an evolving one, but it can produce hard, reliable data needed to plan and execute effective strategies that meet customer requirements.

## CONCLUSION
Even though there are still major imperfections in some of the company's performance models, the management at EG&G Idaho is convinced more than ever that such a process is mandatory if any company is to achieve high performance uniformly across the organization. This company, like many others, has not been able to adequately define measures in some areas, such as one-of-a-kind research engineering or development activities. However, it is having success in convincing its managers that outstanding performance cannot be achieved unless one can define and measure performance.

# Quality at Kodak's Parts Services: Evolving Into a State of Mind

**Thomas M. Hally**
**John R. Bauer, Jr.**
Eastman Kodak Company

Eastman Kodak Company, founded by George Eastman in 1880, is very much involved with the growing traditional imaging markets it has always served. Products for this market include still and motion picture films, consumer cameras and supplies, films for the printing industry, and medical and industrial x-ray films, to mention only a few.

Kodak also is a multi-billion dollar supplier of commercial and information imaging systems for today's electronic office. In recent years the company has developed a wide range of health and nutrition products for the burgeoning life sciences industry. And it is underwriting a variety of small venture groups, both within and outside the company, as an investment in the future.

Kodak's more than 121,000 employees worldwide serve a global marketplace from manufacturing and marketing facilities in some 45 countries with sales outlets in over 150 countries. The firm is headquartered in Rochester, New York.

## INTRODUCTION

The concept of quality throughout Eastman Kodak Company has always been recognized as a necessary ingredient in the recipe for satisfying its customers with a competitive product or service. However, the proportion of quality within the product of service can vary among operations depending on the emphasis management places on this key ingredient. Continuing for a moment with the recipe analogy, if the chef is consistently rated more heavily for cost effectiveness and volume output than for uncompromising quality, the end product will be inexpensive and quickly prepared, but most likely, will not completely meet the customers' expectations.

The story to be told here is how Kodak's parts services operation has improved its recipe for providing top-quality parts-logistics services to customers. The *secret* to improvement of the recipe is blending quality into everyday thinking throughout the organization, thereby *evolving* quality into a *state of mind*.

The key word here is *evolving*. Parts services' new way of thinking evolved as a result of a number of things:

- A change in the corporate culture and philosophy surrounding job security and performance, as well as the relative role of quality in employees' everyday tasks;
- A new parts services management team committed to becoming a *world-class* service-parts logistics operation;
- Management's drive to assess the company's *true*, versus perceived, performance quality level;
- Looking at the business from the customer's viewpoint;
- Setting quantum-leap service and quality goals, then challenging both supervisors and other employees to meet them;
- Giving employees full responsibility and accountability for delivering top-quality parts orders;
- Encouraging customers to provide continuous feedback on quality;
- Reeducating employees on the correct relationship between quality and quantity;
- Monitoring quality information closely and providing timely feedback at both the team and employee level;
- Demonstrating commitment to high-quality standards by consistently rewarding superior quality results and by addressing less-than-satisfactory quality;
- Reinforcing service expectations throughout the service-supply network (vendors, carriers, planners).

These are the key ingredients for transforming Kodak's parts services organization. Each ingredient plays a role in making quality a state of mind at parts services.

# A CHANGE IN CULTURE

By now it is common knowledge that Kodak, like many other large manufacturing companies, has gone through a significant downsizing and reorganization over the past few years. This process has caused a reawakening of employee awareness that the company is vulnerable to competition if quality sights are not raised to world-class levels. As a result, employees are actively involved in upgrading work processes and striving to deliver top-quality products and services.

# A NEW MANAGEMENT TEAM

The reorganization also resulted in an influx of new quality-oriented managers and supervisors who, in the case of services, are committed to high standards in the service-parts logistics operation. The new management team places strong emphasis on the role quality, versus quantity, plays in the product mix. They are very much aware of the hidden costs associated with quality errors and poor service, and continually strive to "wring out" these costs. Their high expectations zero-defect work are critical to establishing the operational culture and performance expectations that employees must share if the company is to succeed.

# ASSESSING CURRENT PERFORMANCE QUALITY

The process of assessing current performance quality means taking a hard, cold look at the quality state of the business. In the larger sense, they needed to take stock of the service level and accuracy of the orders their customers were receiving. Were customers getting the best service or was there room for improvement? More specifically, they needed to develop a profile of the quality feedback they were getting from customers to determine how they were performing. This profile would represent total team results, although, more importantly, it would be developed at the employees level.

## Service Level

After the new team took over, it reviewed service levels to customers and determined that there was much room for improvement. With the current distribution process and work flow, a routine replenishment order was taking three days from the point of availability in the warehouse to carrier pickup. In addition, the transmitted field-engineer and district replenishment orders were being queued in the system for consolidation and release once per week per district.

While it wanted to keep shipping expenses to a minimum, the team felt the lead time to customers was unreasonable, especially in the western United States. Furthermore, it felt the long lead times were probably causing unnecessary high levels of field inventory for parts that were in good supply and high levels of emergency orders for parts in lower supply.

Internationally, the service levels were significantly lower, with orders taking four to eight weeks to arrive, depending on the country. The ramifications noted above for U.S. customers were magnified for the rest of the world. Clearly there was an opportunity to make a quantum leap in international service.

## Accuracy

There have been times when quality seemed to receive less emphasis than quantity. As a token effort toward quality monitoring, occasional quality audits were done on in-process orders. These audits showed a 99.9% accuracy; therefore, overall results were assumed to be 99.9% accurate. Unfortunately, the audit process approach was less than satisfactory, with no clear audit trail to the person responsible for an error. At that point in time, there were three employees involved with the warehouse-processing of every order: picker, merger, and packer.

## Quality Feedback

Clouding the quality picture further, there was no systematic effort to gather, track, and report trends on quality feedback from customers. This effort was left to occasional management field trips and trip-report action items, unless an error caused a major customer outburst which gained instant recognition and attention.

## THE CUSTOMER'S VIEWPOINT

Once the company had assessed its performance position, it was time to put itself in the role of the customer's to determine how to restructure its business practices to best meet their needs. Those at Kodak asked themselves when they would like to have replenishment orders shipped if they were the customer. They felt the answer was simple: as soon as possible. They also knew that, as a customer, they would want and *expect* top quality from a company like Eastman Kodak Company. It was clear they had much to do in preparation to meet those expectations.

## QUANTUM-LEAP CHANGES

To go from where the organization was to where it had to be in order to meet customers' requirements, there was the need for significant or quantum-leap change in the way it did business. The place to begin the change had to be in the outbound distribution process where there was control over the work process and much room for efficiency gains.

Management challenged outbound's supervision and group leaders to restructure the work flow in such a way that routine orders would be processed and shipped the same day they were received in the warehouse, or *here today, gone today.* Through total involvement of outbound employees, functions were redefined, and handling was greatly reduced to the point that three-day in-house time was reduced to one. This change had other significant quality results (discussed below). To further reduce replenishment-cycle time, the queuing of field-replenishment orders was changed to allow each district to release orders to the warehouse twice, versus once each week.

On the international front, the company made some systems changes and worked closely with carriers to enable it to ship directly from its docks instead of routing shipments through the central distribution organization. This resulted in a reduction of transit time to seven calendar days versus four weeks at comparable shipping costs—definitely a giant improvement in service.

## EMPHASIZING RESPONSIBILITY AND ACCOUNTABILITY

The change to the outbound work process mentioned earlier resulted in the company's first big step toward building quality into its organization, for example, by providing an incentive for doing the job right the first time.

The initial move was to consolidate all three stock-service order-processing steps—picking, merging, and packing. This resulted in both reduced handling and a direct audit trail for quality monitoring and feedback. Employees are now responsible for filling the customer's entire order except for some special-handle parts which are easily traceable to the person who picked them. When a group of orders (a batch) is assigned to a stock-service person, he or she signs out a defined batch number on a daily work log. This log is maintained as an audit trail. Should the person's personal identification stamp not to be included with the customer feedback, the company can reference back to the person who signed for the batch which contained that order.

The accountability is put in place through the establishment of a quality-monitoring system with tight procedures. When customer feedback is received, a quality record is maintained at the employee and team levels. Outbound group leaders maintain for each of their people a quality log which contains a chronological and detailed record of quality results, both positive and negative. When an error is received by the group leader, a thorough evaluation of the situation is done *with the employee* to make sure there is complete understanding of where the mistake occurred. In many cases, it is determined that the pick-merge-packer was not responsible after all; that is, a prepacking or vendor packing error was the culprit, or perhaps it was a misidentified part. In these cases, the error is redirected to the appropriate work center for resolution and accountability. This latter process is critical to employee acceptance of a quality-monitoring system: it must be *fair*.

## ESTABLISHING CUSTOMER FEEDBACK

Over the years, contact with the field organization, the largest customer, had diminished, leading to a lack of consistent quality feedback. The field engineers got in the habit of adjusting their inventory record for shipping discrepancies and got on with their business. The company was not hearing about any errors being made. The problem here is lack of a quality database for evaluating organizational and employee and quality performance. Developing customer feedback was critical to establishing performance benchmarks. To rekindle customer feedback, a series of steps was taken.

Initially, the company had to increase our visibility in the field, which it did through frequent field trips. Another approach was to visit field-engineer training classes to describe Kodak's operation, its dedication and approach to quality, and its desire to hear from them when things do not go right. To increase the chances of this happening, it had to make it easy for the feedback to take place. It tackled this on two fronts.

First, the customer-service operation established a one-window concept for customer concerns called the *help desk*. The distribution operation followed suit with their own help desk to troubleshoot the customer's problem from an inventory point of view. Secondly, a customer survey card was put in every order leaving our operation. These cards were postage-prepaid; they requested basic feedback on order accuracy, packaging, and delivery quality.

## REDEFINING THE RELATIONSHIP BETWEEN QUALITY AND QUANTITY

When implementating the new quality system, the company found its most difficult task was to convince employees that quality must be judged independently of quantity. The old school believed if your output was 20% higher than expectations, then more errors should be acceptable as well. This mode of thinking belongs more to the *get the work out at any price* approach. Yet, what about those customers who get stuck with the results, the extra errors?

Kodak has taken a significant step toward addressing this problem by restructuring the performance appraisal (PA). Until 1987, *quality* was a subset of *productivity* on PA. By definition, quantity and quality were linked, both in management's and the employee's eyes. The new PA ranks quality and quantity separately as key job factors with quality coming *first* in the sequence. As a result, it can command the heavier weight in the overall performance equation.

## QUALITY EXPECTATIONS FOR EMPLOYEES

Quality goals and expectations must be set for the organization as a whole and, *more importantly*, for the individual employee, at whose level quality must be incorporated into the work. Supervision must establish the employee-level expectations and closely monitor the customer feedback on every employee.

At the employee level, the goals and expectations become much simpler. Each person must strive for zero defects. Supervisors rate employees on how close they come to zero defects in relation to expectations for the job. The employee is challenged to find that level of output at which he or she can effectively perform while meeting or exceeding quality goals for his or her work group.

Of course, exceptions to this approach occur when there is a significant difference in time worked in this function. When the experience level is low, the individual can be benchmarked against the average error per work week for the group. Once expectations can be determined, it is critical to advise the teams and individuals how they are stacking up on a reasonably frequent basis. Each employee in the operation gets two informal reviews and at least one formal PA each year. The outbound operation has initiated a quarterly "travel log" where the group leader dedicates a block of time to observe the employee perform his or her job up close. Pluses and minuses are documented and discussed.

## REWARDING SUPERIOR QUALITY RESULTS

When employees exceed quality expectations, they should be recognized by supervision and management so as to reinforce the quality process and let them know their efforts are truly appreciated—outside the scope of normal pay-for-performance guidelines. A fairly recent event in the organization is an example of this reinforcement. An employee came up with the idea of a No-Error Week. Management liked the concept and agreed to support the employees with whatever time and resources were required to make it happen. Employees got heavily involved in the preparations by sponsoring several "dry-run days" and mini-media events to pique everyone's interest. No-Error Week came and went, with remarkable results. A review of activity showed 13,000 orders and 50,000 line items shipped; 8,000 customer calls; 199,000 parts received and put away; 5,200,000 computer keystrokes; and 20,000 different parts prepacked during the interval, with 10 reported mistakes.

Management recognized these outstanding results by putting on a first-class dinner for all employees during working hours. The entire operation was shut down for two hours while employees enjoyed a roast beef dinner and heard all about the fruits of their hard work from many levels of corporate management.

## THE IMPORTANCE OF THE SERVICE SUPPORT NETWORK

A responsive service support network is critical to the culmination of the company's service expectations. First and foremost, parts planners must work closely with suppliers to make sure there is stock to ship—*here today, gone today.* Secondly, as caretakers of the business unit's stock, all employees must respect the integrity of the inventory to minimize unnecessary stockouts. Finally, carriers need to be constantly aware of company needs and be responsive to meeting them while remaining flexible.

## CONCLUSION

Returning to the example of the quantity-driven chef and those key ingredients required, it is clear that a great deal of groundwork must be done, first, to change the employee's thinking from quantity to quality, and then to put in place those tools to monitor, give feedback, and rate the results of the person's work fairly.

Those at Kodak parts services are working hard to create a world-class logistics recipe known as *here today, gone today* and are continuing to refine the philosophies, policies, and key ingredients that will satisfy their customers' service parts needs with zero defects.

# Improving Service Quality In Transportation

**Roy W. Mayeske**

3M Corporation

3M was founded in 1902 in Two Harbors, Minnesota, when five businessmen incorporated the Minnesota Mining and Manufacturing Company to mine a nearby mineral deposit for grinding wheel abrasives.

Early technical innovations began to produce success and in 1916 the company paid its first dividend—6 cents per share. The world's first waterproof sandpaper was developed in the early 1920s. In 1925, masking tape, 3M's first step towards diversification and the first of the family of Scotch brand pressure-sensitive tapes was developed. Scotch cellophane tape was introduced for sealing packages and the development of transparent tape gave 3M its first realization that it had potential outside of industrial markets.

One of 3M's newest products is a bioelectronic ear which provides sound to a deaf person by electrically stimulating the inner ear. The user is able to detect sounds such as fire engine sirens, car horns and doorbells, as well as hear voices at normal conversational levels.

Currently employing more that 82,000 worldwide, 3M's growth has come through the desire to participate in any market in which it can make a contribution, rather that attempting to be dominant in just a few. The stock which was once traded two shares for a shot of bar whiskey, has split seven times. One original share has become 384 shares, selling for about $85 each.

## INTRODUCTION

Transportation of goods and materials creates place, time, and utility value. This is an old, well-known principle. The application of quality improvement concepts to transportation service is, however, of much more recent vintage. What follows is an overview of how service quality emphasis has reshaped 3M's transportation strategy and improved performance.

In this author's view, the main purpose of 3M's transportation organization is to be a low cost provider of quality transportation service that meets the expectations of internal 3M customers, as well as those of external customers who purchase 3M products. The organization's mission comprehends three roles: being a partner with carriers in providing 3M with high quality transportation service; being a support for 3M's marketing effort by creating added value for 3M products in the marketplace; and being an industry leader.

## OVERVIEW

Congressional action deregulated airline transportation in 1978, and motor carriers and railroads in 1980. During this time 3M re-emphasized quality in all its areas, including service performance.

Prior to deregulation of the transportation industry there was little opportunity to purchase transportation services in the same manner as other less regulated goods or services. For the most part, an adversarial relationship existed between transportation carriers and transportation service users. Regulatory agencies often settled disputes between the two factions. There was very little, if any, service or price differentiation between carriers in the same mode of transport. Transactions were usually conducted at arm's length. "Partnerships", (as defined below) between carriers and users were non-existent, but deregulation brought the opportunity for dramatic changes in carrier-user relationships.

Beginning in 1980, 3M's senior management began to re-emphasize quality by creating a corporate staff quality-group. This group, now known as "corporate quality services," was charged with developing a quality framework for application throughout the company worldwide. The transportation organization was introduced to the new 3M quality improvement process early in 1982. Quality training initially focused on awareness and on the development of a good attitude toward quality improvement. A variety of quality improvement tools and techniques have been provided since that time. More recently, training has centered on managing service quality, and using it as a competitive weapon.

On a corporate basis, 3M looks at quality as a process for continuous organizational improvement and increased customer satisfaction. It is a process with an ultimate goal of total quality management throughout the organization. 3M's corporate quality logo refers to "world class quality" as a "way of life," a part of its business culture. Quality is defined as "consistent conformance to customer expectations." Quality at 3M is customer-driven and oriented to growth and profit.

In pursuit of quality performance, 3M thinks five essentials guide the process:

1. Management commitment and leadership
2. Consistent conformance to customer expectations
3. Prevention and specific projects enable attainment of continuous quality improvement objectives
4. Errors are unacceptable
5. Quality measured by customer satisfaction indicators

## PARTNERS IN PROGRESS

Looking back at the period 1978 to 1980, one can see the opportunities resulting from transportation deregulation. Under regulation, 3M used a large number of carriers with a limited commitment to any given carrier. For the most part, one carrier was no better or worse than another. Since various regulatory agencies controlled freight rates, the routing (purchase decision) was not greatly influenced by price. Deregulation opened the door to carrier-user arrangements that address unique user requirements. It also presented an incentive for carriers to be innovative in providing specialized services that met user needs. For the first time, it made sense to dramatically reduce 3M's carrier base and to identify a select number of carrier "partners." To take advantage of this opportunity, the Transportation organization developed a program called "Partners In Progress."

It began to view carriers as business partners and structured agreements around innovative, unique services tailored to 3M's needs. The carrier partner was viewed as a part of the total business strategy and was awarded a large, or the largest, share of business in a particular traffic lane. Volume and price commitments were made and as a result, prices became stable, predictable, and directly related to the value of the service. One could look beyond pure transportation costs and could evaluate distribution costs. A written business planning process was followed.

Partners In Progress gave the Transportation department a good start on establishing a manageable carrier base and on developing service strategies. What was missing were a systematic means to establish service performance targets, a measurement system to quantify actual service performance, and accountability for results. Enter the quality improvement process.

As 3M began to position quality improvement activities for internal application by the Transportation organization, the use of performance improvement concepts and techniques had obvious application to the business relationship with carriers. Partners In Progress, therefore, gave way to a total quality performance process with carriers, a process called "Partners In Quality."

## PARTNERS IN QUALITY

The quality partnership embarked upon can be defined simply as 3M and carriers working together for quality transportation service. Partners In Quality is really a system for communication. 3M determines its service requirement and communicates that requirement to the carrier. Performance standards (figure 1) and measurement bases are mutually agreed to, as are performance review periods. A corrective action procedure, which can be initiated by either 3M (figure 2) or the carrier (figure 3), is available for recurring problems that cannot be resolved by customary means. The Transportation department's requirement emphasizes predictable and reliable service. The Partners In Quality improvement process has been geared to that goal.

In mid-1983, 3M introduced Partners In Quality to carrier executives during a meeting in St. Paul. The focus at that time was on carrier executive management and that focus has continued to the present. It is a matter of principle that management—both at 3M and at a carrier—must lead the quality process. The emphasis from the beginning has been that quality improvement is management-driven.

During the St. Paul meeting, carrier executives were told of 3M's desire to work with them, in harmony and mutual respect, in order to obtain agreed-upon performance in the following major areas:

- Transit time
- Pickup and delivery
- Billing and rating accuracy
- Equipment supply and condition
- Proof of delivery (LTL)
- Documentation and notification
- Loss and damage prevention
- Shipping and receiving hours
- Safety

Later in 1983, regional meetings were held across the U.S. to introduce Partners In Quality to other levels of carrier management and to 3M plant and warehouse personnel—the people who would be charged with implementing Partners In Quality and sustaining it on a daily basis.

During these regional meetings, 3M personnel explained their service requirements to the carriers; both parties began to discuss and agree upon written performance standards. A performance standard form had already been developed for this purpose. The form contains 3M's service requirement, the measurement basis that will be used to monitor performance, and the frequency of performance service reviews. The form also contains the carrier's acknowledgement of the service requirement and its commitment to perform to 3M's expectation. In order for a performance standard to take effect, the carrier must agree to it. The carrier has the opportunity to suggest modifications to the standard during the performance setting process.

# 3M CORPORATION

| | |
|---|---|
| **3M** | 3M Location |
| | Carrier Name / SCAC |
| | Type of Standard |

**Completed by 3M**

3M Transportation Requirement

Performance Measurement Method

| Authorized 3M Representative | Title | Phone ( ) | Date |
|---|---|---|---|

**Completed by the Carrier**

Carrier Capabilities:

☐ Will perform to the 3M requirements as stated above.
☐ Will perform to the 3M Requirements with the following modifications:

| Authorized Carrier Representative | Title | Phone ( ) | Date |
|---|---|---|---|

**3M**

Performance Standard

☐ Set according to the 3M requirement

☐ Set according to the 3M requirement with carrier modifications as noted.

☐ Unresolved, Reason:

Effective Date _____

Review Period _____ Months

FIG. 1. TRANSPORTATION PERFORMANCE STANDARD

**3M**

| Carrier Name | Carrier SCAC |
|---|---|
| 3M Location | |
| 3M B/L or Purchase Order | Date |

**To ►** _____

_____

_____

| 11 ☐ Pick-up | **3M** |
| 12 ☐ In Transit | Transportation Ref. No. |
| 13 ☐ Delivery | |
| 14 ☐ After Delivery | |

**Carrier Performance Checklist:**

**Completed By 3M Location**

| **Pick-Up** | **In Transit** | **Delivery** |
|---|---|---|
| 21 ☐ Missed Pick-Up | 31 ☐ Tracing Failures | 34 ☐ Early |
| 22 ☐ Early | 32 ☐ Equipment Breakdown | 35 ☐ Late |
| 23 ☐ Late | 33 ☐ No Delivery Deviation | 36 ☐ Damage |
| 24 ☐ Wrong Equipment |     Notification | 37 ☐ Shortage |
| 25 ☐ Condition of Equipment | | 38 ☐ Wrong Location |
| 26 ☐ Driver Problem | | |

**Follow-Up**

45 ☐ Incorrect Billing
46 ☐ Late Billing
47 ☐ Proof of Delivery
48 ☐ Claim Problem

**Other**

49 ☐ Note Below

**Please Note**
- Details of Problem
- Frequency of Occurrence
- Costs
- Action Taken to Solve
- Recommended Corrective Action
- Other Pertinent Information

Problem Description:

This Problem Is:

01 ☐ High Cost   $ _____

02 ☐ Recurring    _____ Times/Wk, Mo, Yr

| Submitted By | Date |
|---|---|

Corrective Action Taken:

**Note:** A status report should be made within 30 days of receipt.

| Completed By | Date |
|---|---|

FIG. 2. TRANSPORTATION CORRECTIVE ACTION REQUEST

# 3M CORPORATION

**3M**

| Carrier Name | | Carrier SCAC |
|---|---|---|
| 3M Location | | |
| 3M B/L or Purchase Order | | Date |

To ▶ _____

| 16 | | Pick Up | **Carrier** |
|---|---|---|---|
| 17 | | In Transit | Transportation Ref. No. |
| 18 | | Delivery | |

## Shipment Checklist:

**Completed By Carrier**

| **Freight** | **Paperwork** | **Packaging** |
|---|---|---|
| 51 ☐ Not Ready | 61 ☐ No B/L | 71 ☐ Damaged |
| 52 ☐ Shortage | B/L Error: | 72 ☐ Not Labeled |
| 53 ☐ Overage | 62 ☐ Freight Description | 73 ☐ Illegible Labels |
| 54 ☐ Damaged | 63 ☐ Weight | 74 ☐ Slip Sheets |
| 55 ☐ Improperly Staged | 64 ☐ Piece Count | 75 ☐ Hazardous Leak |
| 56 ☐ Delivery Problem | 65 ☐ Address | |

**Equipment**
81 ☐ Trailer Not Ready
82 ☐ Trailer Not Sealed
83 ☐ Trailer Overweight
84 ☐ Power Loading Equipment Not Available

**Other**
95 ☐ Note Below

**3M Personnel**
91 ☐ Appointment Not Honored
92 ☐ Dockman/Checker Unavailable

**Please Note**
- Details of Problem
- Frequency of Occurrence
- Costs
- Action Taken to Solve
- Recommended Corrective Action
- Other Pertinent Information

Problem Description:

| Submitted By | | Date |
|---|---|---|
| Location | | |

Corrective Action Taken:

**Note:** A status report should be made within 30 days of receipt.

| Processed By | | Date |
|---|---|---|

FIG. 3. CARRIER CORRECTIVE ACTION REQUEST

A key element of Partners In Quality is the mutual agreement on the performance standard. Once the carrier agrees to a performance standard, it is expected to conform to the standard 100% of the time. Performance standards are updated or reaffirmed annually, or as often as required to reflect changing business conditions.

To facilitate the performance-standard-setting process, a video presentation was shown at the St. Paul meeting for carrier executives and at the regional meetings. The video depicted representatives from a carrier and 3M negotiating performance standards. The video portrayed the give-and-take in the negotiation process which 3M believed was necessary to get "buy-in" and commitment. The goal was to create an ongoing two-way communication process.

3M subscribes to the old adage, "If you can't measure it, you can't manage it." The most thorough performance standard is of little value if the actual performance is not measured, monitored, and reviewed by the partners. Carriers have been encouraged to measure their own performance. Likewise, 3M's performance is measured. Carriers need to know what their actual performance is, as well as to become aware of service deficiencies which require immediate action as they occur. In the case of less-than-truckload (LTL) shipments (under 10,000 pounds), carriers measure their performance. The carriers use a special code to indicate situations beyond their control that may cause substandard performance, such as unloading delays caused by the receiver. 3M takes the carriers' data and puts it into formats that allow one to look at overall performance, as well as specific origin-to-destination performance, in a variety of ways.

An overall evaluation rating for carriers from the composite of their actual performance as specified on the performance standard form is developed. There are assigned values to the individual performance criteria. After the measured performance is reported, a weighted average is applied to each criteria in order to arrive at an overall rating for a carrier. The carrier's performance is reviewed with the carrier as required, or as specified in the performance standard. Despite a heavy reliance on quantified performance data for carrier evaluation, one cannot overlook the importance of qualitative information. The carrier that finds a way to meet extraordinary service receives extra consideration.

As the Partners In Quality process has evolved, the Transportation organization continued to reduce its carrier base and, in most instances, to eliminate backup carriers for specific traffic lanes. Carrier partners know that they are being relied on to perform to the agreed standard and that there is no one available to bail them out.

## Benefits

Several benefits have been derived from the quality partnership with carriers. Electronic data interconnects have been established with selected carrier partners for billing and payment, manifesting, mail, and customer/carrier/ shipper data transmissions. Loading and unloading dock congestion has been minimized at 3M locations and at customer facilities by using a limited number of carrier partners. Some numbers may help illustrate this point. Up to the early 1980s, about one thousand LTL carriers were used. Now fifty carriers handle 87% of all LTL shipments. For export/import ocean shipments, forty carriers now handle shipments previously handled by about one hundred carriers.

Similarly, 7 truckload carriers are utilized, down from about 240. The dramatically reduced number of truckload carriers has made it feasible to establish a sophisticated computer driven load control center which optimizes routing for upwards of 300 truckloads per day. The load control center concept represents a direct enhancement to the transportation strategy in support of 3M's just-in-time manufacturing and distribution goals. In addition, it enables one to track carrier performance closely.

Another benefit from the quality partnerships with carriers has been a reduction in administrative expense, both for carriers and for 3M. The latter does not spend much time in the "courtship" which is traditional in buyer-supplier relationships. The partners concentrate on meeting performance targets and on developing innovative ways of doing business. Mutually beneficial volume-price arrangements have been established that permit 3M to meet its low-cost provider goal. Being a low-cost provider does not necessarily mean using the lowest cost carrier. It means using the carrier that provides the best utility of service in its application to meet customer expectations.

The Partners In Quality process has been supported in various ways within the Transporation organization. A quality improvement plan is developed annually to support the organization's strategic business objectives. Specific objectives related to Partners In Quality are identified in the annual plan. The cost of quality (the expense incurred due to substandard performance) associated with Partners In Quality is tracked and reported on a quarterly basis.

A quality performance steering committee, in conjunction with Transportation management, oversees the activity of two quality improvement teams (QITs). An external QIT focuses on the Partners In Quality process to strengthen 3M field location support. An internal QIT facilitates quality training, quality circles and task teams, recognition, and communication of quality activities. Both QITs establish performance benchmarks and accountability for results.

Quality improvement projects which require intensive effort to accomplish have been facilitated by using resource people. Under this arrangement, an individual is pulled out of the mainstream of the Transportation organization's activity and assigned to a project full time. They concentrate their efforts solely on completing their project. In one instance, a resource person worked eighteen months with LTL carriers and within 3M to enhance the carrier service performance management reports. When the project was completed, the resource person was reassigned within the organization.

### Transportation Quality Achievement Awards

Without doubt 3M's transportation service has improved due to the emphasis on service quality and carrier partnerships. Transit timeliness is now averaging 95% or higher for most transportation modes, and there has been steady annual improvement. Future improvement is expected to be slower than in the past; however, the focus will continue to be on the 100% performance target.

At the end of 1986, it was decided to recognize those transportation companies that had recorded superior performance, as measured against the mutually agreed standards. Eleven companies were selected to receive the first annual 3M Transportation Quality Achievement Awards. Two airlines, an air freight forwarder, four motor carriers, and four ocean carriers were recognized. As a public recognition for the accomplishments of the award winners, 3M placed an announcement in the *Journal of Commerce* and sent press releases to seven trade publications.

3M shipping and receiving locations have the day-to-day task of making Partners In Quality work with the company's carrier partners. At the end of 1986, the company also introduced an annual recognition program for 3M locations that excelled in implementing and sustaining the Partners In Quality process. Each location received an award plaque, similar to that presented to carriers. Each plaque has space for ten individual year plates. This challenges both carriers and 3M locations to earn recognition each year.

As mentioned previously, it is important to keep the transportation quality process focused on carrier executive management, since they must lead the quality improvement process within their companies. To keep them informed of the activities within 3M, a Partners In Quality newsletter is published for the carrier executives, who can then route the newsletter through their organization.

In their roles, carriers often function as an extension of 3M. They may be the only direct contact a customer or vendor has with the company and, therefore, may play a critical role in the 3M quality performance process. Carriers have the responsibility to perform in exact conformance to the agreed standard. Their performance is a direct reflection upon 3M. Those who perform to 3M's expectations make an important contribution to the success of 3M, and they reap major benefits that a partnership brings: an ongoing relationship and the opportunity for new business.

### CONCLUSION

Just as 3M requires excellence from its people, it expects high performance from companies that provide transportation services. In both cases one needs to manage quality the same as one manages employees, equipment, materials, terminals, or any other business facet. A system that fosters quality awareness, individual responsibility, and accountability for results must be an important process in any company. Certainly, these ingredients are essential in performing transportation services that consistently meet 3M's requirements. In short, it is just as important for carriers to have a quality improvement process as it is for 3M; for both it's equally important to make quality a way of life.

# Identifying Service Objectives

**John Lane**
Polaroid Corporation

The Polaroid Corporation, founded in 1937, produces and services photographic and electronic imaging equipment. There are five Polaroid Service Centers in the United States and another twenty-six authorized service centers located in cities across the country.

Polaroid employs approximately twelve-thousand people who are headquartered in Cambridge, Massachusetts.

## CURRENT MISSION OF CONSUMER SERVICE

The traditional role of the product service group in manufacturing companies is a simple one: to rectify failures or other product defects either by warranty repair or replacement. At Polaroid, the consumer service division, in addition to performing those traditional functions, acts as the conduit through which the customer communicates back to the manufacturer. The consumer's impact on manufacturing through the marketing process is significant.

Each year Polaroid's consumer service group goes through a detailed planning effort. Although it is not a profit center, its planning, goal-setting, and business accountability procedures are essential. The method is to set objectives for the coming year, identify strategies, and lay out action plans. The business plan is summarized in a concise mission statement that brings the consumer service group's charter for the year into focus. The mission statement for 1988 reveals what the corporation can expect from the consumer service division: *Our objectives are designed to seek out and move us closer to our customers; to make us a more effective communications link between Polaroid and the marketplace; to add value to our products as perceived by users; to influence the corporation in the creation of new products; and to build a flexible organization designed to do the job.*

Everything they do in the coming year will be measured against the objectives prefaced by this statement. The business plan is not their job description; it is not what they *are*, but what they must *become*. It describes the gap between where they are now and where they are going. The following ten objectives are the service criteria against which their performance will be measured.

1. Assure, improve, and measure customer satisfaction
2. Provide a forum for consumers to speak to Polaroid on product performance and customer attitudes
3. Manage costs and income effectively
4. Improve teamwork and communications throughout the network
5. Design timely and useful management reporting systems
6. Formalize a program for job redesign and career development
7. Manage the new training concept
8. Define and execute service responsibility in new product development
9. Define and publicize the role and corporate responsibility of the consumer service organization
10. Develop a global approach for worldwide service.

## THE SERVICE ORGANIZATION

Although Polaroid's consumer service, a part of the marketing division, is a worldwide organization, this chapter addresses the U.S. operations only. There are five Polaroid service centers in the United States housed at regional marketing centers. These are full-service facilities that are able to answer questions regarding all Polaroid products; they are staffed to do in-house and field repairs on both consumer and industrial products. An additional twenty-six authorized service centers are scattered throughout the country. These are independent camera repair businesses authorized to do warranty work.

Consumer Services eagerly offers training at the centers, via a toll-free telephone line, or by mail to customers on how to use products. About 80% of these transactions are created by the need for information rather than by problems. The other side of the traditional business is to repair or replace inoperative equipment.

Caveat emptor has no place at Polaroid. Products are backed with liberally interpreted warranties in the belief that customers deserve fair value. The relationship with consumers is never adversarial: service representatives treat customers well and they come back to buy cameras and film. Polaroid photography is part of their personal and professional lives.

## MONITORING SERVICES

Consumer services consist of what they say to customers and what they do for them. The quality of what they say is measured in terms of the accuracy of the information given. How well they restore complex hardware back to efficient operation can be tested functionally. These activities are the core of the business and must be performed flawlessly before doing anything else.

How to monitor the quality of this business is no mystery. Internal control procedures give a good reading of day-to-day quality: How many times does the phone ring before it is answered? Are answers accurate and concise? Are letters answered within a day or two? Do repair technicians correctly diagnose problems and return hardware to specification in a reasonable turnaround time? Quantitative matters such as these are dealt with routinely—routinely, but not effortlessly. Monitoring, training, and updating are never-ending, costly and time-consuming endeavors.

Service representatives take customers and themselves very seriously. They have nearly a million customer contacts each year. Service representatives determine who their customers are and what they think about them. Since they want their service to be viewed as something valuable that differentiates them from others, expecially the competition, customer satisfaction is measured. Especially with lower-priced products, dissatisfied customers tend to give up and move away silently, grumbling in their underground network, but not directly challenging the manufacturer. The mission objectives clearly show that what customers think is of critical concern to Polaroid.

To get a fix on the quality of services as perceived by the customer, they developed a follow-up questionnaire for consumers regarding the level of satisfaction with the service or repair work performed. This gives service representatives not only a reading of quality, but also a very important opportunity for a second chance at a customer they might be losing.

It is important for any group to examine, or from time to time reexamine, what business they are in. It seems a naive question and one that many of us would answer casually. It may not be so simple. A service group is out there in the world in a way that no other element of a manufacturer's organization can be. There are ways to exploit this marketplace presence. Selling, for example, can be an important part of the group's charter. Polaroid's view of its service effort, however, is as an enhancer and facilitator of the picture-taking experience. They leave selling to the professionals.

Polaroid has always thought that the service group's intimate relationship with consumers can benefit both the customer and the corporation. Clearly, information-gathering can be an appropriate use of the service network, especially when it serves to enhance reliability, add value in the market, and improve current and future products.

Despite any company's claims to be customer-oriented and market-driven, its product is manufactured within the walls of a factory, very much isolated from the market: the customer is remote. Working in the isolation of the factory, manufacturing engineers have traditionally relied on process controls to evaluate quality. These controls have become extremely sophisticated. Engineers are so comfortable with these controls that they even use them to evaluate themselves: that is, if the process is good, *we* are good.

Input from the field is solicited, but usually it is late, sketchy, contradictory, and inconclusive. While many have been uneasy about this approach, it is the way things have gone throughout Polaroid's manufacturing history. Yet, to go from process-control-based quality indicators to performance-based criteria would take a philosophical leap. A growing intuition has pointed them in this direction.

## SPECTRA EARLY RETURNS
An opportunity to experiment with fresh market data presented itself a couple of years ago with the introduction of the new camera system, Spectra. Completely new products seem to carry an implied license to innovate. Furthermore, the highly energized people who bring new products on line can usually find the extra time to try something new; and of course, they are much less vested in the status quo.

About a year before the product's introduction, consumer service, in collaboration with the camera division, joined the Spectra manufacturing program. Their job was to work at the factory as the project took shape. This arrangement had two benefits: first, it gave them a more fundamental understanding of all aspects of a new product than they ordinarily would have; second, a genuine rapport grew between the two groups. Service and manufacturing have always had good relations in the past, but working together in a new way, on a day-to-day basis, created an atmosphere of trust that would become essential if the credibility of data became an issue.

The major objective of the program was to get performance data back to the factory in order to effect corrective action. It was essential to return information quickly. Time lags in the product distribution and defect-return cycle have previously been so long that data once received could not be used on-line. The customer has been remote in time as well as distance.

Consumer service headquarters in Cambridge, Massachusetts, was the clearinghouse for all product returns and analyses. The service representatives who respond to the toll-free telephones were key players in the program. The instruction materials packed with each camera told consumers that if they experienced any problem with their new Spectra, they should call the 800 line for consultation. Telephone representatives are highly skilled in analyzing the likely cause of the customer's problem. To make a photograph, three elements of a system must be synchronized: the camera, the film, and the photographer. While the company goes to great lengths to make its products user-friendly, some consumers are confounded. A little clarification can often go a long way.

If there appeared to be a camera defect, the customer was asked to bring the camera to one of thirty-two service centers for replacement. Where geography permitted, this was the ideal solution from the customer's point of view, since all service locations were able to give expert training on how to use the product and could work directly with the customer. They could do a definitive analysis of the cause of the defect and, if necessary, make the exchange on the spot.

All defects were returned to Cambridge by overnight express. There were no field repairs in the early return period. If the customer was unable to go to one of the centers, a replacement camera was shipped via overnight express. The defective unit was returned by the same carrier. Failed cameras could thus be replaced and returned to Cambridge from anywhere, nationwide, in a matter of a few days.

If a caller's problem was not a malfunction, but a misunderstanding of the system, a telephone representative could usually give adequate instruction over the phone. The customer was advised of the solution and the data recorded. Even raw data like that, without physical evidence, was analyzed and evaluated. If a film defect appeared to be the problem, the film was replaced directly to the consumer, and the defective material was analyzed and tabulated.

Data collection was part of the service encounter, not a separate function. The collection of data although important never hindered or compromised service. New products are always celebrities, and the high priority given to Spectra system data gave even greater status to the Spectra owner and his needs.

In Cambridge, a group whose members came from consumer service, product design, quality, and manufacturing was dedicated to analysis of film and failed cameras. The group quickly created a reliability profile of the product in the field; once significant problems were identified, solutions were proposed.

The manufacturing group now had the timely and reliable information they previously lacked. Some of the problems isolated by the Spectra early-returns program have been easy to correct; others, more difficult. Working within the essential process controls of the manufacturing world presents innumerable challenges. Scheduling, productivity, yields, and the myriad aspects of running a profitable factory make *awareness* of a problem and *solving* the problem two very different matters. To assume that there are easy solutions to hard problems is simplistic.

The net result of the program has been overwhelmingly positive. Cameras produced today are significantly more reliable than those made in the early months of the Spectra early returns program. Those improvements were dramatically hastened by the early-returns program. In fact, because of the relatively short life cycle of modern products, many changes could not have been made, had it not been for the speed of this program.

Very soon after the Spectra introductory period, a companion product called Onyx was introduced. This was essentially a new, top-of-the-Spectra line, but, it was, marketed separately and could be tracked by a similar early-returns program. The results showed a significantly higher reliability leading directly to increased customer satisfaction.

This experiment has been an exciting and satisfying one. Will it become the paradigm for future product rollouts? While it has potential as a model, like all good experiments, it raised as many questions as it answered. It showed that faster data collection and analysis can significantly affect the quality of the product that reaches consumers.

This was an expensive program, as pilots usually are. If those on the service side expect to do this level of data collection and analysis as a routine procedure, and it appears they do, they will have to make some organizational adjustments to accommodate it. The same is true on the manufacturing side. You cannot shut down the line every time a camera fails in Iowa, but if that field data can be available on a timely basis, it can be factored in along with other controls.

# THE BOTTOM LINE

Service, as they see it at Polaroid, is a rewarding business. It attracts intelligent and highly motivated people who put a great deal of themselves into their work. But while good, customer-oriented service is part of the corporate culture, it is not purely altruistic: good service pays off.

In order to be profitable, Polaroid has to bring customers back repeatedly to buy film and eventually to buy new camera models. It is highly unlikely that an unsatisfied customer will ever come back. In the end, all functions will be measured in light of contributions to the profit and loss picture. Sometimes that contribution is hard to quantify. Unfortunately, short-sighted economic policies can raise havoc with fragile corporate elements like service.

The emphasis at Polaroid is to focus on results. In service, no less than in other disciplines, identifying the desired result is at the heart of setting objectives. Lining up the service organization with corporate direction and profitability requirements is the only way to achieve the high-level support that a service group needs. You have to demonstrate pay-back that exceeds cost. You can do this either with good numbers or with good sense, but you have to do it.

# Publishing, Printing

R. R. Donnelley & Sons
James Graham

The New York Times
Leonard R. Harris

The USA TODAY
Donald B. Berryman

# Service Quality at R. R. Donnelley & Sons Company

**James Graham**
R. R. Donnelley & Sons Company

R. R. Donnelley & Sons Company will celebrate its 125th anniversary next year as a leader in the printing industry. Donnelley produces over four billion pieces of printed literature a year including books, magazines, catalogs, directories, technical manuals, and financial documents. The twenty-four domestic manufacturing plants and numerous sales and service centers that produce and distribute these publications are found in major metropolitan areas as well as in smaller communities in the U.S., England, and the Far East.

## INTRODUCTION

Service quality at R. R. Donnelley & Sons Company is a story within a story. The quality of the service provided by R. R. Donnelley & Sons can best be understood within the large context of the company's history, the history of the United States printing industry, and the history of printing. Donnelley has become the nation's largest printer as a direct result of a tradition of quality products, strong customer service, and close and cooperative employee relations.

The process of putting ink on paper has changed dramatically since Gutenberg's day. What began as a simple, hand-operated press that printed one sheet of paper at a time has grown to a modern web offset press, 130 feet long, one story high, that weighs 200 tons and prints multiple-color images at the average rate of 2,200 feet a minute.

*Preliminary work*—work done prior to putting the plates or cylinders on the press, was performed entirely by craftsmen skilled in retouching film or assembling the artwork and text on individual pages. Today these steps are part of electronic prepress operations that convert pictures into streams of computer information and make color corrections electronically. Typesetting has grown from the days when each letter was selected by hand and placed into position in a line, to using a beam of light to form characters. Once upon a time typed manuscripts received from publishers were handset into type *galleys*, then returned to the customer after proofreading for a final okay. Today, it is not unusual for the type to be set on a computer at one location, transmitted via satellite to another location, then converted to characters by means of a photographic process.

No longer are most magazines published to meet the general interests of a huge market. Now interests and markets are highly specialized. As a result, a magazine may have East and West Coast editions, or one version for dairy farmers and another for cotton farmers. The magazine or catalog is tailored for a specific customer's interests. New computer, printing, and binding technologies enable magazine publishers and direct marketers to achieve specialization in their publications.

In terms of economic impact, the printing and publishing industries constitute approximately three percent of the gross national product. The printing industry, for the most part, is made up of small businesses—with almost fifty thousand companies in the U.S. alone. Of these, nearly eighty percent have fewer than twenty employees.

An astonishing number of factors affect the printing process and the quality of the printed product. These factors are found in the manufacturing process and in the functions that support it, such as customer service, sales, accounting, engineering, and employee relations. Donnelley does not manufacture a product for which set specifications exist, like those for an automobile or a circuit board; the requirements differ for every product Donnelley manufacturers. For this reason, controlling the quality of the product and service for any particular customer is a highly individualized matter. This challenge must be met at every step of the sales, manufacturing, and distribution process. Also, because of the specialized nature of each product, the measurement of success is not always easy to quantify. Certainly every department in the company documents its standards and attempts to measure its performance; yet, probably every one of them would conclude that its success has to do, more than anything else, with people who are dedicated to their work and do their jobs well.

Donnelley traces its predecessor companies back to 1864. The company is based on simple values: honesty, integrity, industry, competence, pride, and dedication. The founder of the company, Richard Robert Donnelley, was persuaded early of the importance of distinguishing between publishing and printing. The publisher selects, edits, prepares, and then markets the printed product; the printer is responsible only for printing and, in some cases, designing and distributing it. In this way, the printer does not compete with its own customers.

## Donnelley's Philosophy of Business

Underlying Donnelley's growth is a philosophy of doing business (summed up in the word *commitment*) that remains constant today. Employees are committed to each other, to working together as a team, and to identifying and solving problems together. This commitment promotes personal satisfaction, job satisfaction, and a better product. A second commitment is to two groups outside the company; suppliers and the communities in which Donnelley operates. The company provides financial support to a broad range of public service activities and causes. At the manufacturing level, it builds plants designed and landscaped to enhance the communities, and that are efficient and productive. A third commitment is to excellence. This results from combining good materials with good design, and superior craftsmanship with careful handling. This is the work of dedicated people in all phases of the services Donnelley offers customers. The fourth, and most important commitment, is to customers.

Delivering quality and service in the printing industry is a challenge because every job is unique. Donnelley employees must produce new products continually, on exact schedules. The original copy, film, paper, printed signatures, work in progress, and final product all require the utmost care when being moved or stored. Consequently, the selection and training of employees is fundamental to the company's philosophy of business. Their dedication and cooperation have a fundamental impact on the company's competitive strength.

Donnelley has long made it its business to serve customers with the best, most technologically advanced equipment available. This enables the company to accommodate the growth, quality, and schedule needs of its customers. In the past five years, the company has invested nearly one billion dollars in the latest technology, new plants, new equipment, and training programs. In less than ten years, it has added twelve manufacturing divisions and eighteen sales offices. If a customer increases the circulation of its publication, which increases the amount of needed press time, production schedules can still be met even if they are lengthened by only a small amount to allow for the increased circulation.

## Human Resources

The company is organized into seven product groups, each of which has several manufacturing divisions that operate with a great deal of independence. To a certain extent, this gives them control of their own destinies: to participate in the development of their own technology and in the scheduling of work for customers.

Except for in-plant printing okays, direct customer contact is infrequent for most areas of the company. General management is typically not involved with a specific printing job; personnel people usually do not work with customers, nor do computer programmers. These people are behind the scenes of the production. Yet, they are as essential to the provision of quality service as are the people who provide service directly to the customer, so their roles in delivering service quality are also subject to rigorous critical reviews.

Fundamental to the company are its people, a fact which underscores the importance of the recruiting and selection process. Through the testing and interviewing process for new hires and transfers, all departments attempt to determine the attitude of a candidate toward service quality as part of that individual's ability to do the job. The next task is to train and develop employees. Training at Donnelley is both centralized and decentralized: divisions provide their own apprentice and employee development programs; the corporate office provides sales, supervisory, managerial, and various other kinds of training.

A key role in the plan for service quality is that of the Donnelley sales representatives. From their first day with the company, they are trained in a consultative approach to sales, which is based on the belief that they cannot provide their customers with the best plan unless they understand the customers' business goals and work as partners to achieve them. Each job is usually a major investment for a customer, one from which they expect a substantial return. That requires careful planning.

Sales people along with staff from the manufacturing division are expected to develop manufacturing and distribution plans for customers that take advantage of the best-priced paper, ink, printing, and binding processes. They know how to get the most out of mailing lists, by reducing duplicates and maximizing postal discounts. Through good teamwork, they can also develop manufacturing plans in conjunction with mailing list strategies to identify prospective customers so that a catalog customer does not receive more orders than can be fulfilled in a reasonable time. They can work with customers to test new markets prior to a major mailing, or rework a plan to fit within a customer's tight budget.

## Service to the Customer

At Donnelley, everybody bears responsibility for the outcome of any printing job. Obviously sales representatives cannot do the job alone, so their ability to work well with customers is as important as their ability to work with people in areas of the company whose expertise will also affect the quality of product and service to the customer. The sales representative, then, is committed to the careful planning of a job. This planning has the purpose of creating optimum manufacturing plans, avoiding overtime expenditures, providing an affordable paper supply, and allowing for postal discounts and distribution economies. These are key elements in customer satisfaction.

By involving division and staff personnel with the customer's needs, each employee is made aware of the importance of his or her job in the delivery of a good product. The objective is to ensure that, for example, in a pressroom, employees working on a given press know what the customer's requirements are, how important they are, and what their responsibilities are in fulfilling them. Sales representatives sometimes bring customers into the plant to meet with the people who bring their jobs to life.

Also critical in providing quality service is the Donnelley customer service representative, (CSR). To the customer, the CSR is the manufacturing division. These people are selected not only for their technical expertise, but also for their attitude toward quality of service. They are trained in printing technology as well as company procedures and policies and their performance is monitored closely and supported with daily production meetings.

Planning meetings are held before production begins with CSRs, customers, and the individuals who will actually be performing their work. These planning meetings allow for brainstorming, foreseeing problem areas, and opening communication channels. Customers repeatedly express appreciation that division representatives are eager to sit down as a team with the CSR, make evaluations, and offer suggestions and solutions. Such willingness exhibits a commitment to the delivery of quality service.

The maintenance of proper security is another major area of customer service. The confidentiality of prices, information about new products, mailing lists, securities offerings, and acquisition statements—all require an intense level of security. Sales trainees who are rotating in jobs throughout the divisions are cautioned against even touching any printed material delivered from the press without a pressman's prior approval; no printed matter leaves the floor without that approval. All employees are educated in the ethics of strict confidentiality.

## Maintaining Standards

Because each printed piece is specialized, the first responsibility is to establish exactly what the customer wants. This does not happen just once; it happens repeatedly during the life of a book, magazine, or catalog. It begins at the conceptual stage with the original design and marketing plan; it occurs again at every stage in the sales, manufacturing, and distribution cycle, and when it is in the hands of the final customer—on the bookshelf or magazine stand. Quality procedures are important throughout the operation because the process encompasses the contract, product, service, and the delivery schedule. This process is ongoing, reflecting the varying requirements of each separate job.

To maximize equipment resources, the corporate manufacturing services department coordinates and schedules production work across the company. The planners in this department take original specifications and schedule the work appropriate to Donnelley equipment and divisions. This function is critical at the beginning of the cycle to assure that press and binding time are available. The company has sufficient presses and binding lines to provide the security of backup capabilities if problems arise, such as severe weather conditions.

Once a schedule is established, the job enters the production cycle. At the prepress stage, the instructions are extremely specific and highly technical, as in this example:

- Films furnished ready for platemaking are to be right reading emulsion down.
- Films are to be of a dimensionally stable polyester base with thickness of .004″, lith-type, high constrast, emulsion; minimum image density of 3.0 as measured on a transmission densitometer.
- Type and other image areas not intended to bleed must be held 5/16″ from trim.

Quality for a printer cannot, in this company's view, be defined as simply meeting a customer's expectations. Donnelley's *quality obligation* is, wherever practicable, to exceed the customer's expectations. All employees are responsible for assuring that the quality of the product being manufactured meets the customer's expectations. Good, in-depth technical training, combined with a clear understanding of the importance of maintaining consistent quality, is the key to quality performance.

Quality tests, reports, and on-the-floor inspections provide information and ensure that the job specifications and quality tolerances are being met. Divisions monitor themselves with daily reports from manufacturing, shipping, and customer service in a spirit similar to that of an intensive care staff of a hospital; when the shifts change, management evaluates the vital signs of every job in progress. Customer service representatives and division management teams perform periodic reviews of product quality during trips through the manufacturing areas. Furthermore, they try continually to improve service by carefully reviewing all comments from customers or salespeople about job performance or interpersonal relations. In response, they may adjust work loads, make assignment changes, or even reassign personnel when circumstances warrant.

## Information Management

Any information is subject to variation, even customer specifications. While it is difficult to define what is the *most* important part of providing customer satisfaction, certainly ensuring the accuracy of customer requirements is essential to serving them well. For this reason, the management of information transmitted among departments within a division, and between divisions and the corporate office is critical. Once established, the customers' specifications for size, paper, and delivery dates are entered into a computer where the information is carefully controlled and made accessible only to authorized individuals. Changes must be approved by department managers. Computer-based information systems perform many repetitive functions to ensure the accuracy of information far above what a human can provide on a daily basis.

Superior information management is further assured by daily production meetings, daily reports concerning specific performance criteria, and frequent customer approvals during production. Typically, the customer is present for color approvals, working closely with the press operators and quality analysts to achieve the desired colors. This helps to avoid the *generation gap* in which the first generation copy (presumably the customer's requirement) differs noticeably from the final copy produced on press.

## The Manufacturing Process

Printing, from start to finish, is an enormously complicated process that is strewn with dozens of pitfalls—any one of which can spoil an important job. A press operator from one of the divisions described this recent event to illustrate the difference that one person can make and the importance of attitude on the job:

Just the other day we were running a form of a catalog that contained many high-priced items. This had been running extremely well for us, both in terms of matching the color requirements and producing a beautiful job for one of our customers. We had been running a very expensive sheet of paper through the press that really did a nice job of showing off the merchandise. The paper was manufactured at the paper mill over a number of days. Unknown to us at the time, the paper that was manufactured on the second day at the mill contained a significantly higher percentage of moisture than the paper that was run during the first day at the mill.

When this moist paper started to run through the press, it shrank to the point that we were not able to get the four color images to line up perfectly over the top of one another. When I say they were not lined up perfectly, in the pressroom this means they were off by 3/150th of an inch. On a running press we change one roll to another without stopping the press, so when we changed to the first roll of the moist paper, we were unaware that a problem existed. Since the printing press was running about 35,000 impressions per hour, it did not take long to produce a significant number of catalogs that would not be right. The first person to notice that something was wrong with these catalogs was a material handler who was responsible for removing the printed product from the press. She noticed this within the first 100 copies that were printed and called it to the attention of the pressman. The problem was corrected and the remainder of the job was completed on schedule.

Equipment can be re-engineered to prevent problems from occurring; this is often done at the suggestion of the individual craftsperson. Recently, one division formed a communications team consisting of a press operator, an engineer, a quality analyst, and a technician to investigate a press that was causing problems. Through this cooperative effort they were able to discover a solution that further improved product quality.

## CONCLUSION

R. R. Donnelley's product is service. The quality of service is found in the company's philosophy, business practices, employee relations, standards of written specifications, and service to customers. Service quality is measured in terms of the success in conforming to and exceeding the customers' requirements.

Certainly, the best measure of quality is the level of satisfaction customers have with the service provided. Donnelley is pleased with the large number of customers who have grown with it over a long period of time, and with new customers who join each year knowing the company is willing to work with them through any obstacle to deliver a quality product. Inevitably, because of the vastly complicated business of publishing and the technical complexity of printing, problems arise. Strong working relationships between customer and printer and a high standard of service quality are essential to success. Donnelley aspires to be the "House that quality built." Only through service quality can they deserve the title.

# Being Good Is Good Business

**Leonard R. Harris**

The New York Times Company

The New York Times is a communications company with newspaper, magazine, broadcasting and cable TV operations, and has equity interest in the forest-products business for the manufacture of paper, its primary raw material.

Founded in 1851 by Adolph S. Ochs, the then called *New-York Daily Times* had 9,000 copies in circulation on the first day of business. Today, the *New York Times* is bought by more than a million people each weekday, and by more than 1.6 million on Sundays.

*The New York Times* is located one half block west of Times Square which was named in honor of the paper in 1904. The company employs 10,500 people, of whom 4,500 are engaged in the daily creation, production and distribution of *The New York Times*.

# INTRODUCTION

A meeting of executives, much like any other meeting. Paper coffee cups, a scattering of cardboard plates with Danish pastry and (for the health conscious) bran muffins. Legal pads, sharpened pencils—and the question before the group was the company's next annual report.

What should be its theme? It could have been growth: The New York Times Company's revenues have risen from $1 billion in 1983 to $1.7 billion in 1987. Net income in that period more than doubled, reaching $160 million in 1987. In terms of return on investment, the company's 1976-1986 growth rate ranked 13th among the Fortune 500 companies listed in 1987.

"No, not growth," said Arthur Ochs "Punch" Sulzberger, chairman of the company and publisher of *The Times*. "There's too much attention to growth for the sake of growth. Lots of companies grow. Let's emphasize the things about us that are really distinctive."

"Excellence," someone suggested. "This company is fanatical about excellence."

"But excellence is getting to be the new business cliche, whether you achieve it or not," said Walter E. Mattson, the president and chief operating officer. "Anyhow, you can't just talk about excellence—you have to show it, live it. All day, every day, in everything you do. The people out there decide what's excellent—they have the ballot, not us."

"Well," someone said hesitantly, "we happen to be one helluva good marketing company. One of the best in the communications industry. In practically every one of our fifty operations, we're the market leader. We can demonstrate that we really combine the urge to be good, to be great, with imaginative ways to market our products. Maybe what we ought to stress is the *marketing of excellence*."

"That's it," another person murmured, and Punch and Walt nodded in agreement, and the people at the conference table began to gather up the cups and the torn packages of sugar and Sweet'n Low. Silently they had agreed—*that* is what their company was all about.

Originally called *The New-York Daily Times*, the newspaper from which the company later took its name was founded in 1851. In its early decades it had magnificent moments, perhaps the finest of all being its exposure of the corrupt Tweed Ring in New York City, a gang of municipal leaders who had fleeced the city for scores of millions of dollars a year for four years.

Nonetheless, by 1896 the circulation of *The Times* remained the same as in 1851 and it was close enough to bankruptcy so that a young man from Chattanooga, Adolph S. Ochs, was able to buy it for a borrowed seventy thousand dollars.

Virtually unschooled, at work as a sweeper and deliverer in a newspaper office by the time he was eleven, Ochs was one of the "born newspapermen" of that time—men such as Greeley, Bennett, Pulitzer. As publisher of *The*

*New York Times* (at age twenty he had become founder and publisher of *The Chattanooga Times*), he "invented" such lasting contributions to journalism as letters to the editor, a magazine section, the book review. At a time when only scandal sheets sold for a penny ("the penny press" was then a synonym for sex and violence), Ochs decided that there was a vast potential market for a good and upright paper priced at a penny. In a few years, *The Times* was selling over 350,000 copies a day.

Most of what the paper earned went back into the paper to employ more writers, more editors. It became the good, gray *Times*, more and more the paper of record, and from 1918 (when the first Pulitzer Prizes were awarded) until 1935, the year when Mr. Ochs died, *The Times* had won six Pulitzers, far more than any other newspaper in the country. (As of 1987, the newspaper and its staff had won fifty-eight Pulitzers, still far ahead of any other publication.)

"In recent years," as Punch Sulzberger recently put it, "we've seen that you don't have to be gray to be good. We're known for being innovative. And we've grown beyond being a one-product company serving one city. Now we're a regional and national paper, printed in ten plants across the country." The company now also publishes thirty-five smaller-city newspapers in ten states, mostly in the Southeast but as far west as Santa Rosa and Santa Barbara in California, as far north as its prizewinning weekly in Kennebunk, Maine.

It publishes the world's bestselling magazine for women, *Family Circle*, along with such popular leisure magazines as *Golf Digest, Tennis*, and *Cruising World*. It is in the electronic broadcast industry, with five television stations, two classical music radio stations, and one of the largest clusters of cable TV systems in the country. Its news service has some 550 subscribers in the U.S. and abroad, newspapers and magazines reaching 85 million buyers. It has substantial equity interests in four paper mills, three in Canada, and one in Maine—which is logical, since paper is its primary raw material.

When the first vague outlines of the annual report to be titled "The Marketing of Excellence" took shape, its editor had a disquieting thought. What, he wondered, would be the reaction of the men and women in the newsroom and on the editorial board to something that might sound crass—the "marketing" of their "product"? He posed this question in a note to Max Frankel, the distinguished Pulitzer-Prize-winning journalist who serves as executive editor of *The Times*.

Frankel's reply: "The news department doesn't wince at the thought of marketing its information, features, and services. Indeed, the editors and reporters routinely examine their many products with a creative desire to improve upon yesterday's edition. Good marketing has to start with outstanding products—the kind we daily produce, yet also daily pursue."

Whether in Kennebunk or Lakeland, Florida, whether in the newsroom of *The Times* or at Channel 3 in Memphis, the men and women of The New

York Times Company daily seek excellence in four areas of the newspaper business: technology, newspaper content, employee relations, and
management.

## TECHNOLOGY

Walt Mattson began his career at *The Times* as an assistant production
manager, after working at newspapers as an advertising representative and as
a linotypist while earning degrees in accounting and electrical engineering.
He made his way up to general manager at *The Times* during a period when
the newspaper unions of New York were rigidly opposing, with almost
ruinously long strikes, any change from the slow, noisy and even dangerous
"hot lead," manual printing machinery of an earlier century. A Linotype at
its fastest could produce thirteen lines of type a minute. Today's photocomposition units can produce thousands of lines a minute. The press printing
plates then in use weighed forty pounds each. Those now in use weigh an
ounce-and-a-half.

Sulzberger, Mattson, and the editors of *The Times* knew their newspaper could not grow until they won the right to modernize. And unless they
won that managerial perogative, *The Times* would almost certainly go the
way of other New York newspapers that had recently died—the great *New
York Herald-Tribune*, the *World-Telegram*, the *Journal-American*, the *Mirror*,
the *Sun*, and others.

Without new technology, *The Times* could not follow its readers who
had moved to the suburbs. Nor could it follow many of its leading retail
advertisers, stores that had followed the population shift by leaving the city
for the suburbs. Its pages could not reflect the changing lifestyles of the
time. It could not rapidly report on business. It could never compete with
the tube.

Briefly, clearly, The Times Company did win that war. It was won in
1974 without a strike. An era ended, a new one began. At this point in that
new era—early 1988—the daily circulation of *The Times* is over 1.1 million
copies, while the Sunday circulation is above 1.6 million copies. And the
company has committed itself to the finest technology not just for *The Times*
but also for every one of its other operations, since only with the finest in
equipment and materials can a communications company communicate.

### What is on the menu?

For *The Times*, a four hundred million dollar facility in Edison, New Jersey,
scheduled to begin operations in 1990 dedicated to the production of the
massive Sunday edition (in November 1987, a twelve-pound, one-ounce
edition was published, a record almost certain to fall in 1988). The Edison
plant will print color in such advance Sunday sections as the Book Review,
Travel, and Arts & Leisure. It will use robotic materials-handling equipment.

The plant is the size of twenty-two football fields under one roof. It is expected to be the most modern newspaper plant in the nation.

For the regional newspapers, the plans are much the same, albeit on a smaller scale. Between 1985 and 1988, new facilities were built for fourteen of these smaller-city papers. In 1989, three more new plants will be built.

The television stations in Huntsville, Alabama, and Wilkes Barre/ Scranton, Pennsylvania, are new. The building housing NYT Cable TV is new, and for the cable company's two-way service it uses the most advanced home converter in the industry—so far ahead of others that NYT Cable TV's "take rate" for films and events is the highest in the industry, more than three times greater than is typical of other systems offering such two-way services as "pay-per-view."

The classical music radio stations are moving into the most modern broadcast facilities in New York. A new mill in Clermont, Canada, in which the company holds a 49% equity interest, is the most modern facility of its kind in North America. Each of the other mills is at, or on the way to being state-of-the-art.

The Times Company is computer-intensive. At *The Times*, for example, reporters and editors type their copy into terminals; their material is stored until edited, then sent by the central computer system for photocomposition. New processors and terminals now being installed will also be part of a system that paginates the paper and then makes page plates, replacing an operation that required stories and ads to be individually placed by hand before completed boards could be plated.

A unique example of computer use is now found in the tri-state area among some advertising agencies devoted solely to preparing such classified advertising as real estate and help wanted. These agencies can now use in-agency computers to prepare and enter ads by telephone lines directly into *The Times'* computers, where the ads are sorted into their appropriate categories, alphabetized, and produced as full pages. The classified advertising that comes in on-line represents 82% of the total carried by *The Times*.

At eight plants of other newspapers, a daily national edition is printed for early-morning delivery or newsstand sale in all major cities. To accomplish this, the newspaper uses satellite transmission. Thus, *The Times* is a national, regional, and city newspaper, able to use technology to "zone" its editions so precisely that the smallest classified ad—for a used car being sold by a New Jersey resident, for example—may upon request appear only in copies sold in New Jersey; or, if that "used car" is a Cord, may appear in all copies sold nationally.

## CONTENT

When Max Frankel wrote a memo about marketing to the editor of the annual review, he said that the restless, relentless examination of the paper by its editors and writers led to periodic innovations in the way they gather and present the news.

In November 1987, *The Times* introduced new pages and columns on education, health, participatory sports, child-rearing, nutrition, fashion, the law, and consumer affairs. These were natural extensions of the magazine sections that the newspaper had introduced over the years and that had profoundly influenced American journalism: lifestyle sections dealing with food, home, sports, weekend entertainment, and science. *The Times* publishes the only full seven-day-a-week business section in the country. The editors know that not every reader can, or even wants to, read every page of the newspaper each day. "It's nice to know it's all there, though," is the common conclusion.

"Special to The New York Times" is a line of small type seen under bylines throughout the paper. These lines signify that the report has been written by *The Times*'s own staff correspondent or reporter, and is an exclusive; it is not a report filed by a wire service. *The Times* has a thousand men and women on its news staff, including its correspondents in thirty bureaus abroad and in some twenty bureaus throughout the United States. In areas of news coverage, the needs of the reader grow ever greater, and a good newspaper must serve those needs, perhaps even before they are recognized by the public.

A newspaper in Ocala, Florida, or in Wilmington, North Carolina, does not need a thousand people on its newsroom payroll; but the belief at The Times Company is that those papers have the same obligation to serve their readers as does the flagship newspaper. A case in point is the *Leesburg* (Florida) *Daily Commercial*, which in eight years has been able to grow its weekday circulation from 9,200 copies to 23,800 copies, and its Sunday circulation from 9,500 copies to 26,000 copies. The keys to the growth were doubling the plant and installing new equipment—and significant staff increases, from twenty-four writers and editors to thirty-eight by year-end 1987. This strong staff enables the paper to cover the news in all the communities it reaches; the company's Florida newspapers have their own bureaus in the state and national capitals, and can, if they so choose, also subscribe to The New York Times News Service.

Punch Sulzberger says that publishing a good paper is not only the right thing to do. He says it is also good business. And indeed, advertising in Leesburg's *Daily Commercial* during this period grew from an average of 8,000 inches a month to 30,000 inches a month. Perhaps most significantly, during the years from 1980 through 1987, the newspaper was honored seventy-seven times in state and regional newspaper competitions. This emphasis on news and information is prevalent throughout the company. The broadcast group is proud of the fact that its television station in Wilkes Barre/Scranton, Pennsylvania, WNEP-TV, has the largest share of audience of any station in the top fifty markets where all three networks are represented.

## EMPLOYEE RELATIONS

Despite having 10,500 employees in operations in eighteen states and abroad, The New York Times Company has set up an open-door policy that can lead an employee directly to the office of its chief executive officer, Punch Sulzberger. An employee who feels that he or she is not being treated fairly, with dignity and respect, and absolutely without bias and bigotry, can take that complaint to the top.

As do most companies, The Times Company has generous employee benefits. The company also has an employee assistance program that goes far beyond the typical help given to alcoholics and drug addicts; any member of an employee's family can turn to the program people for help with any personal problem, whether it be debts or difficulties with teen-age children, compulsive gambling or anorexia, in-law troubles or learning difficulties.

New York City is a labor town, and labor unions have been a fact of newspaper publishing life there since the mid-nineteenth century. Of 4,500 Times employees, 4,200 are union members, and there are fourteen unions. As this chapter was being written, new labor agreements with the unions were being negotiated. The lead union in this collective bargaining process was the pressmen; they signed a six-year agreement, which has since served as the model for two more union agreements.

Throughout the company, there are intern programs to aid minorities, and throughout there are black executives and women in such executive roles as publishers and editors of regional newspapers, vice president of *The New York Times*, general counsel, and treasurer. Management is dedicated to assuring that theirs is a company in which each person progresses according to ability and dedication, without artificial impediment.

## MANAGEMENT

When New York City was close to bankruptcy, and when then-obdurate unions were still attempting to sweep back the waves of technological progress, and when middle-class New Yorkers were fleeing to the suburbs, The New York Times Company was itself a sick company. At that time Punch Sulzberger set forth these goals: win the right to advance into the twentieth century in technology; diversify into other areas of the communications industry and into other areas geographically; and manage the company so that it would win the respect from the financial community that it had won from journalists around the world.

In the 1987 Fortune 500 listing, the company was listed as 219th for revenue, 121st for net income, and 38th for earnings per share. Sulzberger thinks that he is achieving his goals. As to tomorrow? In a prefatory note to the current annual report, he wrote, "In each of our operations, our goal is identical and unchanging. It is to seek excellence."

Do problems remain? Yes. There is no solution as yet to the problem of ink rub-off. Perhaps, however, by the time this book goes into a second edition. . . .

# A New Commitment
# To the Customer

**Donald B. Berryman**
USA TODAY

The Gannett Co., Inc., launched *USA TODAY* on September 15, 1982. By September 1987, after five years of publishing *USA TODAY*, the circulation department had launched thirty print sites; opened distribution offices in twenty-seven metropolitan markets; placed more than 120,000 newspaper vending machines; opened more than 300,000 new store outlets; and had developed a subscriber base of more than 500,000 customers. In five short years, *USA TODAY* became the second largest newspaper in the country, as measured by net paid circulation, with 1.6 million customers; and the number one read newspaper in the country with more than 5.5 million readers daily.

# THE BIRTH OF A COMMITMENT

Even in the newspaper's infancy, *USA TODAY*'s innovative use of color and hundreds of concise, informative articles was something new to the industry. In addition, while the editorial product broke with journalistic traditions and lead the publishing industry into a new era, the circulation side of the business fought with the age–old problem of distributing a daily newspaper to homes and stores.

The fifth birthday of *The Nation's Newspaper*, in September 1987, will be remembered for its record-breaking circulation growth and the fact of having its first profitable quarter. Apart from that, it will be remembered also by the circulation staff as the year the paper became committed to service quality.

*USA TODAY*'s commitment to service began at its annual meeting with Gannett executives in November 1986 in Cocoa Beach, Florida. The meeting was a brainstorming session where department heads reported on the past year's progress and, more importantly, progress expected for the next year. The circulation team's message concerned circulation gains, cost reductions, restructuring successes, and a plan to be profitable, as expected, in the coming year. This was the first time that someone from *circulation customer service* had given a report at an annual meeting. In fact, the customer service report lead the circulation presentation. In itself, that fact was a sign that the company's top executives recognized the importance of service. Providing customers with quality service was a way for them to continue their growth and hold onto those customers who loved the newspaper.

The presentation was delivered by seven circulation executives and the company's president. When it came time for the CEO, John Curley, to wrap up the meeting, he was happy with the circulation performance and talked about the challenging year ahead. The chairman and founder of *USA TO-DAY*, Al Neuharth, gave the closing remarks; however, before his remarks he decided to run a test. He handed that day's issue of *USA TODAY* to the deputy chairman, Jack Heselden, and asked him to call the 800 toll-free number (that is conveniently located on the front page of each section) of the national customer service center. Jack dialed the number. After the phone rang twice, it was answered by an ACD digital recorder. The recorded message explained that all respresentatives were busy but to please hold for the next available representative. The next recording came on twenty seconds later with a blurb about the latest promotion. Two and one-half minutes went by before a customer service representative answered the phone: it was the longest two and a half minutes in the short career of the recently promoted director of customer service. The message from the chairman was clear: "If I was a customer or potential customer of *USA TODAY*, I would not wait two minutes." This brief but powerful moment changed the focus for the entire customer service operation. That day in November 1986 was the beginning of *USA TODAY*'s *new* commitment to the customer.

The mistake in the service plan that lead to the infamous phone call was associated with the reports and statistics that monitored performance: the ones being used did not give a true picture of how they treated the customer. Management was watching a service level in customer service that only monitored the percentage of calls answered. They were also letting other departments, like systems and finance, affect customers by not making software enhancements fast enough or not processing payments before a customer was cut off for nonpayment.

Nineteen eighty-seven became the year of the customer. Management set out to make the customer's needs the top priority. Their goals that year were several: (1) to define service quality for *USA TODAY* customers; (2) to set up measurements to monitor performance; (3) to set goals to improve the level of service in order to meet the customer's needs; (4) to involve all circulation personnel in service quality improvement; and (5) to set up the training of circulation personnel to include both the new standard for service and the employee buy-in program.

## DEFINITION OF SERVICE QUALITY FOR *USA TODAY* CUSTOMERS

### Customer Surveys
The first area of concentration was the national customer service center which averages twenty-five hundred phone calls a day. Focus was placed on those customers who called to start a subscription, stop delivery, or complain. A group of representatives was set up to call those same customers hours after they called the center and ask them various questions such as how they were treated when they called the center. Did they wait on hold? Did they remember the representative's name? Was he or she helpful and knowledgeable? How did they find the *USA TODAY* number? And finally, How would they rate the newspaper's performance? Letter surveys were also sent to those customers who could not be reached by phone.

### Three Areas of Service Improvement
The results were very interesting. Customers calling to stop delivery told the phone representatives, "No one asked me why I wanted to stop." Some customers who had called because they were upset over a delivery or a billing problem had since calmed down and now regretted stopping delivery. The best information came from those customers calling to complain, although they were a mixed bag indeed: some were extremely happy with the polite and professional attitude of the representatives, while others thought their call was mishandled. After finding the customer phone surveys to be very beneficial, the company made three changes to improve service to different groups of customers.

First, from *those calling to start delivery*, customer service realized that the customers were already familiar with the newspaper. Customers were asked which offer prompted their call so customer service could trace the call to a promotion. If the customer did not remember or called from a referral, they would be given a standard discount offer. This occasionally caused a problem if the subscriber had seen another offer in the paper with a premium or special rebate. In this case customer service quickly switched their standard offer to match the one running in the paper. It was a simple change that, as the surveys quickly detected, reduced the number of customer complaints.

Second, contacting those *customers who stopped the paper* helped to uncover two areas for improving the level of service. They found that when aggravated customers called in to stop the paper, customer service representatives did not always ask the right question to define the complaint and get to the root of the problem. Most representatives were practicing *conflict avoidance* by just processing the cancellation request. When calling the customers back to verify the stop, they made the call hours or occasionally a day later. In most cases, the customer had calmed down and was much better at explaining the real reason for stopping. Usually, it was the result of a late or perhaps a missed delivery. When the verifiers called back, they were often successful at getting the customer to continue delivery while customer service worked on fixing the problem.

To improve this situation, more emphasis on dealing with aggravated customers was incorporated into the training and retraining sessions with customer service representatives. They also assigned a group of representatives to contact all those customers whom a customer service representative flagged as *an aggravated stop*. The representative waited twenty-four hours before calling to see if the customer would agree to continue delivery while the problem was fixed. A follow-up was made on these customers to insure that the reason for their dissatisfaction was corrected. This program has paid many dividends in improving customer satisfaction and increasing the number of resold cancellations by 11%.

The other improvement area that was revealed in the survey to customers who had cancelled was the high number of business addresses that appeared on the lists. Apparently many subscribers had the paper delivered to their business address. In most cases they also billed the subscription to their business account. It took longer for businesses to send a check and in the meantime the delivery would stop. Because the customers submitted the request from their business office, they assumed that the company's stopping the delivery was a delivery problem and not a cancellation for nonpayment. Of course, the subscription restarted automatically when payment was received. By that time, many customers had already called to complain or had changed their mind after their unhappy experience and had cancelled delivery.

This also presented an easy fix. Customer service representatives asked subscribers, when they called to *start* delivery, if their address was a business or residence. Business addresses were given a different code so as to give the new customer a longer period before the subscription is stopped for nonpayment. This has worked very well. Early results show that business cancellations have decreased.

The phone representatives, following up with those *customers who had called to complain*, found similar results to surveys of customers calling to stop. The customer service representatives were always rated highly for their phone manners; still, either they left the customer with the feeling that they did not probe far enough or they did not say the right thing to persuade them to continue service. Most of the complaints were about late or sporadic delivery. The customer felt that because the problem continued no one cared about fixing it. In many cases, the customer service representative did not get enough information to help determine the cause of the late papers. They were procedurally doing all the right things by logging the complaint on the customer's record but they failed to make the customer feel as though the problem would be fixed. Sharing these results with the customer service representatives and adding some extra role playing to training sessions helped to give them the right words, phrases, and feeling of confidence that the problem would get fixed, so they could pass that feeling onto the customer.

## Generalization about Customer Needs

By means of the phone surveys customer service was able to learn what kind of service gave customers the desire to continue a subscription. The results enabled them not only to make the changes already mentioned, but also to define a high level of service for customers. They discovered that customers are busy and do not have time to make more than one call to correct a problem with their account. Secondly, customers dislike waiting on hold, for any duration, when they call the customer service center. Thirdly, many of our customers become dependent, set on a routine of reading the paper everyday, so they demand consistent, on-time delivery everyday. Fourthly, being a daily newspaper, the company found they had to fix things very quickly; that is, if a stopped paper was not restarted immediately, the customer was reminded of it daily. Lastly, most customers were very happy with the professionalism of the customer service representative, but customers did not have time to detail their problem and rarely had a bill or account number to help locate their account.

## New Standards for Services

Customer service used this information to set the standards for improving service. These standards included (a) every customer request will be handled with one phone call; (b) every call into the national customer service center will be answered within twenty seconds or four rings; (c) all customer orders will be started in four days; all customer letters will be answered within forty-eight hours of receipt; all customer complaints will be resolved within five days; and (d) an average customer call should last no more than two minutes.

## MEASUREMENTS TO MONITOR PERFORMANCE

Once the task of gathering customer needs and laying out the standards to meet those needs was finished, the tools to monitor performance were needed. An analysis of needs showed they were a long way from where they needed to be. Some reports currently in use needed modifications, and most of the reports needed did not exist. It was crucial to have reports that would keep them in touch with customers and foresee customer need changes.

An internal committee was formed to assess the kinds of reporting needed. This group was made up of two representatives from customer service, one each from the systems and finance areas, and one representing the field operations. In two months, the committee found many ideas for new reports and enhancements to existing reports. The measurements fell into three areas. First, they decided to measure the progress of subscription fulfillment; second, to monitor all calls into the national customer service center to assess the level of service to each customer; and, finally, to monitor delivery.

The first area, customer order fulfillment, was one of the toughest areas to build a reporting process around because it was not centralized. An order could be handled by a number of departments and outside vendors, depending on the promotion or customer response vehicle. For example, a customer could send a coupon to an outside fulfillment house to be keypunched, put on tape, and then processed by the internal subscription processing department; or the customer could send an insert directly to the subscription processing center. If no sweepstakes or other special handling was needed, the order was keyed into the subscriber files by company staff. The quickest and most efficient way to handle a customer order was if a customer called the national customer service center where representatives would key their order directly into the subscriber files with no delay.

All of this was complicated even further after the customer was either routed to home delivery or mail. If a subscription was routed to mail (the service available was determined by zip code), the order was entered into the centralized mail subscriber file and the order would start three days later. If the subscription was routed to home or office delivery by a carrier, then the order was sent to one of twenty-seven field offices to be entered into their subscriber files. Given this many variables, customer order fulfillment was a tough process to measure.

With a new sensitivity to the customer's needs in mind, four days from the day the order was routed was set as the goal to get the subscription started. Making this happen in four days would be another challenge, but now they had the measurement tools in place to determine how long it should take to start all orders.

The second area of focus was monitoring the calls into the national customer service center. In this area, the reporting became much easier. A myriad of reports already existed that indicated how customer calls were being treated. The service level (the percentage of calls answered within twenty seconds), the average customer talk time (the time representatives spent on each call), and the call trend report (a daily report showing the number of new orders, stops, complaints, etc., compared with the previous day's and with the average of the previous four weeks) were monitored. Once customer service managers focused their efforts on those statistics that really affected the customer, they saw immediate results of improved service.

The third area they intended to measure was actual delivery service to customers. This was a bit more difficult to quantify since the only real gauge was customer complaints. Reports were set up that made it easier to monitor the service level by showing total customer deliveries and the number of complaints logged against those deliveries. This is a standard measurement in the industry called complaints-per-thousand subscribers. The *acceptable* industry average in complaints-per-thousand deliveries is one.

Management began compiling these complaints-per-thousand reports and sending them to all the top circulation executives. This had some effect on those markets with very poor performance, but the real improvement came with a simple change in the format of the report. It was changed to rank field markets from best to worst and was sent to every field office. When those at the bottom saw their standing, it was not long before they put plans of action into effect to improve delivery and make it possible to face the other market managers. Aside from this report, customer service is still working to perfect ways to measure actual delivery service. They send surveys to new customers and follow up with phone calls.

## GOALS TO IMPROVE THE SERVICE LEVEL TO CUSTOMERS

Now, with the measurement tools and the expected standards in place, the next step was to set a time frame to achieve those standards. The year 1987 was already slated as the year of the customer. The process of changing the emphasis to provide quality service would be an evolution. Customer service set three dates to review and assess their progress. First was the kickoff date to explain the new focus to the executives and field general managers. This was conveniently done at the year-end meetings held annually in Washington, D.C. These meetings included discussions of what quality service meant, what needed doing in the coming year to improve service, and what the improved service would mean to the customer.

The next date when overall operations would be discussed was in June. The topic of service was added to the agenda so that an assessment of progress in individual areas would be discussed as well as performance by each market operation. The final target date was in November at the annual meeting/brainstorming session at the chairman's house in Cocoa Beach. Management hoped to give a report of substantial progress there.

The timeline was set, and the service quality plan was in motion. The overall goal for 1987 was to set up within the organization a service structure centered around providing and selling quality service as well as a quality product. That became the USA TODAY circulation department's mission.

## INVOLVE ALL CIRCULATION PERSONNEL IN SERVICE QUALITY IMPROVEMENT

This was the most difficult part of the plan. How could an organization that is spread across the country be united in a crusade to improve service? The company president came up with the idea of a USA TODAY Service Day which would involve everyone in the company. It would be a day devoted to providing *perfect service* to customers and would get people practicing for it in the meantime.

Service Day was a great success. It became the talk of the entire circulation organization. No market wanted to be the only market with complaints. It became a from-the-bottom-up fix. Every complaint, starting in March after the Service Day announcement, was scrutinized to see what could be done to prevent it from occurring again. The organization was abuzz with ways to provide perfect service. Customer complaints dropped dramatically each week. When Service Day finally arrived, customer complaints were at an all-time low. Except for New England where there was a freak snowstorm, the field operation had its best delivery day ever.

The process of working up to Service Day and the information gained trying to provide perfect service helped to reduce customer complaints by 36% in 1987. Service Day was entered into the calendar as an annual event.

## TRAIN AND EDUCATE PERSONNEL IN QUALITY SERVICE

An ongoing commitment to quality service exists in the programs developed from experiences in 1987, especially in the programs for ongoing training of circulation personnel. It was concluded that every person in the organization must be committed to providing a high level of service to customers to make the programs work. Efforts to provide training to improve service at every level have been increased.

In one short year a great deal was learned about customers and the organization, and about how to make things happen. It was a simple process that has paid, and will continue to pay, many dividends. The company listened to customers, set standards for better service based on what it heard, set up ways to measure service, set goals to achieve the new standards, and put together a plan involving the whole organization to insure its success.

The most important thing learned about providing quality service is that it takes a long time and a large commitment to make a difference. *USA TODAY* realizes that it has just *started* down the road to perfect service.

# Retailing

Lazarus
Daniel G. Bukey

# The Lazarus Customer Service Evolution

**Daniel G. Bukey**

Lazarus

Lazarus, named after its founder Simon Lazarus, is a division of Federated Department Stores. It was founded in 1830 and currently employs a staff of fifteen thousand. Lazarus is headquartered in Cincinnati, Ohio.

## INTRODUCTION

It is the Lazarus objective to differentiate itself from the competition, in each of its markets, through an ever-evolving customer service selling effort. This applies to all aspects of its business, both on and off the selling floor. The company knows that each customer is precious and that every course of action undertaken by Lazarus must be with the customer in mind. Lazarus employees are customer-driven: they know the customer comes first and that their every action must satisfy the customer.

The Lazarus commitment to the long-term development of selling professionalism is ever improving. Full commitment by the Chairman of the Board and top management is needed to successfully implement service quality programs. To that end a Vice President of Customer Service was appointed to spearhead the drive for a customer-driven sales force. The following measures have been implemented in each of the Lazarus department stores:

- A task force containing employees from each staff level of the store to ensure a bottoms-up mentality and buy-in, makes recommendations for programs to improve service quality. One result of the task force is the "think like a customer" strategy.
- The creation of a Store Merchandising Service (SMS) organization (responsible for the analytic, distribution, and information functions) enables sales managers to concentrate on selling supervision.
- Training classes at all levels of the selling organization were developed. Sales managers and sales associates are trained in the latest techniques to be a professional selling force.
- Measurement systems were developed to ensure that the expectations of customers are met.

### Training Programs

An extensive and ongoing training program for new hires, management, and other employees is in place in order to provide the highest level of professional service to each and every Lazarus customer.

For newly hired personnel a three day program discussing the Lazarus customer service philosophy, policies, and procedures (returns, gift wrap, alterations, etc.) plus hands-on cash register systems training is required. Emphasis is placed on productivity, methods of goal setting and performance reviews. The following sales training techniques are also taught to new associates:

- Associates learn how "thinking like a customer" will increase their sales and improve selling productivity. Through self-assessment and video tape exercises, associates learn how to handle common customer service challenges and problems.
- Associates are taught advanced selling skills and proven techniques to effectively service more than one customer at a time.

- Training is provided on techniques used to build sales in the fitting room and on wardrobe building as a technique to sell additional items to customers. Lazarus customers' needs are fulfilled as associates "put together" the right items and fashions during every sale.
- Each store has Personal Clientele departments in which associates learn how to provide quality personalized service to preferred customers. Associates practice how to converse with customers to learn their preferences and interests. They become skilled at anticipating their customer's needs and learn to follow-up with their customers to develop an ongoing professional service relationship.
- The Lazarus return and adjustment policy is discussed and through video and experimental exercises, associates learn how to determine customer's needs in order to sell alternative products to customers who are returning merchandise.
- Understanding why customers make "big ticket" purchases like carpet and furniture and what influences their decisions to buy are discussed.

Lazarus believes that the training of the training staff is very important to the success of the associates as well as to the bottom line of the company. Store management is trained in effective sales leadership techniques. They attend an overview of the program taught to associates that addresses the role of the sales managers and the importance of following up with sales associates to reinforce selling skills. Sales managers learn how to lead by example and motivate associates through the observation process which develops and refines selling skills and, ultimately, increases customer satisfaction. Through a program called the "one minute coach" managers are taught how to communicate brief on-the-job coaching skills. Utilizing role playing and video tape feedback, managers are taught how to convey job standards and expectations, give positive feedback and constructive criticism.

## Incentive Programs

An hourly productivity goal setting process is in place. Every associate is striving to meet their productivity goal through a professional selling effort. A monitoring process is in place so that each associate is informed weekly of his or her results versus goals. Recognition programs in place in each store ensure that high producers are singled out for their efforts. Action plans are used to help associates performing under their goal.

A program for rewarding outstanding selling (PROS) will be in place in stores in 1988. The key components of PROS are:

- An incentive program which includes compensation, benefits, and recognition.
- High minimum standards for all associates including new hires. Individuals who cannot achieve the minimum standard will not remain in selling.

- Rapid salary advancements while maintaining a fixed selling cost.

## Selling Services

Competitively, superior customer service is the cornerstone of Lazarus' sales growth strategy. Customer service includes not only selling service but those things which make it easy for customers to shop in Lazarus' stores, such as:

— Appropriate merchandise signs
— Size marking... Marc Bric size markers are on all garments.
— Dress code..."three piece" rule is in place for all selling associates. Professionalism is built through this differentiater.
— Store directories... free-standing store directories are in place in all stores.
— Constantly reinforcing treating customers the way they want to be treated: with warmth, sincerity, and exceeding the customer's expectations of a salesperson.
— Evening delivery service is available as a convenience to the customer.
— All merchandise is prepared (sized, categorized) off the floor. This expedites floor setup and ensures that selling associates are available to the customer.

## MARKETING CUSTOMER SERVICE

The marketing of customer service includes constant recognition and communication to all associates. Customers are also informed through the following means:

- **White Carnation Program** - All Lazarus store executives wear a white carnation for identification. This approach was initiated by the founder, Simon Lazarus, in 1851.
- **The Lazarus Guarantee** - Lazarus promises service, selection, and satisfaction. If ever a customer is not fully satisfied, the store manager is available with a quick phone call. Signs at each register display this promise. Also, full sheet signs picturing the store's associates are posted throughout every store, promising satisfaction and identifying the store manager's name and phone number to ensure that all customers are fully satisfied.

## Recognition

Lazarus will become the number one retailer only if Lazarus is the place to shop because of its people and the enlightened manner in which they serve the customer. Effective and productive people must be employed and provided with an environment that serves to retain them. Management knows that its people must be "turned on", highly involved by choice, optimistic and view the workplace as important and fun. To facilitate this, many recognition programs are in place:

- **The Red Apple Award** - Sales associates are eligible to receive apple awards through nominations from customers (usually in the form of letters or telephone calls). Stores have annual "applefest" events which recognize outstanding customer service by associates.
- **The Star Award** - Star awards are given to those employees nominated by an associate or executive within the company. A star award may be awarded for any one of the following criteria: customer service, teamwork and cooperation, and specific incidence of excellent performance.
- **Executive of the Month** - Each location selects an executive of the month based on overall performance. A photograph of the executive is placed in the executive office area.
- **Associate of the Month** - An associate in each store is selected based on overall productivity, teamwork and customer service. An annual luncheon is held for the the winners of this award.
- **Best Seller Award** - Best seller certificates are given monthly to the associate in each merchandise area who has exceeded his or her goal by the greatest percent. Photographs of the winners are placed in the employee lounge.
- **Ten Dollars for Outstanding Customer Service** - Monthly Professional Shopping Reports are completed and anyone who scores a perfect one hundred is rewarded with ten dollars.
- **Insight** - A corporate monthly newsletter for employees highlights new products and concepts, introduces new personnel and lists winners of recognition awards.
- **Storewide Meetings** - Each week a meeting is held in each location to recognize all who achieve outstanding customer service.

## MEASUREMENT: LISTENING TO CUSTOMERS

To ensure that customer expectations are being met Lazarus has the following measurement techniques in place:

**Professional shopping program.** Outside professional shoppers rate the professionalism of sales associates' advanced selling skills. This process measures Lazarus' progress and indicates areas in need of assistance. These outside shoppers also rate the stores' appearance, neatness, staffing, visual presentation, and name badge use as well as dress code.

**Focus groups.** Each store holds focus groups quarterly to brainstorm about customer expectations. All information from these customer focus groups are fed back to the appropriate individual so that an action plan can be implemented.

**"Tell it to the chairman".** Postage paid postcards are available in all stores giving customers the opportunity to express their likes and dislikes. Over

25,000 cards are received annually and of those 80% contain positive remarks. If a problem exists, the area affected is notified and a resolution is expected within forty-eight hours.

**Customer service action center.** A toll free number for all inquiries including credit and merchandise problems is in place. Again, quick resolution is the key and forty-eight hour resolution time is the standard. Incoming calls are monitored and complaints are recorded and tallied to identify weak spots or areas in need of improvement.

**Staffing.** A traffic profile study was conducted at each store to indicate peak shopping periods on a daily basis. Staff scheduling is based upon this information so that personnel resources are used as efficiently as possible and to ensure that enough associates are on duty and available to answer any customer inquiries.

## RECRUITMENT

Recruiting by sales managers is done by visiting stores in local malls to search for sales talent. The new PROS program (discussed earlier) will be used to encourage salespeople from other retailers to join Lazarus. In addition, first day coverage for benefits such as medical, dental and store discounts is offered to new associates while many other companies require waiting periods of thirty days or more.

## EVOLUTION

If any store is to differentiate itself from the competition, it must become "customer driven". The management must develop a sense of self-determination and proprietorship that leads to this customer service mindset. Lazarus believes the basics of its "think like a customer" strategy must be consistently implemented and that it must foster a customer service mentality that nourishes its evolution to be "customer driven" Patience is the key; evolutions take time. Standards must be set, frequent measurements taken, a "listening post" available, and constant improvement expected. Each customer is precious and through the quality customer service selling effort, can be won, one at a time.

# Rubber and Plastic Products

Firestone, Inc.
Raymond Wachniak

# Forming Quality Improvement Partnerships

**Raymond Wachniak**
Firestone, Inc.

Firestone, Inc. was founded in 1900 and today is one of the world's largest manufacturers of tires for automobiles, trucks, and agricultural equipment. Firestone is also a major supplier of automotive maintenance and repair services in the United States with approximately 1,500 company-operated tire and automotive centers and thousands of independent dealers. In addition, Firestone produces and sells single-ply rubber roofing systems, synthetic and natural rubber, air springs, and molded rubber products.

The company is headquartered in Chicago, Illinois and employs 54,000 people worldwide.

## A PARTICIPATIVE PARTNERSHIP

No one ever said that making continuous improvement in quality was easy. And when the objective of such improvement means solving the identified number one service quality problem in America, a national effort is required. This article describes how industry and education have joined forces in a participative partnership to create an ongoing, long-term solution to this service quality problem.

Many top managers have recognized that the role of the quality professional has changed and are implementing many diverse strategies to achieve "world class" quality. These strategies have covered a wide spectrum of tactics from quality circles to company-wide quality control, from statistical process control to quality function deployment. The participants in this partnership represent one or more of the following organizations: the American Society for Quality Control (ASQC), Firestone, Inc., the Vocational Industry Clubs of America (VICA), the National Institute of Automotive Service Excellence (ASE), and educators from various schools around the country. It all began with a survey on the quality of service in America.

## THE ASQC/GALLUP QUALITY SURVEY

In 1985, the American Society for Quality Control commissioned the Gallup organization to conduct a public opinion survey about American-made products and services. The report showed that more than half (51%) of those interviewed rated American products at or near the top of a ten-point scale used in this survey to evaluate quality; some 128 accorded them the very highest rating for quality and 53% believed that products made in America by American-owned companies are most likely to meet their expectations for quality (see fig. 1).

The survey also found that consumers overwhelmingly expect the quality of American products to improve, both in relation to present quality levels and to the quality of foreign-made goods. Other important findings in the ASQC/Gallup survey deserve mention:

- Consumers rate brand name, product performance, and durability as the most important factors that they use in judging the quality of products.
- In evaluating services, the public cites various attributes related to the performance of service personnel—such as courteous and helpful treatment—and the ability to satisfy the customer's needs as most important.
- Consumers report that they would be willing to pay a substantial premium to get the quality they desire in consumer products.
- Respondents named the companies they associate most frequently with high quality: General Electric, General Motors, Sears, and Procter & Gamble head the list.

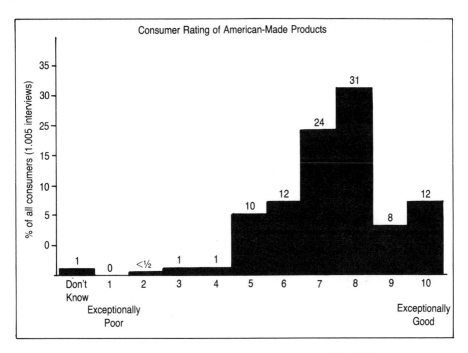

FIG. 1 CONSUMER RATING OF AMERICAN-MADE PRODUCTS

- Respondents also offered opinions on areas needing improvement in the realm of service quality. Consumers also expressed opinions on the factors determining quality, on the perceived quality of specific services, and on the areas of potential service improvement.

## Rating the Quality of Service

To learn more about customer's impressions of the services they receive, the survey asked this question: *Using a 10-point scale in which "1" means the quality of service is very poor and "10" means the quality of service is very high, how would you rate banks, hospitals, airlines, insurance companies, hotels, auto repair, and local government?*

Banks are most likely to receive the highest (10) rating from consumers for quality of service. About one in five consumers (18%) rate banks 10, and a majority (52%) give banks a rating of 8 or better. The service provided by hospitals is also favorably evaluated; 15% of the consumers give top ratings to hospitals, and a total of 44% rate them 8, 9, or 10 with regard to the quality of service. Airlines also get high marks for service: 47% rate airlines 8, 9, or 10 (though about one in five could not evaluate airlines). About as many rate insurance companies highly (11%) as rate hotels highly (8%). However, hotels have a slight edge when the three top ratings are considered

**457**

as a whole. Least likely to be rated high for quality of service is one's local government or auto repair services (see table 1). In addition, it was noted that one's opinion regarding the quality of these services is *not* strongly influenced by having used the service recently.

## Consumer Perception of Service Quality: Factors

When asked the question, *How do you determine the quality of services rather than products?* consumers mention a long list of considerations (see table 2).

Given the intangible nature of the subject, many of the attributes mentioned overlap and represent subtle differences rather than clear distinctions. Courtesy and the ability to satisfy the customer's needs are the most frequently cited criteria for determining quality (21% and 18% respectively). Also important are one's own past experience and the recommendations of others. Most other highly rated attributes related to the performance of the personnel, for example, promptness, helpfulness, friendliness; but some consumers mentioned other considerations such as the price of services, the organization's reputation, and so forth.

## Service Quality Complaints

Other questions asked: *Within the past year or two have you ever used a service, of any kind, that you thought was of poor quality or needed improvement?* A majority of consumers (56%) reported using, in the past year or two, a service which was of poor quality or needed improvement. Among those encountering such an experience, four in ten (41%) mention automobile repair. The

TABLE 1.
RATING QUALITY OF SERVICE

| Rating of Quality | Banks | Hospitals | Airlines | Insurance Companies | Hotels | Auto Repair | Local Government |
|---|---|---|---|---|---|---|---|
| 10 | 18 | 15 | 11 | 11 | 8 | 8 | 6 |
| 9 | 9 | 9 | 10 | 6 | 7 | 5 | 4 |
| 8 | 25 | 20 | 26 | 17 | 26 | 13 | 12 |
| 7 | 17 | 16 | 15 | 15 | 20 | 13 | 14 |
| 6 | 7 | 10 | 7 | 10 | 10 | 12 | 11 |
| 5 | 12 | 13 | 9 | 18 | 14 | 20 | 19 |
| 4 | 4 | 5 | 1 | 8 | 1 | 8 | 8 |
| 3 | 3 | 4 | 1 | 5 | 1 | 6 | 7 |
| 2 | 2 | 2 | 1 | 3 | 1 | 4 | 5 |
| 1 | 2 | 2 | 1 | 4 | 0 | 6 | 8 |
| Don't know | 1 | 4 | 18 | 3 | 12 | 5 | 6 |
| Total | 100% | 100% | 100% | 100% | 100% | 100% | 100% |
| Number of interviews | (1.005) | (1.005) | (1.005) | (1.005) | (1.005) | (1.005) | (1.005) |
| Average | 7.2 | 6.9 | 7.4 | 6.3 | 7.2 | 5.8 | 5.6 |

TABLE 2.
INFLUENCING FACTORS

| Factors Influencing Consumer Perception of Service Quality | All Consumers (Percent) |
|---|---|
| Courteous/polite treatment*** | 21 |
| Satisfy your needs | 18 |
| Past experience | 13 |
| Recommendations | 12 |
| Promptness | 12 |
| Price | 11 |
| Attitude of personnel*** | 10 |
| Helpful personnel*** | 9 |
| Friendliness*** | 8 |
| Reputation | 7 |
| Advertising | 6 |
| Personal attention*** | 6 |
| Cleanliness | 6 |
| Availability | 4 |
| Services are good | 4 |
| Efficiency | 4 |
| Trouble free | 4 |
| Convenience | 3 |
| Dependability | 3 |
| Company name | 2 |
| Variety of services | 2 |
| Accuracy | 2 |
| Length of time in business | * |
| Miscellaneous | 4 |
| No answer | 8 |
| Total | 179** |
| Number of interviews | (1.005) |

*Less than one-half of one percent.
**Total exceed 100% due to multiple response.
***Personnel performance attributes.

services provided by banks and insurance companies are also likely to be seen as needing improvement by consumers. Similarly, governmental services and health care are also mentioned relatively often. In contrast, eating places and retail stores are least frequently the sources of dissatisfaction with the services provided (see table 2.) While the report was very interesting, it did trigger some individuals to take action. What follows are the beginnings of a quality improvement plan with specific focus on improving the quality of automotive repair services — nationwide.

TABLE 3.
SERVICE QUALITY COMPLAINTS

| Type of service | All who experienced poor service % | All consumers % |
|---|---|---|
| Auto repair | 41 | 23 |
| Banking | 18 | 10 |
| Insurance | 16 | 9 |
| Government | 15 | 8 |
| Hospital | 15 | 8 |
| Airline | 8 | 4 |
| Repair (other than auto) | 7 | 4 |
| Hotel | 6 | 3 |
| Fast food/restaurant | 3 | 1 |
| Retail store | 2 | 1 |
| Miscellaneous | 3 | 2 |
| No answer | 1 | * |
| Total | 135 | 73 |
| Number of interviews | (593) | (1,005) |

*Less than one.

## Scoping the Target Population

The Department of Commerce Statistical Abstract released in 1987 estimates the population of automobiles, trucks, and buses in America to be 170 million. Exact numbers as to the dollars spent on vehicle repairs per year are not easy to find. Estimates range from 60 billion to 85 billion dollars annually. These repair services are performed by national and regional service organizations, car dealerships, and local repair centers and garages. The largest market share enjoyed by any single organization in the automotive repair service industry is about 4%. Clearly, there is a one single dominant force that commands a large market share.

## A PARTNER—FIRESTONE, INC.

One of the partners in this national effort to address the automotive service issues is Firestone, Inc. The Firestone automotive service company has about 2% market share which is achieved by a network of over fifteen hundred company-owned retail stores. These retail stores service about nine million vehicles annually.

## Mastercare Objectives

Based on market research and direct feedback from customer focus groups, Firestone developed MasterCare. A concept of complete automotive service; Firestone's quality objectives for MasterCare are numerous:

- Clean stores; courteous, professional employees
- Exact estimates given prior to servicing the vehicle
- Use of protective items to keep the vehicle clean
- Performance of preventive maintenance appraisal on all vehicles, with customer authorization
- Quality control sign-off to insure the vehicle is fixed right the first time
- Service completion on the vehicle at the time promised
- Return of replaced parts, upon request
- Contact of the customer after service work
- A nationwide MasterCare service warranty.

## Setting Quality Performance Standards

For each of the quality objectives a set of measurable standards were established to measure MasterCare performance as well as to benchmark the major competition. The principal means of determining compliance with established standards is through a sequence of quality audits conducted under a program called MasterCare Shopper program. The shopper program performs telephone, in-person, and post-customer-service audits by an independent third party, an approach that replicates, in many ways, the one used to make independent financial reviews required of U.S. companies. From this shopping activity and other informational sources, the findings of the Gallup/ASQC survey were confirmed.

Additionally, it has been determined that one of the key variables in fixing a person's automobile is the level of skill of the technician. While many organizations in the automotive service industries spend a great deal of money training technicians, there always seems to be a shortage of technically trained and qualified people. A plan was conceived to explore the feasibility of a national syllabus to be used in training automotive technicians in vocational, secondary, and post-secondary schools. To attempt such a venture, Firestone looked to the Vocational Education Clubs of America (VICA) to form a partnership.

## A PARTNER—VICA

VICA is a national organization of 300,000 students and teachers (of which some 30,000 are studying to be automotive technicians), 1,470 clubs, 470 organizations, 51 state organizations, and the national organization in Leesburg, Virginia. VICA is perceived in different ways by different audiences. To teachers, it is a training program; to industry, it is one of the most effective ways around to become involved in the future of vocational education;

in towns across America, its students are known for community service projects; and to student members, VICA is their own organization.

VICA provides students with one of the most important things anyone can have, *opportunity*: the opportunity to compete in contests; to gain community, business and peer recognition; and to work as part of a team. The key is that VICA students are learning by experience, about themselves and about their skill area. Moreover, they're learning because they enjoy what they're doing. VICA is aimed at students enrolled in public vocational programs—in high schools, vocational technical schools, junior and community colleges, and in co-op programs. The total population in vocational education is three million. VICA members are enrolled in trade, industrial, technical, or health occupation programs; they will graduate as tomorrow's auto technicians, drafters, printers, dental technicians, bricklayers, and so on. They are developing the vocational knowledge and skills needed to begin a career.

### Skill Olympics

VICA has programs that work because they are geared to student interests. One of the clearest examples of how VICA works can be seen in the Skill Olympics, a program that creates an excitement for skill excellence through competition and recognition. The Skill Olympics involves vocational education students coming together to compete for gold medallions in trades such as welding, automotive repair, and electronics. They use the finest equipment and race the clock for recognition.

But, it is much more than that. This one day event has taken a year of planning and $8.5 million investment in time, funding, and equipment from industry. For its part, VICA has pulled together the resources, the expertise, equipment, and funding to make the Skill Olympics a reality. Competition begins right in the local community. For students at every level, the Skill Olympics program is a motivator.

By instituting events such as the Skill Olympics, VICA has developed methods of bringing industry and education together. Take a look at the facts: vocational education and industry have not been communicating as they should. Yet, both groups—students, teachers, and school administrators on one side and those in industry on the other—have a significant stake in how these students develop as workers and as citizens. With over 3,000,000 students enrolled in vocational industrial programs in this country, and 1,050,000 looking for jobs every year, the future looks brighter. Members are either just beginning their jobs or will be looking for jobs next year. With vocational education on the rise, there are many more students right behind them.

The Skill Olympics is just one of the methods VICA uses to reach its goal: the goal to combine the efforts of vocational education and industry to develop the committed, motivated work force this country desperately needs.

In support of this diverse background of students with critically needed skills, Firestone and VICA encouraged other organizations to get involved and create an automotive Professional Development Program (PDP).

## DEVELOPING THE PDP PROGRAM

With a grant from the Firestone Trust Fund, a team of leaders from industry, academia, and professional organizations met in a series of workshops to create a plan and an implementation strategy to put PDP in place.

By design, the VICA Professional Development Program (PDP) will be integrated into the automotive technician training program where applicable. The competency tasks have been identified for a two-year program to be presented in a daily three-hour block of time. It is recommended that 80% of the time be spent in the automotive technician laboratory and 20% be devoted to classes on related theory. The following duty areas have each been assigned a recommended percentage of time-on-task (based on a 180-day school year). For example, 20% or approximately 216 hours should be devoted to teaching the service and maintainence of fuel and emission systems. The sequencing of task skills and/or duty-areas (table 4) is up to the discretion of the individual instructor.

TABLE 4.
DUTY-AREAS

| Automotive-Technician Duty-Area | Percent of Time |
|---|---|
| 1. Performing Basic Automotive-Technician Skills and Safe Operating Procedures* | 5% (54 hours) |
| *Safe operating procedures must be practiced daily. | |
| 2. Maintaining and Repairing Engine Assemblies | 10% (108 hours) |
| 3. Servicing Drive Trains | 10% (108 hours) |
| 4. Servicing Chassis | 10% (108 hours) |
| 5. Servicing Brake Systems | 8% (86 hours) |
| 6. Servicing and Maintaining Fuel and Emission Systems | 20% (216 hours) |
| 7. Performing Basic Electrical Services | 22% (238 hours) |
| 8. Servicing and Repairing Heating and Air Conditioning Systems | 10% (108 hours) |
| 9. Performing Shop Management Skills** | 5% (54 hours) |
| **Most shop management skills integrated throughout entire two-year program. | |
| | (Total 1080 hours) |

## General Program Statement

To conduct a high-quality vocational program to train automotive technicians, the following guidelines are recommended:

- The automotive technician student should possess average or above-average skills in reading, mathematics, and communications. It is recommended that automotive technician not have a reading level of less than two levels below their grade level. It is also recommended that students learn basic computer skills.
- The automotive technician instructor can arrange for an exchange of students with other vocational education disciplines when possible and applicable—i.e., welding, heating and air conditioning, electronics, and auto body—to learn basic skills useful in the automotive technician industry.
- The school should provide automotive equipment, components, hand tools and supplies, and secure, safe storage for such items.
- All competency tasks demonstrated and practiced in the automotive technician laboratory must be in compliance with safe operating practices. Approved eye protection, ear protection, clothing, and shoes are essential for the operation of a safe working environment for the automotive technician.
- The automotive technician students nearing program completion can be placed in a trade internship for a minimum of thirty 30 hours. A training plan and evaluation process must be in accordance with state and local guidelines.
- It is suggested that automotive technician students take the certification examination given by the National Institute for Automotive Service Excellence (ASE) upon completion of the automotive technician program.

## Competency Tasks

For each of the nine areas of automotive technician duties, a number of competency tasks have been identified. The total number of tasks recommended for this two-year program is 273. Table 5 outlines the competency tasks for servicing brake systems.

## PDP—A Dual Ladder Program

By design, this program also teaches communication skills, organization, teamwork, and leadership skills, along with technical skills to automotive students. The combined classroom and internship program provides a learning experience as to what American business is all about; second, it helps to develop a positive work attitude and the qualities needed to be a good citizen. These are the skills and work habits necessary for success on the job. For this portion of the program, students work on their own during specified class times. As assignments are completed, it is recorded in a notebook

TABLE 5.
COMPETENCY LIST

| Servicing Brake Systems (Competency List) |
| --- |
| 132. Remove and replace drums |
| 133. Inspect brake lining, drums, and hardware |
| 134. Check and inspect a hydraulic system |
| 135. Recondition drums |
| 136. Check operation of a parking brake |
| 137. Service and/or replace parking brake components |
| 138. Replace steel brake lines and/or fittings |
| 139. Cut, bend, and double International Standards Organization (ISO) flare steel brake lines |
| 140. Bleed brakes manually |
| 141. Bleed brakes with pressure bleeder |
| 142. Remove and replace brake shoes |
| 143. Adjust brakes |
| 144. Remove and rebuild sliding and floating calipers |
| 145. Remove and rebuild fixed calipers |
| 146. Inspect and recondition rotors |
| 147. Inspect and remove pads |
| 148. Repack wheel bearings |
| 149. Remove, replace, and adjust wheel bearings |
| 150. Test and replace power booster (vacuum, air, or hydroboost) |
| 151. Test and service antilock brake systems |
| 152. Remove and replace brake system control valves |
| 153. Inspect and overhaul a wheel cylinder |
| 154. Remove and replace a master cylinder |
| 155. Inspect and overhaul a master clyinder |
| 156. Flush the brake system |

that requires the teachers sign-off. Recognition and awards for completion of each of four levels are built into the program.

The responsibility for verification as to competency for these tasks rests with the teachers. And while the test for technical competency also rests with the teachers, as stated earlier, the general plan is to encourage the automotive technician student to take the ASE certification examination upon completing the program and acquiring sufficient time on tasks.

# A PARTNER: ASE

The National Institute for Automotive Service Excellence (ASE) was established as a non-profit corporation in June 1972 as the result of a joint effort of the domestic vehicle manufacturers and the automobile dealers. Other sectors of the industry have added their encouragement and support to what is now truly an industry-wide program. The goal of the Institute is to organize and promote the highest standards of automotive service in the public interest. Through a voluntary competency testing and certification program, it measures and recognizes the diagnostic and repair skills and the knowledge possessed by automobile and heavy-duty truck technicians, as well as by body repairmen and painters. It also assists in the development of effective training programs.

The Institute has retained the services of the American College Testing Program, Iowa City, Iowa, for test development and administration. Tests are held in the spring and fall of each year, at simultaneous times and dates in over three hundred locations across the nation. This arrangement, coupled with the fact that the tests are changed each time they are administered, assures tight security. A minimum of two years' work experience as a technician is required to be eligible for certification.

## What Good is Certification?

To the motorist, it means that the technician has the know-how to do the job. To the technician, it means prestige and recognition by demonstrating that he possesses the skills and knowledge needed to pass the tests. To the shop owner or service manager, it is an impartial, objective assurance that his or her technicians are competent. It also encourages the technician who does not pass a test to review his manuals or take more training. In both the short and the long run, this will benefit the car owner, technician, and dealer alike.

## How Can One Recognize a Certified Technician?

Certified technicians wear a blue seal with the initials *ASE* in white on a shoulder patch on their work uniforms. A pocket protector carries a card indicating their specific areas of certification. A technician who passes all the tests is designated as a Certified Master Technician. ASE is providing the technical input to VICA to assure that the skills covered in the automotive technicians Professional Development Program are compatible with ASE certification requirements. ASE will also provide the guidelines needed by the schools and automotive instructors to assure that all systems are integrated to meet the common goal.

## CONCLUSION: PDP IMPLEMENTATION

A roll-out and pilot study was started in 150 schools across the country in the fall of 1987. These schools were identified by the Departments of Vocational Education in various states and were linked with a section of the country with Firestone retail outlets. Local Firestone personnel work directly with the schools to help evaluate students' progress. Other companies like General Motors, and Snap-on-Tools support this PDP program by providing vehicles and tools to participating schools. Currently, there are over six thousand students enrolled in the pilot program. And the program will be expanded to seventeen thousand VICA clubs with over 37,000 students enrolled as automotive technicians. This announcement will be a key event at the June 1988 United States Skill Olympics.

This happening, a national effort to improve the Gallup/ASQC identified-number-one service quality problem, is being undertaken by a unique partnership of American industry, state and local school administrations, and professional organizations. The focus is on developing tomorrow's new professionals, those who will be working in many service sectors of American businesses, and on creating a win-win-win situation: for the American consumers, for the service providers, and for future automotive technicians.

# Savings Institutions

Home Federal Savings & Loan Association
James E. Stutz

# Service Quality and Shareholder Value

**James E. Stutz**

Home Federal Savings and Loan Association

Home Federal Savings and Loan Association is a diversified financial services company focused on consumer banking and real estate finance. With assets in excess of $14 billion, it is the 11th largest savings and loan in the United States.

Founded in 1934 in San Diego, California, the company employs more than 4,000 people in its 168 bank branches in California and its nationwide real estate finance services division. In 1983 the company went public.

## INTRODUCTION

The first thing to remember about quality service is that it is only an option. This statement, although true, sounds heretical or, at the least, boorish. Even if that is what they think privately, many people in business would be embarrassed to suggest publicly that it is legitimate to compete for the consumer's dollar without providing quality service. It is too much like being ungrateful for Mom and apple pie.

Perhaps we are conditioned to think that way. The stale and misleading phrase "The customer is always right" seems to pop into the mind almost as readily as other bromides drilled into us in youth, such as "Always wash your hands before dinner." Of course, being adults now, we know the customer is *not* always right. It merely seems impolite to say it aloud.

But maybe we should say it in order to achieve any clarity about the actual importance of service quality to contemporary American business. That importance does not depend on some sort of mercantile machismo. An informed commitment to the concept does not arise from any categorical imperative and erecting some sort of metaphysic around it serves mystification better than enlightenment. Demystifying service quality starts with placing it in the proper context. And the proper context for any company that contemplates raising the quality of customer service involves the question of whether or not such a choice suits the company's business objectives.

What follows is a brief case study of one company, Home Federal Savings in San Diego, which has *chosen* quality service as one centerpiece of its competitive strategy. Quality of service at a financial institution like Home Federal will be defined, but more importantly, its role in the company's business success will be probed. To put it another way, the emphasis will be on how high quality of service increases shareholder value.

## OVERVIEW

Although deliberate, Home Federal's current emphasis on quality could have resulted from intertia as easily as from choice. The company was founded in 1934 at a time when the housing finance sector was being revived—and strictly regulated—by the government under the aegis of the New Deal. Steady growth over five decades has made Home Federal one of the largest and most successful savings and loans in California and the nation.

Until deregulation of the financial industry began in earnest in the late seventies, however, the company's avenues for gaining the competitive edge were exceedingly narrow. Rock-solid regulatory walls kept thrifts apart from banks, and both apart from securities firms and commerce. Federal regulators determined what financial products thrifts could offer and how they could price them. Aside from promotional campaigns—"toaster wars"—thrift marketing emphasis was effectively limited to convenience (primarily a matter of branch location) and service. Generally, quality service to retail customers in this period was more closely associated with thrifts than with banks, who were burdened with the distraction of their commercial clients—traditionally, the bulk of their business. Barred by charter from making commercial loans, a thrift's client base was largely limited to household accounts. This made retail customer service a natural marketing focus for thrifts and offered a way to counter the greater product variety available from banks. Certainly, this was how Home Federal viewed the matter.

The company had long been noted for a degree of diversification unusual among thrifts: traditional savings and home lending activities shared the stage with commercial real estate lending, construction lending, and real estate development. Even so, its retail branch network was among the industry's finest and its customer service reputation was regarded as a distinctive strength.

## A BRAVE NEW WORLD

By the early eighties, however, deregulation had ushered in a brave new world, a world in which the old magnetic poles seemed to shift, making it more difficult for the financial services strategist to find his true bearings and chart the right course. Conventional wisdom was forced to undergo a thorough reexamination. Economic developments made matters even more stressful. The Federal Reserve's anti-inflation campaign pushed interest rates to record heights just as deregulation lifted the limits on what thrifts could pay to attract funds. With investment portfolios dominated by low-yielding, long-term home loans, the unhappy result was an erosion of the thrift industry's capital base.

But by late 1982, the interest rate crisis had eased. A new lending instrument, the adjustable rate mortgage, enabled thrifts to begin restructuring their portfolios and to match assets and liabilities better. As the interest rate picture continued to brighten, an industry dominated by large mutual associations such as Home Federal, looked to Wall Street to rebuild capital. A wave of conversions to stock charters began and gained force. Home Federal converted in the spring of 1983 in one of the largest initial public offerings on record.

A brave new world indeed, one in which conflicting forces seemed to be at work. Deregulation had opened the floodgates to a myriad of new products. Thrifts were free to set their own pricing and terms. Such complexity increased the need to educate consumers and seemed to provide a compelling case for an even more intense emphasis on high quality service. But going public seemed, at first, to bring countervailing pressures. Shareholders now owned the company, not depositors and borrowers, and management's primary obligation was to serve the owners' interests. The focus on the bottom line became sharply magnified; there was pressure to show better and better quarterly results. Cost-cutting became the premise of the new corporate consciousness.

## SHIFTING THE FOCUS

Efficiency, as measured by the ratio of general and administrative expenses to total assets, was not Home Federal's strong point, the market analysts chorused. Unfavorable comparisons were drawn between the company and competitors who emphasized low-budget operations. As the company went public, one analyst went so far as to suggest that Home Federal should hire someone whose job would be simply to fire people.

In this environment, even fifty years of tradition would not alone suffice to perpetuate high quality customer service as a priority. Service quality, like every other aspect of company operations, had to be completely rethought and justified, if at all, only in terms of its contribution to the development of shareholder value. As it turns out, quality service as a priority not only survived in this crucible of corporate introspection, but also emerged, along with a sales culture, as one of the critical underpinnings of the new Home Federal. A sifting of strategic options revealed quality service to be an indispensable tool for maintaining and expanding the company's single greatest source of lasting investment value: a large and loyal customer base which views the company as its primary resource for multiple financial products.

Market analysis provided the key which unlocked the solution. Intensive research revealed that Home Federal's best customers were not to be found in the price- or rate-sensitive segments of the market, but among the "searchers" and "savers": they included, respectively, the younger, upwardly mobile utilizers of credit and basic financial services, plus the older, safety-conscious users of basic investment products. Attracting their business and retaining their loyalty required the provision of value added service. "Value added" has become a familiar phrase to readers of business bestsellers in the eighties, but what does it mean? What puts the "high" in "high quality service" and makes it the linchpin in building and retaining market share?

At Home Federal, two basic principles provide the answer: (1) Quality is what the client says it is; and (2) Quality is everyone's responsibility. If quality is what the client says it is, then obviously an institution had better listen to its clients. There are many ways to do this, formal and informal. Formal means providing clients with definite and easily utilized channels for feedback. Even if the "Express Yourself" boxes (prominently located in each Home Federal branch) rarely yield suggestions of substance, and even if the "We Care" cards with space for comment (which all Home Federal client-contact people hand out after each transaction) bring more bouquets than brickbats, they indelibly define the company's attitude in the clients' eyes.

They cause the company to be perceived as responsive. Clients will return to responsive companies when they have additional needs.

Formal also means proven research techniques—not just the usual closed account survey, but also "focus groups," in-depth interviews in a group setting which elicit clients' views on the quality of service they seek. Focus groups are routinely used by Home Federal, not only to evaluate products, services, and programs already in place, but also proactively to test programs prior to implementation. The company's aim is to know what the client wants even before he asks for it.

But at no time does the client communicate more clearly his definition of quality than when he complains. And at no time are his expectations of quality better met than when his complaints are understood, acknowledged, and *resolved to his satisfaction promptly*. This situation is the crucial one for service quality, the meeting ground of formal and informal client communication, of quality as client-defined and quality as everyone's job. Not all client complaints can be anticipated. Many times, if they are to be resolved promptly, they must be resolved on an ad hoc basis by front-line people. Genuine customer satisfaction cannot wait for the slow workings of some creaky bureaucratic mechanism, for the stately deliberate pace of an Olympian corporate staffer with "authority."

## Applying Quality Service

High quality service is simply unattainable unless the authority to resolve client complaints has been firmly and irrevocably placed in the hands of the front-line employee on the spot. Client-contact personnel must know that they have the authority to act and must know that they cannot be second-guessed. They must firmly understand the company's posture of responsiveness and must be thoroughly confident that the entire company backs them up.

This simple need for front-line power and responsibility has tremendous implications. First, note that the mode of communication it requires is informal. This type of client encounter cannot be handled with a ready-made form that puts everything in boxes. There is no formula, suitable for recitation by rote or for plastering on a wall in poster form, that will tell front-line personnel what to do or will unerringly guide their judgments. It is a one-to-one transaction and can only be guided by training and by corporate values effectively communicated. If a company is committed to high quality service, to earnest responsiveness to customer needs, it must train its employees accordingly. Its internal communications must constantly reinforce the message. It must make its value system clear and make it clearly understood.

Second, front-line decisions must be upheld all the way up the line, even when mistakes are made. True, the customer is not always right, and the front-line decision-maker must take risks no matter which way the decision goes. Judgement calls must be safe from recrimination. That the customer deserves the benefit of the doubt should be company policy. But if the burden of decision falls on the front line, the burden of support rests at every link in the chain of command. Quality is everybody's job.

The posture of responsiveness delineated above is the essence of the concept of *value added*. It is nothing less than the crux of customer retention for a financial institution serving savers and searchers. And it costs very little — nothing, in fact, compared with the expensive media advertising and discount pricing often needed to gain new customers and greater market share. It also forms the basis for successfully cross-selling multiple products to existing clients, a vital imperative for financial institutions in today's sharply competitive consumer arena.

Here is where service quality and shareholder value are connected. High quality customer service is the sinew of Home Federal's marketing prowess. The company serves market segments which value responsiveness over price in the handling of their financial services needs. Building and carefully maintaining a strongly responsive institutional profile are the best and least expensive means of retaining customer loyalty and increasing customer receptivity to highly profitable cross-selling. Finally — and very significantly — responsiveness to customers heightens their tolerance of new fees for services.

If service quality had not set the stage for the successful imposition of service fees (by making them more palatable to customers), Home Federal's recent history might have been sharply different. Remember, when the company went public, securities analysts rapped it for relatively high overhead. Because a retail delivery system is people-intensive and requires considerable technological and logistical support, it easily becomes a tempting target for cost-cutters looking for a quick fix.

But service quality is also the hub of the company's consumer franchise, the heart of its economic viability as an enterprise, and the largest and most durable source of true investor value. If the investment funds it brings in are not always the least costly, they are certainly the most stable. Continental Illinois, a wholesale bank, tottered precariously until regulators came to the rescue. Bank of America, despite all its woes, has found its retail base (the largest in the country) a rock of strength amid recent crises. Efficiency, however, is a legitimate issue. The ability to introduce fees for services has significantly boosted the efficiency of Home Federals' retail system for funds acquisition. It is this author's firm belief that the company could not have achieved this without maintaining high quality service as a corporate priority.

Emphasis on service quality has been incorporated into all areas of Home Federal's operations. The company's success in commercial real estate lending, construction lending, and corporate financial services is based on "relationship" lending. In other words, loan officers focus not on single transactions, but on forging lasting relationships with borrowers with the aim of becoming a financial resource to which they return again and again. On the corporate level, Home Federal's staff functions are organized into service units that relate to line units in the role of service providers to clients.

At Home Federal, high quality service is neither rhetoric nor unthinking reflex. It is, essentially, both a fulfillment of management's promise to shareholders and an indispensable element for success in the company's pursuit of its business mission.

# Tobacco

Philip-Morris U.S.A.
Michael B. Overstreet

# A Service Delivery Measurement and Improvement Program

**Michael B. Overstreet**
Philip Morris U.S.A.

Philip Morris U.S.A., the nation's largest manufacturer of cigarettes, is one of the divisions of the Philip Morris Companies. The other divisions are Philip Morris International, General Foods, Miller Brewing, Philip Morris Credit, and Mission Viejo Realty.

Philip Morris U.S.A. is headquartered in New York City with manufacturing headquarters in Richmond, Virginia. It employs 16,000 people.

## INTRODUCTION

Service is not in the eye of the beholder, especially when it is provided by one division of a corporation to another. In this instance, service must be defined, achieved, maintained, and audited on a continuous basis.

The York Engineering Center is a function of Philip Morris U.S.A.'s engineering department. Its primary mission is to rebuild (literally remanufacture) cigarette-making and cigarette-packing equipment. Its customers are the four Philip Morris U.S.A. cigarette manufacturing factories, two in Virginia, one in North Carolina, and one in Kentucky. York receives this equipment after it has been in production for fifteen to twenty-one shift-years (i.e., after operating for five to seven years for three shifts). York's end-product is a machine that, when returned to the factory, is comparable to a model produced by the original equipment manufacturer (OEM). The question posed by York's management was how well the service being performed by its technical craftsmen was perceived by management at the cigarette manufacturing factories.

## BACKGROUND

Viewed simply, manufacturing of the cigarette itself can be divided into three processes: filter making, cigarette making, and cigarette packing. Each process requires its own specialized machinery.

Filter making has generally been standardized to a single vendor and machine specification, with each machine capable of producing about sixteen thousand filters per minute.

Over the past two decades, industry demand has led to a number of technological advances in cigarette making and cigarette packing machinery, resulting in a number of different types and makes of equipment used in the factories. Depending on the vintage, cigarette-making machine speeds vary from 3,000 to 10,000 cigarettes per minute. Similarly, cigarette packing machine speeds range from 200 to 500 packs per minute. At any given time, there are over six hundred pieces of cigarette-manufacturing machinery in operation in the four factories, with additional equipment used for training, product research, and engineering development.

Because of the growing numbers, variations, technical complexity, and costs of new machinery, the company built and began operating its own machine-rebuilding center in the late 1970s. The York Engineering Center, has evolved to fulfill three primary purposes: to maximize the utilization of company assets; to remanufacture the machinery, whenever possible, to the speed and state-of-the-art of a later version being offered by the OEM; and to incorporate Philip Morris's own operational improvement standards during the rebuilding process.

Three ancillary functions have been added to York's basic mission. Because it could not rebuild all machines required within the established timeframe, some machine rebuilding is contracted to the OEM's local shops. York ensures that machines turned out by these shops are equal to the machines rebuilt at York. The second, a natural extension due to the complexity of the electronics of the making and packing equipment, was the formation of an Automated Test Engineering (ATE) group. Circuit boards that fail in the machines during operation are sent by the factories to the ATE group for computer analysis and diagnosis, repair, and subsequent return to inventory. The third function is a parts warehousing operation. York is responsible for purchasing and storing all engineering development parts, major product size change parts, and, of course, all machine rebuild parts. The emphasis of this paper will be on York's three primary purposes—equipment rebuilding, equipment utilization, and improvement standards.

The York Engineering Center employs 165 supervisory and technical personnel. The one hundred thousand-square feet facility includes the rebuild area, stockroom, offices, and amenities. Organizationally, it is aligned under engineering, with the plant manager reporting to the director of engineering operations and, subsequently, to the director of Philip Morris U.S.A. engineering.

York operates in tandem with engineering's new equipment procurement function to ensure that the company's long-range needs for the most productive manufacturing equipment are met. When a machine reaches the end of its productive life, the company can either replace the old machine with new machinery or extend the useful life of the machine through the rebuild/remanufacture process. This decision can be driven by outside factors, such as desire to incorporate new technologies that provide greater quality and productivity or because newer, faster machinery is required to meet the growing sales volume requirements. In all instances, the decision is based on economics, and the option chosen is the one that provides the highest return on investment. In general, the cost of a machine rebuild is about one-third to one-half the cost of a new machine.

The advantage of buying new machinery is that the OEM may have made a significant quality or productivity increase through design improvements that cannot be reproduced with a rebuild. In fact, over the past two decades, due to industry demand, equipment manufacturers have devoted increasing amounts of effort to such design improvements. In the absence of technological improvements, rebuilding is clearly the superior choice.

## SERVICE DELIVERY

A large organization such as Philip Morris is composed of many smaller interdependent functions which in many respects act as small, independently operating businesses. York Engineering Center is one of these small engineering functions. York's leadership set out to define the three most important product characteristics required by its customers—quality, price, and timeliness of delivery—and thereby increase the quality of its service.

Quality was defined as "doing the right things," instead of just "doing things right." The price characteristic was defined as the value of York's products. Using the classic definition of efficiency (output divided by input), value can be increased by either increasing output or decreasing input. Timeliness was defined as the amount of time it takes to deliver the finished product to the customer when it is needed by the customer.

For the York Engineering Center to properly examine and improve the quality, productivity, and timeliness of its service delivery, four major steps were required. First it *diagnosed its services*. This was accomplished by dividing the organization into its major functions. The second step was to set *service objectives*. Each major function area defined what it should do to provide its service. The third step defined *service measures* and required York's management to construct measurements that would report on the attainment of service objectives and provide information allowing causes of non-attainment to be identified and corrected. The final step was to set *service goals* which challenged the organization to improve by setting long-range goals of attainment.

## Service Diagnosis

Service diagnosis identified four major responsibility areas at York Engineering Center: York machine rebuild, contract machine rebuild, automated test engineering, and inventory and warehousing.

The two rebuild responsibilities represent external outputs. Automated Test Engineering and Inventory and Warehousing responsibilities are both external and internal. The Inventory and Warehousing group processes machine parts in support of rebuild and, at times, to external customers. (Figure 1 presents the York machine rebuild, supplier/customer relationships.)

The remaining steps of the process discuss the York machine rebuild responsibility only. The process followed to identify service objectives, measures, and goals for the other three responsibilities were similar.

## Service Objectives

Four activities completely defined York's service objectives: rebuild equipment, provide technical assistance to factories during installation and start-up of equipment, train customer personnel to operate and maintain rebuilt equipment, and provide machinery-related technical assistance in product (cigarette) design specification changes, machine specification upgrades, and machine documentation.

## Service Measures

This step constructed measurements of the three service delivery characteristics and provided sufficient information to allow causes of non-attainment to be identified, corrected, and/or enable York to change its service policies to meet changing customer needs.

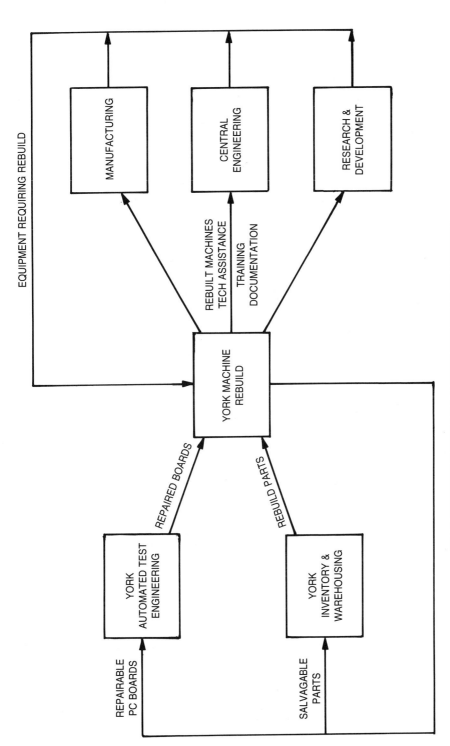

FIG. 1. YORK MACHINE REBUILD SUPPLIER/CUSTOMER RELATIONSHIP

Five measures were developed to evaluate service, two of which are surveys designed for York management to ensure that York's product was truly meeting factory demands; that is, that the rebuilt machines themselves were quality products and that they produced quality products. The interviews provided a formal, ongoing mechanism for feedback, exchange of ideas, constructive criticism, and maybe an occasional compliment from the factory all aimed at strengthening performance in the supplier/customer relationship.

While the purpose of the surveys was generally to ensure that "the right things were being done," the purpose of the other measures was to ensure that "things were being done right." Each measure is described below:

**Machinery Quality Survey.** This survey is in two parts; the first part deals with the installation phase of the rebuilt machinery and the second with the production phase (see figure 2). The installation survey examines any difficulties or problems that occurred while the machine was being installed in the factory. The first part is conducted within two weeks after installation and start-up is completed, and is requested of the factory supervisor having direct responsibility for the installation.

The questions are directed toward determining the machines condition at the time the factory receives it in an attempt to identify items that York, or the factory, could do to make machine installation easier and faster.

The second part of the survey is completed by the factory production supervisor after the machine has been in production three or four months. The purpose is to gain information about the machine's performance, including the amount of downtime (contributing to loss of productivity), product quality levels, and product waste levels.

While the first part of the survey deals more with making sure that "things were done right" (making sure that the workmanship and care for the machine during rebuild were of the highest levels), the second part tries to make sure that the "right things were done." The proof of whether a rebuild was effective or not is how well the machine performs on the production floor after a period of time. The survey questions ask the production supervisor to compare the rebuilt machine's performance to other machines on the floor. Specific downtime, quality or waste causes may be identified which will tell York to add, delete, or modify components of the rebuild process.

**Service Assistance Survey.** This survey was designed to obtain information about service response time, the serviceman's knowledge of the machine, attitude, cooperation, and the quality and quantity of service the York Engineering Center provides to its customers in support of its product. If excessive problems are indicated in the quality of service rendered, additional technical training of York's personnel may be required. If the quantity or amount of service is insufficient, then either York may need to reallocate

PHILIP MORRIS U.S.A.

FACTORY _____     MACHINE TYPE _____
FACTORY NO./LOC. _____     MACHINE NO. _____
INSTALLATION DATE _____

|  | Lowest Rating | | | | Highest Rating |
|---|---|---|---|---|---|
| Installation length and difficulty | 1 | 2 | 3 | 4 | 5 |
| Electrical problems – startup associated | 1 | 2 | 3 | 4 | 5 |
| Mechanical problems – startup associated | 1 | 2 | 3 | 4 | 5 |
| Rebuild workmanship quality level | 1 | 2 | 3 | 4 | 5 |
| York support for machine | 1 | 2 | 3 | 4 | 5 |
| Overall rebuilt machine rating | 1 | 2 | 3 | 4 | 5 |

Comments: _____
_____
_____
_____
_____
_____

Signature: _____     Date: _____

FIG. 2. REMANUFACTURED MACHINERY QUALITY SURVEY

its personnel resources or else the number of "legitimate" service requests are excessive, indicating a need to reexamine the rebuild process itself. Since product service and support is an ongoing process and not directly tied to specific machines, this survey is taken every three-months. It is generally given to factory machine maintenance supervision, but may be given to anyone who routinely works with York's service respresentatives.

Quality Assurance Audits Per Machine. Before York permits a rebuilt machine to be shipped, it must operate and achieve "production floor" quality levels. After a planned tune-and-test period, audits are conducted by manufacturing quality assurance representatives, and by the service representative(s) who will assist with factory installation. This measure then, is simply the average number of times machines must be tested before shipment is approved. (The goal is obviously, once). The measure provides excellent information to identify and analyze recurring problems and trends. In most cases, recurring problems can be traced back to the component(s) of the rebuild process and corrections made in the process itself.

**Rebuild Efficiency.** This measure is a classic efficiency measure of personnel utilization and is defined by:

$$\frac{\text{Standard Rebuild Labor Hours}}{\text{Actual Rebuild Labor Hours}} \times 100$$

Standard labor hours are the labor hour estimates for each machine type multiplied by the number of machines completed during a time period. Actual labor hours are the hours used by York's personnel assigned to each machine type. (Table 1 presents a sample rebuild efficiency calculation.) The information provided permits York's management to track targets, and allows proper management of personnel.

**Scheduled Completion Measurement.** Each year, York's management negotiates a rebuild schedule with each of its customer (factory) locations for the next calendar year. The schedule specifies which machines are to be rebuilt, when they will be removed from service, and when they will be returned to service. This provides a standard against which actual performance can be checked to measure the precentage of machines returned to service on or before the scheduled date. This is York's bottom-line measurement of timeliness. Used in conjunction with the rebuild efficiency measure, it

TABLE 1
REBUILD EFFICIENCY
SAMPLE CALCULATION

| MACHINE TYPE | ACTUAL LABOR-HOURS | ACTUAL/ ESTIMATED MACHINES COMPLETED | TARGET LABOR-HOURS PER MACHINE | STANDARD LABOR-HOURS GENERATED | REBUILD EFFICIENCY |
|---|---|---|---|---|---|
| Cigarette Makers | | | | | |
| Type A | 10,750 | 4.0 | 1,600 | 6,400 | 60% |
| Type B | 9,400 | 2.3 | 3,200 | 7,360 | 78% |
| Type C | 4,900 | 2.6 | 2,000 | 5,200 | 106% |
| Total Cigarette | | | | | |
| Makers | 25,050 | 8.9 | — | 18,960 | 76% |
| Cigarette Packers | | | | | |
| Type A | 0 | 0.0 | 5,000 | 0 | — |
| Type B | 16,800 | 2.8 | 4,800 | 13,440 | 80% |
| Type C | 17,600 | 1.6 | 6,200 | 9,920 | 56% |
| Total Cigarette | | | | | |
| Packers | 34,400 | 4.4 | — | 23,360 | 68% |
| Total York | | | | | |
| Machine Rebuild | 59,450 | 13.3 | — | 42,320 | 71% |

tells York's management how well its customers are being served and how well rebuild personnel are allocated.

As a total package, the five measures allow York to judge how well it is attaining its service objectives and to tell where problem areas might lie. The measures also check and balance each other. The three service delivery characteristics are in many respects of equal importance. Productivity cannot be emphasized to the point of sacrificing quality and timeliness. Timeliness cannot be emphasized to the point of sacrificing quality and productivity. Quality cannot be emphasized while sacrificing productivity and timeliness. The emphasis of these measures is on total service quality.

The two surveys help define and measure quality, and the quality audits per machine measures product quality. The final two measures for productivity (efficiency) and timeliness are necessary to check the importance placed on service delivery quality.

The measures are also balanced by being both internal and external. The internal measures make sure that things are done right; the external measures make sure that customer expectations are met - making sure that the right things are done. The external measures indicate when changes in the objectives are needed, which in turn will create changes in the rebuild process. Or they might indicate that the service objectives are correct but are not being attained with the current rebuild process.

## Service Goals
The measures just described tell York management where they are, but they do not project where they would like to be. To set a course for the future, goals are necessary. The York management team determined long-range goals for each of the measures as follows:

| Measure | YEAR | | | | |
| | 1 | 2 | 3 | 4 | 5 |
|---|---|---|---|---|---|
| Machine Quality Survey | 3.0 | 3.5 | 4.0 | 4.5 | 5.0 |
| Service Assistance Survey | 3.0 | 3.5 | 4.0 | 4.5 | 5.0 |
| Quality Audits Per Machine | 1.4 | 1.3 | 1.2 | 1.1 | 1.0 |
| Rebuild Efficiency | 75% | 81% | 88% | 94% | 100% |
| Percent Machines On Schedule | 100% | 100% | 100% | 100% | 100% |

For the two surveys, York management assumed that the first year level of performance would rate as average, or 3 on the 1-to-5-rating-scale. The last year's goals were set at the highest possible rating. Actual levels for quality audits per machine range between one and two tests before shipment is permitted, thus, the first year's goal was set at 1.4, with the eventual target being 1.0. The measure for rebuild efficiency was set by the standard labor hour estimates for each type of rebuild. The estimates were set so that a substantial amount of room for improvement could be allowed. Delivering machines on schedule was considered too important to tolerate a performance of less than 100%.

## SUMMARY

This paper has discussed the design and application of a service delivery improvement program for a machinery rebuild center supporting a large manufacturing operation. Since the program is new and because this was York Engineering's first experience with a process that attempts to "quantify" heretofore intangible measures, the informed reader may find "holes" in the applied methods. As the program is implemented and refined each year, York will discover these "holes" and correct them. By design, the program is relatively unstructured and flexible enough to allow for such changes. The program is a "change instrument" in the sense that one of its major purposes is to identify changes in customer expectations and subsequently trigger changes in York's rebuild process. If this is achieved the program's purpose will have been fulfilled.

The author would like to acknowledge and thank Al Opengart, director of Engineering Operations at Philip Morris U.S.A., and senior member of IIE for his assistance in helping to focus this article towards service quality, part of the program of excellence, under which the York Engineering Center is managed.

# Transportation

CSX Transportation Corporation
Gary T. Sease

Delta Air Lines, Inc.
R. A. McClelland

Norfolk Southern
Jack R. Martin

# Service Quality: CSX Transportation's Centralized Customer Service Center

**Gary T. Sease**
CSX Transportation

CSX Transportation represents the transportation group of CSX Corporation, the holding company based in Richmond, Virginia. The principal business lines of CSX Corporation are transportation, energy, properties, and technology. In 1986, CSX reorganized its rail transportation units internally into three business units: Rail Transport, Distribution Services, and Equipment. Each unit operates independently under a president. Rail Transport has the responsibility for operating train service, including locomotive management and roadway maintenance of CSX's fifteen-thousand mile core network. Distribution Services is the unit dealing directly with customers through the Customer Service Center and the sales and marketing forces. Equipment manages the CSX car fleet. Another CSX transportation unit has since been formed focusing on the combination of intermodal traffic and the acquisition of Sea-Land Corporation, the Menlo Park, New Jersey based container shipping giant. American Commercial Lines in Jeffersonville, Indiana, represents CSX's inland barging subsidiary.

## INTRODUCTION

What once was a dilapidated freight depot is today a modern brick building that houses CSX Transportation's Customer Service Center. The building looks somewhat out of place, located as it is in a gritty industrial area on the west side of Jacksonville, Florida. Yet a clean, eye-appealing structure amid the stark, strictly utilitarian warehouses seems to indicate just how far CSX's customer relations have progressed in the past three years.

From across the country, an average of four-thousand-plus calls per day are received at the customer service center. For people like Mary Anne Stone, a customer service clerk, a typical day is a mixed bag. Tracing a customer's railroad car, for example, is old hat. A few keystrokes on her quad-screen computer terminal and the information is displayed electronically. Getting that same car rerouted to avoid an unexpected track blockage requires considerably more effort. Through it all, Stone remains unflappable: "I work best under pressure," she says. Stone, who like many of her fellow clerks has varied railroad experience, moved to the customer service center when the customer service functions of the two major CSX predecessor lines, Chessie and Seaboard System Railroads, were combined in Jacksonville (one of two transportation headquarters cities of CSX Transportation, the other being Baltimore, Maryland).

A team approach is the cornerstone of the operation of the customer service center, which employs seventy people and is open from 7 A.M. to 7 P.M. on weekdays and 8 A.M. to 5 P.M. on weekends. Under the center's director are three assistant directors. Each of them supervises senior managers, managers, and assistant managers. Those managers, in turn, supervise the customer service clerks. Two of the assistant directors have specialized duties. One is a computer expert, whose talent is often in demand in the high-tech center. The other has responsibility for some of CSX' biggest customers—the U.S. Postal Service and other intermodal operations, and auto manufacturers (which require the distribution both of their parts to assembly plants and of finished autos). All managers and assistant managers have national accounts for which they are responsible.

## CENTRALIZING CUSTOMER SERVICE

In 1984, James A. Hagen, president and chief executive officer of the Seaboard System Railroad, created a task force to study the problems associated with responsiveness to customers and to recommend improvements. "We knew we had problems and we knew that the old way of doing things had to change if we were to maintain our customer base," says Hagen. "Not only did we want to maintain that base, we wanted it to grow." One member of that task force is now CSX's assistant vice president of customer service; according to him, there was no consistency in the way customer service was managed, and system-wide service complaints were not handled well.

At the time, Seaboard and Chessie were managing customer service in time-honored traditional ways. Seaboard used personnel in its forty-seven field sales offices. Chessie used five regional centers. Neither method, the task force concluded, was satisfactory. Seaboard historically provided customer service through clerks in the field sales offices. Customers did, of necessity, contact their marketing or sales representative, local transportation supervisor, or the executive department. Too frequently, customer service was the job of whoever happened to be nearby when the phone rang. The response to customer problems was fragmented and generally was graded in mail surveys of our customers as *not responsive*. Chessie's five regional centers did not fare much better in similar surveys.

Centralizing the customer service function in Jacksonville was recommended by the task force and other strategic planners. They decided that a centralized environment would enable customer service to be more responsive to customers. For example, better planning could be done for service changes or improvements; also, effective data could be collected that would assist in the long-term resolution of problem areas. The bottom line was to provide them with a competitive edge by making them customer responsive.

Surveys and studies were conducted to understand call volumes, call origins, and the types of customer questions and problems. For instance, they might have a situation in which five customers from different parts of the country complained about cars being delayed in the same yard. Under the old system, those complaints would have been handled by five sales offices and approached on an individual basis. Customer service would have had five isolated problems. Now, all this information is brought together, and they can see a congestion problem at a specific location that could be solved, say, by adding another switch engine. From those surveys and studies came the plan for the customer service center and its staffing. The Jacksonville location was recommended because of its proximity to the future CSX rail transport headquarters; such proximity would expedite problem solving. Work stations at the customer service center were spaced to minimize telephone noise. Sound screens also were installed to muffle outside noises; thus, full concentration could be given to responding to the customer without outside distractions. Communications needs were sized, and WATS lines installed.

Because centralizing customer service was a radical change there was a need to communicate the plan both internally and externally. Various in-house publications were used for the former; customer newsletters and other mailings, for the latter. New customer service brochures were designed and published.

## RECRUITING AND TRAINING OF CENTER STAFF

Mary Anne Stone arrives at her work station at 7 A.M. and scans the daily situation report provided to each clerk. On this day, the situation report notes, among other things, a one-car derailment near Lee, Florida; a snow-storm approaching Chicago; some congestion at intermodal terminals; shortages of wood chip hoppers in Florida, Georgia, and North Carolina; and shortages of one-hundred-ton gondolas for scrap-loading at several locations. The daily situation reports help customer service workers anticipate delays and head off problems.

CSX wanted to provide a positive working environment for its customer service clerks, whose jobs, by their very nature, would be stressful: when customers call with a problem, they already are dealing with a certain amount of stress themselves. Defusing customer anxiety called for a special kind of person. Staffing, because of labor agreements, came from two sources. Some customer service clerks came from The Brotherhood of Railway and Airline Clerks (which has since changed its name to the Transportation Communications Union). A number of customer service clerks working in field sales elected to transfer to the centralized environment. This enabled the department to get off to a quick start. A number of assistant managers/ and managers also came from field sales where they had already been involved in customer service work.

The strength of the staffing, however, came from recruiting efforts. CSX wanted to have a cross section of expertise from all railroad-related departments. A broad mix of experienced employees certainly gave them the edge in handling almost any type of problem that might arise.

The Transportation Communications Union represents the railroad clerical crafts under which the customer clerical functions fall. The company soon realized that because these employees fell under the jurisdiction of this labor agreement there would be almost perpetual turnover of employees who could bid for other openings within that craft, and thus detriment the efforts to respond to customers on a consistent basis. They needed a stable workforce in the center. With that in mind, negotiations were held with the union to protect fourteen of the original twenty customer service clerical positions by designating them permanent and not subject to the bidding process.

A training program was developed that involved one week of intensive instruction in use of the telephones, computers, and other equipment in the center, as well as education about the geography of CSX territory and train operations. Retraining and ongoing training became a way of life for employees in customer service. A fulltime training function was established in the customer service center. Consequently, one-on-one daily training and group training continue to keep all of their people fully informed of changes and new systems. When possible, the customer service center staff takes field trips to area CSX terminals in north Florida and south Georgia.

## CUSTOMER SERVICE CENTER OPENS

By September 1985, Seaboard and Chessie each operated central customer service centers. One year later, in September 1986, both railroads began operating from the Jacksonville center. During its first months of operation, the center's top managers closely monitored the number of inbound calls by clerk, the average talk time, the number of calls delayed, and the number of calls abandoned by the customer. The information helped the customer service center staff to make modifications to speed calls through and to establish parameters on the workload for each clerk.

The customer service center is able to cross departmental lines to get to the heart of problems effectively and quickly; that is due in no small part to the fact that the center has unflagging support from top management. Distribution services president Hagen says the center would not have succeeded without it: "The people in the center, from the director to the clerks, know that they represent one of our most vital links to our customers. Apparently because the operating people understand this, they have had minimal problems in encouraging cooperation to make the customer service center work. The center's intent is not to place blame. Their intent is to correct the problem, report back to the customer as quickly as possible, and take action to keep the problem from recurring."

Some of the tenets of CSX's quality improvement process were already being put to use in the customer service center before the formal corporatewide process began in January 1987. A foundation of their quality improvement process is to urge their employees to perform their jobs right the first time, because it costs money not to. They accept that some problems are beyond their control and are going to occur; but many could be avoided. The data from the customer service center helps to identify those problems they *can control*. The center's staff makes sure the customer is kept informed of delays beyond their immediate control, like weather. Instead of sweeping problems away, they want to document them and see that they do not happen again.

Like most major railroads, CSX is scaling down its work force and route miles; also it is disposing of underutilized or inefficient capital-intensive equipment such as aging locomotives or cars that are too expensive to rehabilitate. Customer service has been affected, yet Hagen argues that quality service is not only deliverable but also more essential than ever in a downsized environment. It would be tempting simply to hire more people but their economic position prohibits that: they have to perform their jobs in a quality manner with the workforce they have.

Estimates of the costs of ignoring quality in service companies run as high as 40% of gross sales. Many CSX customers, faced with strong foreign competition, already have focused on quality and initiated their own quality improvement processes in an effort to regain or maintain their market.

CSX recognizes that its transportation services are a critical link in its customers' abilities to provide quality to *their* customers. In order to be a viable partner with its customers, CSX realizes that all of its employees must understand the importance of quality to its customers and to CSX's future. To support the implementation of the quality improvement initiative, all CSX transportation employees will participate in quality awareness and problem-solving workshops based on the methods developed by quality pioneer W. Edwards Deming, Ph.D. Despite being only one year old, the CSX quality improvement process already is beginning to produce benefits for both customers and the company.

## TOOLS AND MEASUREMENTS
The decision to centralize customer service in Jacksonville was met initially with doubt by the field sales representatives. The Staggers Rail Act of 1980 had partially deregulated the railroad industry and had increased competition, not only with railroads but with the trucking industry. Field sales representatives generally perceived it as a threat because they would lose personal contact with their customers. In a regulated environment, field sales representatives serviced an account rather than aggressively performing a true selling function. Under deregulation, they would seek new business while relying on the customer service center to perform those servicing tasks. It was determined that a centralized customer service center would need good communications in order to keep field sales representatives fully informed of activities of their customers. For example, that way the field representatives would not be blindsided when they called on a customer who had problems that the representative might otherwise not know about. As CSX moved to centralized customer service, management knew the down side was going to be the loss of most of the personal contact with customers, but the benefits outweighed that loss. Some at the company felt that, if given the opportunity, the customer would never want it back the way it was.

### The Audit Trail Log
A customer audit trail log was developed so that the customer service staff could fully document a customer complaint on a real-time computer basis, including the cause of the problem and the steps taken to resolve it. These audit trail logs then were transmitted immediately to field sales representatives. The audit trail log is simple in design. It is assigned an identifying number and opening date. The customer's name and that of the caller are noted, as well as a summary of the complaint and the CSX group—transportation, terminal services, intermodal, and car/mechanical—with the ability to correct the problem. Once the problem is resolved and that information is communicated to the customer, the report is closed and the data are assimilated by the computer for a weekly audit trail log summary. The weekly report makes four-week comparisons of the problems generated by those four major groups and further breaks them down to show which of CSX's nine operating divisions they occurred in. It also shows those problems in a year-to-date graph, group percentage of accountability for problems, and the amount of proactive sales functions handled at the customer service center. Codes specify the nature of the problem for data processing: 204C is

a switching error with the transportation group responsible; 104C is a car marked and/or classed improperly with terminal services responsible; 302C is an improperly loaded container or trailer on a flat car with intermodal operations responsible; 504C is repair facility congestion with car/mechanical responsible.

## Touch Trace

Car tracing and weight-in-transit queries account for an average of 75% of the customer service center's inbound calls. In many cases, shippers want weight information so that they can proceed with billing even before the cargo has completed its journey. In December 1986, customer service staff developed the car location message system called Touch Trace. The tracing and weight information is available to shippers while customer service clerks handle other, more complicated customer calls. Customers calling Touch Trace for the first time listen to brief recorded instructions for using the system and entering designated codes on the telephone keypad. Customers experienced with Touch Trace bypass the instructions. Upon entering a valid initial and car number, the information is electronically generated and spoken back to the caller. At any point during the call, customers requiring human assistance can terminate Touch Trace and get immediate attention from a customer service clerk.

Obviously, Touch Trace is gaining acceptance: its volume of calls more than doubled in 1987. In October 1987, for example, more than forty thousand calls were handled by the car location message system. The percentage of car-tracing calls handled by Touch Trace increased from 26% to 45% in that same period.

## SATISFIED CUSTOMERS

A wall of the customer service center's lunchroom is dotted with framed letters expressing appreciation for its work. The center's director says the letters remind the staff of the potential they have to foster good will toward CSX. Typical of the letters is this one from the traffic manager in Weyerhaeuser's Atlanta office: "I have been transformed from a habitual complainer of your company's service to a satisfied customer." Others single out individuals. A typical comment was that, while not perfect, it is a great improvement over the old system.

That comment came from the rail transportation supervisor at Tennessee-Eastman; it manufactures more than 350 products, including chemicals, fibers, and plastics at its facility in Kingsport in northwest Tennessee. The plant has access to CSX, a competitor railroad, and of course, trucks. The supervisor also said that the previous system of complaining to the Kingsport sales office was ineffective because the field office had little control over transportation, equipment, or terminal problems: "Their ability to accomplish something for me was limited. You were never sure who to call to get something done. When the center opened, you could tell it had total upper management support. That hasn't changed." CSX and Tennessee-Eastman have formed a joint quality action council to explore how both companies can cooperate to improve transportation services. The joint quality action councils have been established with other customers as well.

General Motors uses CSX's XpressRailer service to move automobile parts from Detroit to assembly lines in the Atlanta area. The XpressRailer service uses RoadRailer bimodal trailers. RoadRailer trailers essentially are highway trailers with retractable rail wheel sets. They eliminate the need for separate intermodal trailers, sideloading equipment, and overhead cranes. GM's just-in-time inventory system demands fast, reliable service from those who provide its transportation. The automaker's rail operations manager says he has urged other railroads serving GM to pattern their customer service functions after CSX. CSX management thinks the move to a centralized system was a good one. As the service center director put it, "Even a hiccup in our rail operations generally will create a major problem for us. The CSX center is responsive."

## BECOMING PROACTIVE

The customer service center continues to react to customer problems but the need to become proactive—anticipating or detecting and solving problems earlier—is recognized. Touch Trace, special customer monitoring, bad order notifications via computer, and other electronic data interchange tools are in use or are under development. The special customer monitoring system enables customer service proactively to advise customers when their shipments will be delayed. Touch Trace will be expanded to permit the automated voice computer system to determine when a customer's car has been delayed for mechanical repairs and to call customers direct, notifying them of the delay and the anticipated repair time.

Reactive responses make up about 80% of the customer service center's workload. The goal is to reduce reactive responses to 50% with proactive efforts making up the other half. They hope to solve problems before the customer complains. CSX transportation's vision of customer service in the future demonstrates a commitment to quality, a commitment that supports CSX's goal of becoming the carrier of choice in the 1990s by meeting stipulated customer requirements.

# If the Price Is Right, Does Customer Service Matter?

**R. A. McClelland**
Delta Air Lines, Inc.

In 1924, Huff Daland Dusters opened for business in Macon, Georgia. The world's first aerial crop-dusting company concentrated on the boll weevil in the Mississippi Delta—hence the modern day name—Delta Air Lines, Inc.

Delta began scheduled passenger flights on June 17, 1929 and has continued since without interruption. Today, it is a nine billion dollar corporation, flying 376 jets. It has been profitable thirty-eight of the last thirty-nine years and has paid dividends for thirty-eight consecutive years.

## HISTORICAL BACKGROUND

It is impossible to go a day without a news story on the airline industry. Much of what is being reported dwells on the sensational. Still, there is a great transition underway in the U.S. airline industry. When it is often cheaper to fly from New York City to Los Angeles than to stay overnight in a standard hotel room, something is out of proportion.

Making your product different is the predicament the airline industry now faces. Delta Air Lines has faced this challenge—it has found the competition can do just about anything it can do. Their prices are the same or even lower in certain cases, and Delta flies the same aircraft and routes. So Delta started selling something no one else had topped—*customer service.*

Delta considers superior customer service the cornerstone to its corporate success. However, throughout the industry two questions are currently being debated: If the price is right, does customer service matter? And, Is customer service dead in the airline industry? Why is there so much turmoil and uncertainty within the airline industry? *Deregulation.* In the fall of 1978, the U.S. airlines were deregulated by Congress. This came about after forty years of economic regulation by government. In the past nine years the industry has aged two hundred years as it made the transition to a free-market environment.

### Before Regulation

Was there competition prior to 1978? Yes. In the face of considerable competition, Delta grew from obscurity to world prominence by offering the best customer service possible.

The story of Delta's rise to success can be traced back to 1924. It began as the world's first aerial crop-dusting company and opened for business in the Deep South where the boll weevil was decimating the region's cotton crops. Delta's founder, a Department of Agriculture agent by the name of C. E. Woolman, believed these pests could be controlled by applying a chemical spray from airplanes. He got the chance to prove his point when the Huff Daland Manufacturing Company of Ogdensburg, New York, provided the financial backing necessary to launch the operation. Huff Daland, manufacturers of aircraft, welcomed the opportunity to demonstrate a new use for the airplane.

In 1924 Huff Daland Dusters opened for business in Macon, Georgia (moving to Monroe, Lousiana, the following year), and Woolman became the head of the Dusters operation. The Delta dusting operation was a success. By 1929, the young airline had taught the boll weevil in the Mississippi Delta how to bite the dust.

On June 17, 1929, Delta inaugurated scheduled passenger service. Its service from that June date has continued without interruption. One out of every eight passengers in the United States flew on Delta last year. 1929 was not the best year to launch a new company, especially an airline. Four months after Delta opened for business, the stock market collapsed. Delta was nurtured in the hard years of the Depression and to complicate the problem, it was doing business in what was the most poverty-stricken part of the nation — the Deep South.

In those early years, it was surrounded on all sides by competitors who were far wealthier and larger. Yet, Delta survived. Some say Delta was lucky; others say it was too stubborn to admit defeat. The fact is that the consumer responded to a superior product — a product made outstanding by an employee group willing to work hard in adversity. Their dedication to quality service paid off, and from a modest few employees the airline has grown into a family of more than fifty-thousand. From the original four cities on its route system, it now serves 156 cities in the United States, Puerto Rico, and 11 foreign countries.

The history of commercial air transportation is relatively brief. From the DC-3 era to today's B-747s, L-1011s and DC-10s, only about fifty years have elapsed. The world has become much smaller in those fifty-odd years, and air transportation is the primary reason. Technology has provided the leading edge in a truly remarkable industry. Today the free market now decides which airline survives, which prospers, and which disappears under the horizon. Every carrier is in a competitive battle each day for survival. In recent years, however, the changes in the airline industry have less to do with technology, because of deregulation.

## After Deregulation

In these ten years the industry has moved far away from the situation prior to 1978. Then, there were thirty certificated air carriers. Currently, that number is in the hundreds, with well over a hundred more having gone out of business. In 1978 the national air route system was stable with competition limited to a market's demonstrated ability to support new carriers. Now, carriers come and go at will with no regulatory barriers affecting competition. At that time, pricing was closely monitored by the government. Today, thousands of fares change overnight. Then, bankruptcies were almost unheard of; and mergers and acquisitions, too, were rare. Since then, deregulation has made bankruptcies, mergers, and acquisitions a common event in the industry.

The merger of Delta and Western Air Lines on April 1, 1987, was one of the most significant events in Delta's history. It is the product of three very successful mergers, actually, having merged with Chicago and Southern Air Lines in 1953 and Northeast Airlines in 1972. The merger of Delta and Western has been called "a marriage made in heaven" by airline analysts. The merger brings together the strengths and experience of two of the nation's oldest airlines. The route systems of the two companies fit together ideally, with the combined company offering expanded service to every section of the country. It has the size and resources necessary to compete effectively with any airline in the deregulated environment. As some carriers continue to shrink in size, this merger gives Delta the foundation on which to grow. More mergers and acquisitions in the industry are likely, as the trend toward concentration in the industry continues.

It is likely, when the dust has cleared, there will only be three or four large national carriers, a number of medium-sized airlines, and a constant turnover in the ranks of the smaller carriers. Delta is now the third largest airline in the free world, carrying more than fifty-six million passengers and nearly one billion pounds of cargo and mail each year.

## Dedication to Customer Service

The industry's environment may be in turmoil, but at Delta the winds are calm. Its philosophy remains unchanged. It represents a service-oriented company dedicated to providing a superior product for the consumer. Several hundred airlines market air transportation. Delta intends to sell superior customer service and offer competitive fares as part of its air transportation package. It believes a large part of the traveling public will always want the airline with the reputation for safe, reliable, and people-pleasing service. Price is important, but it is not the only consideration.

The airline can back its claim for superior customer service. In 1987, for the fourteenth consecutive year, official government records show that of the major airlines Delta received the fewest number of passenger complaints per one hundred thousand passenger boardings. Also, for five consecutive years, the readers of *Travel Holiday Magazine* voted Delta their preferred domestic air carrier. Customer service is a state of mind at Delta. No management could impose the constant commitment to good service that exists among its personnel. The company thinks its people are committed because they love their jobs and are proud of their company.

Airline people are constantly exposed to the public. The consumer may be exposed to as many as ten people in the course of a flight. He or she may meet skycaps, ticket agents, passenger service agents, gate agents, flight attendants, and pilots. At other businesses the consumer will likely be in direct contact with only one or two employees. The airline understands the importance of public contact. Service is essential to its business, so it strives to have its personnel at the highest state of people consciousness. The company wants its employees to be happy and wants the "Delta Spirit" to be readily apparent in its service. It is policy to treat the employees the way the customers are treated. The company is proud of the technology of its airplanes, its automation systems, its baggage handling systems, and its facilities. But if there is one thing it wants to be known for, it is the airline people and their world-famous customer service.

## New Focus on Marketing and Pricing

Following deregulation, as the airlines evaluated the many opportunities and also the problems of a new environment, a few clear lines of action emerged. Most notable was a focus on marketing and pricing. In fact, pricing is one of the most critical areas in the modern airline business. In a regulated environment, price changes were approved by the government only after months and months of consideration and the filing of reams of paper. Today, such decisions are made daily and often within minutes.

The objective in this new pricing approach is to keep the price of the product at a level high enough to allow a profitable operation, while maintaining it low enough to meet the many competitors in the field. This is an elusive goal, and pricing is often a source of customer confusion and dissatisfaction. Delta's job would be far easier if it were possible to price each seat on a cost-plus basis. Since this is not the case, the airline relies on a formula that maximizes the revenue each seat produces on a revenue passenger-mile basis.

In pricing its product, Delta uses what is called revenue control. This is a system that uses a complex program to predict with amazing accuracy the number of full-fare and discount seats required to be placed in inventory on a market-by-market and flight-by-flight basis. These inventories are based on historic demand curves and booking trends, taking into consideration any unique element in a given market. With the proper discount-seat mix, it maximizes the revenue for each flight while meeting the need of its customers.

In today's environment in which the consumer is so price sensitive, it is Delta's continuing goal to provide the best service possible at a competitive price and, at the same time, to realize a reasonable profit for the continued well-being of its stockholders and employees. As a free enterprise, Delta obviously cannot sell its product for less than it costs to produce it — neither will Delta ever compromise its high safety standards. The company believes in the old adage, "price sells," but also believes that the traveling public recognizes and appreciates quality service. By all accounts, its employees strongly believe that they operate the finest airline in the world. The company encourages every employee to feel a strong personal responsibility for maintaining this reputation.

## Good Employee Relations

Good relations between management and employees are a time-honored institution at Delta. It is a relationship decades old and one that helps ensure a flight schedule that is always reliable. What is the secret of Delta's success? The simple answer is its *people*. Employee enthusiasm is obvious to the company, and management pursues a number of programs designed to keep all personnel on a personal high for their jobs and their company.

Delta practices a simple organizational structure. The company is divided into six divisions, each headed by a senior vice-president. These people and two others—the president, and chairman of the board—meet together every morning of the work week to review the previous day's operations. On Mondays they have a lengthy meeting to discuss all major policies, problems, and plans. In this way each senior officer is familiar with the total operation on a continuing basis—so much so that any one of them could, in a pinch, administer any other division.

Another strong policy is that of promotion-from-within. No officer with Delta was hired in an officer position. Each one comes from within the ranks before being promoted into an officer's position based upon performance. The chairman of the board and chief executive officer, Ron Allen began his career as a methods analyst over twenty years ago.

Delta not only has senior management personnel who are *interchangeable* in their roles; it also encourages employees to develop the role skills of others. This cross-utilization maximizes productivity; in addition, it offers opportunities for learning new skills and an appreciation for the challenges of other people's problems and jobs. Because of the policies of promotion-from-within and cross-utilization, every person employed by Delta knows he or she has an opportunity to advance. The top job itself is available, based upon someone's performance and ability.

At this airline there is a tradition of no furloughs for permanent personnel. You may call this a Japanese style of management, but the fact is that Delta practiced this long before anyone heard the Japanese might be doing something similar. This policy continued during recessionary periods early in this decade, even when such a practice helped contribute to its first fiscal-year loss in thirty-four years.

An example of the intense loyalty of Delta workers to their company occurred in the closing months of 1982. That was a year of sizable financial losses within the industry, and Delta was no exception. The story began when three flight attendants started talking about the company's financial problems. They took their thoughts to a senior officer, saying, "Delta has been good to its employees for a long time and we think Delta people would like to reciprocate during this difficult period. We want to purchase a Boeing 767 for Delta." Knowing this would require more than thirty million dollars, the amazed executive promised to take the matter before senior management, after realizing the seriousness of the flight attendants. Following the discussion, the company agreed to provide an office and telephones from which the flight attendants and other employee volunteers could mount their campaign to enlist the entire work force of Delta to support their project.

After months of hard work, on the morning of December 15, 1982, one of the most moving and emotional experiences for Delta occurred as thousands of employees gathered at Atlanta Maintenance Base to present an airplane to the company. There, neatly packaged beneath a huge, bright red velvet ribbon was a sparkling new Boeing 767—the very first of Delta's 767 fleet. Indeed, among employees and visitors, there were few dry eyes—it was so emotional. The Boeing 767, named "The Spirit of Delta" is now the flagship of its 376 jets. It is more than an airplane, however: it is a symbol of the shared interest and commitments between Delta and its family of employees.

It is the airline's intention never to lose that spirit. To answer the questions posed at the beginning, If the price is right, does customer service matter? At Delta Air Lines the answer is *Yes*. Is customer service dead in the airline industry? *By no means, at Delta Air Lines*. As far as this airline is concerned happy employees make for happy passengers and superior customer service.

# Service Quality: A Commitment at Norfolk Southern

**Jack R. Martin**
Norfolk Southern Corporation

Norfolk Southern Corporation is in the freight transportation business, specializing in the area of surface transportation using the rail and highway modes. Norfolk Southern's rail companies — Norfolk and Western Railway, and Southern Railway — serve a geographical area of eastern North America. Norfolk Southern's motor carrier subsidiary, northAmerican Van Lines™, serves the continent of North America and offers limited service in Europe and the Pacific Rim. Triple Crown Service™, Norfolk Southern's subsidiary, offers RoadRailer® rail and highway transportation. transportation.

The primary commodities handled by the NS railroads are coal and coke, chemicals, grain and agricultural products, pulp and paper, stone/clay/glass products, automobiles and auto parts, metallic and non-metallic minerals, and intermodal trailers/ containers.

In the motor carrier area, northAmerican™ handles general routes, irregular routes, and trailer-load freight; electronics and computer exhibits; and household goods. Triple Crown™ handles automotive parts, grocery products, beer, and other products.

Norfolk Southern Corporation has corporate offices in Norfolk, Virginia and Ft. Wayne, Indiana and employs thirty-two thousand people to operate both its rail and highway businesses.

# SERVICE QUALITY GUIDELINES

Norfolk Southern does not sell a product in the sense of a tangible commodity for wholesale or retail sale. Its product is its service—transportation of customers' goods. This product is perishable; it cannot be inventoried. It can be sold only when one is ready to deliver the service at the time the goods are offered by the shipper, in the type of equipment dictated by the shipment, and at a price competitive with the customer's transportation alternatives. Although *service* is often thought of only in terms of moving the shipment between two locations, providing the transportation product which is sold to the customer actually requires an extensive infrastructure of physical plant and equipment operated by competent personnel. The resulting network is a system that must be managed by a well-coordinated team of supervisors.

The competitive changes in the transportation marketplace which have resulted from the deregulation of the various carrier modes have *required* Norfolk Southern's common carriers to improve the manner of providing service to customers and of conducting business. To retain traffic, rates are adjusted to compete with the independent operator, and service is tailored to meet the customer's needs.

Norfolk Southern operates under a set of guidelines that define its responsibilities to the shipping public. Each of these responsibilities affects the product which NS sells. First, *safety of operations* covers the safety of railroad and public personnel and property; this includes caring for the customers' shipments in a manner that ensures that the lading is not damaged in transit. Second, *service* provides that a customer's traffic is switched on a regular and timely basis; that the desired equipment is placed at the proper location; that a shipment is handled on time, on the proper train, and in a manner that assures making all of its planned connections so the shipment is completed to the customer's satisfaction. The third responsibility is *cost control*. Although this is often thought of in terms of overtime reduction and the elimination of nonproductive activities required by labor agreements (actions which are perceived to benefit only NS), this also affects the product, since lower operating ratios and transportation costs allow the corporation to charge competitive prices for transportation service.

Another quality emphasized by Norfolk Southern, primarily as a result of the multimodal market competition associated with deregulation in the transportation industry, is that of service reliability. Service reliability recognizes that a shipment which arrives at a consignee's dock earlier than planned can be just as harmful to the customer as a shipment that is late, when the customer's total logistical (transportation, warehousing, handling, and inventory) costs are considered. This has been stressed to the corporation's railway transportation and marketing officers through the following definition of *reliability* that was distributed throughout the company: *The science of business is the science of service; he profits most who serves the best; to this end, it is better to do more than you promise than to promise more than you do.*

Although the "just-in-time" method of inventory control through strict adherence to tightly defined transportation schedules is a current buzz-word in logistics management circles, the railway companies actually developed the practice many years ago with the inauguration of a train appropriately named *The Spark Plug*. This train, which still operates, carries auto parts from Michigan and Ohio to three automobile assembly plants in the Atlanta, Georgia area. These plants operate with inventory for only twenty-four hours' worth of production. If the parts shipments handled on this train incurred delays in transit exceeding one day, these plants might be forced to shut down.

## JUST-IN-TIME GUIDELINES

Recently, some shippers have established industrywide service guidelines that affect interline shipments, as well as those handled locally by NS, and that apply the just-in-time method of inventory control. These guidelines are covered by service contracts that call for the substitution of premium service (air or truck) at the reasonable discretion of the customer and at the expense of the rail carrier that fails to provide the service outlined by the established transit standards.

To manage these multiple-origin, multiple-destination, multiple-carrier shipments, the corporation has implemented a series of computer-generated reports. These allow operations control center personnel to react to conditions that have caused individual shipments, still in transit, to slip from the predetermined standard. A theoretical example of the problem might involve the following: a service contract establishes a six-day standard for a shipment between Boston, Massachusetts and St. Louis, Missouri via an interchange at Buffalo, New York, and establishes that each of the two carriers involved is allowed three days for its portion of the trip. If Norfolk Southern receives the shipment at Buffalo on the fourth day and handles it through its planned intertrain connections without unusual delay, the shipment in question will be delivered to the destination customer on the seventh day, a day late.

However, if Norfolk Southern were to give the shipment in question expedited handling, the lost day could be made up, and the shipment would arrive on time, on the sixth day. It would incur additional costs for this extraordinary service; the need for this expense would arise from a condition created by the delivering carrier. The decision to have NS provide the extraordinary service might be triggered by a request from the customer or the originating carrier, or it could originate from the railway's computer-driven information system, which identifies enroute shipments that might be in trouble. The customer would know that the shipment was slipping away from the standard and might request the originating carrier to substitute premium transportation for the shipment. It might be less expensive for the originating carrier to pay NS for the extraordinary service than to transload all or part of the shipment to another mode and to absorb the freight charge for the substituted service. Similarly, NS could implement the extraordinary service scenario on its own, either to preserve customer goodwill or to recover from an operational failure that might occur after the shipment is received in interchange.

To make the day-to-day decisions (similar to those in the example) that a widespread just-in-time network requires, operations control center personnel have information originating from several sources. This includes data on the day and time of origin, shipment routing, applicable interchanges, transit standards, current status, available options (including costs) for substitute services, names of shipper and foreign-line contacts, and allowable decision parameters. Some of this information is available through interrailroad data exchange, and some must be manually procured and entered into the NS computer files.

## SERVICE RELIABILITY

In addition to the service requirements of just-in-time logistical systems, other shipments also require a high level of service reliability. To measure this required reliability and to allow management to correct service-related problems, the railway has established standards for service corridors that cover hundreds of origin and destination point pairs. The corporate goal calls for 90% of the shipments to arrive at their destination within twenty-four hours of the standard.

Additionally, a study of the service requirements of all of the service corridors led to the establishment of a network of key or *corporate plan* trains to handle time-sensitive freight. These corporate trains are given priority throughout the rail network. Each has a *plan* time to arrive at its destination and to make any required connections or interchange deliveries. Each corporate train is monitored on a real-time basis by both line officers and the operations control center. Any deviation from the standard schedule prompts action for correction. Each segment of every service corridor is monitored to determine if any operational problems are affecting the overall service reliability of the entire rail system. Also, some service corridors are served by dedicated *intermodal* and/or *run-through* trains. These trains by-pass intermediate yards and terminals to provide service for time-sensitive freight, and the run-through trains, which are operated in conjunction with connecting carriers, also by-pass normal interchange yards.

Damage-free service is of the utmost importance to Norfolk Southern. They address this in the following ways: properly designed freight cars, instruction to the shippers concerning loading practices, operation of process control (computer-supported) terminals that minimize overspeed impacts, the training of employees in the proper train-handling and switching procedures, impact tests on board trains and in the terminals to identify trouble spots, and, most recently, the use of the RoadRailer®, a vehicle which is virtually slack-free and damage-free.

Norfolk Southern operates a network of ten computer-supported electronic *hump* yards throughout its rail system. This network is the freight version of an integrated system of ten interconnected hub-and-spoke operations, similar to those used for the transportation of passengers in the airline industry. These modern facilities allow the railway to provide intertrain and interroute connections for the shipments of many of the corporation's customers. To minimize intermediate handling of shipments and to expedite movement, each terminal builds blocks of cars for each geographically significant destination, terminal, and/or interchange location.

## FREIGHT CAR DISTRIBUTION NETWORK

In addition to providing transit reliability (that is, arriving on time and not a day early or a day late), a carrier's total service package must include furnishing the right piece of equipment at the right time to its customers. For example, if a customer orders a 50-foot/70-ton/wide-door boxcar, the carrier cannot furnish a 50-foot/50-ton/narrow-door boxcar and consider the order to be properly filled. Similarly, each freight car must be of the proper quality and cleanliness for the customer's shipment. The railway maintains strategically located cleaning facilities for freight cars and makes extensive use of computerized indicators of the condition of the cars.

In the transportation business, no two cities or stations are exactly alike. One station may terminate more loads than it originates. Another might be balanced in terms of originations and terminations, but the originations could require boxcars, while the terminations primarily produce open-top equipment. To manage the equipment side of the service package, NS handles each subtype of equipment separately. Each subtype is distributed through the use of a computerized demand-and-supply forecast and distribution model. Movement instructions are generated by the model, then fine-tuned as needed by centralized and local car distribution officers, who are in real-time contact with customers and station agents. These functions allow them to provide the right piece of equipment at the right time, while minimizing the system total of empty equipment mileage.

Car distribution managers use a series of computer-generated reports to monitor the system performance relative to the equipment supply. These reports, which are driven by the railway's real-time car movement system, are produced daily, weekly, monthly, quarterly, and annually. Car distribution personnel can receive up-to-the-minute information via CRT inquiry. As conditions change, the car distribution section determines if the change in question is of a temporary or permanent nature. Temporary demand shifts simply require adjustments to the computerized disposition instructions. If a shortage situation persists, however, alternative sources of car supply, such as the increased use of equipment owned by other carriers, are evaluated. In some cases, the customer service engineering department, Norfolk Southern's liaison group between management and equipment suppliers, may recommend the acquisition of new or rebuilt equipment to protect the customers' car supply requirements.

Large volume shipments of bulk commodities, especially coal and grain, are handled somewhat differently. In 1960, the railway pioneered the concept of the *unit train*. A typical unit train handles multiple train-load shipments between one shipper (for example, a coal mine or a transloader) and one consignee (for example, an electric generating plant); uses an assigned set of locomotives and cars; operates in shuttle (*continuous*) service over the same route; and by-passes intermediate terminals.

Also, NS serves and operates several large transloading facilities where commodity interchange between the rail mode and the water mode is accomplished. Serving these facilities requires the handling of numerous train-load shipments, but, due to inconsistent demand and vessel scheduling, these shipments do not fit the continuous nature of a unit train operation. The corporation, as the interface between the mines and the vessels, has to contend with the peaks and valleys that result from a mine's plan to maintain a steady rate of production, a shipping company's need to efficiently schedule the sailings of its vessels, and the general demand fluctuations in the worldwide marketplace.

As an example of this process, Norfolk Southern handles a large volume of coal for export from numerous mines in West Virginia, Kentucky, and the western portion of Virginia to its Pier 6 facility at Lamberts Point (Norfolk), Virginia. The shipping company, which has delivery orders from the foreign destination, applies to NS for a docking permit for a specific vessel within eighteen days of the scheduled docking. At this time, the shipping company furnishes the railway the details of the shipment that the vessel in question is to receive; these details include the total shipment volume, the coal mines (up to six within two districts) involved, the amount of coal to be produced by each mine, and the anticipated sailing date. NS verifies this information with the central offices of the coal companies that have actually sold the coal to the foreign buyer. After NS issues the controlling permit number to the ship line, car distribution personnel arrange for the placement of the necessary empty freight cars at each mine. The car placement schedule for each mine is determined by mine capacity, the amount of coal which the mine is to produce for the particular shipment, and the standard transit time from that mine to Lamberts Point.

As the mines begin to produce the ordered volume of coal, the railway arranges to have the necessary locomotives and train crews in place to handle the shipments, and Pier 6 personnel plan for the arrivals of the multiple-origin shipments. The desired result is to match shipments and transloadings with the available supply of freight cars. This allows Norfolk Southern to maximize the utilization of its freight car fleet and, by minimizing total equipment requirements, to charge competitive rates for its transportation service.

## HIGHWAY AND INTERMODAL NETWORKS

Service in the highway mode, is tailored to the needs of the individual shipper of highway-compatible commodities within certain standardized guidelines. The vehicle is standardized on the basis of the 48-foot-by-102-inch highway trailer, and shipment schedules are standardized on the basis of 450 miles per transit day. A shipper can tailor the available transportation service to its own needs by simply telephoning the centralized dispatching office. For example, if a shipper needs three-day service on a 2,000-mile shipment and if it is willing to pay for the nonstandard service, the dispatching office can arrange for a team of drivers to provide continuous transit of the shipment.

The centralized dispatching office for northAmerican™ trailers and for the RoadRailers® of Triple Crown Service™ is responsible for having empty equipment available to receive the customers' shipments as they arrive. Although many shipments do not require coordination between the corporation's departments that handle the highway and rail modes, RoadRailer® and some conventional intermodal shipments do require such an interface. In these cases, the highway dispatching office and the intermodal operations personnel work together to insure that Norfolk Southern's transportation product is delivered and meets the overall service needs of the customer.

This dispatching function is graded through the measure of daily total loaded-unit mileage. The dispatching office uses the real-time northAmerican Capacity Forecasting and Planning Model™ as its primary tool. This model uses historical, seasonally adjusted demand data for each customer and geographic area, present equipment orders, and inputs provided by the dispatching office to produce a nationwide equipment repositioning recommendation. As equipment is emptied at the various destinations, the drivers and tractors are systematically dispatched to match both the available empty equipment and the current demands.

In recent years, Norfolk Southern has implemented an additional dimension to its package of services, the wholesaling of the transportation product. The primary users of this concept are freight forwarders and consolidators and international containership lines. The corporation provides transportation of intermodal trailers and containers between two terminals for the contracting party, but has no contact with the actual shipper or consignee. These shipments are often handled in dedicated *intermodal* and/or *double-stack* container trains. Occasionally, it provides, through a subcontractor as requested by the retailer, drayage service for the trailers or containers.

## LINES OF COMMUNICATION

In addition to the various services offered to its customers, Norfolk Southern also solicits feedback from customers. Although each mode has a sales and marketing staff, the efforts of each are coordinated at the corporate level to insure that the company speaks with one voice to its customers.

Although the sales and marketing forces provide the primary contact with customers, transportation line officers, freight agents, and train and engine personnel who actually switch a customer's traffic often form the most effective lines of communication between the customer and the railway. Not only are problems solved quickly between these parties, but also potential problems are avoided as a result of this communication link. The corporation, to recognize those employees who give exemplary service to the customers, sponsors Thoroughbred Service Awards. An employee is nominated for an award by his supervisor or directly by a customer. The employees who are selected receive a gift from the corporation and a Thoroughbred Service jacket.

District and regional sales offices communicate regularly with customers in their areas. This communication includes discussions about service problems that need attention and the customers' forecasts of upcoming demand for specific transportation services. When resolving service-related problems, the sales representative works with those in the corporation who actually produce the transportation product for the customer. When the customer desires to establish a new service, the sales representative serves as a liaison between the marketing and operations groups that will be involved in designing and producing the specific product. If the new service requires a new facility, site, or piece of equipment, the representative's available resources include the industrial development, engineering, and mechanical departments.

## CONCLUSION

Although the corporation's motor carriers use the government-maintained system of streets and highways, the rail mode uses an extensive network of privately owned and privately maintained tracks, sidings, yards, terminals, structures, and systems involving communications, signals, and computers. The goal is to provide, at a competitive price, a transportation product acceptable to the corporation's customers. To do this for a multitude of shipments that are constantly moving over interconnected routes, the physical plant must be kept in first-class shape, and the maintenance must not be deferred. To accomplish this, the company makes significant annual capital investments in its physical plant. These expenditures involve replacing conventional jointed rail with continuous welded rail on the main tracks, timbering and surfacing main and auxiliary tracks, constructing new or expanded yards and terminals, purchasing new equipment, upgrading existing computer and communication systems, installing new signal and train control networks, or acquiring specific new routes.

In summary, providing the desired transportation product involves many activities. Although it may be perceived as the only function of the transportation department, the actual movement of the customer's shipment from the origin to the destination is only one piece of the service package. Norfolk Southern is committed to being the best provider of surface transportation available to the freight-shipping community. It recognizes that it will not meet this goal if any of its transportation systems fail to provide quality service to customers.

# Utilities

Bell Atlantic Network Services, Inc.
L. T. Babbio, Jr.

BellSouth Services
John F. Bryant

GTE Service Corporation
D. Otis Wolkins

Nynex Corporation
Robert F. Cummins and Joseph F. Riesenman

Pacific Gas & Electric
Stephanie Amsden

U S West Communications Corporation
Ed Tharp

# Quality Service the Bell Atlantic Way

**L. T. Babbio, Jr.**
Bell Atlantic Network Services, Inc.

Bell Atlantic, headquartered in Philadelphia, is one of the regional holding companies formed in 1984 following the breakup of the Bell System. Bell Atlantic's seven telephone operating companies are Bell of Pennsylvania, Diamond State Telephone (Delaware), New Jersey Bell, C&P Telephone (Washington, D.C.), C&P Telephone of Maryland, C&P Telephone of Virginia, and C&P Telephone of West Virginia. Together they serve nearly 16 million customer lines in a geographical area that is home to the federal government and 85 of the largest businesses in the nation. Bell Atlantic also is the parent company of a number of largely unregulated companies that provide products and services in the following areas: mobile communications, information and communications systems, computer maintenance and software, and diversified financial services.

## INTRODUCTION

In the long run, it is the quality of a corporation's service that distinguishes it in the marketplace. Many customers base their first purchase decision on price, but they buy the second time on the basis of service. The key then is for corporations to focus their attention on those aspects of service that yield a high level of customer satisfaction and, in turn, result in a customer who comes back again.

High quality service at competitive prices is the centerpiece of Bell Atlantic's primary business: providing network telecommunications services. Ever since Bell Atlantic came into being on January 1, 1984, the day of divestiture, its goal has been to deliver the level of service its customers expect.

### Universal Service

The corporation's seven telephone operating companies are committed to communications service that is universal. The telephone penetration rate in the region is 94%, 2 percentage points higher than the national average— and the national average is the highest it ever has been. Testimony to Bell Atlantic's commitment to providing service to all consumers is implicit in results: in every jurisdiction where the corporation's telephone companies provide local service, there are options in place to meet the calling needs and economic circumstances of practically everyone. All seven companies offer economy or low-use service options and they support lifeline programs targeted for low-income families.

But Bell Atlantic's commitment goes beyond insuring that all consumers can afford to hook up to the local network. The quality challenge must be met continuously, from the initial installation through the long-term provision of service. In today's highly competitive, post-divestiture market, a successful company must provide the level of service customers have come to expect if it wants to keep customers' loyalty.

In addition to the obvious advantages to the customer, there are both marketing and financial incentives for the company to provide quality service. Besides the financial incentive associated with customer loyalty, an advantage often overlooked is that high quality costs less to provide than does poor quality. Bell Atlantic receives no extra revenue for sending an installer twice; it simply incurs extra costs. It is expensive to handle a customer complaint or a trouble report. In the final analysis, it is better and more cost efficient to serve the customer well—the first time.

On the whole, most customers today rate the telephone service provided by Bell Atlantic as good as or better than it was before divestiture. A nationwide poll conducted last year by the Associated Press and Media General found that 75% of the people interviewed said the quality of local service has stayed the same or improved since divestiture. That figure was even higher, about 85%, in both a nationwide Gallup survey and a study commissioned by Bell Atlantic in the mid-Atlantic region.

## Eliminating Customer Confusion

Despite the encouraging survey results, telecommunications today can be a confusing business for some customers, especially in light of divestiture-related changes that prevent the telephone company from selling or fixing telephones, and from offering complete end-to-end service. From the start, Bell Atlantic has taken the position that the customer expects quality communications service. It is committed to helping every customer get that service even when Bell Atlantic is not in direct control of the total service offering. In other words, it is not acceptable to say "It's not my job." If it affects the customer's perception of service, then it is the company's job to fix the situation. Therefore, Bell Atlantic

- Uses the power of the mass media—television, radio, newspapers, and magazines—to make it more convenient for customers to do business with the company.
- Funds the Tele-Consumer Hotline operated by the Consumer Federation of America and by the Telecommunications Research and Action Center.
- Underwrote a new federal government consumer pamphlet called "A Consumer's Guide to Telephone Service."
- Redesigned the format of the customer bill to make it more informative and easier to understand.
- Offers maintenance programs through which telephone sets can be loaned to customers when the problem is not in the dial-tone line, but in the set itself.

## Criteria for Performance

Clearly, a customer-focused service philosophy at Bell Atlantic drives current performance as well as corporate goals and objectives. This philosophy translates into a set of quality measurements that are used to evaluate technical competence and customer perceptions of performance. These criteria, called "key service indicators" (KSIs), measure the customer's reactions to how well the company provides service information, reliable dial tone, clear transmission, prompt installation and maintenance, and operator services.

Many of the same KSIs were tracked before divestiture, but they depended primarily on internal measurements (such as the duration of customer contacts, hours to install or repair, and missed appointments) rather than placing the highest premium on customer *perceptions* of service. Fewer external measurements were used then because the corporation believed it understood what customers wanted. This is not to say that it ignored the customer's perspective: it used a variety of sampling techniques, most notably an annual customer attitude survey, to monitor customer perceptions of service quality. But the direct "real time" measurement of quality was based primarily on internal technical criteria.

This began to change in the early 1970s, when the company initiated programs to look at customer satisfaction from the customer's angle. At that point, external feedback was added to the evaluation formula in the form of telephone interviews with customers. A limited use of external results may have been adequate in a monopoly environment, but it is not sufficient in the post divestiture marketplace. This was recognized while planning for divestiture, and more external sources—customer interviews, focus groups, and account team reviews—were introduced into the service measurements. The feedback received from those sources helped to formulate new KSIs.

In 1985, the system was expanded to include not only numerical summaries of customer satisfaction, but verbatim customer comments as well. These comments are further categorized into "alerts" (negative comments) and "tributes" (positive comments) that are returned to the specific office that generated the customer reaction. In total, some nine thousand direct customer comments are received each month. The process helps to identify customer standards, determine market focus and behavior, and watch for warnings of any impending service deterioration. This new approach focused corporate attention more sharply on customer perceptions and provided trend data on the market climate.

## Performance Awards Tied to Service

From the start, Bell Atlantic recognized the effect service quality would have on market potential. It incorporated service thresholds, set at very high levels, as part of the 1984 incentive plan for officers and based the remaining portion on financial performance. In 1985, this philosophy of tying financial incentive plans to service and financial performance was expanded to include all levels of management. Compensation depends on the percentage of "minimum performance levels" (MPLs) met or exceeded in a particular period. If MPLs are not attained, performance awards are either reduced or eliminated.

The use of MPLs has advantages and disadvantages, as do most other measurement tools. Advantages include the following:

- MPLs provide a single benchmark for corporate commitment to service and for the capital and expense levels necessary to maintain service at acceptable levels
- MPLs have enough latitude to encourage individual telephone companies to establish their own corporate service objectives, and to give them flexibility in managing resources based on the corporate culture and on unique market configurations.

Two disadvantages are worth noting:

- MPLs fail to indicate that there are major differences—geographic, demographic, or economic—among the telephone companies.
- Local results can be affected by uncontrollable events like severe storms or mass calling.

Although the concept of MPLs had its roots in the late 1970s, when the Federal Communications Commission requested the establishment of minimum acceptable service levels, Bell Atlantic has refocused the measurements so that direct customer feedback is the measured data, and customer satisfaction and management compensation the result.

The KSI measurement approach and MPL concept promote the delivery of quality service and represent a continuing commitment to improvement. The goal is to maximize customer perceptions of service by anticipating and meeting their changing needs, and simultaneously to maintain the proper balance between service and costs.

## Measuring Customer Perception

Bell Atlantic's service is only as good as its customers perceive it to be. It does not matter if every service measurement indicates an excellent job — what matters is what each customer actually thinks. Bell Atlantic uses an impartial process to gauge customer perceptions. Outside research firms conduct telephone surveys in six marketing areas: residence, small business, large business, directory assistance, customer premises equipment vendors, and federal government. These surveys provide the means for customers, whatever their size, to rate the service provided during service center contacts, installations, and maintenance calls.

To assure that feedback is obtained on current performance, 99% of the customer surveys cover a person or business who has contacted the telephone company within the past thirty days. This contact might have been for installation, repair service, information inquiries about additional services, or directory assistance. The remaining 1% consists of overall attitude surveys of large business customers. In all, approximately five hundred thousand customer interviews are completed annually. The company publishes the survey results monthly in the form of KSIs (fig. 1) and passes on the individual surveys to the affected organizations for further analysis.

Note that individual districts typically have results that are at different levels. For example, figure 2 shows the corporate average and the individual district results that make up the average. It depicts the time from January 1985 to January 1987 and shows a fairly wide deviation from the average, with some districts falling below the minimum performance levels. Concentration on improved procedures, training, force additions, or other activities focuses attention on those districts where the results are lower and performance is open to improvement. This has the effect of raising the average by bringing the lower performers up to a better level.

Feedback from telephone surveys is augmented with face-to-face customer contacts, which include account team reviews and focus group sessions. Account executives from the marketing organizations are assigned to most medium- and large-sized business accounts. Team reviews then are spearheaded by the account executive who, along with other marketing and

CUSTOMER SATISFACTION PERCENTAGES

| SERVICE TYPE | MPL* | APRIL | MAY | JUNE | YEAR-TO-DATE** |
|---|---|---|---|---|---|
| Residence installation | 90.0 | 95.9 | 95.8 | 95.8 | 95.6 |
| Residence maintenance | 84.0 | 92.2 | 91.4 | 90.9 | 91.6 |
| Residence service center | 92.0 | 96.4 | 96.5 | 96.5 | 96.2 |
| Small business installation | 85.0 | 94.1 | 94.3 | 94.6 | 93.8 |
| Small business maintenance | 81.0 | 92.1 | 91.5 | 91.0 | 91.4 |
| Business service center | 90.0 | 95.1 | 95.3 | 95.1 | 95.1 |
| Directory Assistance | 89.0 | 94.1 | 94.5 | 94.0 | 94.3 |
| Large business overall (quarterly) | 82.0 | | | | 93.0 |

*Minimum performance level
**First three quarters

FIG. 1. KEY SERVICE INDICATORS (1987)

Bell Atlantic key service indicators for the second quarter of 1987 show customer satisfaction is high.

operations personnel, regularly meets with customers to review the accounts. These meetings provide excellent forums for gaining insight into customers needs and into the types of telecommunications and information products that might be required in the future.

Focus groups offer another source of information about customer perceptions. The interactions generated by focus groups often provide information about a product or service that rarely surfaces in other surveys. Remarks from the group also can spark ideas for product or service improvements, or for new revenue producers.

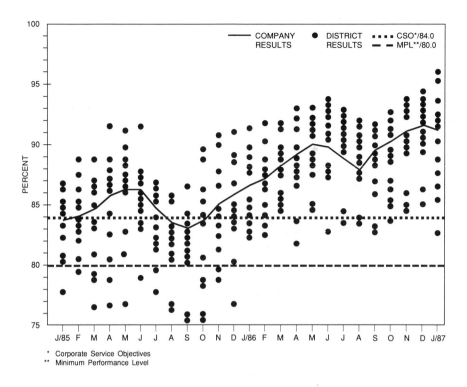

**BELL ATLANTIC NETWORK SERVICES, INC.**

COMPANY RESULTS — ● DISTRICT RESULTS ▪▪▪▪ CSO*/84.0 ── MPL**/80.0

\* Corporate Service Objectives
\*\* Minimum Performance Level

FIG. 2. SMALL BUSINESS MAINTENANCE - DISTRICT RESULTS (Percentage satisfied)

## Hiring and Keeping the Right People

Most often, the impressions customers develop of Bell Atlantic are based on their first contact with an employee. Thus, great care is taken to hire the proper people and to give them the tools and motivation to succeed. Selecting the right person for the right job plays a strategic role in providing quality service. Once hired, employees begin a career of continual training and professional development. Skills-training classes and professional seminars are regularly offered to help employees keep up-to-date in their jobs and to improve their interactions with customers.

The best motivators are, first, to let employees know that they are doing well and that you value their performance; second, to provide opportunities for growth. Publicizing customer compliments and giving honors such as "most valuable employee" serve to recognize front line personnel for their outstanding efforts. Professional growth is promoted through training classes, seminars, tuition assistance programs, and home study courses. These offerings allow motivated employees to improve their educational and training qualifications, and to position themselves better for promotion. Bell Atlantic retains its talented people by providing competitive compensation, recognition for outstanding performance, and growth opportunities for employees at all levels of the company.

### Employee-Customer Contacts

Employee-customer contacts often begin with a call to one of the business offices for service. These customer service centers (business, residence, special services, and interexchange carrier) throughout Bell Atlantic have a wide variety of programs and internal measurements to insure that employees understand and meet the quality-of-service commitment. Customer Service Center supervisors use "service observing" monitoring contacts between their representatives and the customers—to determine if employees are courteous and use a proper conversational tone, whether they collect the right information from the customer, whether they answer the customer's questions correctly, and if the work promised is initiated properly and quickly so as to meet the commitment to the customer.

Project teams are formed within the centers to conduct individual and office "work quality reviews." These sessions evaluate the quality of service provided, analyze feedback from customers, and address any internal problems the center might have. Often, as a result of these reviews, the center organizes interdepartmental teams to develop formal plans to study issues.

Quality installations are a primary concern to Bell Atlantic, both for the technical quality of the work performed and the face-to-face contact with the customer. Installers must pass regular training courses as well as a certification program that measures technical competence and identifies areas where retraining is needed. Installers are trained that doing it right the first time and doing it courteously are far better than trying to reestablish rapport with a customer on subsequent repair visits. Installation supervisors routinely perform "riding exercises" with their employees to identify servicing difficulties and to perform post inspections of installation jobs.

The requirement for quality service does not end after a customer's initial business is secured. Instead, quality service needs to become a way of life that on an ongoing basis will reinforce customer loyalty. Therefore, service technicians receive the same in-depth review of their technical proficiency as do installers. This includes certification programs, internal audits to assure that appropriate methods and procedures are being followed, and regular riding exercises and post inspections by supervisors.

Operator services is another high-contact, demanding function. When customers call an operator for information, they expect immediate response and assistance. Because customer expectations are so high, operators train periodically in order to refresh their skills. Operators receive instruction in responding professionally and developing their voice, personality, and skills in stress management. As proof of the attention on customer satisfaction, consider these statistics on operator services. The average operator handles thirteen hundred directory assistance calls per day. More than 10% of those calls are requests for information on non-published or non-existent numbers, that is, numbers that cannot be given to the calling party. This means that, at a maximum, 90% of the customers surveyed might be satisfied with the service; in fact, the customer satisfaction level for the first three quarters of 1987 was 94.3% (see Figure 1). Attention to how the customer is handled—with a courteous manner—can insure customer satisfaction.

Pay telephones, some of the most visible products, are provided through Bell Public Communications. This group handles service requests and installation, trouble-receipt and repair service, and other special services. All this, of course, remains invisible to the customer, who basically looks for convenient locations and fully functional equipment whenever he or she needs to make a call.

## Feedback Tools

Bell Atlantic uses a wide variety of tools to track the success rate of its operations. Line personnel are updated daily on their technical and service performance through internally generated reports. Regularly scheduled telephone interviews provide insight into the perceptions of customers—from residence customers to the federal government. Account teams discuss service quality with their customers. Marketing research personnel monitor customer perceptions of access, billing accuracy, competence, courtesy, responsiveness, and problem resolution. More feedback is gathered from corporate action teams and focus groups. Using these tools, the corporation can gauge how well it measures up in the customer's eyes and can identify areas that need to improve. Because the key to future success in this highly competitive industry will be to maintain an edge through service differentiation, Bell Atlantic must build on its service strengths and eliminate weaknesses.

In the future, the slice of the competitive pie will depend largely on customer loyalty. Therefore, attention to quality service will continue to be paramount in corporate strategies. Bell Atlantic's mission is to meet customer requirements for high-value information and communications systems and services: That represents an institutionalized commitment to maintaining and improving the quality of service.

# Bellsouth's Approach To Service Quality

**John F. Bryant**
BellSouth Corporation

The BellSouth story began in 1879 with an agreement between Western Union, National Bell, and a group of investors to form the Southern Bell Telephone & Telegraph Company, which later was divided into South Central Bell and Southern Bell. BellSouth is the parent company of these two telephone companies as well as BellSouth Services, Inc., BellSouth Financial Services, Inc., and BellSouth Enterprises, Inc., the holding company for the non-regulated companies.

BellSouth Corporation provides information distribution services as well as local area networks, cellular mobile telephone systems, telecommunications terminals, and advertising and publishing services. It is headquartered in Atlanta, Georgia and employs 97,000 people.

## THE CUSTOMER'S PERSPECTIVE

Concern for providing quality service has long been considered a basic requisite in the planning and operation of the telephone network among the Bellsouth companies. That concern for quality incorporated a commitment to reliability and universal availability and led to the utilitarian acceptance of telephone service. Beyond that, the folklore of each of the former Bell operating companies is full of anecdotes of exceptional dedication to the customer in times of individual and community emergency. In this tradition, the BellSouth Corporation and its regulated operating subsidiaries, Southern Bell and South Central Bell, have embraced a set of corporate values beginning with *customer first.*

Although the operating companies have for decades measured service quality by internal technical criteria, an awareness of the concept of customer perception began in the BellSouth companies in the 1960s. The realization of the need to view telecommunications services from the customers' perspective yielded another set of criteria for determining the level of service quality, one that recognizes customer satisfaction as a prerequisite to the profitability and success of the business. BellSouth seeks a delicate balance between a high level of customer satisfaction and a cost-effective operation.

Internal quality control methods have been in place since the beginning of the telephone industry as mechanisms for monitoring performance levels, uniformity, and trends in all aspects of customer services, and for providing report cards to higher management, state public utilities commissions, and federal agencies. While these internal processes give an accurate picture, in technical terms, of actual service quality in a myriad of specific work functions, they are incomplete in providing a comprehensive view of the corporation's success in recognizing and meeting its customers' needs and expectations. Without the customer's perspective on and input about the provision of communication services, it's possible to devote resources to excelling in a service function that has little impact on the customer's overall satisfaction with services; in addition, one may overlook some aspect of service quality that the customer considers vital. A one-dimensional, self-measurement approach sufficed for a time to manage the developing telecommunications industry in a regulated monopolistic environment, where the customers' expectations were largely molded by the services and standards offered by the provider. With a faster-changing technology and a much more highly competitive society came a more sophisticated customer, with a more complex requirements, a new set of expectations, and a variety of potential solutions from which to choose.

## SETTING OPERATIONAL STANDARDS

In order to maintain their position as premier providers of telecommunications services, the Bell companies in the early 1970s began the development of a program of ongoing customer satisfaction measurements. This program, which encompasses sampling and interviewing techniques, has been expanded and refined in the ensuing fifteen years.

Managing a sophisticated telecommunications network like BellSouth's, which covers the nine-state southeastern region with more than fifteen million access lines routed through one thousand central office switching machines, requires the uniform implementation of standard operational procedures across the two telephone companies. These detailed procedures, or practices, provide functional guidelines for the service order process, customer records and billing, wiring and physical plant maintenance, central office switching operations, the provision of standard and special-purpose circuit facilities, and thousands of other processes involved in providing telecommunications services.

BellSouth's practices are developed typically by teams of subject-matter experts from BellSouth Services working with their counterparts in Southern Bell and South Central Bell, with consultation from Bell Communications Research. The practices define appropriate quantitative measurements that allow the review of recent performance against predetermined objectives and monitor the effectiveness of corrective measures. Audit procedures are also included in the practices so as to facilitate the periodic review of their observance in the field and of the uniformity in their application across the region. Extensive field testing is performed to validate both the operating procedures and the measurement mechanisms in the practices.

In addition to the measurements that are standardized across the region, there are scores of performance measurements that are developed and implemented within departments and geographic areas. Often departments set objectives to ensure a desired level of quality in specific work functions.

## MEASURING CUSTOMER SATISFACTION

Although many years of experience have finely tuned BellSouth's internal service measurements systems, the BellSouth companies have had an equally longstanding concern with customers' opinions of services. Indeed, Theodore Vail (the first president of the American Telephone and Telegraph Company) was concerned about customer satisfaction with telephone service a hundred years ago. And that issue has been pursued by telephone industry executives and managers ever since.

### Telephone Service Attitude Measurement (TELSAM)

The corporation's experience in assessing customer perceptions to determine satisfaction levels led to the development of the Telephone Service Attitude Measurement (TELSAM) program in 1972. The TELSAM process measures customer perception of the service received from Southern Bell or South Central Bell through a structured telephone interview conducted soon after the customer's contact.

The questionnaire's content and flow are developed by BellSouth Services measurements research staff with statistical and market research specialization, working with subject-matter experts from the departments for whom the surveys will be administered. The development of a questionnaire begins with focus groups of customers, who are encouraged in an informal atmosphere to discuss all aspects of their telephone service. Through pretesting and statistical analysis, a list of key service factors most important in determining customer satisfaction is developed. A TELSAM questionnaire is then designed to evaluate these key service aspects, as well as overall customer satisfaction, in a particular service category. Current service categories being measured through this method in BellSouth include installation, repair, and service center functions for both residential and small business customers, as well as operator services.

The administration of the telephone interview process is performed under contract by a market research firm. Each new or revised questionnaire is pretested and refined through actual customer interviews before it is accepted as a valid measurement. A daily sample of customer contacts is taken from each operating company's records and databases for each measured service category. After undergoing an exclusion process to ensure that no customer is interviewed frequently, the statistically determined sample of contact telephone numbers is forwarded to the research firm's interviewing facility. The interviews are brief and fully structured, with standard response categories, to ensure consistency, accuracy, and freedom from bias.

Data from the interviewing center's minicomputer are electronically transmitted to a BellSouth database (discussed below) for monthly detailed reports at various organizational levels. In addition to the categorical responses, provision is made to handle several types of customer comments. If, during the interview, the customer requests further action from telephone company personnel concerning a specific service problem he or she is experiencing, an action comment form is completed and either mailed or called in to the appropriate departmental contact for immediate follow-up. Other nonaction comments made by the customer during the interview are noted verbatim and forwarded to the proper organization.

## Customer Satisfaction Plan (CSP)

While TELSAM effectively canvasses the majority of customers, the complex needs of larger business customers are addressed through a somewhat different process. BellSouth introduced in 1985 a series of customer attitude surveys tailored for medium-sized, large, and very large business customers. These Customer Satisfaction Plans (CSPs) go through a developmental cycle similar to that of the TELSAM surveys, but vary in their sampling universe and delivery. The primary difference in the TELSAM and CSP measurements is that CSP sampling is on the entire universe of those customers, not on a subset who had very recent contact; in addition, the CSP interview itself is based on customers' entire experience with the telephone company, rather than a single experience with a particular service function.

The public relations and marketing research organizations in the two operating companies conduct comprehensive, periodic customer opinion surveys complementing the TELSAM surveys by drawing samples from all residence and business customers. A more comprehensive questionnaire is used to quantify customer attitudes about a variety of service — and nonservice — related subjects. Furthermore, extensive market research is conducted on a continuing basis to ensure that BellSouth remains in touch with evolving customer needs and expectations.

## DATA REPORTING

Management at all levels of the regulated BellSouth entities rely on results from both internal and external measurement plans, as well as on other external barometers of customer opinion, to provide direction in the daily operation of the service functions, in the development of new programs and policies, and in the long-range planning functions of the corporation.

Most of the support systems, (such as the ones mentioned earlier in this chapter) for mechanical operations carry their own data reporting functions; they typically generate daily, weekly, or monthly printouts in a standard format defined in the practice. These reports are used by departmental field managers to monitor their operations and take corrective action where problems are indicated. Most of these systems are not designed to maintain historical data or to provide ad hoc reporting and analysis.

### Centralized Results System (CRS)

To facilitate the systemwide collection of results data, large, service measurement databases were developed in the mid-1970s and collectively termed the Centralized Results System (CRS). The systemwide CRS database and a lower-level counterpart for virtually every telephone company subsidiary contained up to three years' of results from nearly a hundred measurement plans. These databases offered both standard reports and ad hoc retrieval, and made comparative and time-series data available to managers in all departments on a timely basis.

### Integrated Results Information System (INTEGRIS)

This system was maintained in BellSouth for several years following divestiture. Since then, it has been supplanted by an Integrated Results Information System (INTEGRIS). This system features interfaces for the direct transfer of monthly results data from the mechanized operations support and customer survey systems; the system also accepts manual data entry for nonmechanized measurement plans. With a relational-type structure and an extensive menu-oriented user interface, INTEGRIS facilitates access to data at all organizational levels, from the line manager groups through regional summeries, in both standard report forms and ad hoc trend analysis. Much of the service results reports for higher management are in the form of monthly chartbooks depicting current/year ago comparisons of performance and satisfaction trends. Most of these publications of results are generated through graphic subsystems that access INTEGRIS data.

## Key Measurement Program

In addition to the dissemination of service quality information in published form, service results are regularly reviewed in departmental management committees, executive councils, and other corporate forums. A frequent focal point of results-oriented presentations is a set of selected measurements representing service functions vital to the telephone business. This group of key measurements is the most closely watched barometer of service quality levels throughout the corporation.

BellSouth's key measurement program has its roots in a predivestiture Bell System collection of measurements that gave a snapshot view of service levels in each of the Bell companies and helped in the development and monitoring of service improvement programs. The key measurement program in BellSouth has gone through a decade of expansion and refinement; it now includes financial, internal, and external measurements and objectives. The components are carefully selected to emphasize key areas of marketing performance and service quality. The purposes of this program are twofold: as a management report card of current performance and trends, and as a motivational tool to encourage responsive, customer-oriented behavior at all employee levels through the various compensation programs.

## EMPLOYEE INCENTIVE PROGRAMS

Executive compensation plans began incorporating service quality results in their base computations in the early years of the key indicator programs. The overall benchmark achievement numbers have been included in upper management's salary plans for several years. More recently, they were expanded to lower management levels, as a part of the annual Management Team Incentive Award, and to nonmanagement personnel through a similar incentive award program. The team incentive award programs are designed to reward outstanding performance and, in some cases of substandard performance, to penalize salary. These awards, which are based on a matrix of service and financial performance, are intended to motivate employees to achieve the optimal balance of service quality and expense control.

The Achievement in Operations Program is another BellSouth program that recognizes a teamwork approach to maintaining high levels of service quality. This program incorporates most of the key indicators and additional measurements at a lower organizational level than the corporate program. It measures and rewards performance of different functional organizations cooperating in geographic teams; such teams work to resolve problems and ensure high customer service levels.

# CONCLUSION

These programs of internal and external measurements, management reporting, organizational teamwork, and incentive awards work together in enabling BellSouth to realize a fundamental corporate value, *customer first*. Rather than new and revolutionary, they are refinements of practices and philosophies developed and proven through a hundred years of experience in meeting communications needs. Through BellSouth's service quality policies and the systems behind them, its customers are enjoying higher service levels than ever before. BellSouth Corporation and its family of companies are working together to provide Customers with the finest and most advanced telecommunications in the world.

# Creating a Culture For Quality Improvement At GTE

**D. Otis Wolkins**
GTE Service Corporation

GTE Corporation is a leader in the telecommunications industry as well as being a manufacturer of lighting and precision materials. Founded in 1935, it acquired Sylvania in 1959 and changed its name to General Telephone & Electronics Corporation because it was more than a telephone company. This name was shortened to the present in 1982. GTE employs 160,000 and is headquartered in Stamford, Connecticut.

## A NEW ERA OF COMPETITION

During the late 1970s it was becoming clear to senior executives at GTE Service Corporation that several forces reshaping the worldwide automobile and consumer electronics markets could have a similar impact on GTE's competitive positions in the markets it served. Three factors, in particular, shaped GTE's approach to quality: technology, competition, and deregulation.

Advances in technology were coming at a rapid pace in every one of GTE's businesses. Consequently, the normal strategic planning process was barely able to keep pace with the changes that had to be dealt with on a day-to-day basis by each Strategic Business Unit (SBU).

Increased competition from worldwide suppliers was putting pressures on all aspects of the business. These pressures were considerably different from those that had been faced and handled in the past. Many GTE strategic business unit managers were having to cope with new dimensions of competition, as many of the new competitors sought to gain a market share by differentiating themselves in the marketplace in ways that were closely attuned to customer expectations.

Finally, the government's desire to deregulate major industries was certainly going to be felt by GTE's telecommunications business. It was not so much a question of whether deregulation of its telecommunications business would come, but when and in what form. The lessons that had been learned by the major players in the automobile and transportation industries provided some guidance on what could be expected in the communications industry. It was also clear that GTE was rapidly being forced to navigate in uncharted waters and that this uncertainty was going to have a profound effect on how the corporation would be managed in the future.

## THE BEST PROGRAM

It was with this perspective that GTE's chairman and CEO in 1982 launched throughout the company a major program designed to create an environment that would help it meet the new challenges of the future. This program was called the BEST program, and the idea behind it was very simple: find out what it takes to be the *best* in everything that GTE does, and then set about doing it.

Participation in the BEST program was mandatory, for staff functional groups as well as strategic business units. Every unit or function was required to define its competitor and compare its performance in every relevant dimension with its competitor's. That would highlight areas where improvement was needed in order to fulfill the requirement to be the top competitor—the best.

This exercise in competitor comparison is called *benchmarking* at GTE. It served in its early years to show that very few of GTE's businesses were fully competitive in the area of quality. In fact, it came as quite a shock to many of the SBUs (primarily those that were regulated) just how poorly they stacked up to their competition in the eyes of the customer—a customer who was rapidly discovering that quality was a factor over which he had some control.

The BEST program, for the first time in the company's history, provided a clear and focused approach to understanding what it takes to be a market leader in all its businesses. The fact that quality had to be improved across the board inspired the drive to make quality a fundamental value in the management philosophy of the corporation. This value needed to be incorporated into all activities, not just in the traditional sense of defect-free products or services.

## THE GTE QUALITY POLICY

The first step in the process of establishing quality as a basic value was to define quality in terms that would meet the corporation's drive to be the best in every market segment as well as internally. The chairman and his staff decided that they had the responsibility for this definition and in 1984 established the GTE quality policy, which begins with their definition of quality for the entire corporation (see table 1).

Several key elements of this policy are fundamental to the drive to improve the quality of all aspects of its business. First, quality is defined from the customer's perspective. Only the customer can determine whether or not GTE is meeting its quality objectives. Measured against its definition

TABLE 1

The GTE Quality Policy

**Definition**

Quality is conformance to the requirements and expectations of the internal and external customers, throughout the expected period of use of the product or service.

**Policy**

It is the policy of GTE to provide products, services, and customer support of the highest quality in the respective market segments served. In all activities, GTE will pursue quality leadership with goals aimed at achieving error-free results that fully meet the needs and expectations of its internal and external customers. These results require the dedicated efforts of all employees.

**Implementation Requirements**

Every company, group, and Strategic Business Unit within the corporation is expected to develop its own supporting policies and maintain quality improvement programs in the areas of product, service, and customer support and in the area of internal activities:

I. By maintaining a *quality system* that establishes tasks and responsibilities for implementing its quality policies. Periodic reviews of the system are to be performed to ensure continuing effectiveness.

II. By establishing a formal process of *quality planning*, which is integrated with the business's other planning activities and oriented toward achieving highest quality both externally and internally. The process is to be driven by goals for major improvement over the next five-year period.

of quality, then, GTE can do nothing within itself to determine its quality performance; instead, it must look to its customers.

Secondly, the term *customer* is broadened to include internal as well as external customers. Internal operations and management processes fall under this definition of quality. This requires that everyone in the corporation adhere to the quality policy; no employee or function is excluded from the corporation's commitment to quality.

Thirdly, meeting customer requirements—the specification—is not enough. The corporation must also meet customer expectations under this definition of quality, and these are often not written down or as clearly defined as the specifications. GTE, like so many other companies, used to operate on the principle that meeting the *agreed-upon spec* was sufficient, but today we know that is not enough. Customer expectations often go far beyond what is contained in the formal specification document. This element of customer satisfaction required a new thrust in marketing research that was new to many GTE business units.

Fourthly, the policy clearly states that the goal is quality leadership—not as *one* of the top quality suppliers but to be *the* quality leader. The original concept embodied in the BEST program is evident in this policy, a policy that is not to be compromised under any circumstances.

Fifthly, the overall responsibility for implementing this quality policy rests squarely on the shoulders of each line and staff organization. This is not a corporate-driven staff program; instead, each department or SBU is responsible for determining for itself what it must do to achieve the overall corporate objective outlined in the quality policy. There will be no standard program developed at headquarters that is then rolled out to the business units. No one can talk about quality as just "another corporate program," because there is none.

After the quality policy was defined, a new office, vice president-quality services was established to see that this policy was understood and was being implemented throughout the corporation. This office reports directly to the chairman and CEO, sending a clear message that quality is a critical issue and will receive attention at the highest level in the corporation.

## THE QUALITY IMPROVEMENT STRATEGY

A three-fold strategy was adopted to the broad issues raised during the BEST benchmarking effort.

The first of these strategies was to redefine the internal measurements of quality in terms of customer perception rather than those geared to GTE's standards or specifications. This was required for compliance with the new definition of quality. As a result, business units reported a considerable downgrading of their quality performance and came to the realization that a new day had arrived with respect to quality. For the internal functions it meant that staff had to know who their customers were. The exercise to determine this, along with considering how they were going to be measured as a supplier by that customer, brought many revelations about quality performance.

The second strategy was to place a significant emphasis on improving the quality of internal management processes. Many articles have been published on this subject, and the idea of managing processes that cut across organizational boundaries has been around for a long time. The fact was that GTE was not effectively utilizing the principles of process management to improve the quality of its internal operations. Consequently, its cost of poor quality was very high. This deficiency was used to raise the employees' awareness of the importance of measuring and improving the effectiveness of GTE's internal operations.

The third strategy dealt with the quality of the products and services GTE purchased from its suppliers. In the past, performance to quality measures on the part of suppliers had not been a high priority during the procurement cycle and had become a factor only if major problems were encountered. This strategy to improve the quality performance of vendors covered not only the product or service delivered, but also the process by which it was delivered. Since then, GTE has applied its definition of quality to vendors as well as to customers.

These strategies cover the full cycle of quality, from procurement through delivery of products and services, and the after-sale support of these products and services. In the past every SBU had in place some elements of these strategies, but none had programs that addressed all three in a comprehensive quality strategy. Additionally, none of GTE's functional or staff organizations addressed quality to any significant degree.

## MEASUREMENT STANDARDS OF QUALITY

The foundation upon which these strategies are based is measurement. Each SBU and staff group is required to establish quality measures that are relevant to its operations and its customers. These quality measures are fully integrated into the normal operations review cycle in the same manner that financial performance is reviewed ensuring that the strategies exist and are meaningful. GTE subscribes to the theory that if it is not measured, it is not managed.

For each quality measure, an objective must be established that, at some point in time, places the SBU or department in a leadership position with respect to its competition. Since quality leadership is the policy, this needs to be reflected in the objectives. Objectives are annually reviewed and approved by the senior management team of the corporation.

To ensure that quality measures receive sufficient priority in relation to other performance measures, such as financial measures, the quality objectives are tied to the corporation's performance appraisal process as well as the executive incentive compensation program. Every manager, whether line or staff, is required to have quality objectives in his or her annual performance objectives; these objectives must receive the same priority as the financial objectives.

The corporation has implemented this system of establishing quality measures, setting leadership objectives, and placing performance to these objectives on the same basis as performance to financial objectives in the employee performance appraisal and compensation programs. GTE thinks this system will be the key factor in achieving quality improvement as a company management process rather than a company program.

When this cycle is performed properly, it will eliminate the tension between short-term financial objectives and long-term quality objectives. Quality and financial performances are so tightly linked that there is no way they can be managed separately. They must be managed as dependent variables and in the same way. Everyone subscribes to the theory that quality is free; but, if quality issues are not managed exactly as financial issues are, then short-term financial performance will always win out.

The careers of GTE executives in the past depended almost solely on annual financial performance. Consequently, in the early 1980s, GTE found itself in the position of having a good financial performance, but only a fair to poor performance in the quality dimension. It expects the strategies outlined above, to improve its performance in quality and, at the same time, to enhance its financial performance. Evidence in several of the business units has already begun to support this premise.

## The Quality Gap

During 1986 and 1987, as these strategies were being implemented, the corporation began to experience what came to be known as the *quality gap*, a gap between what employees believed managers were committed to and what those managers said they were committed to. It was clear that in many parts of the corportion employees' actions did not match intentions with respect to quality.

In researching this quality gap, it became evident that employees were skeptical about management's commitment to quality, no matter how often or how eloquently a manager expressed his or her commitment. Frustration began to settle in everywhere. The managers, who were now being specifically measured on their unit's quality performance, could not understand why their employees were not *signing up* for the process to the degree required for success. And the employees became frustrated with what they saw as an inconsistency between management's stated commitment and their personal, day-to-day management practices.

## Management Training

It became clear to senior management that managers did not understand how to manage the quality improvement process and to take actions that effectively reinforced the words they used to describe their commitment. For this reason, it was decided that, beginning with the chairman and his staff, every manager in the corporation would receive training in this subject. The first session of a new course, "Quality: The Competitive Edge," was given in August 1987 and was attended by the chairman, the president, and their staffs. This three-day course was designed by GTE's Management Development Center specifically to educate managers on what it means to be committed to and manage the quality dimension in their SBUs or departments. The final objective is to close the quality gap and get all employees to participate in the quality improvement process. The design of this executive course in quality follows objectives established by the chairman and his staff.

The first objective is to provide a solid foundation for understanding the many dimensions of quality. This is accomplished by presenting an historical perspective on the quality movement in the United States. That is an effective way to introduce the quality vocabulary so that a common understanding of quality fundamentals is in place for the remainder of the course. The second objective is to present quality as a strategic tool—a way to enhance a business unit's financial performance while, at the same time, provide a competitive edge in the marketplace. A great deal of attention is given to the strategic planning process and the role quality can play in its formulation. The third objective is to provide a thorough understanding of the quality improvement process as applied to every facet of business. The quality dimension of management processes and the human factors that must be taken into account in managing process quality are major parts of this course.

The final objective, and perhaps the most important, is to establish management practices that provide an environment for quality improvement. This is in part accomplished by studying other companies' efforts to see what factors in mangement practices earn the commitment of the entire work force to improve quality in all company activities. This segment deals with the roles of senior managers in the quality improvement process as individuals and as a team; it is designed to get everyone to examine his or her personal management style against the criteria established for the effective management of quality.

## CONCLUSION

GTE is now in its fourth year of a renewed commitment to quality. Measuring its success in improved quality is very difficult, given the size and diversity of the corporation. Clearly, it has made considerable progress in establishing quality as a major factor in defining success for the corporation, namely, by promoting quality performance as equal in status to any other performance measure.

Currently, there are significant improvements in the corporation's market position with respect to quality. The rate of improvement is higher than before this quality strategy was implemented. (GTE has always worked to improve quality; it is a question of the rate of the improvement relative to the competition that now is critical.) Those at GTE are just beginning to see the cost advantages of improved quality. For instance, in the telephone operations, major network improvement projects (directed toward improved quality of voice and data transmissions) are being financed from the cost savings realized from improvement in the quality of the management process.

There are signs that employees are beginning to believe that this emphasis on quality will be a permanent part of the corporate culture—that it is not just another corporate program that is here today only to be replaced next year by a new one. The company's employee survey data support this. Despite the successes to date, no one in the corporation believes that the job is finished. Even those business units that have now established a quality leadership position in certain market segments do not believe that they can relax for a moment. Like other companies, GTE is learning that you never arrive with respect to quality; that success is only temporary at best.

GTE is now in that period when the momentum for continuing quality improvement is building. Future activities will be directed continually to reinforce the strategies adopted to gain momentum. The people at GTE are finding that, although quality represents a journey, it is an exciting one.

# Telephone Company Quality Measurement In the Postdivestiture Era

**Robert F. Cummins**
**Joseph F. Riesenman**
NYNEX Corporation

NYNEX Corporation was established as a result of the breakup of the Bell Telephone System on January 1, 1984. AT&T, under the consent decree, divested itself of the twenty-one operating telephone companies which then became separate entities organized under seven regional holding companies. Established at divestiture, NYNEX is the holding company for the New York and the New England Telephone Companies. While NYNEX is now much more than a telephone company, it is this facet of our business that this chapter describes.

## WHO ESTABLISHES THE REQUIREMENTS?

Quality is meeting customers' requirements—no more, no less. Therefore, the proper approach to evaluating quality is to find out if you are meeting those requirements. One of the most significant changes for telephone companies in the postdivestiture era surrounds the question of who determines the requirements for products and services. One would intuitively say that the customer establishes them.

In fact, for most of the years the Bell System was in existence, it set the requirements for its products and services. It decided how clear the connection would be (loss and noise); it decided how long after you picked up the telephone before the dial tone was received (dial tone delay); and it decided how many calls could be carried successfully (call completion). And it worked. No reasonable person, regardless of his or her views on the breakup of the Bell System, denies that it developed the best telephone service in the world and made it almost universally available. It did this, however, by raising incredible amounts of capital, thereby creating an enormous embedded investment base. And therein lies the difficulty. As advances were made in technology, the Bell System deployed that technology with one eye on its embedded base. There was no way that the existing equipment could be made universally obsolete and be replaced until it had been depreciated; the impact on rates would be enormous. But then the Bell System controlled the network and all the equipment from station to station.

Nonetheless, there were forces at work to change this. Perhaps the start was the 1969 Carterphone decision which permitted the attachment of customer-owned and -maintained terminals to what had been exclusively the end-to-end network of the Bell System. Without recounting the entire history, subsequent legal and regulatory events introduced competition into the intercity private line market (MCI), eliminated Bell-imposed requirements for special protective arrangements at the terminal interface, and then accepted competition in interexchange services. In essence, the market for telecommunications products and services was deregulated, open to competition by anyone.

About the time that customer equipment deregulation (the ability to connect any functioning equipment to the telephone network) came along, so did advances in electronics, featuring reductions in costs and great increases in the capacity of microcomponents. A variety of products appeared on the market to take advantage of new electronic capabilities, products which were attractive in price and advanced in features and functions. And then with the advent of digital technology and fiber optics, the next generation of technology took over. The market, in relatively a few years, went from the "any color telephone as long as it is black" era to digital PBXs, electronic full-feature telephones, fiber optic-based private networks, and a host of other products and services.

For their part, the telephone companies could continue to establish the requirements for products and services to accommodate their own needs, but they could no longer set the pace for deploying technical advances. They delayed in offering these advanced products and services at increasing risk to the loss of business in key markets. Other companies were listening closely to what the customers said they wanted, were able to utilize the new technologies, and were there to meet new needs at attractive prices, unencumbered by embedded capital bases. In short, the customer began setting the requirements for telecommunications products and services.

What now faces the NYNEX telephone companies is the absolute need to evaluate customer satisfaction by understanding what the customer wants. Because if a company lacks the right requirements, that is, if its products and services do not give customers what they want, a very large percentage of them can go elsewhere for a wide range of competing products and services. And, of course, assuming you know what your customers want, then you must meet those needs to remain competitive.

## OVERALL CUSTOMER SATISFACTION

As NYNEX sees the telephone company marketplace, the generic requirements of our customers include the timely delivery of defect-free products and services supported by a responsive maintenance force and an accurate and readable bill. Within that framework, products and services have specific characteristics which must address the differing needs of customer segments. Most of all, though, the company thinks that customers will stay with it across a wide spectrum of its services, based on their overall perception of how well it understands and meets their needs. So the very first measurement, the one we think is most critical, is overall customer satisfaction.

### Customer Surveys

NYNEX approaches its customers differently based on the latter's size, but in every case it is done through direct contact by an independent research vendor to assure consistency and integrity of results. For the three largest groups this is called the customer attitude survey. A key element is frequency of contact:

- The top three hundred customers: each contacted twice a year
- The large business customer (defined as providing annual revenues exceeding fifty thousand dollars): each contacted annually
- The medium business customer (defined as providing annual revenues of over ten thousand dollars): sampled.

Making contact by telephone, the interviewer tries to speak to the person previously identified as responsible for telecommunications, both voice and data. They are the people in their companies who order communications services, who hear from their customers about how well telecommunication needs have been met, and who catch the heat if something goes wrong. They are asked, first, to rate the overall quality of telephone service over the past six months as either excellent, more than satisfactory, satisfactory, less than satisfactory, or unsatisfactory. The interviewer discusses their responses and notes their replies. These verbatim replies are then subsequently coded into one of the following functional categories for analysis: negotiation, provisioning, maintenance, billing, and other issues (including policies).

Small business and residence customers are also contacted on a sampling basis by an independent research vendor. In this case, however, the call is made to customers who have had recent contact with the telephone company so that they can report how that contact went, what their overall perception of company response was, and how the company addressed the specific need behind their call. The interviewer has different questionnaires for each type of contact: installation, repair, directory assistance, and so forth - which make up the Telephone Service Attitude Measurement (TELSAM). Like the customer attitude survey, it begins by asking for an overall rating of the contact—excellent, good, fair, or poor.

These customer surveys are designed to satisfy the following objectives:
- Track the overall quality of services over time, to see if they are meeting customer needs and expectations
- Provide managers with the specific reasons for customer dissatisfaction
- Monitor the effects which company practices, methods, and operating procedures have on customer satisfaction
- Furnish a customer evaluation of the previously unmeasured qualitative factors, such as the courtesy and helpfulness of the employee contacted.

## Quality Linked to Compensation

Quality is recognized as so critical to the success of NYNEX that overall customer satisfaction is built into the compensation plans of all managers, from officers to first-level managers. Each level has a base salary and a total number of dollars at risk, that is, dependent upon the attainment of company objectives in three areas: quality, finances, and strategy. The idea is to tie at least some part of employee compensation to the success of the company. To NYNEX, quality as perceived by the customer is a critical success factor, and so it is one of the three compensation requirements. The percentage of total compensation at risk increases with the management level.

## CUSTOMER PERCEPTION MEASUREMENTS

Understanding and meeting customer requirements depends on staying close to your customers. Staying close to customers for NYNEX means quite a few things. One key strategy uses internal measurements to provide early warnings of adverse trends before the customer sees a failure.

## Function of Internal Measurements

Perhaps the best example of that is the measurement of the time it takes to deliver dial tone after the customer takes the receiver off the switchhook. The average interval runs about 0.3 seconds, probably faster than most people get the handset to their ear. Yet the company measures that interval during the busiest hour of every business day of the year and relates that interval measurement to the capacity of the central office equipment to provide dial tone. After measuring performance and translating that into equipment capacities, you know when to add equipment because of growth in lines and call volumes. Typically, increased usage is permitted to extend the dial tone interval to 0.5 seconds before equipment is added—certainly not enough time to generate adverse customer reaction. Obviously, there are examples where calling patterns change or forecasts are not accurate. In most cases, however, the daily measurements, tracked and summarized monthly for the information of management, provide a sufficiently early warning to permit adding equipment or rebalancing loads without the customer noticing any difference at all.

The basic characteristics, then, of internal measurements are

- *Sensitivity*, detecting changes before the customer is adversely affected;
- *Timeliness*, providing information soon enough to make corrections before the customer experiences a problem;
- *Relevance*, meeting the key requirements of the customer for the particular product or service.

Thus, measurement of dial tone speed provides information about changes in delivery that are not apparent to the customer, information that can be acted upon in sufficient time to maintain service levels. In other words, such measurement affects an important characteristic of basic service: the ability to make a call, that is, get dial tone, when you want to without waiting.

## Range of Measurements

The range of internal measurements is exceptionally wide. Each switching machine is automatically monitored and measured for specific performance characteristics every hour of every day; computer screening of the data provides critical exception reports to maintenance personnel. Interoffice facilities (trunks) are tested routinely by automatic test devices for transmission characteristics and are taken out of service if standards are not met. The Service Evaluation System (SES) is a computer-based system which measures the customer's experience of call-completion performance. In addition to these, there are other measures which track busy-hour traffic, trunk group busy conditions, and many other aspects of the network where degradation of services can be detected before the customer would perceive the difference.

Detailed summaries are also developed on all troubles detected and reported to us by the customer. The customer trouble report summary contains a comprehensive record of troubles, such as type of trouble and identified cause, which were reported and cleared, along with the average interval from report to clearance. It provides managers with excellent analytical tools to assure that service restorations are timely and to identify trouble patterns.

Because company procedures require the action of a number of functional groups in the provisioning of new equipment, these groups have individual measurements of their role in the overall process. For example, circuit orders are tracked and measurements are made against milestone due dates by department in order to ensure that the overall due date to the customer is met. The special services provisioning plan tracks each new exchange access and intra-lata (local access transport area) service, and the customer installation service plan tracks the provisioning of residential and small business orders. No provisioning service is exempt from this tracking.

Measurements of answer performance and accessibility are made on all customer contact centers to assure that a sufficient number of lines and personnel are available when customers call. These measurements are made on directory assistance, repair service, and business office response intervals.

## The Problem of Internal Measurements

As noted above, due to the complex, functionalized nature of telephone operations, internal measurements are devised for departmental process components. This is important for the measurement of work group performance and for the supervisors of those groups. Yet this very action creates opportunities for work groups to suboptimize performance in favor of their measurement, rather than in favor of the customer. Like a number of other companies, NYNEX has become more sensitive to this issue, and it is seeking ways to accomplish the goal of total customer orientation while retaining work group accountability.

One exceptionally important concept which the company has taken to heart is the idea of the internal customer. In a very large business, very few people actually deal with the external customer. But, in fact, everyone has a customer: the person or work group who receives the output of your work is your customer. The company is trying to animate all employee with this idea, sponsoring work group meetings and discussions, establishing requirements, and writing contracts. Then, regularly each employee needs to ask internal customers, "How am I doing?"

## New Products and the Necessity of Measurements

When major new products and services are introduced, the need for measurements is increased considerably. Given the very competitive nature of the marketplace it is essential that marketing and product managers quickly know how their customers are responding. Adverse reaction must be understood. It may be that they did not understand the market and customer requirements, or it may simply be a failure of execution: they understood the requirements well enough and designed the service to meet the need but failed to deliver. For example, NYNEX introduced Superpath$^{sm}$, a service which offered twenty-four point-to-point circuits in one digital line. Early feedback from the marketplace said that the product was right and it was the right price, but the delivery times were too long; so the company responded by reducing the times substantially.

To attain this kind of response to the market requires that, when you introduce any new products and services, there is a measurement structure sufficiently detailed to gauge how well you are doing. In addition, there needs to be sufficient responsibility and accountability for product management in order to correct any problems and to keep customers satisfied. If a particular product or service cannot be offered in a way that will satisfy a customer's need, then the company will drop it from its line.

In NYNEX's view, quality is a marketing imperative. Nowhere is this clearer than in its policy, enunciated by the chairman, Mr. D. C. Staley, in December of 1985: "It is the policy of NYNEX to offer totally reliable products and services which always meet our customers' needs in a timely manner." The marketplace will be the ultimate test of the company's success in reaching that service goal.

# Hitting the Service Excellence Target

**Stephanie Amsden**
Pacific Gas and Electric Company

Pacific Gas and Electric Company (PG&E) was founded in 1905. As the name of the company denotes, PG&E's primary business is providing gas and electric energy to residential and commercial customers.

This utility, headquartered in San Francisco, California, employs approximately 27,000 people.

# INTRODUCTION

The primary goal of Pacific Gas & Electric Company is to provide the highest level of safe, reliable, and efficient energy and conservation services possible within the rates permitted by the Public Utilities Commission and with special emphasis on courtesy at all times. This long-term commitment to service excellence has only intensified as PG&E has entered an era of competitive challenge in the utilities industry.

It is much easier to hit the service excellence target—and to continue hitting it—when you have accurate gauges to measure your efforts. Still, there's a big difference between random customer contact (for example, while reading meters or when servicing gas and electric lines) and a consistent, ongoing, and accurate process for analyzing and reporting customer reactions to service.

PG&E employs several important gauges of opinion for residential customers: field-located consumer advisory panels; community outreach; investigation of letters or complaints; and feedback from front-line service employees. In addition, a primary gauge of satisfaction with service is PG&E's automatic, ongoing customer satisfaction survey. Slightly ahead of its time when conceived in 1980, the Quality of Services Evaluation (QSE) meshes perfectly with the company's current key marketing strategy elements: customer, price, cost, and leadership. Additionally, while the utility has reorganized into business units and decentralized local field offices have begun to deliver service, the centralized QSE is still able to serve staff efficiently.

This paper will describe why PG&E developed a service survey, how it works, and how the survey results are useful. Implementing the survey involved complexity and required commitment so it is instructive to point out examples of problems encountered while getting the survey system on-line. Of particular interest is how QSE fits in with the Management Incentive Plan (see step 15A/B, figure 1). The description of the survey process reveals a philosophy in which customers are important: PG&E's QSE service excellence process starts and ends with customers.

# ROOTS OF THE QUALITY OF SERVICE (QSE) PROCESS

## Customer Attitude Survey

For twenty years, since the 1960s, PG&E's customer services department, using local office staff to complete all tasks, conducted its Customer Attitude Survey (CAS) to measure customer satisfaction with these residential services:

- Appliance adjustments
- Pilot light work
- Energy cost inquiries (ECIs)
- Power outage service

- Gas leak service
- Service turn-ons
- Voltage adjustments
- Meter sets
- New business

Customer reaction to these services was measured in terms of service quality, courtesy, service scheduling (that is, timeliness), and workmanship.

## Value of QSE

Eventually, in the beginning of the 1980s, customer services developed a plan to computerize the process of selecting survey participants, to electronically tabulate and analyze survey results, and to use the company's automatic bill processing equipment to mail questionnaires. Thus evolved the current-day Quality of Services Evaluation. (QSE measures the first seven CAS items mentioned above; the last two, meters set, and new business, are now covered in separate surveys.) Although QSE has the same purpose as its predecessor (CAS), the service measuring process needed improvement for these reasons:

- The time, labor, and money required in the local field offices were substantial, and the lack of a centralized process sometimes meant duplicate efforts.
- Survey results were slow to be reported.
- Data quality was not high for example, because of small sample sizes.

The QSE incorporates each of these improvement goals. As published in several PG&E reports, the results of independent consultants have verified that QSE is accurate and appropriate. Even though there are thousands more QSE questionnaires than with the original CAS survey, apart from initial developmental costs in the several-thousand-dollar range, the operating costs remain lower than hiring an independent consultant to do the surveys. Centralizing and automating QSE—which saved costs—was feasible because the survey is large, it is ongoing, and the questions do not change over time.

## QSE Questionnaire

One of the first steps in the improvement process was to hold focused discussion groups with employees from all local field offices and to find out what kind of information they needed to deliver quality service. They are, after all, the direct and primary users of the survey output. The field employees identified both service- and nonservice-related factors which they felt influenced customers' perception about service. Information provided by focus groups served as the foundation for the QSE questionnaire, which remains relatively unchanged from its beginning until today. (A copy of the twenty-three current questions, expanded from the original half-dozen in the CAS, appears in this chapter's appendix.) The questionnaire contains these types of questions:

**Service rating questions**
  a. Timely
  b. Overall satisfaction
  c. Phone service representative
    • Courteous
    • Helpful
    • Competent
    • Spoke understandably
    • Handled request okay
  d. Home delivery representative
    • Competent
    • Thorough
    • Courteous
    • Neat
    • Answered questions okay

**Diagnostic questions**
  a. Descriptive
    • Number of times phoned
    • Number of times phoned about bill accuracy
    • When during the week phoned
    • Encountered busy signal when phoned
    • Number of times phoned or visited to get service
    • Amount of time before received service
    • Service received when scheduled
  b. Attitudinal
    • Reasonable rates
    • Meter reading accuracy
    • Efficient management
    • PG&E employees work hard

**Demographic and housing characteristics**

**Open-ended comments**

**Request for PG&E follow-up with customer.**

After the focus group data collection, a team organized and spent about a year in implementing the QSE process. A number of improvements to the original design were added during the first two years of operation, before the process stabilized. These changes are reflected in the flow chart (figure 1), which depicts the key elements in the QSE survey process. Although seemingly a relatively simple task at the outset, improving the residential service survey turned out to be complex and required original solutions to problems since no other utilities with similar internal surveys could be found to use as a guide.

## How the Survey Process Works

QSE questionnaires are mailed monthly to a computer-selected sample of 11,000 to 13,000 residential customers that have requested one of the first seven CAS services mentioned previously. In-house, automatic bill-processiong equipment mails the questionnaires to customers. Results are computer-analyzed quarterly to determine customer satisfaction, both systemwide and also by geographic local field office. The survey's response rate runs between 25% and 35%. Systemwide PG&E customer satisfaction over the past four years has varied between 92% and 85%, while satisfaction with individual services has reached as high as 95%.

## SOLVING PROBLEMS IN QSE IMPLEMENTATION

Following is a brief outline of the QSE process depicted in figure 1. In addition, there are examples to convey a flavor of the type and magnitude of the problems encountered, along with some of the solutions tried. These are offered to realistically portray the process, which is a complex one. Management must be firmly committed to service excellence because, as the problems show, determining current service level is not easy. Of course, these examples are only a few of the hundreds of problems uncovered and solved before the QSE was successfully implemented.

## DATA USES

Even though the QSE questionnaire only contains twenty-five questions, investigating all possible results would involve analyzing data from more than 2,450 pages of computer tables every quarter. You can see how quickly one could be overrun with numbers. But data only becomes useful information when it is communicated in a form that management can understand and can act on easily and quickly. The following list contains examples of QSE data uses which illustrates how QSE data has been turned into usable information:

- Analyses identifying the differences between satisfied and dissatisfied customers, by service type.
- Contrary to *Cambridge Reports' 1985 Value of Electric Service Research*, very little relationship between customer opinions about PG&E as a company and their evaluation of its service was found. It appears that customers' feelings about PG&E do not influence customers' satisfaction with service, and vice versa. Consistent with these findings, then, one cannot expect to mitigate negative customer feelings about, say, rate increases, by projecting an image of a caring and concerned institution.

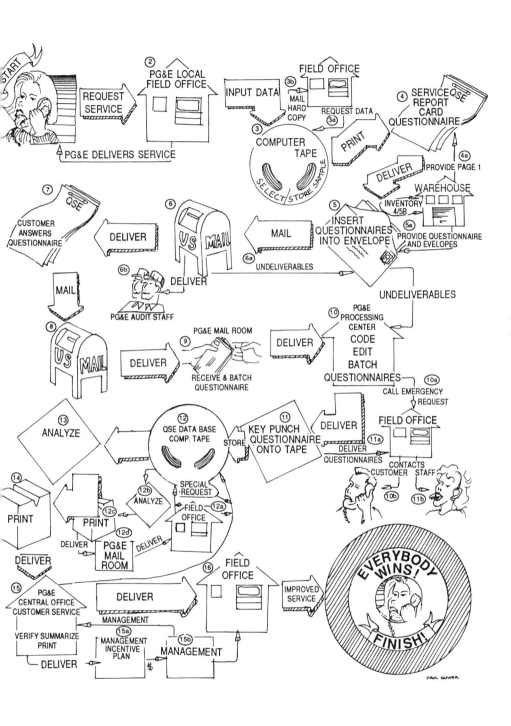

FIG. 1. QSE PROCESS FLOW CHART

- Although there were mixed results depending on the type and depth of analysis, some evidence showed different levels of service satisfaction across billing serials. Customers are billed according to a staggered billing schedule so as to have an even work flow.
- Analysis of customer satisfaction with a new, improved phone system and with by-hour service appointments in a local field office. Likewise, the questionnaire is an evaluation vehicle for pilot testing customer reactions to new programs (especially in local field offices) by measuring before/after and test/non-test area QSE responses.
- Time/trend analyses using variables such as service satisfaction with a particular service type, attitudes about PG&E, or level of busy signals.
- Demographic composition of customer classes disaggregated, for example, by types of service received or geographic location of customers.
- Correlational studies comparing QSE data (for example, satisfaction with service class compared with the total number of service reports) and studies comparing QSE and non-QSE data (for example, service satisfaction and number of service field representatives available to answer phones).
- In-depth analyses of service satisfaction by geographic field office location.
- Analyses of service satisfaction across local field offices (within divisions and regions).
- Analyses of satisfaction across types of service to find out where satisfaction is acceptable and where it is low.
- Time analyses of customers' open-ended comments.
- Analyses of factors associated with customers in geographic areas that favor municipalization and tracking to predict when problem areas require additional attention.
- QSE was one of several already in-place measurement systems used to gauge the effectiveness of PG&E's recently reorganized service delivery system.
- Use of QSE in performance recognition standards (Management Incentive Plan).

TABLE 1
QSE PROCESS: EXAMPLES OF PROBLEMS

| No. | Step | Description | Example of Problem |
|---|---|---|---|
| 1 | Customer requests service | The QSE process starts when a PG&E customer walks into a local field office or calls to request service. | Occasionally, a customer does not receive a questionnaire because the billing address is different from the customer's actual residence (as in the case of renters). |
| 2 | Input service request into data base | When a local field office representative enters service request information into teleprocessing equipment during a phone call, it is automatically entered into the company's main customer data base. | Some changes to teleprocessing screens used to accept customer service requests affected results in two of the QSE service categories. By 1989, all local field offices will have teleprocessing equipment; thus, all will be directly represented in QSE. |
| 2A | Company delivers service | Service can be delivered by phone or may involve a home visit by a service representative. | After a few of the respondents said they did not remember asking for service, the type and date of the serivce were printed on the front page of the questionnaire. |
| 3 | Computer sampling | Every month the computer automatically selects a random sample of all customers who have requested eligible QSE services. | The sampling formula is programmed onto a PC disk so that survey user staff can easily recalculate sample sizes when a change is made that affects the sample (for example, adding new local field offices). |
| 3A/B | Special sample requests | Local field office staff fill out a preprinted form requesting either the entire population or a sampling of customer names and addresses for a specific geographic location. | With a small amount of additional programming, the system offers a feature whereby both the entire population and the sample names and addresses are saved on tape. For example, local field office employees can request a list of customers who have or have not received QSE questionnaires for a particular month. This information has been used to audit our process and for surveys other than QSE. |
| 4 | Print questionnaires | The following information is printed on page 1 of the questionnaire: customer's name, account and control number, code for type of service and service spelled out, code for geographic field office location, date of service, computer page number. | A computer page number was added after initial design to help both our printing and bill processing departments keep track of questionnaires. This is especially helpful during interruptions. |
| 4A/B 5A/B | Supplies | Supplies of QSE Questionnaires and envelopes are stocked and reordered in a central warehouse. | To eliminate running out of supplies, there is an automatic reorder inventory process based on use, not on time. This is necessary because sometimes more questionnaires are used than usual due to mistakes in printing. |

TABLE 1—CONTINUED

| No. | Step | Description | Example of Problem |
|---|---|---|---|
| 5 | Insert questionnaires into envelopes | The bill processing department uses automatic machines to insert questionnaires into envelopes, batch, and deliver them to the U.S. Post Office. | A unique incident occurred when the bill processing department was overloaded and hired an outside contractor to process work. Several months later thousands of unmailed pieces of bills and questionnaires were found in a warehouse. An analysis was made to determine the impact this lack of sampling had made on results. |
| 5C/ 6A | Undelivered mail | The U.S. Post Office returns undelivered mail to PG&E. | PG&E tracks the number of undelivered questionnaires and accounts for them in the response rate calculations. |
| 6/ 8 | Mail delivery | The U.S. Post Office delivers questionnaires to customers and delivers customers' answered questionnaires back to PG&E. | In designing questionnaires and envelopes, you must comply with postal regulations. Also, a process for transferring funds to pay for postage was established. |
| 6B | Audit check | As an audit check of the automatic print and mail process, the program that prints questionnaires was designed to include the names and addresses of selected QSE project staff who receive a questionnaire every month. | Several problems were noticed when receiving the monthly QSE questionnaires: receipt of two questionnaires; print not aligned; mailings not on schedule; no page 2 or return envelope. However, mailing bills takes priority over mailing out questionnaires. |
| 7 | Receive, answer, and return questionnaires | Customers receive a request to fill out questionnaire, fill it out, and return it in the provided postage-paid envelope. | In an effort to increase our response rate, an incentive was offered for returning the QSE questionnaire. However, this practice was stopped when the response rate remained constant. It had been hoped to increase sample sizes and thereby the accuracy of disaggregated results. |
| 8 | See step 6. | See step 6. | |
| 9 | PG&E mail room | Upon postal delivery, the mail room separates out all QSE questionnaires and delivers them to the processing center. | Do not forget to notify your mail room when you make a change in your envelope or address so they will deliver both the old and new styles. |
| 10 | Code, edit, batch questionnaires | The processing center has employees trained to code and edit questionnaires according to instructions. They deliver and pick up questionnaires from the keypunch office and audit quantities. | Go through sufficient questionnaires to develop comprehensive instructions. Go through sufficient questionnaires with each newly trained processing employees to ensure consistency and accuracy. This is especially important with open-end comments. |

TABLE 1–CONTINUED

| No. | Step | Description | Example of Problem |
|---|---|---|---|
| 10A/ 10B | Emergency customer requests | Occasionally a customer will write something on his or her questionnaire that PG&E considers an emergency (for example, a gas leak). In these cases, processing staff call the appropriate local field office for immediate follow-up. | Luckily, there has never been a problem in this area. However, the potential is there because two weeks can pass before all questionnaires are received and sorted. |
| 11/ 12 | Data entry | The keypunch department inputs questionnaire answers onto computer tape. | Keypunch has an internal verification process. So once the questionnaire was designed to be keypunch-compatible, problems were minimized. However, keypunch once contracted out some work during a work overload and the QSE data tape was misnamed. It took some time to discover why the data had disappeared. |
| 11A/ 11B | Original questionnaires | Once keypunched, original questionnaires are delivered to appropriate local field offices. Office employees contact customers who requested this service and return all comments to appropriate employees for either praise or improvement. | It is not usual to include a mechanism whereby respondents can be contacted to answer a question, although this is a natural progression to the open-ended question. Even though this feature adds a lot of time to the process, local office field staff have insisted on its inclusion (and *they* are responsible for customer contact). |
| 12A/ 12B/ 12C/ 12D | Special data requests | Using a "friendly" program and computer terminals located in local field offices, employees access the QSE data base and request more in-depth information than what is reported in quarterly summaries. Each data request is analyzed and printed centrally and delivered by the company mail department; they then deliver this hard-copy report to the requesting local field office. | The QSE Data Management System (QSE-DMS) solved the problem of providing more in-depth information quickly and inexpensively than what is available in quarterly summaries. However, specially requested data base analyses are not weighted, so they cannot be directly compared with overall quarterly system results, which are weighted. This information is useful for diagnosing problems in or across local field offices. |
| 13 | Analysis | The problem that tabulates and analyzes survey results not only calculates questionnaire answers by local field office and system totals, but also weights answers in proportion to the population of service requests, so results will be representative. | The original weighting method was revised to a more proportionate method once data variability was discovered. Addition of new local field offices and a company-wide reorganization have affected the sampling and weighting programs. |
| 14 | Print results | Quarterly summary reports are printed by the computer department. | Formatting changes and revisions to make it easier to pick out the most important weighted results have been added to the computer reports. |

TABLE 1 – CONTINUED

| No. | Step | Description | Example of Problem |
|---|---|---|---|
| 15 | Verify, summarize, print, distribute | Centralized customer services staff verify the accuracy of printed survey results and send out a summary of quarterly results to local field offices and central management, including those responsible for the Management Incentive Plan (MIP). | The report layout has been changed several times over the past four years, and the jury is still out on the best format. |
| 15A/ 15B | MIP | Central office staff transmit system QSE results to the department responsible for calculating the company's MIP results. QSE is one of a dozen or so key company measures against which the board of directors assess the effectiveness of the entire senior management group. Likewise, for employees not covered by MIP, the Team Award Program (also based on MIP objectives) awards cash bonuses. | MIP was not operating at the time QSE was developed. When MIP came into operation, QSE (and all MIP measures) came under careful scrutiny. QSE staff spent a lot of time initially convincing management, users, and auditors that the QSE process produces accurate results. |
| 16 | Data use | When local field offices receive survey information, including specially requested analyses through QSE-DMS, they have information telling them if they have a problem, where the problem is located, what type of problem it is, and some information diagnosing it. They then develop and pilot programs and changes to improve service. | Since QSE was designed as a gauge of service success, it does not contain all the answers for making it clear how to improve. To save money, it was decided to limit the evaluation, mainly because PG&E service is usually good and in-depth research is expensive. |
| 17 | Customer contacts company (again) | The next time this (or any) customer contacts the company, it is able to deliver better services and to satisfy customers better. | Customer services staff had to overcome an initial tendency to "kill the bearer of bad news" before buckling down to the hard task of solving problems and improving service. |

\* *Note:* Each number refers to a step similarly numbered in the flow chart (figure 1).

# CONCLUSION

The customer services department at PG&E is pleased with QSE because it works. It meets PG&E's goals of improving data accuracy and saving local field office time and money. It also provides far more analytical power to management than was originally foreseen. To be sure, establishing an in-house quality evaluation process is complex, time-consuming, and expensive; in addition, it requires staff across many departments and a constant commitment from upper management.

Results of such a process highlight service and keep quality service in the limelight. The results are worth the effort because easy access to relevant information is essential in today's faster-paced, competitive utility market.

More efficient methods of reaching company goals mean the difference between remaining a viable business enterprise and falling behind.

You can't sell in a competitive market—you have to market. That means knowing what your customers think and want, and tailoring your product and services along those directions. There just is not an easy way.

## Works Cited

Pokorny, G. and J. Murphy. 1985. Residential Customer Market Segmentation Study. *Cambridge Reports for the Edison Electric Institute.*

---

APPENDIX
Quality of Services Evaluation (QSE) Questions
PG&E Service Report Card

REPORT CARD:  Please circle the appropriate answer.

1. During the past 3 months, about how many times altogether have you phoned or visited PG&E?
One    Two    Three    Four or more    None

2. During the past 3 months, about how many times have you phoned or visited PG&E about the accuracy of your bill?
One    Two    Three    Four or more    None

THE FOLLOWING QUESTIONS APPLY TO YOUR *MOST RECENT* REQUEST FOR PG&E SERVICE
(Example: new service, bill inquiry, appliance adjustment, etc.)

3. When did you phone or visit PG&E to ask for service?
One a weekday (8am-5pm)    On a weeknight (5pm-8am)    On a weekend/holiday

4. If you phoned PG&E, was it difficult to get through because of busy signals?
Yes    No    Don't Remember

5. About how many times did you phone or visit PG&E to get the service you asked for (not counting busy signals)?
One    Two    Three    Four or more

6. About how long was it before you received service?
Two hours    Four hours    Same Day    Next Day

7. Did you receive your service when PG&E scheduled it?
Yes    No (received it later)    No (service rescheduled)

## PACIFIC GAS & ELECTRIC COMPANY

PLEASE GRADE OUR SERVICE BY CHECKING *ONE* ANSWER WHICH BEST DESCRIBES
HOW MUCH YOU AGREE OR DISAGREE WITH EACH STATEMENT.

| | Agree Strongly | Agree Somewhat | Neither Agree Nor Disagree | Disagree Somewhat | Disagree Strongly |
|---|---|---|---|---|---|
| 8. I received the service I asked for within a reasonable time. | _____ | _____ | _____ | _____ | _____ |
| 9. Overall, I was satisfied with the service I received from PG&E. | _____ | _____ | _____ | _____ | _____ |
| 10. The person I spoke with on the phone (or in person at PG&E office) | | | | | |
| a. was courteous | _____ | _____ | _____ | _____ | _____ |
| b. was helpful | _____ | _____ | _____ | _____ | _____ |
| c. was competent | _____ | _____ | _____ | _____ | _____ |
| d. spoke in understandable terms | _____ | _____ | _____ | _____ | _____ |
| e. handled my request satisfactorily | _____ | _____ | _____ | _____ | _____ |

ANSWER QUESTION 11 *IF A PG&E REPRESENTATIVE CAME TO YOUR HOME.*
(Skip to question 12 if a PG&E representative did *not* come to your home.)

| | Agree Strongly | Agree Somewhat | Neither Agree Nor Disagree | Disagree Somewhat | Disagree Strongly |
|---|---|---|---|---|---|
| 11. The PG&E representative who visited my home | | | | | |
| a. was competent | _____ | _____ | _____ | _____ | _____ |
| b. was thorough | _____ | _____ | _____ | _____ | _____ |
| c. was courteous | _____ | _____ | _____ | _____ | _____ |
| d. was neat in appearance | _____ | _____ | _____ | _____ | _____ |
| e. answered my questions satisfactorily | _____ | _____ | _____ | _____ | _____ |

**563**

PG&E APPENDIX CONTINUED

12. The rates PG&E charges
    for gas and electricity
    are reasonable.
    _____  _____  _____  _____  _____

13. I feel my PG&E meters
    are read accurately.
    _____  _____  _____  _____  _____

14. Overall, PG&E is
    efficiently managed.
    _____  _____  _____  _____  _____

15. Most PG&E employees
    work hard.
    _____  _____  _____  _____  _____

16. About how much was your PG&E bill last month?
    $0-$25          $26-$45          $46-$65          $66-$80          $81-$95
    $96-$125        $126-$150        $151-$175        $176-$200        $201 or more

17. Do you own or rent your residence?          Own _____          Rent _____

18. In which type of residence do you live?
    Single family home    Mobile home    House trailer    Apartment    Condominium    Duplex

19. In which of the following groups does your age fall?
    17 or under          18-24          25-34          35-44
    45-54                55-64          65 or over

20. Would you please volunteer your approximate total annual household income before taxes?
    under $10,000        $10,000-$19,999        $20,000-$29,999        $30,000-$39,999
    $40,000-$49,999      $50,000 and over        Choose Not to Answer

21. Additional comments about PG&E's service: _____
    _____
    _____
    _____
    _____

22. Your responses are confidential and will not be shared with anyone outside PG&E. May we use your
    responses to investigate your inquiry?
    Yes _____                    No _____

23. Fill in the following if you want PG&E to phone you about your comments.
    Name:_____ Daytime Phone (\_\_\_) _____
    The best time to call is between _____and _____.
    Address: _____
    Street                          City                          Zip

# Redefining Quality in an Industry in Transition

**Ed Tharp**
U S WEST Communications Group, Inc.

U S WEST Communications Group is a telecommunications company formed as a result of the divestiture of AT&T in 1984 (one of seven holding companies resulting from that action).

Headquartered in Englewood, Colorado and employing nearly 68,000 people, U S WEST is made up of three principal telephone operating companies, Mountain Bell, Northwestern Bell and Pacific Northwest Bell plus a number of other diversified subsidiaries.

## BACKGROUND: DIVESTITURE OF THE BELL SYSTEM

The world standard for telephone networks is, without question, the Bell telephone network in the United States. Designed and built as a single system, the Bell network has long been noted for its speed, accuracy, and cost-efficiency in switching and completing millions of telephone calls everyday. The 1984 breakup of the Bell System divided that network into seven regional operations. In one of those regional companies, U S WEST, Inc., management felt that the breakup and its primary causes—new technology and growing competition—called for a reexamination of the company's relationship with its customers.

For fifty years, Bell's definition of quality service had been rooted in the policy goals defined by the Communications Act of 1934. The primary thrust of those goals was to put "a phone in every home," and to assure that each phone had access to every other phone. This was achieved by providing local monopolies to the telephone companies and by substituting regulation for competition. Since the goals were to make phone service both affordable and reliable, regulators encouraged long-term depreciation of equipment and measurable standards for service. These, combined with the natural propensity of engineers to set *standards*, led to a highly internalized concept of quality service.

Anyone who worked in the Bell System during the past thirty or forty years does not think of an *index* as something in the back of a book. They know an index is something posted on the wall, such as 98. In an operator service office, this might mean that 98% of all calls were answered within ten seconds. In a business office, it might mean that the installation dates promised to customers were met 98% of the time. In a repair bureau, it might mean that 98% of trouble reports were resolved within twenty-four hours. Everyone knew that a 98 was good. A 97 was not.

In other words, the company had very rigid standards of quality, but they were based on management's (and regulators') perceptions of quality. The target of the prescribed levels was internal efficiency. This resulted in an *averaged* treatment of customers, with little attempt to judge the seriousness of a customer's need. (One cannot say there was *no* attempt to do so, because extraordinary efforts, such as an after-hours' mission to repair a disabled person's phone, were often reported and rewarded. But, generally speaking, customers were told the rules rather than granted the exception. Those rules were seen as necessary to maintain control of the vast Bell network of wires—and workers.)

Furthermore, the sometimes-conflicting goals of low cost and high quality led to elaborate mechanisms to *size the force*. Instead of focusing on customer satisfaction, management monitored the level of customer complaints. When complaints reached unacceptable levels, they hired a few more people to get those installations or repairs done, or to get those calls answered faster.

None of these observations is meant to suggest that the Bell System lacked a service ethic. Indeed, there was constant emphasis on *the spirit of service*. Its symbol was Angus MacDonald, a lineman who donned snowshoes and walked for miles through a blizzard to repair broken lines. His effort was immortalized in a painting that hung on office walls across the company. In fact, Bell people even measured their performance in blizzards, fires, and floods against comparable restoration efforts after previous blizzards, fires and floods.

So the Bell culture provided a long list of standards against which employees, managers, and regulators measured almost every step of every task. There was a lot of emphasis on *quality* — as defined by everyone but the customer. Thus, nobody knew that the customer was less than satisfied, perhaps not even the customer himself or herself, until some eager entrepreneurs introduced new technology (much of it developed by the Bell System) faster than Bell did.

At the same time, the distinctions between communicating and computing were fading. In short order, this new environment outgrew the parameters of the Communications Act. And this new competition not only alarmed the Bell System — it also caught regulators and policymakers almost totally unprepared. While they debated, technology marched onward, creating an environment in which divestiture of the Bell System was perhaps inevitable, (as it seems now in 20–20 hindsight).

## MARKET-BASED MANAGEMENT

As noted earlier, that divestiture created seven regional companies to manage the local Bell networks. Reacting to this environment in which U S West originated, its management undertook a reexamination of the company's relationship with its customers: *Who are they? How can our network not only carry their voices, but also help them manage their time and improve their lives? How can we do a better job of listening to customers and responding to them?*

As that examination progressed, the company's managers and strategists developed a new concept of quality. They sought to redefine the company's output in terms that went beyond rigid, generic, internal expectations of specific customers. For example, meeting a Wednesday installation date 98% of the time is good; but making the customer stay home all day Wednesday because you cannot name a specific hour, or will not come after hours, is not good. This process has led not only to a new emphasis on listening to customers and responding to their individual wishes, but also to a completely new corporate strategy and corporate structure.

A key element of U S WEST's new strategy is *managing markets* instead of managing products, services, or territories. In this way, managers can focus on meeting customers' needs with whatever mix of products and services, at whatever locations, are necessary to solve the customers' information-management problems. Another element in the company's strategy is *performing effectively*, both to control internal costs and to respond to the customer's definition of quality. In fact, the creation of this author's job—vice president of quality management—was a step toward fulfilling both the market strategy and the effectiveness strategy: this position is charged not only with drawing together all programs for quality in the company, but also with ensuring that a market approach to quality is shared throughout the organization. Creation of this position was one of many measures in the company's new approach to customers and to quality, an approach known as *market-based management*.

An internal report described the process as follows: "We have to let the markets we serve define the way we serve them. We've called this focus market-based management and we've adopted it as our new management philosophy." In other words, the company decided it must redefine quality as going far beyond an excellent adherence to engineering (or regulatory) standards. It had to define quality, instead, as satisfying the customer's needs with the right solutions to the customer's problems. That includes good products and good services. But it starts with good listening.

By 1986 U S WEST faced the challenge of pushing this idea into every part of the organization. Planners began restructuring the company's existing businesses into lean, effective market units. At the same time, it was building efficient, centralized groups to support those market units with common services. As a first step in this process, strategists brought many Mountain Bell, Northwestern Bell, and Pacific Northwest Bell functions under common management. This allowed the development of better focus and consistency in meeting customers' needs. The company also began a market unit planning process. Planners were asked to determine the markets U S WEST served, the appropriate strategies for succeeding in those markets, and the opportunities that existed to meet customer needs in new ways.

Many of the changes were invisible. More apparent to the company's customers was bringing under common management the groups that provide connections to long-distance carriers, coin telephone service, and services to customers in government and education. Large customers began almost immediately to comment on the improved quality of U S WEST's service. What they were noticing, initially, were *simplification* (especially, having one point of contact) and consistency (that is, having the same procedures at Northwestern Bell in Minneapolis as in Mountain Bell at Boise).

By 1987 the company began naming specific market units, such as home and personal services, government and education markets, large business, and general business. In each of these market units, management is charged with determining how customers use and distribute information, and how U S WEST can improve those processes—at a profit to the customer and to U S WEST. Today, all functions of the three Bell companies and leadership of the market units are under common management. They operate under the umbrella name U S WEST Communications. In short, the essence of U S WEST's move to market-based management is redefining quality from the customer's point of view. This effort is becoming apparent throughout the organization.

## IMPLEMENTATION OF SERVICE QUALITY IMPROVEMENT
Here are a few examples, some old and some new, of U S WEST's approach to quality management.

### Service Measurement
In the past, a sampling of customers was asked how well the company was meeting its standards: for example, *Did the installer arrive on Wednesday, as scheduled?* The results were reported in the indexes discussed earlier. After divestiture, U S WEST developed a new management tool it called the Market Perception Survey. This study is based on customers' definitions of good service: *Were you satisfied or dissatisfied with our service? Why?* Customers' verbatim comments are used not only to measure but also to guide the company's behavior.

### Employee Input
U S WEST operates a widely recognized employee suggestion plan, which received and evaluated 5,481 employee suggestions in 1987, accepting 689. These ideas were credited with either reducing expenses or increasing revenues by a total of twelve million dollars and with improving service in dozens of small but important ways. Another vehicle for developing employee ideas is called The Aviary. This facility offers employees both time and money to develop ideas that show promise for improving the quality of U S WEST's products, services, or processes, as well as for developing new products.

### Resource Allocation
More than half the jobs in America involve the creation, distribution, processing, and interpretation of information. It is a big business, nationally and internationally. To monitor this gigantic market, to assess what it means to the company and particularly to its customers, U S WEST created a separate, strategy-level organization reporting to the office of the chairman. Known as U S WEST Strategic Marketing, the organization includes market researchers and other specialists who focus on the information-management functions that customers will want in the years ahead.

A companion organization focuses on the technology customers will need to fulfill those functions. Known as U S WEST Advanced Technologies, this group of scientists, engineers, and technicians both evaluate and develop new technology. The office of the chairman has approved spending up to 3% of the company's total sales on research and development by 1990.

## Management Behavior

The acid test of market-based management, with its new emphasis on quality from the customer's point of view, is the behavior of management. From the beginning, U S WEST has made it clear that quality service and customer focus are more than just buzzwords or just another program from headquarters. Management bonuses are based on two components, service and earnings, weighted equally.

Workshops in market-based management are taught by the officers themselves to hundreds of senior managers and professionals. The company's new vice president of sales in home and personal services, has visited every service representative in the fourteen states the company serves. She stays in touch with those service reps through newsletters and reply forms. When the company's officers gathered for a planning retreat last summer, the featured speakers were customers—not only business customers, but also *ordinary* residential customers. The company's magazine features success stories of people who focus on quality, both inside and outside the company. One was Mrs. B., a 92-year-old who sold her family's furniture during the Depression and eventually built the largest single-store furniture business in the nation.

U S WEST's president has made it clear that Monday-morning meetings and management appraisals are to spend more time discussing *customer* items than *business* items. When customer-contact employees suggested that they themselves dress more professionally, management said yes. When customers suggested longer hours, management said yes. In fact, the three Bell companies today offer 24-hour home-phone centers, where customers can call, toll-free, with questions and requests about their service, their bills, or U S WEST's products and services.

Employees are empowered to make many decisions on their own, because the customer is more important than *the rules.* Instead of *Wednesday* installations, the company will schedule appointments for *3 p.m. Wednesday*—or even *3 a.m.* Among other steps in 1988, the company is contemplating sending each of its nine million customers a report card. On a smaller scale several years ago, one of the U S WEST companies used the card to find customers with *little irritations* that could be resolved before they became big irritations. When the company fixed these problems, the most common customer response was "Here's a company that cares about the quality of its work."

## CONCLUSION

U S WEST viewed the breakup of the Bell System not as an ending, but as a beginning. Reevaluating a hundred-year heritage of carefully measured, averaged service, the company has redefined quality from the customer's point of view.

The company's primary strategies today are to effectively focus upon and meet customers' needs for quality products and services in the information age. The key is enabling employees to provide the kind of service they know the customer wants, needs, and deserves. The key word is *quality*.

# The Service Quality Effectiveness Model

A significant conclusion drawn from the case studies in *When America Does It Right* is that there is no single best way to achieve successful service quality operations. All of the case studies represent highly successful implementations. While similar principles and strategies have been applied, no two processes are the same. Each company has gone about it in a different way. It appears, in fact, that this individual uniqueness is a key to success. The managers of these companies have tailored their processes to their organizational cultures and customer needs, adapted appropriate technologies to their individual environments, and have been creative in dealing with human factors.

What follows is the service quality effectiveness model which presents the operational factors needing to be addressed to achieve a successful quality process. The model provides guidance and direction, yet is non-prescriptive. To illustrate this point, notice that the Quality Awareness segment of the model highlights the need for group and individual awards, but does not prescribe non-financial awards in preference to financial awards. The model is designed to facilitate the kind of creative initiatives that make for high quality achievement.

Figure 1 shows an illustration of the model. The central focus is on the customer, recognizing that all organizations have both internal and external customers. The importance of working effectively with the internal customer can be seen in IBM's "Business Process Management" approach. IBM views internal, cross-functional analysis as a key to dealing successfully with dynamic business change. By defining who the internal customers are and by giving emphasis to horizontal operating processes and objectives, their method bypasses functional and operating unit boundaries that may limit efforts to improve operating performance. Also, by definition, process flow management calls for the total involvement of suppliers and customers to better understand business requirements.

Having defined who the customers are, it is important to appreciate that productivity and quality are mutually complimentary goals. In case after case it has been demonstrated that thrusts to improve product and service quality lead to direct cost savings and indirect benefits (i.e., increasing market share and retaining existing customers).

There are seven service quality effectiveness success factors shown in the model. Together, these factors form a proven approach to improving service quality operations. There is no priority intended in the order of their presentation. To achieve the highest levels of customer service, it is vital that attention be given to all of the factors.

# CUSTOMER SATISFACTION AND BEYOND

## Measuring Customer Perceptions
- **Type of Measurements.** Written surveys, telephone surveys, focus groups, on-site interviews, mail-back cards.
- **Objectivity of Measurement Process.** Use of outside firm, use of staff group, statistically confident sample size.
- **Translating Customer Perceptions Into Improvement Actions.** Number of improvement programs, implementation results, impact of change on customers' perceptions of issues.

## Trends
- **Five Year Time Line**
- **Identifying Individual Factors**
- **Significance of Factors to Total Trend**

## New Initiatives
- **Number of New Initiatives.** Impact on quality performance of product/ service.
- **Magnitude.** Degree of impact in both internal and external business areas, level of investment.
- **Creativity.** Extent to which new initiatives reflect new thinking, risk taking, and leadership within industry.
- **Consistency.** Number and significance of new initiatives over the last five years.

## Competitive Analysis
- **Benchmarking.** Identifying present and future competitors and their respective key customer service factors, developing comparative measurements, implementing an ongoing measurement system.
- **Actions to Improve Competitive Position.** Programs to go beyond present levels of service, plans and results to improve service where rated at or below that of competition.

## Negative Service Indicators
- **Loss of Customers.** Trend in customer attrition, identification of causes for attrition, process for solutions and corrective action plans, analysis of the number of customer complaints, frequency distribution by type of complaint.

## Preventing Customer Attrition

Market segmentation and analysis, root cause and problem anticipation analysis, customer surveys and feedback, and customer retention incentives, programs, and results.

# QUALITY ASSURANCE

## Measurement of Service Performance

- **Design of Internal Measurement System.** Determine areas of business significance; establish service contracts; set key process control parameters; determine business objectives and establish standards for accuracy, timeliness, responsiveness, and intangible service factors; design reporting system.
- **Design of Third Party/External Service Delivery Measurement System.** Determine key performance criteria, develop performance standards, select third parties, build performance standards into purchase contracts, establish service performance reporting system, perform on-site reviews.

## Managing For Continuous Improvement

Establish multiple level performance feedback reports, provide continuous error and service problem review process, plan for corrective action and report on results, conduct a weekly executive review of total performance achievement with pinpointing responsibility to reverse negative trends, plan for future investments to improve quality.

## Performance Audit

Establish clear customer service and quality assurance policies and procedures, create an independent staff function to conduct reviews of quality assurance and operations functions, determine appropriate frequency and scope of audits, design format for reporting findings, plan for follow-up actions and progress reporting to resolve all open issues.

## Comparability of Quality Measurement Process

Where multiple business units exist assure consistent design, maintenance, content, and control of customer service and quality assurance policies and procedures; establish procedure and policies change approval process; develop a consolidated service quality performance reporting system to include all business units; require management commentary on variances to acceptable performance levels; emphasize comparability in audits; encourage exchange of information on positive performance between business units.

# METHODS, SYSTEMS, AND TECHNOLOGY

## Methods Improvement Analysis

Establish systematic operations review process with dual emphasis on productivity and quality, utilize professional methods analysts to direct and facilitate review process, involve all levels of the organization, stress results orientation, quantify benefits, utilize multiple approaches and analytical tools, establish periodic progress reporting, set improvement goals.

## Systems Quality Assurance

Utilize project management techniques to establish and monitor system design and implementation timeframes, assign independent group responsibility for final acceptance testing and implementation approval, establish key performance indicators and monitor with trend analysis.

## Technology — The Strategic Variable In Product Differentiation

Establish ongoing responsibility for applied technology research; determine state-of-the-art applications in key business areas; evaluate potential impact on service quality through introducing new technologies; establish reporting on number, trends magnitude, and results on quality performance; evaluate competitor's use of technology; develop knowledge engineering capability for expert systems applications.

# QUALITY AWARENESS

## Creating a Quality Culture

Top management initiation and involvement in the total quality process over time, creation of a quality belief statement for the company (what people believe about their company's intention to deliver quality is more important than all the systems and technologies brought to bear on the quality issue), incorporate quality improvement plans into overall annual and strategic business plans, establish a tiered quality performance and evaluation reporting system highlighting key performance indicators for senior management, provide training in quality techniques to everyone in the organization, create multiple recognition awards and incentives for quality performance.

## A Quality Awareness Process

Continual highlighting of quality through company media, contests, and promotions; bring focus to exceptional and sustained quality performance through group and individual awards; invite headquarters and external dignitaries to participate in quality awareness programs.

# TRAINING

## Quality Orientation

Quality orientation should involve *all* individuals in the company and should include such factors as:

- the company's competitive situation and the importance of quality in its industry,
- the balance needed between productivity and quality,
- a personal message from the chief operating officer or the chief executive officer of the company indicating his support of and belief in the importance of quality,
- how the company measures service quality,
- the quality performance reporting system,
- the importance of meeting and exceeding customer expectations,
- how customer service level standards are achieved,
- the need to comply with federal and state legislation,
- how quality performance results are presented to management,
- the importance of high levels of quality performance to personal career development and to the future success of the company.

## Training in Quality Techniques

Train everyone in the company. *Senior management* training highlights include the service quality goal setting process, key service quality programs, management visibility in creating or enhancing a quality culture, and customer requirements.

*Middle management* training includes quality orientation in resource allocation, program development, program maintenance, and promoting customer partnerships.

*Supervisor* training covers the tools and techniques for managing a quality program, feedback mechanisms to improve quality, and maintaining the program.

*Technical personnel and workers* are instructed in tools for measurement and control, planning, and improvement. Detailed instruction is provided in understanding and applying the concepts of reliability, responsiveness, assurance, empathy, and achieving a quality presence.

# INVOLVEMENT

## Employee Participation in Quality Improvement Programs

Quality improvement programs in this context include quality circles and suggestion systems. The extent of participation is as important as the programs themselves and is measured by such factors as the number of programs in place, number of employees involved, five year trend in employee participation rates, and results achieved.

## Feedback on Quality Performance

Continued employee involvement in quality improvement programs is enhanced by rapid feedback and high visibility. Use automated systems to provide daily performance feedback to individuals, supervisors, and managers. Company media may be used to highlight high achievers and outstanding units. Numerous opportunities should be created to display quality performance statistics.

## Management Visibility

Management visibility takes several forms and is a crucial factor in developing successful quality processes. The creation of a quality credo by senior management is one way to increase management's visibility. A quality credo not only establishes management's involvement and commitment to quality, but further, provides direction, focus, and purpose to the entire organization.

Other ways to increase management's visibility are to create quality components within business plans, make periodic statements on quality in public and in-house media, integrate a quality policy into formal vendor relationships, create quality forums with key customers, and personally participate in quality recognition events.

# RECOGNITION

The most successful service quality companies in the United States use numerous approaches to recognize outstanding quality performance. Recognition is linked to meeting customer needs; both internal and external customers needs are considered and recognition is largely non-financial.

## Programs for Team Recognition

- **Weekly Executive Meetings on Quality Performance Results**
- **Quality Club for High Achieving Units**
- **Quality "Hotline."** Designated quality experts available to advise employees on proper procedures.
- **In-House Newsletters, Bulletins and T.V.**
- **Quality Awareness Month.** A month long series of contests and recognition for outstanding quality performance.
- **Department Recognition Awards for Outstanding Quality Performance**
- **Display of Departmental Quality Performance Trends**
- **Quality Circle Presentations to Senior Management**
- **Dinners for High Achieving Units**

## Programs For Individual Recognition
- Quality Employee of the Month
- Incentive Awards/Gift Certificates
- Display of High Quality Achievers Photographs in Board of Directors Conference Room
- Quality Commendations for Individual Customer Satisfaction Efforts
- Video Taping and Display of High Achievers' Comments on Quality
- Photographs and Commentary in Company Publications
- Quality Contest Awards

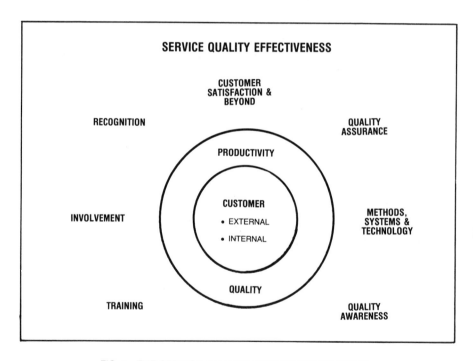

FIG. 1. THE SERVICE QUALITY EFFECTIVENESS MODEL

# Belief Systems

Belief systems are the single most significant driving forces in the business world. Our economy and business structures are based on a complex set of beliefs. Whether a company chooses to organize along centralized or decentralized lines, adopt a participative management philosophy, introduce wage incentive plans, invest in research and development programs or change its position regarding the importance of quality, the decisions are fundamentally based on beliefs.

It took a long time for a large part of America's business leadership to recognize that achieving high levels of quality was a *management* issue and responsibility. The belief seemed to be that *others* were to blame for poor quality; that the government or the unions or poor worker attitudes were the cause of our quality and productivity problems. All the while America had its quality stars. Companies like Warner-Lambert, Firestone, Metropolitan Life, Eastman Kodak, American Express, Mack Trucks, Caterpillar Tractor, Hewlett-Packard, Digital Equipment, Delta Air Lines and many others were there to serve as role models.

Importantly, many of the stories told by the contributing authors to this book demonstrate that every company has the resources needed to change. The deciding factor is whether their beliefs will motivate them to change. Implementing new beliefs, particularly under adverse conditions, becomes a powerful element and expression of leadership. Getting rid of the "sunk cost" in beliefs that no longer work has been a strength of American leadership in all walks of life. In fact, it's one of the things we are best at.

Fortunately, the record shows that creating a strong, positive quality belief system is a money-making proposition. One of the companies contributing to this book, for example, had a warranty system based on a lack of trust, inspection that relied on after the fact detection of poor quality, long and complicated claim processing and ineffective use of warranty data. A complete change in their warranty system and improved product quality has resulted in their reducing warranty costs by 50%, reducing warranty staff administrators by two-thirds, increased customer satisfaction and the ability to market new services. Ford Motor Company, in its case study, reports that it created a "total customer focus" and reaped the benefits of increased market share, customer satisfaction and a sense of gratification among its employees.

In many companies, implementation or rededication of its energies to superior quality performance begins with creating a "quality credo". Most often, the credo is presented in a one or two page statement highlighting quality management principles. In some cases, the statement on quality is imbedded with a corporate policy statement with a separate vehicle used for emphasizing quality. A third approach may be seen in the National Westminster Bank's broader statement of their management beliefs that includes a major section on their commitment to quality. In reviewing the credos, several principles surface as being most significant and are found to apply across a broad range of industries.

**Customer driven quality standards.** There is general agreement that quality performance should be measured against customers' perception of and needs or requirements for service rather than by internal criteria.

**Enthusiasm.** Service quality is viewed as including intangible factors such as attitude, demeanor, tone of voice, responsiveness and other personal attributes. Where manufactured goods are involved, the above ingredients are seen as enhancing the product in the delivery and maintenance phases of operations.

**Consistency.** Consistency in the service context refers to applying the organizational and individual discipline required to provide the same level of service quality in all customer relations today, tomorrow, forever.

**Total involvement.** There are no limitations on delivering service quality performance. "Customers" are interpreted in the broadest sense to include all internal organizational units and individuals, external customers and business partners (i.e. vendors, suppliers, sub-contractors, etc.).

**Response to change.** The quality credos reflect a concern with the need to constantly evaluate and react to customers *current* perception of service quality delivery.

**Cost effectiveness and product value.** There is a strong trend towards combining high levels of quality and productivity as inseparable corporate goals. These top companies are saying that they can have it all — reasonable cost/price structures accompanied by a level of quality that serves as a product differentiator in the marketplace.

**Integrity.** The meaning of integrity in a customer service sense is best described as "promising what you can deliver and delivering what you promise".

**Pro-active quality management.** Great value is placed on seeking, anticipating and solving operating and customer relations problems before they happen versus maintaining a "fire brigade" and "hero" culture that gives greater recognition to straightening out a mess.

**Community.** Attention is given to the need for developing and maintaining quality, community relationships. Executive and employee support and involvement in community affairs is protrayed as being in the company interest.

The Quality Credos shown on the following pages represent the best thinking on the subject in America. A lot of hard work went into their development and they have been an integral part of creating the kind of "quality cultures" that have resulted in outstanding service quality performance.

# AT&T

## Policy

Quality excellence is the foundation for the management of our business and the keystone of our goal of customer satisfaction. It is, therefore, our policy to:

- Consistently provide products and services that meet the quality expectations of our customers.
- Actively pursue ever-improving quality through programs that enable each employee to do his or her job right the first time.

## Intent

Quality will continue to be a major, strategic thrust in AT&T. It lies at the heart of everything we do.

Through active planning in every function in the company, we will strive to provide products and services that consistently meet all quality, schedule, and cost objectives. Furthermore, we will dedicate ourselves to continually improving the quality of our products and services by focusing on our processes and procedures.

Every employee is a part of our quality system.

- Each of us will strive to understand and satisfy the quality expectations of our customers (meaning the next internal organization in the process as well as the eventual end-customer).
- Each of us will strive to identify and eliminate the sources of error and waste in our processes and procedures.
- Each of us will aid the quality-planning and improvement efforts of others for the good of the corporation as a whole.

## Responsibilities

Each business group president, entity head, and senior staff officer is responsible for:

- Communicating our quality policy to each employee.
- Clarifying specific responsibilities for quality.
- Developing and reviewing strategic quality plans and objectives on an ongoing basis.
- Implementing a quality management system to carry out the plans and achieve objectives.
- Monitoring and continually improving the level of customer satisfaction.
- Monitoring and continually improving the defect and error rate of internal processes and systems.
- Developing joint quality plans with suppliers and other business partners.

- Implementing, funding, and reviewing specific quality improvement programs.
- Providing education and training in quality disciplines for all employees.

# BELLSOUTH CORPORATION

## Customer First

We deliver our service in a manner that causes our customers to perceive value added. We will know their preferences and perceptions and market our products and services accordingly. We will judge our performance against the standards of the customer. Only by satisfying our customers are we able to provide an attractive return to our stockholders and opportunities for our employees. A promise to a customer by an employee commits all employees to help fulfill it.

## Respect for the Individual

We provide our people full opportunity to contribute to the success of the business through individual participation and challenging responsibilities. We believe our people are capable, loyal, and concerned about the success of the business. We encourage them to use their own initiative to satisfy customers and improve profitability, and we respect their opinions and ideas. The dignity of each individual is central in the way we conduct our business.

## Pursuit of Excellence

Our mission is to be the leader in our industry and that calls for excellent performance in every part of the business and by each employee. We will pursue excellence in the quality of each product, service, and contact. We debate the issues, but once a decision is made, commitment is expected from everyone. The success of an integrated, multi-functional matrix organization depends upon excellent teamwork. Our integrity, as a company and as individuals, will always be without question. Through excellence, we will meet or exceed the expectations of our stockholders.

## Positive Response to Change

We must create positive change in our industry. In today's world, constant change is inevitable. Our people must be future oriented and inspired by change, with a commitment to help mold change to BellSouth's and its customers' advantage. We will meet the challenge of change with an aggressive and innovative approach to the way we market and service our customers as well as the way we run the business internally.

## Community Mindedness

The vitality of our business is directly impacted by the quality of life and opportunity in the cities and states where we operate. We will work, as a company, for the betterment of the communities where we operate, and encourage our employees to do likewise.

## CATERPILLAR TRACTOR CO.

### Product Quality and Uniformity*

A major Caterpillar objective is to design, manufacture, and market products of superior quality. We aim at a level of quality which offers superiority for a broad range of applications.

We define quality as the combination of product characteristics and product support which provides optimum satisfaction to customers.

Products are engineered to exacting standards to meet users' expectations for performance, reliability, and life. Our goal is to build products to comparable quality standards, wherever they may be manufactured, and with maximum interchangeability of parts and components.

Product quality is constantly monitored. Our policy is to offer continuing product improvements—and better values—in response to needs of customers and requirements of the marketplace.

We strive to assure users of timely after-sale parts and service availability at fair prices. From our experience, these goals are usually best achieved through locally based, financially strong, independently owned dealers committed to service. We back availability of parts from dealers with a worldwide network of corporate parts facilities. We provide a wide range of assistance to dealers to help assure high quality support for Caterpillar products.

---

*Excerpt from Caterpillar's, "A Code Of Worldwide Business Conduct And Operating Principles".

## CSX TRANSPORTATION

At CSX Transportation, quality is defined as "meeting agreed-upon customer requirements by doing right things right the first time". It is the firm belief that the customer is the only one capable of defining quality and that all employees have a customer, either internal or external.

Identification of customer/supplier relationships and determintion of customer requirements, taking into account the supplier's capability to meet the requirements, is the critical first step in producing quality. If the involved processes are not capable of consistently meeting the requirements, then the process must be changed. Continuous improvement of all work in an effort to meet changing customer requirements is the key to CSX's future.

Five key concepts of quality improvement are stressed at CSX. These five building blocks of quality are: customer focus, total involvement, measurement, systematic support and continuous improvement.

## The Five Building Blocks of Quality

### Customer Focus (meeting needs)

CSX is in business to serve its customers. All our work, as individuals and as a company, should be generated in response to a customer's requirements. We have to work with our customers to identify what they really need from us and find ways to meet those needs at a profit to the company. We are all links in a chain that is devoted to meeting customer needs.

### Total Involvement (taking responsibility)

Everyone at CSX is personally responsible for generating Quality at every level, and in all facets of his or her job. Quality must be both a top-down and a bottom-up commitment and effort. Top-down because only senior management can lead the corporate culture change that is required to make quality the only acceptable way to do business. Bottom-up because employees are the experts at doing their jobs and improving their work.

### Measurement (tracking progress)

To manage the quality process, we must accurately measure how well we meet the needs of our internal and external customers, and eliminate unnecessary measures. The people who do the work should do the measuring and display their results graphically when possible.

### Systematic Support (coordinating efforts)

All systems in the company must support the quality improvement process. These systems include MIS, performance and development plans, and corporate planning. Reward and recognition, both formal and informal, must be consistent with quality objectives and initiatives.

### Continuous Improvement (finding a better way)

Quality is a journey, not a destination. We need to do things better today than yesterday and better tomorrow than today. We must constantly look for ways to solve problems, eliminate waste, prevent errors, make improvements, and improve consistency. It's important to constantly question the systems and procedures we use to do work without worrying about who is responsible for that old way of doing things.

# CUMMINS ENGINE COMPANY, INC.

## Cummins Quality Policy

The quality policy of Cummins Engine Company is to provide products and services which consistently meet or exceed the standards set by our customers on time and at the lowest cost.

**Quality is a customer determination.** We first must determine who our customers are, and what their needs are. In order to serve our external customers well we must identify our internal customers and fully meet their expectations. Meeting customer needs in a quality way goes beyond shipping Cummins products without defects. It includes all aspects of work i.e. the way we answer the phone, the quality of a typed document, the correctness of a service publication and the accuracy of an engineering analysis.

As quality improves, customer expectations rise. We must identify and deal with these new expectations better than our competitors.

Each entity is responsible for establishing and maintaining processes and procedures which ensure that the changing needs of their customers are clearly understood and continuously met.

**High quality means lowest total cost.** High quality is achieved by continuously minimizing waste, reducing variability and continuously improving all phases of our work. This means fewer redesigns, better product introductions, less scrap and rework, and lower cost of sales. It also means greater internal efficiency, lower field failure costs, and increased sales.

For the customer, high quality means lower operating cost, lower purchased price, maximum availability, safe products, more predictable performance, and higher profitability, which all lead to greater customer satisfaction.

Each entity is responsible for establishing measurement systems which ensure that product and process quality is measured during development, manufacture, sale, and customer use of the product.

The cost of attaining the necessary customer oriented quality levels will be measured in order to monitor progress toward improvement.

**Total quality—a way to improve work.** Each individual employee is responsible for the quality of his/her work. The Cummins Total Quality System Procedures form the basis of our prevention oriented quality improvement effort and all Cummins people are expected to conduct their work in accordance with those practices.

# DELTA AIR LINES, INC.

## The Delta Mission

Delta is a transportation company whose primary business is the air transportation of passengers, cargo and mail in domestic and international markets.

We shall strive to satisfy the needs of the market by providing quality transportation services within the framework of ethical and legal behavior. We shall maintain a level of earnings sufficient to support our growth and provide our shareholders with attractive returns on their investment over the long-term.

## The Delta Beliefs

We are a group of people with a family spirit and a shared mission. We respect the contributions of each family member as we work toward that mission.

Our shared mission is a sincere commitment to providing the safest, finest air transportation in the world.

In order to preserve the first two beliefs for all time, we must manage financial resources carefully.

## DIGITAL EQUIPMENT CORPORATION

### Digital's Quality Statement

"Growth is not our primry goal. Our goal is to be a quality organization and do a quality job, which means that we will be proud of our product and our work for years to come. As we achieve quality, we achieve growth".

*Excerpted from Digital Equipment Corporation's Policy Book*

## EASTMAN KODAK COMPANY - PARTS SERVICES DIVISION

### Mission

Parts services is commited to be the world leader in the quality of its parts logistics and support services. We will judge this quality by how well we maintain excellence in customer satisfaction, meet the needs of our people, achieve corporate goals and create a climate of continuous quality improvement in all line and support functions.

### Vision

To be viewed by Kodak customers and prospective customers as an organization recognized internationally as a leader in service parts logistics who is easy to do business with and committed to providing "quality" service that exceeds their expectations for timely, accurate and effective delivery of service parts.

To be viewed by Kodak Business Units as an essential element in their overall operating plans as:

- A business partner sharing in common goals and objective to assist in developing and implementing diverse KBU service strategies involving Kodak Manufacturing, OEM Vendors and CES Field Service organizations worldwide.
- A low cost provider of 24 hour/7 day customized customer service delivered according to the terms and conditions contracted for between the KBU and their Kodak customers.
- An organization that provides high quality interactive on-line/real time service part and customer status information that contributes to the KBU's development of a differential service strategy advantage which makes Kodak products more attractive to customers.
- An organization that assures a high level of integrity in protecting and maintaining inventory placed in its possession.
- A provider of customized logistical services for the worldwide distribution of high technology service parts.
- To be viewed by its employees as an organization that is entrusted with the assets of others and who significantly contributes to the success of its clients. As an opportunity to develop a career in diverse areas such as customer relations, materials management, transportation, sales and inventory logistics.
- To be viewed by the General Manager of CES as a source of new revenue by developing strategies for seeking new customers for its services both within and outside of Kodak.

## EG&G IDAHO NATIONAL ENGINEERING LABORATORY

Our belief is that quality is achieved when all employee actions are guided by the following:

- The only reason we are here is to serve our customer's needs.
- A simple organization with decision making at the lowest level is mandatory.
- Performance is paramount—we must be faster, better, and cheaper than the competition.

## FIRESTONE TIRE AND RUBBER COMPANY

### Statement of Policy

Quality is a philosophy and continues to be a principle of the Firestone Tire and Rubber Company.

Customers and users to the company's products or services expect them:

- To be fit for the ordinary purposes for which such products or services are intended;
- To comply with applicable laws, regulations or standards in the countries in which they are installed or marketed;
- To conform to any applicable warranty or authorized representation;
- To be safe if operated in a prudent manner in accordance with any needed instructions;
- To perform satisfactorily for a reasonable period of time with proper use, care and maintenance; and
- To receive prompt, dependable service if or when needed.

It is the company's policy that Firestone rank highest in earned reputation for meeting these expectations.

## Intent

A Quality management system and function shall exist in each operating unit to make certain:

- Acceptance and performance requirements of the company's products and services are met;
- Cost of quality goals for each operating unit are achieved;
- Personnel performing quality related activities are provided required communication, education, and training.

## Responsibility

Each manager of an operating unit is responsible for the establishment of an effective quality system.

The head of the Quality Assurance Department in each operating unit shall typically report directly to the unit manager and be on at least the same organizational level as the departments whose performance is being measured, i.e. Manufacturing, Tech Services, Engineering, etc. The head of the Quality Assurance Department shall represent his unit in the Quality Councils.

The Director, Corporate Quality Assurance, shall establish and implement, as necessary, administrative policies, standard practices and guidelines in support of this policy; provide advice and counsel through specialized staff services, including education and training and professional development in quality sciences; and assess the effectiveness of the quality systems by performing periodic audits.

## APPLICATION OF POLICY

### Quality System

Operating Groups will institute an effective quality system to ensure quality products and services in support of this policy.

The quality system is an intrinsic part of the business system and requires a series of carefully planned events and activities which include but are not limited to the following:

- Establishing appropriate quality organizations to determine the customer quality needs and delineating specific quality requirements and standard practices.
- Reviewing product design and development and reviewing information for feasibility, performance, productibility, inspectability, reliability and safety.
- Controlling the quality of purchased goods and services and controlling product during manufacture and, where applicable, during installation and service.
- Controlling inspection and test equipment, special processes, nonconforming materials, handling, shipping and storage.
- Obtaining feedback information from products as manufactured and in use, and utilizing information to improve or maintain product quality.
- Performing periodic quality audits of the system, procedures, products and processes and taking corrective action where appropriate.

## FORD MOTOR COMPANY

### MISSION
Ford Motor Company is a worldwide leader in automotive and automotive-related products and services as well as in newer industries such as aerospace, communications, and financial services. Our mission is to improve continually our products and services to meet our customers' needs, allowing us to prosper as a business and to provide a reasonable return for our stockholders, the owners of our business.

### VALUES
How we accomplish our mission is as important as the mission itself. Fundamental to success for the company are these basic values.

- **People.** Our people are the source of our strength. They provide our corporate intelligence and determine our reputation and vitality. Involvement and teamwork are our core human values.
- **Products.** Our products are the end result of our efforts, and they should be the best in serving customers worldwide. As our products are viewed, so are we viewed.
- **Profits.** Profits are the ultimate measure of how efficiently we provide customers with the best products for their needs. Profits are required to survive and grow.

# GUIDING PRINCIPLES

- **Quality comes first.** To achieve customer satisfaction, the quality of our products and services must be our number one priority.
- **Customers are the focus of everything we do.** Our work must be done with our customers in mind, providing better products and services than our competition.
- **Continuous improvement is essential to our success.** We must strive for excellence in everything we do: in our products, in their safety and value—and in our services, our human relations, our competitiveness, and our profitability.
- **Employee involvement is our way of life.** We are a team. We must treat each other with trust and respect.
- **Dealers and suppliers are our partners.** The company must maintain mutually beneficial relationships with dealers, suppliers, and our other business associates.
- **Integrity is never compromised.** The conduct of our company worldwide must be pursued in a manner that is socially responsible and commands respect for its integrity and for its positive contributions to society. Our doors are open to men and women alike without discrimination and without regard to ethnic origin or personal beliefs.

## GENERAL MOTORS

## UAW-GM

### Quality Network

The leadership of General Motors and the UAW is jointly committed to securing General Motors' position in the market and the job security of its employes in every phase of the corporation through an ongoing process of producing the highest quality customer-valued products.

The parties agree that the production of world-class quality products is the key to our survival and jointly commit to pursue the implementation of the following jointly developed quality strategy:

- Ongoing UAW/GM top leadership commitment and involvement to a corporate quality strategy.
- Voice of the customer is understood and drives the whole process.
- Ongoing education and training to support the quality improvement process.
- Communication process to support the quality process.
- Create a plan and structure for a joint process for implementation.
- Total involvement for continuous improvement and elimination of waste.
- Reward system which supports the total quality process.

# GTE SERVICE CORPORATION

## Definition
Quality is conformance to the requirements and expectations of the internal and external customers, throughout the expected period of use of the product or service.

## Policy
It is the policy of GTE to provide products, services and customer support of the highest quality in the respective market segments served. In all activities, GTE will pursue quality leadership with goals aimed at achieving error free results that fully meet the needs and expectations of its internal and external customers. These results require the dedicated efforts of all employees.

## Implementation Requirements
Every company/group/SBU within the corporation is expected to develop its own supporting policies, and maintain quality improvement programs in the areas of product, service and customer support and for internal activities:

- By maintaining a *quality system* that establishes tasks and responsibilities for implementing its quality policies. Periodic reviews of the system are to be performed to ensure continuing effectiveness.
- By establishing a formal process of *quality planning,* which is integrated with the business's other planning activities and oriented toward achieving highest quality both externally and internally. The process is to be driven by goals for major improvement over the next five year period.

# THE HERMAN MILLER MANDATE

At Herman Miller, problem definition and problem solving result in products, systems, and services that improve productivity and the quality of life in working and healing environments. In a special way, we are committed to design excellence and leadership. Through research we seek to discover new solutions to our customers' needs. We recognize that this commitment requires us to adapt to significant change, and we are prepared to do so.

We will serve users in selected international markets, recognizing cultural differences and especially the needs of our multinational customers.

We are committed to quality and excellence in all that we do and the way in which we do it.

At Herman Miller, we are committed to the participative process of working together. We achieve our goals by each having the right and responsibility to contribute in our individual areas of competence, to own problems, and to be held accountable for results. We believe that people are our most important resource and are committed to enabling their development and to providing equal opportunity to each person.

We believe that all career employees should be able to own stock in the corporation. We believe that participative ownership, practiced with fidelity, can make this an exceptional company.

We will consistently strive to achieve equity for our customers, participating owners, and investors.

We will build quality relationships and a sense of fairness with our vendors and dealers.

We seek to be socially responsible. We share a concern and responsibility for the quality of the environment in which we and our neighbors live and work. We recognize that we are more than participating owners in our company: We are also members of families and communities. We are committed to the nurture, support, and security of the family.

We are committed to offering a unique investment opportunity to investors who identify with our goals and values and who wish to have a meaningful ownership share in the company.

Appropriate financial results are essential. They enable future vitality and must be integral to annual and long-range planning and the implementation of those plans.

At Herman Miller, growth and job security must be a consequence of our problem solutions, of the potential in our programs, and of the performance of our people.

## HEWLETT PACKARD

### OBJECTIVE

To provide products and services of the highest quality and the greatest possible value to our customers, thereby gaining and holding their repect and loyalty.

HP's view of its relationships with customers has been shaped by two basic beliefs. First, we believe the central prupose of our business—the reason HP exists—is to satisfy real customer needs. Second, we believe those needs can be fully satisfied only with the active participation and dedication of everyone in the company. The essence of customer satisfaction is a commitment to quality, a commitment that begins in the laboratory and extends into every phase of our operations. Products must be designed to provide superior performance and long, trouble-free service. Once in production these products must be manufactured at a competitive cost and with superior workmanship.

Careful attention to quality not only enables us to meet or exceed customer expectations, but it also has a direct and substantial effect on our operating costs and profitability. Doing a job properly the first time, and doing it consistently, allows us to employ fewer assets, reduces our costs, and contributes significantly to higher productivity and profits.

Providing innovative, reliable products is a key element in satisfying customer needs, but there are other important elements as well. HP offers many different products to many different customers, and it is imperative that the products recommended to a specific customer are those that will best fulfill the customer's overall, long-term needs. This requires that our field sales people, operating individually or in well-coordinated teams, work closely with customers to determine the most appropriate, effective solutions to their problems. It requires, as well, that once a product is delivered, it be supported with prompt, efficient services that will optimize its usefulness.

Our fundamental goal is to build positive, long-term relationships with our customers, relationships characterized by mutual respect, by courtesy and integrity, by a helpful, effective response to customer needs and concerns, and by a strong commitment to providing products and services of the highest quality.

## HOME FEDERAL SAVINGS & LOAN ASSOCIATION

### QUALITY MISSION

At Home Federal, we aim to be nothing less than the premier provider of quality financial products and services in every market we serve, from retail banking in California, to real estate, corporate finance and investment services in selected U.S. markets.

Our passion for quality is anchored by the principle of respect—respect for clients, respect for shareholders, respect for co-workers. Respect for clients means continually making an extraordinary effort to understand and be responsive to their financial services needs—an effort which distinguishes us from our competition, earns strong client recognition, and ensures a loyal and growing client base. Respect for shareholders means a commitment to productivity and profitability. Respect for co-workers means working in harmony for common goals, moved by a shared vision of corporate and personal success.

## MACK TRUCKS, INC.

### The Mack Mission

We serve our customers around the world through the innovative design, engineering, manufacturing and servicing of trucks and vehicles that meet their needs at low life cycle cost.

## Mack Corporate Strategies

- Create a productive organizational climate that encourages creative contributions from Mack people.
- Provide support to a strong and competitive field organization.
- Maintain an effective global support system of parts and service availability for Mack products.
- Communicate effectively with our customers.
- Maintain and strengthen product differentiation and high quality.
- Build on our reputation for a distinctive, durable product.
- Compete on value, deliver products with the lowest life cycle cost.
- Build for long-term strength, rather than short-term results.
- Eliminate non-productive assets.
- Capitalize on our synergy with Renault.

## METROPOLITAN LIFE INSURANCE COMPANY

*Quality is the key to our future success.*
Met Life customers are our first priority: without customers, there is no reason for a business to exist. *Exceeding* the *expectations of our customers* will make Met Life "the *Quality* Company".

### Implications

- All of our people must understand *who* their customers are, and *what* their customers expect, regardless of whether those customers are internal or external.
- Meeting or exceeding the expectations of internal customers and especially Met Life sales representatives in our various lines of business is a high priority as a precedent to satisfying external customers.
- Our activities must be customer-driven.
- High quality performance should be expected and appropriately rewarded; inferior performance should not be tolerated.

## NATIONAL WESTMINSTER BANK USA

### Statement of Quality

National Westminster USA will develop and deliver products and services that conform to customers' financial and information requirements. Our goal is to be recognized as the premier quality bank in each of the markets we serve.

All marketing, products, processes, systems and training will be designed to prevent errors and to provide customers with consistently high levels of quality, which we will continuously monitor.

If errors or service problems do occur, emphasis will be placed on timely and courteous resolution, including appropriate communication with the customer.

Success will be measured in terms of our ability to meet customer requirements, and employees will be rewarded for quality performance.

## Quality Program

Quality represents the everyday expression of our value system. It is the means by which we carry out the strategies and achieve the goals set forth in the Mission Statement.

The Bank's commitment to quality is thorough and long-term. It is how we intend to differentiate ourselves and, at the same time, achieve a cost advantage over our competitors. In addition, customers are willing to pay a premium for high-quality services.

## Customers

The everyday things we do to better serve customers are obvious, but they bear repeating. These actions apply to everyone because, even where there is no direct customer contact, everything we do is related to serving customers:

- We listen to our customers to determine their needs and then attempt to fill those needs.
- We respond in a thoughtful, professional and timely manner.
- We deliver our products and services error free and in a consistent manner.
- We price our products and services fairly.
- We are always respectful and courteous.
- We do our work in essential staff areas as cost effectively as possible, because we invest our principal resources in customer-driven activites.

## Communities

In all our community activities we seek to reflect the Bank's commitment to quality and excellence while helping others.

This is a dimension of our job that goes beyond day-to-day duties. It involves community service: giving generously to the United Way, donating blood, and taking leadership roles in significant community organizations.

We furnish substantial community support on the corporate level as well. Our contributions budget has grown each year and provides major funding for education, health care, community welfare and the arts. In addition, we have chosen to direct significant portions of our corporate communications budget to sponsorship of quality arts projects.

## Parent

Superior quality in everything we do is the only way to meet the dual responsibility we have to our parent of enhancing its reputation and meeting our financial goals.

High-quality work is key to enhancing the NatWest name. But it is also critical to achieving our new financial goal, because we must do this by improving margins rather than by expanding assets. Quality banking involves several things:

- Wider lending and investing spreads.
- Increased fee and service-charge income, which can be expected if we deliver quality products consistently.
- Expanded demand deposits.
- Higher credit quality, resulting in lower credit costs and fewer non-performing loans and charge-offs.
- Reduced tax liability.

An additional element that enhances our reputation as a quality institution and ensures that we achieve our goals is consistent prudence both in the extension of credit and in our asset/liability management activities.

## Ourselves

The competence, dedication and hard work of our staff are the essential ingredients in our success. We need quality people. Therefore, we are very selective in hiring, and take training and promotion from within very seriously.

We closely monitor salary and benefit trends and seek to be fully competitive, increasing compensation levels in relation to those of our peers as the performance of the Bank improves. On an individual level, we reward according to contribution.

We have developed a variety of programs to improve communication: an expanded NewsBeam, staff and management bulletins, staff meetings, special surveys and the like. We constantly seek new ways to increase communication at all levels of the Bank.

We encourage leadership by example, creating an environment that is caring, trusting, fair and enjoyable.

By doing quality work, each of us contributes directly to achieving the Bank's goals. In the process, we also foster a stimulating work environment and enhance our individual well-being.

## NAVISTAR INTERNATIONAL TRANSPORTATION CORPORATION

## Mission Statement

We believe our people are the source of our competitive advantage which is created by:

- Making "Service to the Customer" the primary goal of all Navistar people.

WHEN AMERICA DOES IT RIGHT

- Continuously improving the quality of our efforts and thereby the overall productivity of the organization.
- Working together in the spirit of teamwork and coopertion to achieve our common goals.

Only by continually focusing on creating value for our customers can we create value for our shareowners, and reward our employees, who are the source of competitivenes.

## PHILIP-MORRIS U.S.A.

## A Credo for Engineering Operations

We believe that the foundation of the company's success lies with its employees. Improvement in the services we provide is contingent upon continued commitment to excellence in the way we do our jobs.

We believe that an environment of *innovation and creativity* must pervade our efforts. Our future depends upon our ability to view the tasks before us with fresh perspectives, to question old habits and ways of thinking, and to have the courage to propose and implement alternative approaches. We will encourage "experimentation" while minimizing overanalysis. We will also encourage risk-taking in pursuit of higher levels of service and quality and will tolerate productive failure. We will, within our corporate policy, reward those who succeed as innovators.

We endorse simplifying operational bureaucracies while providing our service at optimun *quality and responsiveness*. We will build on individual strengths, share all available information, and delegate authority and autonomy to those who can most effectively accomplish the job. We will trust our own integrity to get the job done without excessive checks and balances.

We will ensure that an environment of *fairness and trust* exists and will strive to know what is happening first-hand, through active communication. We will support this environment by providing necessary training so each of us can become confident and enthusiastic about our jobs and company. Together, we will energetically seek our answers to our customer's needs.

We recognize that conservatism and predictability lead to stagnation and mediocrity. It is incumbent upon all of us to listen to customers and company needs, to react, decide and take the necessary action. We must acknowledge that every action, no matter how small, must be performed in a sincere, prompt, courteous and caring fashion. Together, by accepting the core values of this Credo, we will be doing our job and contributing to our company's prosperity. We must make it happen, not just talk about it.

# PHILLIPS 66 COMPANY Plastic Resins Division

## Quality Policy
Our fundamental policy is to be a responsible supplier of quality resins and services to our worldwide customers.
- Quality is a strategic business principle for plastic resins.
- Our commitment to quality assures our customers of products and services that meet their expectations.
- Quality is the responsibility of every employee.

# REYNOLDS ALUMINUM

## Credo
Every Reynolds employee has a responsibility to produce products or render services that meet our customers' expectations. No one has the right to accept or ship an unsatisfactory product.

Our products and services must conform to their requirements, as expressed in a specification with measurable characteristics, and exemplify pride in workmanship. They must be reliable, offered at a reasonable cost and delivered on time. Reynolds objective is to be the quality leader in everything we do.

# WARNER-LAMBERT

Our mission is to achieve leadership in advancing the health and well-being of people throughout the world. We believe this mission can best be accomplished by recognizing and meeting our fundamental responsibilities to our customers, employees, shareholders, suppliers and society.

To Our Customers *we are committed* to providing high-quality health care and consumer products of real value that meet customer needs. We are committed to continued investment in the discovery of safe and effective products to enhance people's lives.

To Our Employees *we are commited* to attracting and retaining capable people, providing them with challenging work in an open and participatory environment, marked by equal opportunity for personal growth. Performance will be evaluated on the basis of fair and objective standards. Creativity and innovation will be encouraged. Employees will be treated with dignity and respect. They will be actively encouraged to make suggestions for improving the effectiveness of the enterprise and the quality of work life.

To Our Shareholders *we are committed* to providing a fair and attractive economic return, and we are prepared to take prudent risks to achieve sustainable long-term corporate growth.

To Our Suppliers *we are committed* to dealing with our suppliers and all our business partners in a fair and equitable manner, recognizing our mutual interests.

To Society *we are committed* to being good corporate citizens, actively initiating and supporting efforts concerned with the health of society, particularly the vitality of the worldwide communities in which we operate.

*Above all,* our dealings with these constituencies will be conducted with the utmost integrity, adhering to the highest standards of ethical and just conduct.

## WINNEBAGO INDUSTRIES, INC.

### Corporate Quality Statement

It is the policy of Winnebago Industries, Inc. to provide products and services of a quality that fully and consitently meet the initial and continuing needs of our customers.

Quality is no longer defined as conformance to manufacturing standards and specifications, but rather as a measure of performance excellence in every aspect of our business.

Products and services must incorporate features of performance, durability, reliability, safety, and appearance that consistently reflect favorably on the company and its employees.

It is not possible to create quality by inspection. It must be designed and manufactured right the first time.

The success of Winnebago Industries begins and ends with its people. Every individual must do everything possible to satisfy customer needs. We must strive for never ending improvement.

Delivering products and services that consistently meet our customer requirements will ensure a satisfactory relationship and a continuing and thriving business in the future.

To achieve this goal, we at Winnebago Industries, Inc. have made a corporate commitment to "A Total Quality Process".

## U S WEST, INC.

Goal—It is U S WEST's goal to become the preeminent marketers of communications products and services in our industry—excellence in service/quality is our standard. We will measure our success by what our customers tell us.

Service Quality Goal—We will make our service U S WEST's competitive advantage.

# Subject Index

## Customer Feedback Mechanisms

## Product Design For Service Quality
- *Delivering Quality Service to the Caterpillar Earthmoving Customer.* Redpath, James E., p. 195

## Programs for Quality Awareness
- *Customer Service Strategies.* Karpas, P., p. 41
- *Forming Quality Improvement Partnerships.* Wachniak, R., p. 455
- *Nothing New Under the Sun.* Sparks, Len, p. 233
- *Quality Improvement at National Westminster Bank.* Deutsch, H., and Metviner, N. J., p. 84
- *Service Quality: A Warner Lambert Priority.* Doane, Allan H., p. 373
- *Service Quality at Phillips 66 Company's Houston Chemical Complex.* Railsback, D. Lynn, p. 361
- *Service Quality: Our Most Strategic Weapon.* Rasmussen, MaryAnne, p. 105
- *The Lazarus Customer Service Evolution.* Bukey, Daniel G., p. 447

## Quality and Market Penetration
- *Being Good is Good Business.* Harris, Leonard R., p. 429
- *Creating a Culture for Quality Improvement at GTE.* Wolkins, D. Otis, p. 535
- *Evolution of Performance Measurement.* Fray, Earl, p. 383
- *Improving Service Quality in Transportation.* Mayeske, Roy W., p. 401
- *Making Friends is Our Business.* Rammes, William L., p. 29
- *Quality Improvement in the Service Sector.* Kilderry, K. W., p. 144
- *Quality is the Foundation of Our Business.* Raine, R. A., p. 274
- *Service Quality in Phillips 66 Company's Houston Chemical Complex.* Railsback, D. Lynn, p. 361
- *The Management of Product Stewardship.* Thurman, Carl C., p. 64
- *The Quality Improvement Process at BASF Polymers Group.* Buller, Manfred, p. 55

## Quality and Productivity
- *A Service Delivery Measurement and Improvement Program.* Overstreet, Michael B., p. 481
- *AT&T: Building on a Quality Tradition to Ensure Quality Service Delivery.* Coleman, Roberta, p. 125
- *BellSouth's Approach to Service Quality.* Bryant, John F., p. 528
- *Delivering Quality Service to the Caterpillar Earthmoving Customer.* Redpath, James E., p. 195
- *Making Friends is Our Business.* Rammes, William L., p. 29
- *Nothing New Under the Sun.* Sparks, Len, p. 233

## Quality and Public Relations
- *Making Friends is Our Business.* Rammes, William L., p. 29
- *Quality Service the Bell Atlantic Way.* Babbio, L. T., Jr., p. 519

## Quality Audits
- *Making Friends is Our Business.* Rammes, William L., p. 29
- *Quality Customer Service.* Fischer, Merrell J., and Roseland, Paul R., p. 282
- *Quality Improvement at National Westminster Bank.* Deutsch, H., and Metviner, N. J., p. 84
- *Quality Improvement in the Service Sector.* Kilderry, K. W., p. 144
- *Quality in Computer Services: Maintenance, Repair, and Support Services.* Smith, Jack, p. 133
- *Quality Service the Bell Atlantic Way.* Babbio, L. T., Jr., p. 519
- *The Herman Miller Quality Audit: A Corporate Report Card.* Pukanic, Ray, and Holm, Dick, p. 175

## Quality Culture

## Quality Incentives

## Quality Measurement

## INDEX